CINEMATEXAS NOTES

CinemaTexas
NOTES

The Early Days of Austin Film Culture

EDITED BY
LOUIS BLACK
WITH COLLINS SWORDS

UNIVERSITY OF TEXAS PRESS ❧ AUSTIN

Requests for permission to reproduce material
from this work should be sent to:
  Permissions
  University of Texas Press
  P.O. Box 7819
  Austin, TX 78713–7819
  utpress.utexas.edu/rp-form

♾ The paper used in this book meets the minimum
requirements of ANSI/NISO Z39.48–1992 (R1997)
(Permanence of Paper).

Library of Congress Cataloging-in-Publication Data

Names: Black, Louis, 1950– editor. | Swords,
    Collins, editor. |University of Texas at Austin.
    Department of Radio-Television-Film.
Title: CinemaTexas notes : the early days of Austin
    film culture / edited by Louis Black with Collins
    Swords.
Description: First edition. | Austin : University of
    Texas Press, 2018. | Includes bibliographical
    references and index.
Identifiers: LCCN 2017030872
ISBN 978-1-4773-1543-9 (cloth : alk. paper)
ISBN 978-1-4773-1544-6 (pbk. : alk. paper)
ISBN 978-1-4773-1545-3 (library e-book)
ISBN 978-1-4773-1546-0 (non-library e-book)
Subjects: LCSH: Motion pictures—Texas—Austin. |
    Motion pictures—Texas—History. | Culture in
    motion pictures.
Classification: LCC PN1993.5.U78 C56 2018 | DDC
    791.430976431—dc23
LC record available at https://lccn.loc.gov
    /2017030872

doi:10.7560/315439

Dedicated to Ed Lowry, our editor, teacher, fellow Program Note writer, mentor, and friend, who personified the best of CinemaTexas!

And to those no longer with us but much missed: Brian Hansen, Chuck Shapiro, Rita TheBerge, David Boone, Brent Grulke, and Richard Dorsett

CONTENTS

PREFACE

HOW THE PROGRAM NOTES WERE CHOSEN FOR THIS ANTHOLOGY

For about fifteen years, CinemaTexas Program Notes were written and published to accompany films shown at Jester Auditorium. Probably close to 1,500 sets were produced. Preparing this volume, we faced the monumental task of deciding how to whittle that number down to a workable anthology. Toward that end, we solicited suggestions from former CinemaTexas writers, asking them to choose their favorite sets of Notes. Collins Swords, Asher Ford, and Graham Carter read through dozens and dozens of Notes and chose most of the pieces featured in this book. So many great Note writers over the years authored so many truly terrific Notes, making this work challenging.

The team above, along with Alexa Harrington, also carefully transcribed each entry for this volume verbatim. Initially, we attempted to reconstruct the Notes as they originally appeared on mimeographed pages; however, after much deliberation, we decided to remove the film credits, director filmographies, suggested readings, and copyright sections from each Note in an effort to minimize the page count. We have included an original Note as an appendix for visual reference.

A number of writers are represented by multiple entries, such as Ed Lowry, Nick Barbaro, D. N. Rodowick, Lauren Rabinovitz, Ann Laemmle, Michael Selig, Steve Fore, and Valentin Almendarez. The driving idea behind this anthology is to present some truly outstanding writing by the graduate students who programmed and ran CinemaTexas. Singling out any of these writers does all a disservice, including the many talented writers not represented in this volume. For this reason, we hope this book will be the first of several volumes. Our concentration has been on providing a wide range of CinemaTexas's best writers, weighing in on films, both classic and far more obscure, as a demonstration of the remarkable value of this archive.

SPECIAL THANKS TO:

Dan Ackerman, Sheri Alpert, Chris Anderson, Mark Alvey, Valentin Almendarez, Nick Barbaro, Marjorie Baumgarten, Greg Beal, Courtenay Beinhorn, Steve Blackburn, Jackie Blain, Rob Blech, Missy Boswell, Scott Bowles, Debbie Burke, Rod Buxton, Jackie Byers, Anthony Cagle, Sam Calvin, Stephanie Canada-Worthington, Hollis Chacona, Candace Costis, Anne Craig, Gregory Cundiff, Stephen Derrickson, Guido DeVita, Michael Drew Dorsey, Ellen Draper, James Elliot, Steve Fore, Hugo Gamarra, John Gibson, Olive Graham, Kelly Greene, Mike Grossberg, David Hansard, Steven Harding, Cheryl Harris, Don Hartack, John Henley, Sam Ho, Burnes Hollyman, Don Howard, Karen Kington, Ann Laemmle, Joanne Lammers, Kristin Laskas, Stephen Lee, George Lellis, Eddie De Leon, Jon H. Lewis, Paul Little, Marie Mahoney, Geoffrey Marks, Peg Masterson, Pamela Menteer, Kevin Moran, Horace Newcomb, Nina Nichols, Kris Niebergall, Marcia Norcia, Linda Obalil, Thomas O'Guinn, Tim O'Malley, Lorrie Oschatz, Carolyn Perkins, Alex Plaza, Ron Policy, Keith Price, Lauren Rabinovitz, Charles Ramírez Berg, Joe Rape, Steven Reddicliffe, Jimmie L. Reeves, Carolyn Reitz, Leslie Rodier, D. N. Rodowick, Gwen Rowling, Alicia Rutledge, Michael Sænz, Gregory Sanders, George Saunders, Jeff Sconce, Tom Schatz, Ann Rowe Seaman, Chris Secrest, Michael Selig, Chuck Schapiro, Kay Sloan, Darby Smotherman, Warren Spector, Mike Sullivan, Rita TheBerge, Ronald Thomson, Richard Vickrey, Kathleen Walker, Robert Walker, Chris Walters, Wiliam Van Watson, George Wead, Tinky Weisblat, Brian L. Wilson, Cicely Wynn, Ray Ydoyaga

Many more to come.

———

LOUIS BLACK

CINEMATEXAS NOTES

Introduction to CinemaTexas

SEVEN NOTES ABOUT CINEMATEXAS PROGRAM NOTES

1. FIRST OF ALL, WHAT WAS CINEMATEXAS?

CinemaTexas was the film programming unit of the Department of Radio-Television-Film at the University of Texas from the early 1970s to the mid-1980s. It was supervised by a faculty member and run by graduate students. The films were supplemental "labs" for students enrolled in the RTF Department's film classes. At its height, films—all 16 mm prints that were projected in Jester Auditorium—were screened twice each night, usually at 7 and 9 p.m., four nights a week, Monday through Thursday, with each evening dedicated to a specific class. Tuesdays, for instance, were always the night for the undergraduate film history survey, RTF 314. Other film classes, both graduate and undergraduate, took up the other nights. Most of the audience were students enrolled in RTF classes, but the films were open to all UT students, faculty, and staff, as well as to the public at large for a modest ticket price (originally tickets sold for 75 cents).

There was one full-time staff member, along with a paid projectionist, and undergraduate students assisted (as paid "work-studies") with the as the most complete listings available. (Subscribers could contact us to join our mailing list and receive free copies of the Notes. That list grew steadily, and included the National Library of Australia, the British Film Institute, and the queen of film critics at the time, the *New Yorker*'s Pauline Kael.)

5. HOW WERE THE NOTES PRODUCED?

There were four graduate student writers each semester, one for each CinemaTexas screening night. The students received three special-projects-course credit hours for writing one set of Notes per week for the entire semester, which typically meant fourteen or fifteen essays per term. The graduate student assistant director/note editor was given a paid graduate assistantship.

From my experience, on a weekly basis, it worked like this. You tried to watch your film as soon as it arrived. As I said, you'd watch it on a Steenbeck editing machine or a projector, and you watched it as many times as you liked, taking notes throughout. Then you'd do the necessary library research to find the two critics' notices you would quote, as well as to familiarize yourself with the film, its director, its place in film history, and the conditions of the film's production. That meant going to the Tower, which in those days was the main UT library. Because the *New York Times* usually had the most complete cast and crew credits and most films could be found there, you'd begin looking up the film in the reference section of the library on microfilm or, later, in a series of reference books published by the *Times* that collected all their reviews. Later, you'd compare the *Times*'s credit listings with the film's. Then you'd look in periodical indexes under the film title, director's name, or star's name, looking for reviews written when it was released. Other newspapers besides the *Times* ran film reviews, especially *Variety*, the *Los Angeles Times*, and the big city papers, so did magazines like *Time, Newsweek, The Atlantic Monthly*, and *Harper's*. Once in a (great) while, you might find an interview with someone connected with the film, or a feature on a star or something, but those weren't as common as they are today. Remember, the *auteur* theory was still being hotly debated, and though films had a central place in the entertainment world, they were just beginning to be taken seriously as art.

Then you'd go upstairs to the stacks where the film books were kept (in the Dewey Decimal System, that was the 790s; in the Library of Congress Classification, it was PN 1993 to 1999) and walk the aisles of film books.

You could first check in the card catalogues, but I found them to be difficult to use and they were often hit or miss (or maybe it was just I was using the wrong key words). Anyway, you'd spend an afternoon or two up in the film stacks, looking shelf by shelf for any book that might have something on your movie of the week.

Then you'd start grinding out your essay. When you were stuck coming up with a lede, you could start with the easy stuff: complete credits; the "this is a great movie" quote, the "this movie is trash" quote; the director's complete filmography. The filmography Bible was Andrew Sarris's *The American Cinema: Directors and Directions, 1929–1968*, which listed the film credits for the best-known American directors. If you were doing a foreign film, you did some serious digging to unearth the director's filmography. Sooner or later you had to write your essay: five hundred to 750 words on the significance of the film. (The essays got longer as the years went by.)

You tried to get it to the student editor by the morning of the screening. Or early the afternoon of, though George frowned on this. There were, he'd say, professional expectations, no different than any other publishing enterprise. He'd attack the draft immediately, and I had his input in less than thirty minutes. In my case it was typically slashing it in half, cleaning up writing mistakes and typos, and suggesting better examples and movie references, and why hadn't I looked up what this or that critic has written? Then I had an hour or two to revise and resubmit. That was usually approved, with various subtractions and additions, which George generously reviewed with me.

Then that draft was handed over to the CinemaTexas typist/office manager. At the very beginning that was Vicky Tubbs, after that it was Karen Kington, followed by Pam Menteer. They were full-time staffers and they earned every penny of their salary because they did much more than type the final version of the Notes. They ran the office, coordinated film deliveries and pick-ups, answered the phone, tracked down MIA Note writers when their drafts were late—in short, they kept the CinemaTexas ship afloat.

The Notes were typed on mimeograph stencils, which needed to be proofread by the editor. Mistakes (or, worse, last-minute changes) required a special cover-up correction liquid, which was typed over when it dried. If there was an illustration, it was cut out from a film catalogue and pasted in place. Then the Notes were printed, using a Gestetner machine, on colored paper. Finally, the pages would be stapled together and the work-study would take them over to the Jester Auditorium box office in time for the

7 p.m. show, along with a roll of tickets and the change box. (At the very beginning, the Note writer ran the box office too, from 6:30 to 9:15.)

The office staff and editor would do it all over again the next day, and the Note writer began focusing on next week's film. On every second or third Friday, we'd gather in the afternoon and help Vicky or Karen or Pam prepare the Notes that were mailed to our subscribers.

6. HOW LONG WERE THE NOTES PUBLISHED?

From 1972 until 1986. There were three separate generations of Note writers. The first, founding generation was from 1972 to 1975 or 1976. It was driven by the vision of George Lellis and the writers who worked under him: Greg Sanders, Mike Sullivan, Valentin Almendarez, Carolyn Perkins, Robert Walker, Courtenay Beinhorn, Anthony Cagle, Keith Price, Kathleen Walker, and me. These Notes were, as George says, journalistic/impressionistic/ *auteurist*. In our defense, I would say that at least they were accurate and based on the film, not our memories of it. And, remember too, that film studies as we know it today was just being born, and *auteurism* was still new enough that folks were still arguing about it, and we felt we were promoting a radical new approach to film analysis while also arguing that movies be regarded as art. The early Notes were short, but when George left for a year to study in Paris, I took the opportunity to make them longer and longer. Soon a twelve-page set of Notes was not unusual.

The second generation, roughly 1976 to 1982 or 1983, was the Ed Lowry era. As editor, Ed was the heartbeat of the CinemaTexas crowd that included Louis Black, Marge Baumgarten, Brian Hansen, Warren Spector, D. N. Rodowick, Lauren Rabinovitz, Nick Barbaro, Rita TheBerge, Marcia Norcia, Greg Beal, Holly Chacona, and Ann Rowe Seaman. During this period *auteurism* began losing ground to other approaches, particularly semiotics, structuralism, and, with the publishing of a seminal book, *Hollywood Genres* by new RTF faculty member Tom Schatz, genre criticism was also in the ascendance. In addition, there was much more attention paid to cult films, exploitation films, and so-called drive-in movies. The notion was the classics had been attended to, and film critics needed to shift their focus to popular movies that were connecting with audiences but unfairly dismissed by establishment reviewers and scholars.

The third and last generation, from 1983 to 1986, moved further in the direction of film as popular culture, in a confident and mature way. The

CinemaTexas programmer was Chuck Shapiro, and the Notes were written by grad students like Chris Anderson, Steve Fore, Mark Alvey, and Jeffrey Sconce (who would later write the film-as-popular-culture manifesto, *"Trashing" the Academy: Taste, Excess, and an Emerging Politics of Cinematic Style*). Meanwhile, film viewing was changing. Home video was making it easier to access films. Films on VHS soon threatened theatrical screenings and theaters began closing nationwide. The large crowds that regularly flocked to watch movies at Jester Auditorium during the 1970s began shrinking. RTF classes began moving their screenings to regular classrooms rather than large auditorium-sized venues. Film distributors began losing money too, and they let their films deteriorate horribly. It was only a matter of time before it was better and cheaper to show a film on VHS than spend hundreds on a 16 mm print that was scratched, torn, probably damaged, and very likely incomplete.

It was time for CinemaTexas to close up shop.

7. IN THE END, WHAT WERE THE CINEMATEXAS PROGRAM NOTES?

Love letters to cinema.

All of us Note writers were infatuated with the movies. Like any young lover, we didn't know what to do next, how to nurture, develop, and deepen that relationship, how to understand why this single-minded devotion—go ahead and say it, obsession—was consuming our lives twenty-four frames per second.

Too young to know that you never understand love, we tried grasping it by watching movies, reading everything about them, debating and arguing about them.

And, once a week, we'd try to use words to describe our loved one as best we could. As carefully, happily, crazily, and honestly as we could.

And we did it in public; we were so far gone we didn't care if everybody knew it. In fact, it was better if they did, because maybe they'd see what we saw and they'd fall for movies too.

That's what CinemaTexas Notes were—weekly chronicles straight from the heart of a movie lover.

———

CHARLES RAMÍREZ BERG

Reflections on CinemaTexas

GEORGE LELLIS, LAUREN RABINOVITZ, D. N. RODOWICK, AND LOUIS BLACK

I

It was not hard for me to choose which grad school to attend in 1971. Of the four or five I had applied to, only the University of Texas at Austin, probably flush with oil money at the time, had offered me a graduate assistantship. Little did I know what I was getting into.

It turned out the assistantship was to run CinemaTexas, a film series that showed movies two nights a week. These were the "labs" for film criticism courses, as this was before the days of VHS or DVDs, and so there had to be 16 mm screenings accessible to the students that would not cut into class contact hours. I worked under Ron Policy, a faculty member who seemed to have unlimited confidence in me and who was always positive, ambitious, and good-natured. I learned the ropes of ordering films, getting them to the projectionist, selling both season tickets and individual admissions, accounting for and depositing the receipts with the bursar, filling in attendance reports for the distributors, and getting the movies sent back on time.

Near the end of the fall semester, Ron, who had the clearest vision of what CinemaTexas might become, proposed that I write Program Notes for the two spring series, one in support of RTF 314, the introduction to cinema course which surveyed the history of film, and the other for a special topics course he was doing on the films of Otto Preminger. I was game. For that Spring 1972 semester, I was the sole writer for CinemaTexas. Ron gave me a free hand to fashion them the way I wanted.

I had a couple of templates in my mind, mainly the Program Notes used by the Museum of Modern Art in New York, where I spent many an afternoon of my adolescence as a geeky film buff from Queens. But those were often just a listing of the complete credits and a few extended quotes from critics. I would be writing a short essay on each title. Because the 16 mm prints would come in anywhere from a week before the screening to the day before, I often had to work quickly, to screen the movie for myself, apply any research I had done, and pen a couple of pages about it.

My first movie was Paul Leni's *The Man Who Laughs*, a silent film adaptation of the Victor Hugo novel made in the late Hollywood period by a German filmmaker associated with the German Expressionist movement. For those first notes, I made a decision that was to shape almost all the Program Notes to come. I began the Notes with a pair of quotes—one positive and one negative, indicating that the film, like most, was neither unanimously praised nor derided. My idea was to give the students a chance to make up their own minds. I wanted them to feel free to like or dislike the movie they saw, but even more, to be able to see it from different perspectives.

This pattern of beginning with both positive and negative points of view was one I carried on, and one that I encouraged other writers to use. Sometimes this was difficult to achieve. I remember having a hard time finding a negative quote for Orson Welles's *Citizen Kane*, and had to resort to a review from the time of its release, since more contemporary critics had lionized it almost universally. Similarly, I had to cast about to find an even remotely positive review for 1968's *The Girl on a Motorcycle* (also known as *Naked under Leather*), which was shown for a course that dealt in part with cinematographer Jack Cardiff, who was hired as both director and photographer for it. (For cultists, it also featured Marianne Faithful as one of its stars, which in retrospect is absolute justification for screening it.)

I was striving for a kind of cinéphilic sophism, whereby one might be able to argue for or against any film, depending on the assumptions and standards one was starting out with. This goal came largely out of the experience of taking a class in film criticism with Manny Farber at New York's School of Visual Arts in the summer of 1968. The class was life-changing for me, since it led to my first published pieces of film criticism. When I signed up for the class, however, I had no idea how important Farber was—or was to become—since he did not have the recognition then that he has now.

One moment in Farber's class stands out. I had written a short piece in which I flippantly insulted a film. Farber's reaction was something like this: "You don't need to do that. If you describe the film well, really well, there will be no need to say whether it was good or bad." Related to this idea was his attitude that often qualities some critics find "bad" are the most interesting ones. "Bad" acting is often more interesting than "good" acting—an axiom that was to develop into a full-blown aesthetic by someone like Rainer Werner Fassbinder. The important thing was to describe the performance accurately and vividly. Similarly, holding a shot "too long" may result in your seeing things in the frame you wouldn't otherwise notice. Where one critic may see incompetence, another may see style.

Almost all CinemaTexas criticism will, by today's standards, be characterized as "journalistic" or "impressionistic." In the early 1970s, when cinema studies was still a relatively new discipline, there was not the obsession with critical methodology which, for better or worse, characterizes the field today. The upside of this is that we could have fun with the whole process of showing and writing about the movies we enjoyed. We were to expand to three nights a week and later to four, so that we needed to engage other writers—some graduate students, some talented undergrads—as Program Note writers. This only enlarged the critical mass of the operation, creating a staff of writers who would encourage one another and rise to the challenge of trying to write good, well-researched, provocative film criticism under tight deadlines.

We had a blast doing it. I remember one promotion I did for *King Kong* in which I dressed in a gorilla suit in the Texas heat and handed out fliers in the middle of campus. The front-page picture in the *Daily Texan* the next day carried the caption, "Gorilla My Dreams." Similarly, we got the bright idea of stapling a Kleenex to each copy of the Program Notes for *Imitation of Life*, so no one would have to use bare fingers to wipe away tears. At the same time, my colleagues and I were getting valuable experience at researching, writing, and editing.

A few years ago, I was looking at the December 4, 2014, issue of the *New York Times* which contained a review of the Mario Monicelli comedy *The Passionate Thief*, a work from 1960 with Anna Magnani and Ben Gazzara.

The movie must have never opened officially in New York until a restored copy was shown at Film Forum, yet I had written CinemaTexas Program Notes about it. We scooped the *New York Times* by forty years!

No period in my life has been as much fun.

———

GEORGE LELLIS

II

Writing is usually an isolating kind of activity. Alone with one's thoughts, notes, and anxieties, one taps out phrases and sentences on the computer keyboard, building to a finished work of some satisfaction. Much of my career as a film scholar has been given over to just this kind of activity, and predating computers, I tapped out workable drafts on an electric typewriter. But, when I was a graduate student in the late 1970s, writing for Cinema-Texas never fully fit into this paradigm of authorship.

An anatomy of writing Program Notes for CinemaTexas entails a multi-part process. First, there were the often-heated discussions among the Note writers over who got to take on which movies. (I remember being pretty amiable myself about which films I would be assigned.) Armed with a list of films—some of which I was familiar and passionate about, others about which I knew nothing—I would hit the library and do typical background research. Finding out about the director and looking up past reviews were standard operating procedure for most of us.

Seeing the assigned film in the late 1970s meant waiting for the 16 mm print of the film to arrive in the CinemaTexas office anywhere from a few days to a few weeks before its official screening date and then checking out the film and a 16 mm projector. But, rarely did I undertake this activity as a lone individual. Weekends were given over to group viewings of the films that were sitting in the office. Generally unsupervised, the graduate student members of CinemaTexas took turns bringing movies and the projector home, then screening the films with each other. I saw most of the CinemaTexas films, not just the ones for which I was responsible, with at least one or two other people and as many as six or seven. Nobody had reference then to the term "binge watching," but that is exactly what we did. On a regular basis.

So many of my recollections of the films on which I wrote are really remembrances of the discussions shared after the screenings, when we would swap ideas about the films and their textual properties. There were differences among us in how we viewed films and film criticism, but this "playtime" of CinemaTexas was an opportunity to test out the theories and generalizations about cinema that we were learning in our graduate seminars (and our Notes had a captive audience in the students required to attend on-campus weeknight screenings of the films). *Auteurism* still formed a strong critical backdrop to what we did, and it often served as a unifying thread. It was otherwise a time when close readings of films, film semiotics, and formal analysis reigned. Sure, there were a few daring enough to apply psychoanalytic concepts, just starting to form a vogue in film studies, and others laying down a Marxist approach. But, in general, we took each film as valuable in its own right and our own positions as cinephiles quite seriously.

So many of the films that I viewed, regardless of whether or not I was writing about them, formed a personal canon for me that I have carried throughout my life and used as the examples in film courses that I teach, hoping to attract yet one more generation to love the same films that I do. On occasion, a CinemaTexas film discovery led me to further research and exploration. I first watched Maya Deren's experimental films as a CinemaTexas Note writer, and I was assigned to write the Program Notes. In this instance, I watched the films with others and, even though I went home and wrote the Notes by myself, my head was filled with ideas about the films from shared conversations after each of the short films. These ideas, which I polished and translated into my own, really belong to a collectivity. The set of Notes that I wrote became a germ of an idea for my doctoral thesis and then for my first book, *Points of Resistance: Women, Politics, and Power in the New York Avant-Garde Cinema 1943–1971.* Sitting in a friend's living room and hashing out the films' meanings, I had no idea that the interpretations being tossed around would be so sustaining over such a long period of time.

Discussions about the films didn't just take place in each other's living rooms. One could always drop into the CinemaTexas office and, more than likely, find at least a few of the Note writers hanging out there with then editor Ed Lowry. Ed took everyone's prose and made the points clearer, the rhetoric more polished.

Indeed, in addition to viewing the 16 mm films in our homes, one could sometimes drop by the CinemaTexas office and view a film on the Steenbeck flatbed editing table that resided in the back room and was used primarily for taking photographs of individual film frames to accompany the written

Notes. It was a type of viewing that has been lost and never fully recaptured by the ability to fast forward or "rewind" a videotape, DVD, or Blu-ray. We would sit there in the dark, two or three of us clustered around the table, peering at the machine's small viewer, and watch a film unreel slowly shot by shot, rewinding and reviewing a shot sequence over and over. It was a type of viewing conducive to the close readings of films that so many of us did and that our critical models were publishing. It felt like we couldn't really "know" a Hitchcock film or a Welles masterpiece until we, like the critics we were reading, had reviewed particular shot sequences in slow motion multiple times. In this regard, I remember watching Kenneth Anger's *Scorpio Rising* with Ed in this manner, resulting in Ed producing one of the best set of Notes that ever came out of CinemaTexas and were subsequently the basis for a published article in the film journal *The Velvet Light Trap* ("The Appropriation of Signs in *Scorpio Rising*," Summer 1983).

So, by the time I regularly made it home to write my Program Notes on my typewriter in my small apartment, my head was filled with the comments, conviviality, and conclusions of my peers. Our Notes were always on individual films. But individual films belonged to larger groupings by *auteur*, style, mode of production, or country, and the Notes rarely lost sight of that. I like to think that the best of them are about bigger ideas than individual movies or, better yet, that through individual movies they uncover big ideas.

—

LAUREN RABINOVITZ

III

I moved from Houston to Austin, Texas, in spring 1974. My game plan was to give up my day job working at a record store to become a full-time professional musician and singer-songwriter. I had attended university classes in Houston on and off but in a completely derisory way, and at this point in my life could not imagine that I was approaching a major crossroad. CinemaTexas screenings and Program Notes would turn out to be a glowing signpost there.

Six months of underemployment (I exaggerate, no paid employment) as a musician rekindled my interest in a college degree. What brought me to the University of Texas campus most often was the plethora of film societies and nearby repertory cinemas. I was for most of my young life a cinephile and avid reader, and with its abundance of movies, bookstores, and live music, Austin was the nearest thing to heaven I could imagine. In those pre-video days, the only way to explore systematically Hollywood genres and *auteurs*, national cinemas, or international art cinema was to haunt those student-run film societies and commercial repertory theaters. In retrospect, it was the best education in film history and criticism that one could possibly imagine.

When I arrived in Austin, CinemaTexas was already screening double features four nights a week. I remember avidly collecting and reading the Program Notes, even hoarding Notes for films that I hadn't seen. With classic undergraduate naiveté (no excuse for it; I was already four years older than everyone else in my classes), it never occurred to me that there were film studies courses being taught in the School of Communication and that there was a Department of Radio-Television-Film, or that CinemaTexas screenings were supporting academic classes. I thought everyone was doing it for fun, which of course, they also were.

I deeply admired the mysterious authors of those Notes, and never once imagined that within a year or two, I would be writing them myself. Academically, I was in another universe then, studying world drama and comparative literature in the Humanities Program (another school of the university, another world). I was under the spell of Professor Neil McGraw in the English Department, a specialist in world dramatic literature and a charismatic and generous teacher whose example inspired me to pursue graduate study and to become eventually a teacher myself. At some point, like many of the same time and age, I discovered Roland Barthes and, seduced by his thought and writing, discovered in turn the world of French structuralism, which was echoed in my passion for Peter Wollen's *Signs and Meaning in the Cinema*, which showed me another way of thinking and writing about film.[1] In the 1970s, I was also an avid reader of *Film Comment*, and especially the criticism of Robin Wood who was and will remain my model for engaging deeply with film style. And then I discovered retroactively that in 1973 *Film Comment* published some essays on "cine-structuralism" with a bibliography assembled by Charles Harpole and John Hanhardt. What?! My rabbit hole grew deeper and deeper as I began to special order books like

---

1. See, for example, my foreword to the fifth edition of *Signs and Meaning in the Cinema* (London: British Film Institute/Palgrave Macmillan, 2013): vii–xvi.

the English translations of Noël Burch's *Theory of Film Practice* and Christian Metz's *Language and Cinema*, often waiting anxiously for months for them to arrive. I was busy buying every book about "film theory" I could lay my hands on from André Bazin and Siegfried Kracauer to Sergei Eisenstein and Stanley Cavell.

From here the dominoes began to fall, and other fortuitous encounters emerged. The first was the arrival of Millicent Marcus in the Department of French and Italian as a newly minted PhD from Cornell University. "Penny," as most of us knew her, offered a course on Italian cinema that was immensely popular. (Later I discovered that Ed Lowry was in the same class, though we didn't know each other at the time.) It was immensely demanding as we were required to write short essays on every film screened, but at the same time, immensely rewarding. This is where I really began to learn how to write, and Penny became a generous and lifelong mentor. Suddenly I had another exemplar—someone teaching *film* at a major university. I still didn't realize that such rare creatures existed. Toward the end of my senior year, I also took a seminar on Bertolt Brecht with the extraordinary and still-missed Professor Betty Weber. She was the mentor who alerted me that there was a doctoral student in Radio-Television-Film who had just returned from studying in Paris, and who was finishing a dissertation on "Bertolt Brecht, *Cahiers du Cinéma*, and Contemporary Film Theory." His name was George Lellis, and he was still managing CinemaTexas. We arranged to meet at the CinemaTexas office.

George knows this, I'm happy to say, but there is still no way of measuring the impact this meeting had on my life. I had already discovered that there was a center in Paris co-sponsored by the University of California-Berkeley and the Council on International Educational Exchange, where one could study film with figures like Raymond Bellour, Christian Metz, and Thierry Kuntzel. I deeply wanted to go but for two impediments—I had no money and I couldn't speak French. I'm sure he doesn't remember but for me reminding him, but out of that conversation George basically plotted out the next three years of my life. From George's report on his own experiences in Paris, I knew I had to study there. On his recommendation, I decided that after graduation, I would enroll for a master's degree in Radio-Television-Film while continuing to save money and to improve my pitiful college French. The idea was to go to Paris the following year and to return to finish my MA, if the mood struck me. If I remember correctly, George also inspired teacher, sympathetic but rigorous editor, is among the standout writers at CinemaTexas. Ed Lowry was a graduate student and the director and editor of CinemaTexas (sometimes a combined job, sometimes two jobs). More importantly, and more than any faculty member, Ed Lowry seemed like he had seen practically everything, and he brought a humanist sensibility and brilliant mind to film study. His Notes on any number of films are so remarkably fresh, appropriate, and provocative. We are planning on following this anthology with one devoted to and offering the complete works of Ed Lowry.

Over the next couple of years, while in graduate school, I would watch between one and three movies a day, every day. Every couple of weeks, I wrote a set of Notes. There were many Note writers who took what they did as seriously as I did.

What follows is the written evidence of those times.

———

LOUIS BLACK

PART I

USA Film History

I

While those Note writers who subsequently pursued academic careers have moved in diverse methodological directions, the most commonly invoked theoretical foundation at CinemaTexas was the *auteur* theory—which was not concurrently a common feature of courses in the RTF Department (and other film studies programs of the time)—although both Note writers and RTF faculty were also adopting other analytical tools, including structuralism, semiotics, and genre theory.

The frequent recourse to *auteurism* at CinemaTexas was never an ahistorical biographical endeavor or an uncritical celebration of a director's back catalogue. Rather, Note writers typically considered filmmakers in relation to the industrial and artistic contexts in which they worked, the audiences for their films, and most broadly, how their work could be understood within the social, political, and cultural dynamics of their historical moment.

This section offers a necessarily incomplete overview of American film history, from the silent period through the revisionist Hollywood films of

VOL. 5, NO. 9
SEPTEMBER 18, 1973

Intolerance (1916)

DIRECTED BY D. W. GRIFFITH

I do not intend to imply that Mr. Griffith's ingenuity has not improved on Mr. Barnum's. He has discovered another great amusement of the American public, and has exploited it—the moral lesson. An easy generalization—that intolerance is the only sin which keeps earth from being paradise—is richly suggestive....

The attempt is not to stimulate the imagination, but to gorge the senses. Even this attempt is unsuccessful, because the illusion is not played for honestly; one is astounded at the tricks, the expense, the machinery of production, more often than one is absorbed by their result. One might enjoy a quarter of it, stretched out to the full time. But as it is, one prefers Messrs. Barnum and Bailey. | GEORGE SOULE, *The New Republic*, September 30, 1916.

This film, so gigantic and complex in its pretensions and yet so simple and basic in its approach, cannot help but create a lasting and deep impression on anyone who sees it. At times it achieves the intensity of a vision; one feels that the images on the screen have no recognizable counterpart in reality, so forcefully are they conveyed. And yet they are real, and so real that one can hear the screaming mass of hysterical crowds, the smell of blood, or the perfume of a young girl's hair. *Intolerance* shows, clearer than any other of Griffith's major works, his ability to construct large and spectacular scenes comparable only to a military manoeuvre, alongside his equally powerful talent for lifting the simplest gesture, facial expression or the most basic and elementary of situations into the realms of the highest artistic achievement attained in the medium of motion pictures. This fact alone commands our respect of him as one of the most important of the figures in the development of cinematic art. | PAUL O'DELL in *Griffith and the Rise of Hollywood*

Do you know we are playing to the world! What we film tomorrow will stir the hearts of the world—and they will understand what we're saying. We've gone beyond Babel, beyond words. We've found a universal language—a power that can make men brothers and end war forever. Remember that. Remember that, when you stand in front of the camera! | D. W. GRIFFITH to his performers, quoted in *The Movies, Mr. Griffith, and Me*, by Lillian Gish.

D. W. Griffith was in a peculiar position. Once disdaining to stoop so low as to work in the cinema ("I haven't reached the point where I have to work in films," he responded to an offer to work in the movies), he was now "Dean of the American Cinema." Once a failed playwright, he was now the creator of the controversial landmark in American cinema, *The Birth of a Nation* (1915). But it was a monument erected seemingly overnight, and the sleepy populace was not prepared for such an edifice. Because of his portrayal of the Negro it aroused fiery questions. (Is he a racist? Or a wrong-headed historian? Or simply a fourth-rate philosopher with a camera?) They were not yet stilled when he released *Intolerance* in September 1916.

With *Intolerance* Griffith hoped to accomplish two goals. He needed to better himself as the director of *The Birth of a Nation*, and he wanted to show that he was not a racist but a defender of love and truth. To do so, he devised an overwhelmingly panoramic vision of intolerance, following four tales in history simultaneously, all of them united in theme. The linking device was the image of the cradle, being gently rocked by the woman, earth mother of the ages, with the three fates nearby, like maternal aunts, relatives of our destiny.

He ended with a film costing 1.9 million dollars and eight hours long. It was trimmed to about three hours for final distribution. (The movie you see

Intolerance. Courtesy of the film still department of Anthology Film Archives.

tonight is an approximation of that original. After World War I, Griffith cut *Intolerance* to make two pictures from it: one of the Babylonian struggle called *The Fall of Babylon*, and another, *The Mother and the Law*, which is the modern story in *Intolerance*. In so doing, Griffith cut up the original negative, so what we now view is a patched-up version of the 1916 original.)

The size and scope of *Intolerance* is astounding. And doubly so when considered with the fact that the whole plan was always in the head of Griffith. There was never any written script prepared or used. No detailed architectural designs were ever drawn up. The buildings were built, much in the same way the film was, piecemeal, with Griffith explaining what he wanted, or perhaps scribbling down hastily a sketch of what the walls of Babylon should look like to his chief carpenter. No one but Griffith knew exactly what would be shot next, or why, or what after that.

Seen today, *Intolerance* is primarily a huge, entertaining spectacle. (The audiences it first played to are said to have had a difficult time following the transitions from period to period.) As Paul Rotha suggests, the lavish sets in *Intolerance* are the stuff spectacles are made of. But Griffith went beyond mere spectacle, and the reason his is more engrossing than anybody else's is the fact that he must have realized he *had* to go beyond grandeur. Griffith's film is aesthetically delightful as well as being a great show.

Consider the photography. "The task I'm trying to achieve is above all to make you see," he has been quoted as saying. And to get us to see, he constantly plays with our eyes, shifting the interest point here and there on the screen (he opens various scenes by unfolding it slowly, using the iris, from one corner or another), or by changing the shape of the frame altogether (in the battle sequences when towers or assaulters scaling ladders are seen, the frame reshapes itself, excluding all but these elements), and of course by making each frame as visually interesting as possible (his formations are absorbing: his players seldom act alone, there is always something else happening, either in front or behind, or to the sides—even to the edges of the frame). He leads us, visually, exactly where he wants us to go. The screen was a precious rectangle for Griffith, each small section of it important to him.

Griffith's heroines are bold, full-blooded, healthy women. The Mountain Girl (Constance Talmadge) strides up to her auction two steps at a time, and eats onions during the proceedings. Later, in what must have been a particularly fortuitous bit of improvisation to catch on film, she bites a goat's ear while playing with it. Mae Marsh struggles violently for her baby, and goes to any lengths to free her husband. Strong-willed girls these, struggling to make their own fate despite the odds. These are heroines we have to cheer for, and indeed, the Babylonian and modern episodes are the most magnetic of the four stories largely because of them.

The fact that he had to cut it down from eight hours is one of the reasons his editing is so taut and economical. The chase scene, a standard element by then, was moved to the fourth power by showing all climaxes concurrently. The tension here is regulated solely by editing. By making some of the main actions so abrupt (especially the murder of the Musketeer), Griffith is not only demanding more and more of his audience, but also approximating the way violent actions occur in reality—"It all happened so fast!" Eisenstein no doubt was influenced, and took the technique of editing for effect to its ultimate in *Potemkin* (1925) and *Ten Days That Shook the World* (1928). (See *Ten Days* on October 2.) And it is no coincidence, I think, that much of Ivan the Terrible's character and operatic presence is prefigured here in the stagey Belshazzar.

If *Intolerance* is now a critical success, it was a 1916 box-office failure. Griffith never quite recovered from the picture's losses. Some feel this lack of financial independence undercut his creativity afterwards, that he never overcame the disappointment of having the message he'd dreamed of showing the world—peace, love, brotherhood—rejected by the world's masses. At any rate, *The Birth of a Nation* and *Intolerance* marked Griffith's artistic peak, and it is sad to hear him speak of the dream that was *Intolerance*:

> Perhaps I was dreaming too big a dream when I conceived *Intolerance*. I was reaching out—stretching beyond my talents. I was trying to say something beyond my talents. I was trying to say something to influence the whole world. Maybe it's not possible to reach out and speak with a message of compassion for the entire world. I should have confined myself to America and the English-speaking people—or to the Western world.

—

CHARLES BERG

VOL. 22, NO. 1
JANUARY 28, 1982

Sunrise (1927)

DIRECTED BY F. W. MURNAU

One would hesitate to call *any* film the finest of its era, though as a climax to the art of the silent film, one could certainly defend that statement if it were applied to *Sunrise*. But quite certainly, it is a textbook illustration not only of what the silent film could achieve despite the lack of dialogue, but, on the contrary, what it could achieve *because* of it . . . | WILLIAM K. EVERSON, *American Silent Film.*

The most beautiful and subtle of all late silent films to come out of America, *Sunrise* earned Murnau a critical and professional acclaim achieved by few emigres. Hollywood directors, including John Ford, adapted and absorbed his style, and American film gained a new depth to its vision, soon sadly to be blinded by the eruption of sound. | JOHN BAXTER, *Hollywood Exiles.*

Hollywood's dominance of the world film market has been challenged but rarely in the eighty-odd years since the birth of the motion picture. Perhaps the most serious challenge was that posed by the German film industry during the 1920s. The Germans boasted at the time a nearly unmatched collection of talent, led by such notables as directors Fritz Lang, Ernst Lubitsch and F. W. Murnau, screenwriters Carl Mayer, cinematographers Karl Freund and a host of other top-flight artists and technicians.

Hollywood's response to the German challenge was simple: bring all of that talent to the United States. Make the top German filmmakers offers they couldn't refuse; simultaneously weaken the German film industry and build up Hollywood. F. W. Murnau was one of the hordes of European film-makers lured to sunny California with promise of huge budgets and total artistic freedom.

The director of *Sunrise* came to film by way of the theater. Like so many of Germany's top filmmakers, he began as a student of Max Reinhardt and later worked as a stage director in Berlin. He directed his first film, *Der Knabe in Blau*, in 1919, and a scant three years later assured himself a place in the film history books with *Nosferatu*, a remarkable (and unauthorized) adaptation of Bram Stoker's novel *Dracula*. Murnau proved himself no flash in the pan two years after that, directing *The Last Laugh* from a script by Carl Mayer. *The Last Laugh* was a huge critical success, a fact not lost on at least one Hollywood mogul—William Fox. On the basis of the success of *The Last Laugh*, Fox signed Murnau to a four-year contract at $125,000 for the first year and escalating to $200,000 in the fourth. The contract called for a minimum of one film a year, with Murnau receiving a $125,000 bonus for any extra films. Murnau signed with the understanding that his first film would be an adaptation of Hermann Sudermann's tragedy "Excursion to Tilsit," and that he would encounter no studio interference.

Carl Mayer, the leading screenwriter in Germany and the man respon-sible for the script which became the groundbreaking Expressionist film, *Cabinet of Dr. Caligari*, was hired to write the screenplay. He and Murnau had the film completely planned before Murnau left for Hollywood. Arriving in the United States, Murnau found Fox as good as his word, interfering in the filming of *Sunrise* not at all: no one but Murnau, cinematographers Charles Rosher and Karl Struss and the film editor saw any of the film until it was completed.

This independence was remarkable in and of itself but seems even more so given the extravagance of Murnau from the time he began shooting. Several studio executives balked at the expense involved in realizing Mur-nau's vision, but William Fox, anxious to release a prestige picture of the sort Murnau had already become famous for, vetoed all attempts to limit Murnau in any way.

Sunrise. From the core collection production photographs of the Margaret Herrick Library, Academy of Motion Picture Arts and Sciences.

And Murnau went to town. Several scenes in *Sunrise* required huge, specially designed sets and even huger crowds. But the sets were not ordinary sets and the crowds weren't ordinary crowds. Murnau wanted to make the city in *Sunrise* large and intimidating. To this end he used forced perspective sets with slanting walls and ceilings which made a set look much larger than it actually was. He actually hired crowds of dwarves to fill the backgrounds, again making the sets appear larger. Rain and duststorms, an important part of the plot, were shot indoors using a mechanism which frequently malfunctioned, requiring expensive retakes.

Shooting at a lake in California, Murnau spotted just the tree he needed for a particular scene. He had the tree trucked back to the studio to be built into a set. When the tree's leaves withered under the lights, 300 Mexican laborers were hired to glue fake leaves on it. When these withered, the process was repeated. Murnau got his tree.

To achieve his stunning and much noted moving camera shots, Murnau and cinematographer Charles Rosher devised a system of ceiling-mounted rails from which the camera could be suspended. The camera was thus freed to move in any direction: up, down, diagonally, even in a complete circle.

The result of all this expensive trickery was *Sunrise*, released in the fall of 1927. The film was something of a critical success, though opinion was far from unanimous. In addition, the film received quite a bit of attention from students of the film as art, being written up in several fledgling film journals. On the positive side:

> Mr. Murnau's talent as it appears in the direction of *Sunrise* . . . is a talent that takes the camera on neglected rather than new terms, making it primarily an eye for motion-beside-within-motion, a retina reflecting an intricately flowing world. The camera moves as the eye, and the eye, with the camera, makes journeys, steering gently along the path of the subject it follows, is caught into long perspectives that plunge into the screen, swerves around corners, becomes involved in elaborate fleeing lights and shadows, all the exciting mixture and quarrel of vision. Here is camera technique pushed to its limits, freed from pantomime and parade against a world as motionless as a backdrop. In the same way that a man walking becomes a more complicated and dramatic mechanism when seen from a moving train than from an open window, so the people in this adapted Sudermann story are heightened and realized in their joy and despair by having their action set against action.
>
> Not since the earliest, simplest moving pictures, when locomotives, fire-engines, and crowds in streets were transposed to the screen artlessly and endearingly, when the entranced eye was rushed through tunnels and over precipices on runaway trains, has there been such joy in motion as under Murnau's direction. He slaps down the cramping cubes of sets and makes, whenever possible, walls of glass and steel that imprison in their clear geometry the intersection of long smooth lines of traffic, people walking, trains gathering speed. When the rare shot shows human gesture against a static background, the stillness is an accent, after the rush of a full and moving screen. | LOUISE BOGAN, *The New Republic*, October 26, 1927.

And on the negative:

A song of two humans. Heads or hearts? Neither—hands made this. It is very elaborate. There is no psychology, no insight, nothing we have been waiting for. The technique—Oh, damn technique. . . . The cinema should be the means of this age to express what this age feels and there is nothing of this age in *Sunrise*. . . . Trying as it sets out to do to be of no place and every place, of all time and no time, it succeeds quite elaborately in repeating the superficialities of every age whilst giving expression to none of the complexities of this. | **ROBERT HERRING**, *Close Up*, March 1928.

Critical response may have been mixed; industry response was overwhelmingly positive. Many filmmakers, notably directors Frank Borzage and Edgar Ulmer, freely adapted Murnau's style to their own needs. In addition, the film won three of the first Academy Awards to be presented. Charles Rosher and Karl Struss won the Oscar for Cinematography; Janet Gaynor, who plays the wife in the film, was named Best Actress; the film, though not even nominated for Best Picture, was honored for having the "Best Artistic Quality of Production."

Unfortunately, the film was a commercial disaster, a failure from which Murnau never really recovered.

Artistic, probably, from a directorial point of view, but the plot was too simple and dragged out to excessive length. Small town patrons not very enthusiastic regarding its merits and there were as many knocks as words of praise. The intelligentsia of the large cities may go wild over Mr. Murnau's art, but the people in small towns don't appreciate it quite as much. | *The Motion Picture Almanac*, 1929.

As a result, Murnau's subsequent films were made under strict studio supervision, even to the extent on one occasion of having sound added to a completed silent film, without Murnau's approval. He made just two more films for Fox, never fulfilling the terms of his contract, and, after completing the independently-produced *Tabu* (1931), he died as a result of injuries sustained in an automobile accident. He was at the time on the verge of signing a contract with Paramount Pictures, a contract which could have revived his career.

Sunrise is often considered to be the aesthetic high point of Murnau's career (though a strong case can be made both for *Nosferatu* and *The Last Laugh*).

> [In *Sunrise*] Murnau, the gangling ex-art historian, had created something new
> in film, an alternative to the intense Expressionism of his avant-garde contem-
> poraries and the slick professionalism of the mainstream. In Murnau's world
> the camera glided sinuously through landscapes made unreal by mist or shim-
> mering light, confronted individuals whose lives existed only in part on the
> physical level, analysed emotions and motivations so obscure that one still
> finds astonishing the vividness with which they leap into the mind. | JOHN
> BAXTER, *The Hollywood Exiles.*

Baxter hits here upon two points of more than passing interest. The first
is the importance of the sinuously gliding camera to Murnau's critical reputation. Murnau is best remembered as a master of long takes and a relentlessly moving camera. But Baxter hints also at Murnau's versatility when he
described *Sunrise* as an alternative both to Expressionism and the slickness
of mainstream Hollywood cinema. Murnau was far from a johnny-one-note
director, a fact overlooked by too many critics and historians.

As *Sunrise* so amply demonstrates, Murnau's visual/narrative style was
a unique blend of apparently disparate elements borrowed from nearly
every school of filmmaking. *Sunrise* incorporated elements of German
Expressionism, mainstream Hollywood filmmaking techniques, Soviet
montage and nearly everything else under the arc lights. It may be that
Murnau's genius lay not so much in his inventiveness as in his ability to create an intensely cohesive and personal style from radically disparate sources
where most filmmakers would have been left with a visual patchwork quilt.
Eileen Bowser describes *Sunrise* as moving freely "from subjectives to realistic style":

> It has fluid movements, double exposures, multiple images, slightly
> distorted sets, a magical use of lighting, all of which contribute to the
> emotional tensions.

Sunrise is a film of oppositions, of clashing imagery and clashing styles. The
way the film looks varies with the emotional state of the characters. Somehow, Murnau makes inconsistency a virtue.

He is able to get away with stylistic inconsistency because his plot, provided by the meticulous Carl Mayer, is so carefully and self-consciously
structured. The film's story neatly doubles back upon itself, forming a

perfect circle. Each scene in the first half of the film has a nearly identical, though opposite, counterpart in the second half (see figure 1). The film begins with a montage of vacationers from the city traveling to the country. The film ends with one of those travelers, the city woman who acts as the catalyst for the film's action, leaving the country and returning to the city. An illicit embrace between the Man and the Woman from the City is balanced in the second half by an embrace between the Man and the Wife. A boat ride in which the Man, at the spiritual mercy of the Woman from the City, attempts to drown the Wife is balanced by a later scene in which the redeemed Man, reunited with his Wife, attempts to save her from drowning as they return home. A trolley ride early in the film in which the Man and Wife are held suspended between the city and the country, between love and hate, trust and fear, spiritualism and godlessness and, perhaps most importantly, between the ordered community of the country and the confusion of the city, is balanced by a later trolley ride in which the reunited Man and Wife have resolved their differences, conquering the oppositions of the first half. The country couple's trip to the city—their vacation—balances the city folks' vacation in the country. Every scene, every action has a mirror-image counterpart. Each scene is, furthermore, shot in a style appropriate to the action in that scene.

Molly Haskell points out that *Sunrise* is all oppositions, a film built dialectically:

> The oppositions in *Sunrise* . . . are between sunrise and sunset, the country and the city, good and evil, salvation and sin, devine grace and black magic, natural and unnatural acts, and finally the blonde, beatific wife (Janet Gaynor) and the dark, sultry city woman (Margaret Livingston) in their struggle for The Man's soul.

In this light, Murnau's stylistic flourishes must be seen as more than simple inconsistency and, certainly, more than mere puffery. For all its stylistic flourishes (if not *because* of them) *Sunrise* remains a remarkably engaging and moving film, having lost none of its aesthetic and emotional charm over the years. Most films seem to strive for realism, hiding their artificiality. Murnau would have none of this. He reveled in artificiality, making no attempt to engage in a fruitless search for something resembling realism.

of developing his character. "Frank Capra," says Sennett in his autobiography, *King of Comedy*, "wanted Langdon as soon as he set eyes on him. Harry has the kind of dough-faced, baby innocence about him, combined with malice, that delighted Capra. . . . Langdon was as bland as milk, a forgiving, small cuss, an obedient puppy, always in the way, exasperating, but offering his baby mannerisms with hopeful apology. Frank Capra's enormous talents first showed themselves when he saw this as something he could photograph."

Indeed, it seems that unlike other notable Sennett graduates, such as Chaplin and Keaton, Langdon was not responsible for the character and style of wit which made him the successful vehicle of many fine Sennett shorts. Historical hindsight shows this to be a tenable assumption. Langdon's star rose powerfully in 1926, just after he quit Sennett taking Edwards and Capra with him as directors. After a brief success with Capra, whom he fired after *Long Pants* was filmed, he began to direct his own features. They were received with mixed reviews, and by 1929 his star was nearly extinguished. He died in 1944, broke and nearly forgotten, leaving behind a string of unnoteworthy performances.

Gerald Mast tries to defend Langdon by outlining comic traits that are unique to Langdon the man. His stock-in-trade was ultimately his physiognomics: that pasty baby-face, sexually ambiguous, both infantile and devilish, which prompted James Agee to characterize him both as "an elderly baby" and "a baby dope fiend." Within any comic situation, Langdon was the master of one expression: the blank state broken by one hard blink of disbelief. The Langdon character rarely reacts to the comic world and never comprehends it. The characters of Keaton, Lloyd, and Chaplin were all dependent on physicality and manic activity. Carried to the frontiers of circumstance by the most improbable of screen events, they could bypass disaster with a balletic sidestep or an inventive twist of imagination executed with faultless timing. The improbability of circumstances was always surpassed by the improbability of their reaction: this is the dynamic key to the best of the silent film comedies. Langdon, however, is uniquely unqualified by these criteria. His comedy resides in the absolute superficiality with which he regards each situation and the impregnable innocence that carries him through each gag.

Keaton and Chaplin had characters with depth and irony, but Langdon was ultimately transparent and never ironic because he never understood the irony of his own position. He strove for pathos in an attempt to emulate and transcend Chaplin, but he never realized that, whereas pathos was the essence of "the little tramp" which enabled Chaplin to transcend his audience, it was the lack of pathos in Langdon and the audience's ability to comprehend his irony while he did not, which made his character successful initially. In retrospect, Capra's assertion that Langdon never understood that pathos resided in his *comedy* and not his *character* seems obvious. He was a brilliant medium for better comic minds than his own who knew how to manipulate his film environment; but once he took the reins into his own hands, that world collapsed around him.

In this respect, *Long Pants* may be Langdon's last good film. Gerald Mast explains the film by developing a thematic conflict between appearance and reality (a metaphysical concern more characteristic of Mast than of Langdon) that is not without some justification. However, the essence of Langdon's character is in his resolute inability to comprehend reality at all beyond the level of appearances. *Long Pants* at its funniest plays off this inability and the superficiality of Langdon's expression which summarizes it. The best example is perhaps his encounter with the "dummy" policeman which he is unable to convince, connive, or threaten away from a seat atop the crate in which his "darling" is cached. Later, a real policeman replaces the dummy, and a box containing an alligator is substituted for the real one. Langdon, thinking he finally knows the score, bops the policeman with a brick and carries off the box with the alligator. The comedy of the scene lies in his dazed and surprised expression as he tries to comprehend exactly what is going on while the screen events remain one step ahead of his plodding mentality.

This type of comedy at its most awkward is revealed in an earlier scene where Langdon tries to murder his betrothed. His inability to shoot right off the bat and his concern that the girl not be looking and have a "comfortable place to land" is some consolation for his desire and conviction to murder her. The superficiality in this case reflects a basic selfishness and stupidity concerning death that is unconscionable in a comic world. His eventual entanglement in barbed wire and a bear trap is little compensation for the inanity that Chaplin or Keaton would easily have avoided or surpassed.

All in all, the key to Langdon's comedy resides in his inability to recognize the absurdity of his own situations. Where Chaplin, and especially

Keaton, were able to match and surpass those absurdities, Langdon was rendered more impotent by them. Perhaps he lost his audience when he tried to equal them, and thereby sank as he undermined the foundation he was trying to build upon.

——

DAVID RODOWICK

Sherlock Jr. (1924)

DIRECTED BY BUSTER KEATON

You very often use gags which couldn't be managed except in films. For instance, the scene in Sherlock, Jr. *where you are dreaming yourself into the picture, and the scenery keeps changing. How did you get the idea of this scene?*

That was the reason for making the whole picture. Just that one situation: that a motion picture projectionist in a theatre goes to sleep and visualizes himself getting mixed up with the characters on the screen. All right, then my job was to transform those characters on the screen into my (the projectionist's) characters at home, and then I've got my plot. Now to make it work was another thing; and after that picture was made every cameraman in Hollywood spent more than one night watching it and trying to figure out just how we got some of those scenes. | BUSTER KEATON interviewed by John Gillett, *Sight and Sound*, Winter 1965–1966.

Self-referentiality has come to be the calling card of the "modernist transformation" which has been most ostensibly effected by directors in the French New Wave; but if this is the case, Keaton's *Sherlock Jr.* may be more contemporary than most modern films. As Keaton implies above, the dream/

> There are films like *The Big Parade* and even *All Quiet on the Western Front*
> which condemn war, but implicitly, by their nostalgic tone, their uncritical
> non-incisive pacifism, their placing of the blame on the lesser individual and
> the stay-at-home, their sympathy with the protagonist, their excitement, their
> comic interludes, make war interesting. Their little condemnations are lost,
> amid the overwhelming pile of films in which war is a farcical holiday, or a
> swashbuckler's adventure. | HARRY ALAN POTAMKIN, *The Eyes of the Movie*

Seen today, *All Quiet on the Western Front* is to this viewer a mixed aesthetic success, an uneven film filled with inconsistencies and unamplified levels of meaning. Long, static, talky sections of film alternate with elaborately edited, manneredly visual sequences. Explicit, anti-war didacticism coexists with naturalistic, slice of life touches of human observation. The acting is at times stilted, at times affecting. Sergei Eisenstein is said to have likened the film to a PhD thesis in its technical perfection, but the work comes across not as a clearly structured argument, but rather as an indirect progression toward its conclusions, an interrupted, deflected trajectory which reaches its destination only after passing by innumerable peripheral points.

This film, the most famous of its director, Lewis Milestone, acquires its most provocative meanings from four central preoccupations:

1. *Reality/Unreality.* The first third of *All Quiet on the Western Front* consists of variations on the problem of perceiving the wartime experience as it really is—both for the recruits experiencing it and the audience. On the most obvious level, the former students come to see the falseness of their schoolmaster's noble proclamations about war. Their initial experiences are a mixture of idealism, camaraderie and fraternity party adventure, mixed with bitter shocks and the steadily growing realization of their eventual destiny.

Consider the sight of their first nighttime battlefield. It is on the one hand an attractive display of fireworks, on the other a chilling threat. There is danger, but a sense of distance from it as well. It is hardly arbitrary to the narrative that the first injury sustained by one of the group is blindness, and that the victim is Behm, the one hesitant recruit who could *foresee* the implications of their enlistment. A short time later, in the barracks, a soldier awakens screaming from a bad dream. "Everything's all right, you're dreaming," he is told, as though the waking reality were any better. Still later, Franz thinks he feels pain in the toe of a foot that has been amputated. Near the end of the film, we learn that Detering has walked off the battlefield to

All Quiet on the Western Front. From the core collection production photographs
of the Margaret Herrick Library, Academy of Motion Picture Arts and Sciences.

go home and help his wife with the harvest. As the recruits enter training,
they are told, "Forget what you've been, and what you think you're going to
be." The reality of war is different, and it is not always what one's perceptions would indicate.

This theme is picked up again when Paul and his comrade discuss the
picture of a girl on a poster in the canteen, while they themselves are seen
by us as reflections in a mirror. Two scenes later, the soldiers have landed
themselves a trio of Frenchwomen for the night. War is like love—part illusion, part reality, and it is the fatal confusion of the two that makes war so
monstrously fatal.

The emphasis on the contrast between the war experience as on the one
hand a false projection and on the other an oppressive reality is suggested
on a visual level in the presentation of the first battle. There is an alternating
montage between shots of the camera panning across the attacking French
(or are they British?) troops, and shots of the German machine guns mowing
them down. The troops fall; the Germans continue to shoot. The editing

level exists almost exclusively in the dialogue (e.g., the discussion of who starts wars, or Paul's return to his school); one could almost imagine a dubbed version of the film which would turn it into a pro-war tract. Although much of what it presents is horrible, there is a glamour to the horror, a fascination.

This very argument has been used against *All Quiet on the Western Front* and other war films as far back as the 1930s, with leftist critic Harry Alan Potamkin (quoted above), and more recently by Paul Goodman in his essay, "Designing Pacifist Films," as well as by several other commentators writing in the Grove Press anthology, *Film: Book 2; Films of Peace and War.* Goodman asserts that most anti-war films are not effective because of this fascination at seeing taboo (violent) images, the audience's guilt at this material and its subsequent resentment at being made to feel this guilt, and the production of the emotion of pity to insulate the audience against the films' more direct political messages. Thus, films like *All Quiet* may well be self-defeating in their subconscious glorification of that which they despise. (A directly contrary argument is made by Jacques Belmans, who asserts—and to this reader less convincingly—that even pro-war films often have an anti-war effect because the graphic presentation of war's violence and its resultant psychoses inevitably produces, even when made heroic, images that are fundamentally repulsive and which most audiences have difficulty accepting.)

World War I was a far more vivid memory to audiences of the 1930s than it is to us today, and it is doubtless unfair to evaluate the film's social significance solely by the standards of our time. But one wonders if the picture might not be justly considered a distant cousin to today's disaster films. Coming as it did at the beginning of the depression it may have provided audiences with a sort of consolation by showing them situations significantly more desperate than people were experiencing at the time. One may also consider the way in which it was part of the popular mythology of the early thirties to blame (rightly or wrongly) the problems of the depression on the First World War, to see a cause and effect relationship between the two events. (Obvious example: the "Forgotten Man" number in *Gold Diggers of 1933*.) Thus, it is fair to speculate that *All Quiet on the Western Front* represented in its time both an escape from a dismal economic situation, and someone, or something, to blame for it. It is nonetheless a shame that the film ends not in accusation (which might have given it a little more constructive purpose), but bathos. As the soldiers turn around and address the audience, the message becomes clouded into a "we are all responsible" state-ment rather than one directed at those economic and political interests that may be considered most fundamentally to blame for the war that everyone thought would be over in a couple of weeks.

—

GEORGE LELLIS

VOL. 24, NO. 1
FEBRUARY 9, 1983

Mr. Smith Goes to Washington (1939)

PRODUCED AND DIRECTED BY FRANK CAPRA

Frank Capra understood, perhaps better than any other Hollywood director of his time, the necessary relationship between romantic comedy and social conventions—and between Hollywood movies and American ideology. From the earliest stages of his career as a gag writer for producer Hal Roach and as writer-director on some of Harry Langdon's best silent comedies, Capra refined his comic style that pitted the "little guy" against the faceless, inhuman forces of "the system." Perhaps Capra's own career provided the blueprint: he was himself an immigrant hustler who, as legend has it, bluffed his way into filmmaking. With personal experience informing his sentimental optimism, Capra's homespun heroes repeatedly overcame society's depersonalizing influence. His films were filled with self-sufficient individualists, good neighbors, and benevolent institutions. | THOMAS SCHATZ, *Hollywood Genres*.

I hated being poor. Hated being a peasant. Hated being a scrounging newskid trapped in the sleazy Sicilian ghetto of Los Angeles. My family couldn't read or write. I wanted out. A quick out. I looked for a device, a handle, a pole to catapult myself across the tracks from my scurvy habitat of nobodies to the affluent world of somebodies.

I tried schooling, a technical education. . . . I pondered other quick leaps: bootlegging, prize-fighting, the ball and bat, con games. When I finally found my vaulting pole, it was not made of bamboo, glass or metal. In fact, it was not a pole at all. It was a magic carpet—woven with the coils and ringlets of a wondrous peel of limber plastic, whose filaments carried the genetic code of all the arts of man, and from which the abracadabra of science conjured up the hopes, the fears, the dreams of man—the magic carpet of FILM! | FRANK CAPRA, *The Name above the Title.*

Actor-director John Cassavetes's statement that "maybe there wasn't really an America, maybe there was only Frank Capra" perhaps goes as far as any single statement can toward understanding the pervasiveness, as well as, paradoxically, the hermeticism of Capra's vision of America. For Capra, the viability of American society is maintained through adherence to small town values, good old-fashioned neighborliness and a belief in the "Golden Rule." These values are bolstered by the strength of good men who are prepared to lead their communities and assert the rights of individuals, despite the forces which undermine the common man. Yet, in a very real sense, Capra's America never existed anywhere but on film; by the 1930s, small town America was an ideal that had been transformed by nostalgia into utopia. Critic Morris Dickstein writes in *American Film* (May 1980):

> The small town is already an anachronism in these films, an idea; it's where the hero comes from; its values are now embodied in his charac-ter, not in any fixed sense of place.

Yet it is unfair—and ultimately unrewarding from a critical perspective—to label Capra naive. With Capra's storybook conception of America—which pits gangly prairie heroes against jaded politicoes and industrialists—there is a strain in Capra's work which acknowledges, albeit cautiously, the darker side of American culture. His films take cognizance of the extent to which American institutions are controlled by monied interests. At times, Capra bludgeons audiences with a realization of the powerlessness of the masses to effect a permanent change in this order, only to mitigate the mag-nitude of his admission through the triumph of a folk savior like Jefferson Smith. The uniqueness of Capra's vision, then, derives from his ability to

> It's a funny thing about men, you know, they all start life being boys . . . and that's why it seemed like a pretty good idea to me to get boys out of crowded cities and stuffy basements for a couple of months out of the year and build their bodies and minds for man-sized jobs, because those boys are gonna be behind these desks some of these days. | JEFFERSON SMITH in *Mr. Smith Goes to Washington*

And while Smith acknowledges that he wouldn't have been able to succeed against Taylor, et al., without Saunders, she is primarily valued for her hearth-tending, morale-building skills, not for her intelligence.

> Dad always used to say the only causes worth fighting for were the lost causes. | JEFFERSON SMITH

> The dopes are going to inherit the earth, anyway. | DIZ MOORE in *Mr. Smith Goes to Washington*

Ultimately, the central conflict in *Mr. Smith Goes to Washington* is not between the Taylors and the Smiths but between naive idealists like Smith and cynics like Saunders, Diz and, most importantly, Paine. Paine's initial compromise with Taylor, his willingness to be Taylor's lackey for the sake of power, represents one option for the erstwhile idealist. The line between social morality and capitulation to monied interests is exceedingly thin. The poignancy of Paine's dilemma derives from the fact that compromising with Taylor is a viable option. Paine's attempted suicide represents a desperate acknowledgement of his failure to choose the morally correct option, the option that would preserve his personal identity and his liberty but not necessarily secure his political future.

More than this, Paine's crisis is a familial one. In the absence of Smith's father, Paine's best friend, Paine must serve as surrogate father to Smith. He fails miserably to live up to Jeff Smith's conception of him as a moral leader and a fighter of lost causes. That Smith's impassioned filibuster convinces Paine of the meaninglessness of his position in the Senate contributes to the film's emotional power and makes Smith's final struggles take on a different meaning. In a sense, Smith and Paine's conflict is depoliticized, if only in those moments when they exchange knowing glances, establishing a bond which transcends the political arena.

Yet, Jim Taylor's machine still rolls. Capra is unable or unwilling to advocate the steps that would be necessary to truly undermine the Taylors of the nation. He is implicitly against redistribution of wealth, seeking rather to bolster small businessmen than to equalize society. Indeed, fighting Taylor *is* a lost cause. And if Taylor's formidableness does not render Smith's final triumph hollow, it should serve to qualify the audience's exuberance about the promise of life in these United States. The question for Capra's heroes, however, is not whether they win, but whether they unite with other little guys. They hope that a lot of little jabs will temper the excesses of greed. The question for Capra is not even whether the little guys can effect change but whether they can maintain faith in a meaning for their existence which they cannot know.

> You cannot overestimate the fact that there is some reason for their [people] being here—some reason to live, some reason for the creation of life, some reason for the cosmos to be here. Why we're here is not given us to know as yet; but if you can follow whatever is biological, if you follow what is spiritual, you can find a reason for being. | "Capra Today," *Film Comment*, November-December 1972

——

MARIE MAHONEY

VOL. 15, NO. 1
SEPTEMBER 12, 1978

Citizen Kane (1941)

DIRECTED AND PRODUCED BY ORSON WELLES

From the moment its planned production was announced it was sneered at. Cruel jokes about its director and aspersions on his masculinity tickled the funnybone of many of Hollywood. When word went about that it was to be a satirical biography of the world's most influential man, other influential men trembled, fearful of the great one's wrath. The president of Metro-Goldwyn-Mayer tried to buy it and burn it before anyone saw it. And in its first release, hardly anyone saw it anyway.

Many more people have seen *Citizen Kane* since its fateful first-run; but like those wealthy, tuxedoed arts patrons who doze through Susan Alexander's operatic performances, many come to *Kane* because they are told it is "art." *Kane* is one of a handful of films which have earned the status of a "classic." Yet nothing is more likely to render a vital, meaningful work dead than that one word. Immediately we are apt to perceive a work so labelled as cold and forbidding, like Kane's Xanadu, with its wrought-iron "K" at the gate. Part of the problem is that a few writers have called *Kane* "the greatest movie ever made," and nothing could live down such an appellation.

Citizen Kane has become folklore. Practically every American film since

Citizen Kane. From the core collection production photographs of the Margaret Herrick Library, Academy of Motion Picture Arts and Sciences.

1941 has owed something to it, and it remains the standard against which subsequent films, including those of its own director, are judged. It did not get this big by being an empty exercise in virtuosity. If Welles's filmic tricks, dazzling as they are, did not have a purpose, *Kane* would be only a footnote to film history.

WELLES TAKES HOLLYWOOD

Citizen Kane was the joint product of a 25-year-old whiz kid, a slightly sour and slightly whimsical screenwriter, a group of actors infected by the whiz kid's magical charisma, and a group of technicians who, having finally been given something challenging to do, made the absolute most of it.

In 1931 Orson Welles had travelled to Dublin, Ireland and presented himself to the director of the Abbey Theatre as a great New York star. His gall was more impressive than his lie, and considering that he was all of 16 years old, there was nothing to do but hire him. Welles returned to America shortly thereafter, and in 1938 he and John Houseman founded the Mercury

Theatre. This enthusiastic experiment in modern repertory theater, spear-headed by Welles's bravura acting and imaginative productions, was soon the most vital thing on the New York stage. Meanwhile, Welles had become known to radio listeners as "The Shadow," and soon the Mercury Theatre was making weekly broadcasts. One of these broadcasts, that of Halloween, 1938, was an adaptation of *The War of the Worlds* done in radio-newscast style. This self-reflexive use of the medium inspired a panic that affected hundreds of thousands of Americans. Welles was now the most infamous man in entertainment. He was 23.

With great fanfare, the Mercury troupe arrived in Hollywood the following year. Welles had accepted a movie contract, not because it was a new medium to conquer, but because Mercury needed money to do *Five Kings*, an amalgam of several Shakespeare histories that was to be the biggest production in theatrical history. (It was never staged, but vestiges can be seen in Welles's 1965 *Chimes at Midnight*.)

The offer Welles accepted came from RKO-Radio Pictures. RKO (Radio-Keith-Orpheum) gave the world *King Kong* and the Fred Astaire-Ginger Rogers musicals, but in 1939 Kong was dead, MGM was grabbing the musical audience, and the company was wracked by a tug-of-war between its two principal stockholders. Perhaps because they had nothing to lose, RKO had given Welles a contract of unlimited artistic freedom, something that hadn't been granted since the days of pioneer moviemakers.

Delightedly declaring that he now had "the world's biggest electric train" to play with, Welles plunged into serious film study, viewing every major and minor film he could get, reading Eisenstein and Pudovkin and with his Mercury partners, preparing treatments for his debut. RKO rejected his first project, Conrad's *Heart of Darkness*, on the grounds of excessive expense. His second and third proposals were also rejected. Snickers began to be heard. The whiz kid had been in Hollywood a year and nothing was coming of it. The old-timers waited for the thud of his face hitting the floor.

Enter Herman Mankiewicz, a newspaper writer and critic with George Kaufman and Marc Connelly in New York who had been one of the first to heed the call of Hollywood and one of the first to grow cynical about what he'd done with his talent. He is remembered today as an indifferent genius, a corpulent, undisciplined innovator of the snappy 1930's dialogue film. For a time he was a producer at several studios, but he always managed to get fired. As a producer, he gave the Marx Brothers, and their writers, free rein to create *Monkey Business*, *Horse Feathers*, and *Duck Soup*; as a writer, none of his dozens of scripts would ever gain him the immortality of the one for *Kane*.

What Welles and Mankiewicz came up with was nothing less than a semi-biography of William Randolph Hearst, newspaper tycoon, formulator of mass opinion, one of the world's wealthiest men, lover of actress Marion Davies, and by all accounts a man with a raging fascist-dictator complex. Hearst was the founder of sensationalistic "yellow journalism," and the shrill tone of his newspapers' reportage is said to have brought about the Spanish-American War. Like Kane, he built a fabulous, medieval fairy-tale castle called San Simeon (which can be seen in the aerial newsreel shots of Xanadu). His newspapers were so widespread they could influence opinion on any subject, including, presumably, the value of spending money on movies and the need for government censorship thereof.

The spectre of the giant Hearst slamming his fist down on tiny, vulnerable Hollywood scared the movie bosses to death. En masse, they tried to persuade RKO production chief George Schaefer to cease filming; he refused. Meanwhile Welles's crew, realizing they had a subject with some teeth in it, rolled up their collective sleeves and gave the neophyte kid more effort than the oldest veteran could command. With what was by 1940s standards a limited budget, they created, through judicious placement of lights and set pieces, illusions of grandeur and immense space. When Welles wanted to stage several shots in manners beyond the scope of extant technology, cinematographer Gregg Toland simply designed a brand new lens. It might have been the happiest, most enthusiastic cooperative effort in movie history, had it not been for the politics of pressure.

With shooting completed, the legendary gossip columnist Louella Parsons, who worked for Hearst, requested a screening. She was shown a rough cut, stormed out of the screening room, and began a campaign of invective against Welles. All mention of RKO productions—not just *Kane*—was banned in the Hearst papers. With their fears confirmed, the other studios renewed attempts to muzzle RKO. Louis B. Mayer offered Schaefer the full amount of production costs and lab work if he would relinquish the negative and all prints. The Hollywood community in general, already resentful because a kid had been given his way, began to be openly, publicly rude to Welles. *Kane* was completed and ready by early 1941, but the publicity and the pressures prevented its release until late spring.

Already, the New York and Los Angeles critics who had been at the earlier press screenings declared that Welles had done just what everybody had challenged him to do—made a better movie than anyone else. Almost unanimously the critics considered it the most exciting thing to come from Hollywood since *The Birth of A Nation*. With this endorsement, Welles demanded that RKO release his film. So they did.

It is popularly believed that 1941 audiences found *Kane* too ambiguous and puzzling, that they weren't at all prepared for it. More likely, they simply didn't get a chance to see it. It got substantial bookings only in metropolitan areas; the Fox West Coast theater chain paid for exhibition rights to the west and midwest, then refused to exhibit the film. It was a case of too much pre-publicity. Despite the accolades, exhibitors and public had come to see *Kane* as something less than a sure thing. It did not actually lose money, but its initial profits were not great enough by Hollywood standards to make all the effort worthwhile. The film community never quite forgave Welles; and at the 1941 Academy Awards ceremony, all mentions of *Kane* or Welles drew boos and hisses. Mankiewicz and Welles were given a screenplay Oscar, but Mankiewicz was never again to do remotely satisfying work and Welles was never again given such freedom.

It is said that not until the early 1950s did William Randolph Hearst see the film, at which time he wondered what all the fuss was about.

AMBIGUITY IN BLACK-AND-WHITE

"The best way to understand *Citizen Kane*," writes David Bordwell, "is to stop worshipping it as a triumph of technique." A basic reason that *Kane* is misunderstood is that many think of it as the great fountain from which sprang all of the modern film techniques. Orson Welles, this idea says, singlehandedly invented the ceilinged set, the deep-focus shot, the long take, the invisible dissolve and the masked cut, bequeathing them for more practical uses to less brilliant souls.

No film can work solely as a catalog of camera tricks. The narrative cinema is a synthesis of arts and crafts—theater, dance, writing, photography, music, sound recording—with its peculiar qualities of editing and camera movement. A narrative film—that is, one which attempts to tell a story— works best when the filmic attributes are brought to the story's aid. Because Welles's use of technique is so dense, one may find it more riveting than any other aspect of *Kane*. But Welles did not "invent" any of the techniques used; all were features of the classic studio film. James Naremore defines the "classic studio" film as one that "used chronological narrative, invisible editing, minimal acting and a muted photographic expressionism—everything designed to immerse the audience in 'content' and make them forget the manipulations of style." In other words, all the possibilities of film technique were devoted to disguising themselves. Welles, however, used these techniques in a very different way; instead of hiding them in his story, he magnified them to intensify the story.

Kane is structured somewhat like a detective story: the audience is presented with a mystery and a character who will attempt to solve it. This character spends the balance of the film taking testimony from various parties involved, and duly draws a conclusion. But *Kane* is not a classic detective story in which a basically orderly world has gone out of kilter and must be set in balance. It is more akin in spirit to the "hardboiled" detective stories of Dashiell Hammett and Raymond Chandler; that is, *Kane*'s world is an ambiguous one where there are no quick answers. Ultimately, the process of the search takes on more meaning than the conclusion; the only conclusion to be drawn is that there is no conclusion. Rather than offering clear-cut moral choices and consequences with obvious villains and heroes, *Kane* clearly states, in boldest black-and-white, that there is no black-and-white. The protagonist is not entirely good and those who oppose him not entirely bad; and ultimately, like Thompson the reporter, the audience must accept that it cannot make a clear decision about the hero.

This approach went entirely against the grain of Hollywood tradition, and, more than his stylistic flamboyance, made Welles dangerous to the established order. Yet, by committing itself to ambiguity, *Kane* ushered in a new era of American film. The morally questionable central character was now permissible, and psychological approaches to story construction and *mise-en-scène* could be employed. Within a very few years of *Kane* (and *The Maltese Falcon*, also 1941) the chiaroscuro lighting effects and the pervading sense of gloom were incorporated into the *film noir*, which was to vie with escapist musicals for the audience's attention over several ensuing years.

Kane's basic ambiguity is made manifest through the narrative's flashback structure and by the film's self-reflexivity. Our portrait of Kane is painted by a group of people who knew him, presenting their stories in a more-or-less chronological order with certain overlaps. But even if the facts they relate are in agreement, we must remember that each of their stories is colored by bitter experiences, by the passing of years and by their various points of view. As we gather more facts we know less, and as we near the end we are farther from the truth.

Kane's self-reflexivity is evident in the way that Welles's virtuosity will not let us forget we are watching a film, an arrangement of light, shadow and sound that can approximate or distort real time and space; neither will he let us forget that it is he, Orson Welles, who is doing the manipulating. The first words, other than "Rosebud," spoken by Welles are, "Don't believe everything you hear on the radio," an almost in-joke reference to the *War of the Worlds* broadcast. And his remark to Thatcher on assuming control of the New York *Inquirer* could be Welles's own statement about making his first film: "I don't know how to run a newspaper. I merely try everything I can think of." Thus, the ambiguity is given yet another dimension—not only do we react ambivalently to Charlie Kane, but our response to the film is qualified by our being flatly told it isn't real and by the overwhelming persona of director-actor-writer Welles.

The most remarked-upon technique utilized in *Citizen Kane* is the deep-focus shot. Normally, a lens's focal point is limited to a small area of the space it encompasses. The technique Welles and Toland developed renders all planes with the lens field in equal focus; distant objects will be as sharp as objects within a few feet of the lens. (Actually, deep-focus was "reinvented" by Toland with his new wide-angle lens; it had been a common feature of the types of film and lenses used in silent days, but had disappeared when sound forced a switch to new equipment.) Obviously, a technique like that is too subtle to be meaningful unless it has point. In *Kane*, it is first used at the boarding house where Mrs. Kane signs over her son to the banker Thatcher. Welles, whose background was in theater, understood the significance inherent in simple placement of characters. This stage sense, combined with deep focus, yields moments like that in Mrs. Kane's living room. She, making a wrenching decision, is closest to the camera and so dominates the frame, yet she is rather pinched up against its edge; Thatcher, goading her on, is a bit farther away but more directly facing the camera, reinforcing his position; the whining, ineffectual Mr. Kane hovers in the background, to the side; and all the way back, frolicking in snow, both framed in and trapped by a window, the boy Charles Kane, whose life is about to change forever.

This shot is echoed years later at the Enquirer office during Kane's gigantic party: as Leland, left foreground, announces his changing feelings about Kane to Bernstein, right middle ground, we see a reflection of Kane, frolicking with a dancing girl, in a window rearground center. There are multiple meanings here: Kane, who has just hired away the complete staff of his rival newspaper and is about to launch his own personal war, is like an exuberant child, yet is already being corrupted by his own ego and ambition; hence, the hint of the boy Kane is an ironic, poignant one. The shot is also a fore-shadowing of the divergent positions his friends Leland and Bernstein will take toward him: Leland (on the left) will desert, Bernstein (on the right and wearing a Rough Riders hat) will remain loyal.

Another celebrated deep-focus shot is reportedly a composite of two separate shots, but it is one of the more strikingly composed single shots in all of film. Susan Alexander Kane, wan and demoralized by her enforced singing career, has attempted suicide. She lies unconscious, horizontal in the middle of the frame. In the extreme foreground, by far the largest object in the shot, is the bottle of pills she has taken. In extreme rear right is the door to Susan's room, which is soon broken open; with a very few strides Kane is beside the bed, looming over her. Susan is now enclosed by two vertical shapes, both of which represent the means of her death.

It should be pointed out that use of the wide-angle lens frequently causes a slight, almost imperceptible distortion of the image, so that our perspec-tive is forced and unnatural. In his book on Welles, Naremore points out that such a forced perspective causes a normal shot-reverse shot edit to be more jarring and unsettling than it would be otherwise; and he suggests that this forced perspective, giving something of a dream quality to the whole film, is the true significance of the deep-focus shots.

Also adding to this dream quality is the film's lighting style, heavily influ-enced by 1920s German Expressionist cinema and the theatrical lighting of Max Reinhardt's famous stage productions. Generally speaking, this style hinges upon an unnatural arrangement of light and shadow which empha-sizes a scene's air of foreboding or psychological disturbance. Prime exam-ples in *Kane* are the scene in the Thatcher library, the deathbed sequence and the encounters between Kane and Susan in Xanadu's living room. Nor-mally, deep-focus is difficult to obtain in less than full light; Kane's use of shadow springs not only from artistic aims but from economic necessity. Xanadu's gigantic living room, for example, is made up only of a chair and large fireplace, the rest being empty set. By shrewd placement of light and shadows, Welles and Toland not only created an immensely foreboding scene but saved great expense on unbuilt walls.

Another much-discussed feature of *Kane* is the incessant forward move-ment of the camera. Welles always has been one of the most fluid directors in terms of camera movement; a constantly shifting image means a constant shifting of relationships and boundaries, so that we are never quite sure where we are. Because Toland's wide-angle lens would have made a side-to-side pan rather ungainly, the movement is predominantly forward. Luckily so, as it proves to be a perfect metaphor for the film's inquisitive nature and the curiosity it inspires in the audience. Two scenes in particular illustrate this.

The very first thing we see is a "No Trespassing" sign. The camera immediately trespasses, moving up over the fence. In a consistently forward motion, it takes us over the grounds of Xanadu, where we are confronted with various images of faded luxury: a deserted golf course, a sinking pier. We are creeping toward the one lighted window in the place. Eventually we are right outside the window; suddenly, in the first of several masked dissolves, we are on the other side of the window, in the room. What follows for the next minute or so is right out of 1920s German Expressionism; it takes the curiosity that has built up and scrambles it into almost supernatural confusion. Such confusion can only be answered by the most straightforward of answers: the newsreel that follows.

The second most obvious example of the "peeping camera" is in the visit to Susan Kane at her nightclub. Here the camera, in a movement almost identical to the one previously mentioned, first floats above the club, then swoops down upon the skylight, which it proceeds to *pass right through* by means of another dissolve. Since Susan is the first witness questioned, the camera movement—thrusting this time, rather than creeping as before—is saying, "Now let's get some answers." There are other, more subtle uses of the forward camera, some of them imperceptible; but throughout, it remains supportive of the film's search for its protagonist.

Welles brought to films a background in theater and in radio. His "Mercury Theater On The Air" had been a pacesetter in radio drama, experimenting with the manipulation of time and space using sound. The *Kane* soundtrack is a culmination of these experiments. Welles uses overlapping dialogue in the projection room sequence; adds to the illusion of space in Xanadu by using echo to indicate distance; and, in the celebrated "lightning mixes," bridges great gaps in time by dividing one sentence between two eras. Also noteworthy is Bernard Herrmann's score, the first effort of one of Hollywood's greatest film composers. Herrmann structured the score around two themes: a slow and ominous lower brass arrangement which characterizes Kane's power and which is heard in the first sequence; and a lighthearted passage for woodwinds which appears when we meet the child Charles, and which represents "maybe something he lost, or something he never had."

These few examples should give an idea of *Kane*'s complexity on multiple levels. The film is so tightly interwoven that, like Joyce's *Ulysses*, everything that happens is intimately bound up with everything else. It is, like good art, a reconciliation of opposing forces—the naturalistic cinema tradition of Lumière, and the heavily manipulated, stylized tradition of Méliès. Welles has blended these basic filmic traditions in such a way as to produce a stylized reality and a realistic dream world. The film is so satisfying on so many levels that it simply defies appreciation through one cursory or even active viewing. A film that can please when seen repeatedly is a good film; but a film that demands more than one viewing does not fit within the Hollywood tradition, and from that point of view *Citizen Kane* may be considered a failure. There are also many films that please well enough the first time, only to be limp dead things thereafter; the men who razzed Orson Welles made lots of them.

A few years ago, Pauline Kael published an essay entitled "Raising Kane" in which she claimed that the sole, indisputable author of the screenplay was poor besieged Herman Mankiewicz. The fury that raged around her from film writers all over the country was enough to take away one's breath. A film that can still get people so stirred up must have plenty of life left.

———

JOHN HENLEY

VOL. 21, NO. 3
(REPRINTED FROM VOL. 11, NO. 3)

North by Northwest (1959)

PRODUCED AND DIRECTED BY ALFRED HITCHCOCK

Hitchcock has tapped a deep vain of primal emotion in his audiences. In fact, he is the existential poet of the cinema *par excellence*, and his extensive gallery of haunted, hunted men and women suffer for us all, victims of the age of anxiety....

Unlike the bulk of his imitators and epigones he does not just manipulate his audience, he *converses* with us.... *North by Northwest*, which Hitchcock considers his most representative American film (and maybe his best) ... described with a perspicuity we weren't to realize fully until a decade later, the political landscape against which the anxiety is set. | JAMES MONACO, *Take One*, Vol. V, No. 2.

Q: Near the beginning, in the mad car chase, one knows that Cary Grant can't be killed this early. So why is one excited?

Hitchcock: That again is purely the use of film in terms of the substitution of the language of the camera for words.... It's the mode of expression. And the use of the size of the image. And the juxtaposition of different pieces of film to create emotion in a person. And you can make it strong enough to make them forget reason. You see, when you say that Cary Grant can't possibly be killed so early in the film, that's the application of reason. But you're not permitted to reason. Because the film should be stronger than reason. | Interview with Hitchcock, Ian Cameron and V. F. Perkins in *Interview with Film Directors.*

Perhaps better than any other director, Alfred Hitchcock achieves a cinema of emotion. Others may be able to evoke an equally intense response from an audience, but most often it springs, not from their method, but from the subject or plot with which they are dealing. Hitchcock, on the other hand, transforms emotion and conflict into cinematic form—the image, the sound, the *mise-en-scène* becoming the means by which we are moved. Such outstanding sequences as the shower murder in *Psycho,* the climb up the mission tower in *Vertigo,* the explosion of the service station in *The Birds,* and the slow retreat down the stairway from the murder of Anna Massey in *Frenzy* come immediately to mind. Yet no single film in Hitchcock's *oeuvre* seems to contain so many outstanding moments or to achieve so consistently and completely the transformation of subject matter into what Hitchcock likes to call "pure cinema" as *North by Northwest.* In its unbroken series of elaborate set pieces placed end to end, interspersed with brief moments of contemplation, and orchestrated with the care of a symphonic composition, the film deals with those subjects, themes and relationships Hitchcock dearly loves to treat in such a way as to create for the audience a visual, aural, visceral experience of them.

On the level of plot, its extended chase is rather picaresque and deceptively flippant. On a thematic level, it provides the viewer the kind of moral workout which Hitchcock delights in, its treatment of the relationship between Roger Thornhill and Eve Kendall being quite as serious as *Notorious* or *Vertigo. North by Northwest* depicts an America in which movement and aggressiveness have become a way of life, in which an inability of people to trust one another has hopelessly isolated the individual, in which the society's anonymity and coldness (especially in its conducting the Cold War against Communism) have betrayed its own idealism by reducing the individual to a meaningless status.

Like numerous other Hitchcock films (e.g. *The Thirty-Nine Steps, Saboteur) North by Northwest* takes for its subject the innocent man accused of a crime he did not commit, but compounds the problem by having him mistaken for a man he is not. This addition reflects the film's preoccupation with

North by Northwest. From the Ernest Lehman Collection at the Harry Ransom Center.

anonymity, as Thornhill is forced to attempt to prove his own identity. His kidnapping comes with the unexpectedness of Judgment Day, suddenly forcing the glib, Manhattan ad executive to become the hero of a spy film, to shed his complacency and take aggressive action, to make judgments of his own about life and death which dwarf any decisions he ever faced on Madison Avenue.

As Robin Wood has noted, a key to the resolution of the dilemma in almost every Hitchcock film is the decision of the hero and heroine to tell one another the truth, to commit themselves to mutual trust. Yet in *North by Northwest*, the elaborate web of lies and play-acting suggest the extreme unlikeliness of such an understanding. In the scene in which Eve Kendall hides Thornhill in her train compartment, the layers of treachery are at their height: Eve lies to the police for the benefit of Thornhill, whom she has tricked for Van Damm, whom she is spying on for the CIA. At this level of role-playing, her true feelings are almost indiscernible. Only when the lies have been swept away and she and Thornhill talk sincerely for the first time (in the forest in front of Mt. Rushmore) do they reach a point where they are no longer isolated. Her statement that life has been bad because men like Thornhill "don't believe in marriage" conveys something more than the frustration of a subservient woman seeking the security of matrimony. It is not the institution of marriage which is being discussed. (Thornhill's reply to her charge is that he has been married twice. "See what I mean," she returns.) The question is one of establishing an honest relationship with a person of the opposite sex and has little or nothing to do with Thornhill's first two marriages since it requires the kind of faith for which one is willing to risk one's life.

The irony is that in the world of *North by Northwest* (which prefigures the elaborate intrigues and lies of the sixties' spy pictures) that trust is not only virtually impossible but almost consistently is shown to be unwise. Disguise and concealment are always the safest choices. In fact, as long as Thornhill claims he is Thornhill, Van Damm believes he is a sham; once he pretends to be Kaplan, Van Damm believes him. Trusting the Intelligence man who saves Thornhill's life means allowing Eve to be murdered by Van Damm. Thornhill must, then, make the moral choice to defy his authority and to rescue Eve on his own. Their relationship is infinitely more important than fighting the Cold War, since the government and society waging the war have ceased to care for the individual (that ideal which Communism was supposedly trying to undermine all along). The trick is knowing when to trust and when not to. And the decision must be made with inadequate information. Mustering the trust for an honest relationship has become a leap of faith at vertiginous heights.

DIRECTION AND DEPTH/LANDMARKS AND LANDSCAPES

I am but mad north-north-west. When the wind is southerly I know a hawk from a handsaw. | *Hamlet.*

The thing that amused me about Hitchcock is the way he directs a film in his head before he knows what the story is. You find yourself trying to rationalize the shots he wants to make rather than the story. Every time you get set he jabs you off balance by wanting to do a love scene on top of the Jefferson Memorial or something like that. He has a strong feeling for stage business

and mood and background, not so much for the guts of the business. I guess
that's why some of his pictures lose their grip on logic and turn into wild
chases. | RAYMOND CHANDLER (on working on *Strangers on a Train*), *Raymond
Chandler Speaking*.

North by Northwest is a symphony of cinematic space. From the moment
Saul Bass's brilliant credit sequence scurries across the screen we are cued
to the lines, the depth, the directions which will determine our experience
of the film. A totally green screen. Lines move out spontaneously, automat-
ically forming a grid seen from an angle. The credits move along and across
the lines as if projected on this imaginary, oblique screen. The abstract lines
become those of a glass skyscraper in which we see reflected the movement
of the crowd in the Manhattan street below—horizontal movement seen in
an awesome vertical mirror. It is both an acknowledgement of the movie
screen (life viewed and distance perceived upon a flat, vertical surface) and
a key to the angles which pervade the film. The milling crowd moves hori-
zontally on ground level and, as the final sequence of the credits shows, the
seeming chaos is in fact the result of a multitude moving quickly, efficiently,
and with purpose (going home from work). Speed and anonymity are conveyed in these establishing shots which become the primary properties of
the modern America Hitchcock depicts. These are the crowds into which
Thornhill can plunge for safety at Grand Central Station and at the train
station in Chicago, which protect him from being assassinated at the auction, whose collective astonishment allows him to escape from the United
Nations Building after Townsend's murder.

The vertical reflection of the street in the credit sequence suggests
Hitchcock's perspective. Hitchcock's films reveal a preoccupation with the
vertical line, the plunge into space, the fear of falling. A man hangs from
the torch of the Statue of Liberty in *Saboteur*, Oliver stands atop a cliff on
the verge of suicide in *Rebecca*, the White Cliffs of Dover figure prominently
as a threat of death in *Suspicion*, a murderess clings to a rain gutter dangling over a courtyard in *To Catch a Thief*; and it is of no small importance
that Hitchcock's most solemn film, fraught with images of height and falling, is called *Vertigo*. In *North by Northwest*, height and vertical perspective
suggest danger. The most frequent threat of death is that of falling: from
the winding road above the rocky shore near Glen Cove, from the ledge
outside the hospital window, from the underpinnings of Van Damm's house
perched on a precipice, and, of course, from Mt. Rushmore itself. Danger

is frequently signified by a high-angle camera position. During Thornhill's first meeting with Van Damm, the camera looks down on the group from the ceiling from the point at which Van Damm suggests they "get down to business" until Thornhill walks away from the others toward a more oblique angle almost under the camera and, isolated in the shot, hears Van Damm suggest our hero may not survive the evening. After the murder of Townsend, Hitchcock provides a shot from the top of the UN Building of Thornhill, no larger than a speck, fleeing the scene. This shot, the first from so extreme a height and only the second looking directly down (the first is when the wheel of the car Thornhill is driving goes off the road by the sea) punctuates the scene, equating Thornhill's predicament with a vertiginous perspective and prefiguring the final terrifying sequence on Mt. Rushmore. In the scene immediately following, in which a group at the US Intelligence Agency decide to let Thornhill fend for himself, the camera once again is placed at a high angle as the final line, "Goodbye, Mr. Thornhill—wherever you are," is spoken, and Thornhill is plunged even further into danger. Other high-angle shots appear in the crowd scenes at the stations in New York and Chicago—the crowds providing Thornhill's cover, while the angle suggests his danger. At Van Damm's house, we see the conspirators from a high angle—but this time with a difference. The perspective is Thornhill's point of view and, though it still suggests his and Eve Kendall's danger, it establishes a relationship between them. They are no longer isolated and Thornhill is for the first time more interested in her safety than in his own. When Van Damm decides to do away with Eve, Hitchcock accompanies his statement that he will throw her from the airplane ("This matter is best disposed of from a great height . . . over water") with an ominous camera movement from eye-level to a position above Van Damm's head.

It seems clear that being on a level physically above one's pursuers is quite dangerous. When Thornhill goes to Kaplan's hotel room, he endangers himself by leaving the safety of ground level, forcing himself into a position where he must ride in an elevator with his would-be assassins to reach freedom. Closely related to the danger of ascending from the lowest possible point is the danger of enclosure. As long as Thornhill can keep moving, he is safe. Once he settles or is trapped, danger threatens. From the opening scenes of brisk horizontal movement, Hitchcock shows us that this is a world of aggressiveness and speed. People fight for taxis; Grant steals a taxi from a waiting man by outwitting him, playing on his sympathy. The incident is closely related to his statement, which follows immediately, that in advertising there is no such thing as a lie. Thornhill's world is one of dog-eat-dog. Self-interest prevails and success is signified by the ability to move as quickly as one can from place to place. There are almost too many vehicles of transportation in *North by Northwest* to list (cars, taxis, buses, trucks, planes, and trains, to name the most obvious) and each must be taken aggressively (taxis are fought for, Thornhill must hide to get passage on the Twentieth Century, he must steal a farmer's pickup to get back to Chicago and Van Damm's car to save Eve). (Ironically, Hitchcock misses the bus.) Entrapment (in the kidnappers' car, in Townsend's library, in Kaplan's hotel room, at the auction, in the hospital) deprives one of the ability to move, of the ability to protect one's self-interest. Entrapment, however, can take many forms, and the lines of the corridors in the Plaza Hotel or in the Twentieth Century, which recede toward the center of the frame and toward infinity, suggest another form of helplessness. Being trapped and physically above one's surroundings is the most dangerous position possible, the position which finally forces Thornhill and Eve to climb down onto the Mt. Rushmore monument. Safety seems to exist only on ground level.

Yet in the cornfield sequence, Thornhill discovers that even where one should be the safest, in the open and on land so flat there is no conceivable way of falling anywhere, danger can still approach from an alien and physically higher level. For Thornhill is still isolated and deprived of mobility. The lines of the highway, in the high angle establishing shot which dwarfs him much as did the shot from the top of the UN Building, recede into the distance much like the lines of the train and hotel corridors. The bout with the crop duster suggests the existence of danger where such is almost inconceivable and corresponds to Thornhill's willingness to be entrapped by Eve Kendall. It is she who has sent him to die in the cornfield. The human necessity of establishing a relationship with a person of the opposite sex is undercut by the basic need for survival. There is no way for Thornhill to realize that on a speeding train he has allowed himself to be cornered by a pretty woman he believes he has met by chance, any more than he could expect a life-and-death encounter with that plane "dusting crops where there ain't no crops."

The relationship between Thornhill and Kendall is closely coordinated with the dangers they face and with the determining motifs of speed and entrapment. Establishing contact between people means the cessation of movement, the denial of self-interest. It means trusting someone in a world where trust seems to have disappeared. And it is a terrible risk which means laying your life and safety in someone else's hands. Thornhill must once again force himself onto a higher level (literally the level of Van Damm's house) and thus into danger, risking death, not in self-interest as he did in ascending to Kaplan's hotel room, but in the interest of the woman he loves. The enormity of the risk is reflected in the enormity of the entrapment—this time atop Mt. Rushmore in the climactic scene of vertigo to which the film has been leading.

In its use of famous landmarks and archetypally familiar landscapes, *North by Northwest* resembles a multitude of other Hitchcock films (the Scottish moors and the London Palladium in *The Thirty-Nine Steps*, the windmills of Holland in *Foreign Correspondent*, the Statue of Liberty in *Saboteur*, the Riviera in *To Catch A Thief*, Albert Hall in both versions of *The Man Who Knew Too Much*, the redwood forests and the Golden Gate Bridge in *Vertigo*, to name a very few) and such "location" films as Henry Hathaway's *Niagara*. Setting events of a film in familiar locations and exploiting the natural possibilities of a well-known area add a dimension of recognition for the audience, calling up myriad associations with regard to the chosen sites. The response of the audience to such settings is rarely intellectual, but is evoked emotionally as a "feeling" about the place. It seems significant that Hitchcock utilizes such locales at every opportunity, since he prefers to work almost subliminally on his audience. *North by Northwest* makes remarkable use of our natural responses to such places as the United Nations, Grand Central Station, the Plaza Hotel, and the flatlands of the Midwest. But the scenes on Mt. Rushmore are among Hitchcock's finest moments. As Thornhill and Kendall scramble across the rocky faces of the presidents, they are reduced to the size of insects in relation to the mammoth heads. There is a good deal of humor in the sight of people running frenetically around the solemn faces of the founding fathers of which Hitchcock was quite certainly aware (the original title proposed for the film was *The Man in Lincoln's Nose*). But there are darker and more disturbing implications which we feel as well. The problems of our hero and heroine are dwarfed by the monument as surely as is their physical appearance, and the faces—unmoving, passive, staring off as if toward a visionary ideal—are disturbingly cold. In one shot, Hitchcock frames the couple with the enormous, stone eye of Thomas Jefferson staring off disinterestedly behind them. Like the monument, the government which it represents is too large, too cold, too uncaring to worry about the lives of individuals.

With its emphasis on movement and depth, it is not surprising that *North by Northwest* becomes a film of elaborate chase and pursuit nor that its title is one which reiterates its preoccupation with direction. The title suggests perhaps the actual direction in which the film's locations are moving, though its course from New York City to Chicago to Rapid City is probably closer to west-northwest. An even more practical explanation of the title might come from the fact that the airline Thornhill and the Professor use to travel from Chicago to South Dakota is Northwest Airlines. Quite literally they go north by Northwest. But the flight itself is never seen and seems in no way central or even significant to the film as a whole. Finally, the direction in the title seems to have been taken from a line in *Hamlet*. It is the direction in which Hamlet says he is mad—a seeming absurdity. Thornhill's journey north by northwest is mad as well, as meaningless in its direction as his being mistaken for Kaplan in the first place. Yet, to paraphrase *Hamlet* again, there is method is in this madness. Thornhill's flight follows the pre-established route of the fictional Kaplan—it is an absurdity which takes on a sensible form. The true "madness" of the film is not Thornhill's attempt to save his own skin, but his willingness to risk it for Eve Kendall. Even though she has arranged his death once, Thornhill is willing to make the leap of faith to end his isolation. It is an absurd decision, romantic and quite unlike the ad executive in the opening sequences. The final scene of the film shows Eve dangling from Mt. Rushmore, held only by Thornhill's grip on her hand. He encourages her to pull herself up while she frantically says she is unable to do so. Hitchcock suddenly cuts to Thornhill pulling Eve into the upper berth of a train compartment following their marriage. The transition is absurd. Our intellect tells us that she is still hanging above the precipice; Hitchcock's happy ending assures us that everything turned out all right. In its impossibility, the ending parallels the unlikeliness of the kind of trust the couple show one another. Admittedly it is the only way for an honest relationship to exist. But Hitchcock is also willing to admit that in the disturbingly modern world of *North by Northwest* such trust is madness.

———

ED LOWRY

Corruption of the Damned (1965)

DIRECTED BY GEORGE KUCHAR

Made by George Kuchar. Written by Ruthy. Dedicated to Abe Chaplan, M. D. Starring: Mike Kuchar (John, the vengeful anti-hero with hate in his heart, hair on his chin), Larry Leibowitz (John's brother, a body too big to be controlled by a peanut), Steve Packard (Paul, who made love with his body, made waste with his bowels), Mary Flanagan (Cora, a girl with a reputation as long as her hair), Gina Zuckerman (Aunt Anna, too much woman for even a mob to handle), Donna Kerness (the top-heavy medium with a built-in set of crystal balls), Floraine Conners (Connie, big and blond with a gut full of liquor on a empty head), with Gina's husband, Michael T. (big business was his line, big bosoms were his curve), Larry's mother, Francis (the mother, a mammoth woman of over-developed mother instincts).

It is not surprising that now, in the twilight of the theatrical cinema, a great theatrical director should emerge. Einstein was called the last of the classical physicists, and Newton the last of the great geometers. These philosophers had to master everything that came before them, in order to break through into new worlds. Similarly, George Kuchar has mastered all of the new archaic techniques of the theatrical cinema, and forged them into something so different, that comparison is only superficial. . . .

Kuchar's films are overtly insane. Anyone who lived in such a world would be mad inside an hour. Perhaps the Marx Brothers might survive, but I doubt it. Godzilla, King of the Monsters, might have a better chance. But the utter insanity, the insanity of perverted cliche, is the genuine unwholesome appeal of Kuchar's outlook. *Corruption* might seethe with violence and sex, the two most attractive things you can put on the screen, but beneath them a twisted outlook pervades. Something is very much wrong with the Kuchar world.

For example, Larry Leibowitz plays a momma's boy in *Corruption*. He follows Mike, his brother in the film around on his odyssey, looking like the original schmuck with ear flaps.

He and Mike are confronted in a junk yard by their mother, who threatens to machine-gun them down if they don't come home and eat supper. I suppose that a Thompson Sub-Machine gun is part of every clinging mother's arsenal in the world. When they refuse, she is unable to gun them down, and stabs herself after they leave. Larry, unaware of this development, or very much else, is cleansed, or transformed, by his sick odyssey. In a fit of spleen, he tosses his earflaps to the ground, and becomes a man!

The belly laughs conceal the true amorality and misanthropy of George Kuchar's films. But we should be grateful to any filmmaker who can make us laugh so hard it hurts. Name a film you have seen recently that had any real laughs in it. Kuchar has too many laughs to be taken seriously by many, but someday he will be recognized. Beneath the laughs lurk a mirror of our beliefs, the middle-class cliches we live by. | LEONARD LIPTON, *Film-Makers' Cooperative Catalogue*.

What can I possibly say about this film? | NICK BARBARO, April 16, 1978

George Kuchar's *Corruption of the Damned*, like all of his other films, is no more than a glorified home movie. But then, it doesn't need to be any more than that. Kuchar's feeling for the conventions of the medium is so finely tuned that he is able to convince us that all films, even the most elaborate Hollywood productions, are home movies.

Corruption is a collection of the moldiest of cinematic cliches held together by a bare pretense of a plot. Each scene, each character and each individual image is a classic of its type: lovers frolicking in a cemetery, Dear

John letters, biker gangs, a seance in a thunderstorm, a dramatically slow burning fuse on a bomb, a car plummeting off a cliff and exploding—the list could go on forever. Kuchar and his bizarre troupe of actors (he uses the same cast in many of his films) imbue these ridiculous scenes with an even more ridiculous sense of unreality. My personal favorite image in the film is a shot of the fakest-looking windswept model trees ever filmed. But precisely because they are so obviously fake, it is clear that they are Symbolic.

Of course, Kuchar parodies symbolism, exposing it as pretension. This may seem ironic, since *Corruption* is one of the most symbolic films ever made. But then it is also one of the most unconventional, conventional, immoral, moral and amoral films ever made. It stands as proof of the cyclical, circular nature of the universe: if you go as far as you can in one direction, you will return to the starting point. Kuchar extends Hollywood's traditions to their illogical conclusions and the result is a film diametrically opposed to just about any tradition you could think of.

——

NICK BARBARO

Necrology (1971)

DIRECTED BY STANDISH LAWDER

Directed by Standish D. Lawder. Cast (in order of appearance): Mario
Uzzo (Taxi cab driver), Elvira Valenza (Deaf mute woman), George
Niedermann (German businessman, retired [living in Brazil]), James C.
Quinn (IBM salesman), Salvatore Pullano (Man with ulcer), Dick Fortino
(Trumpet player), Dominic Pulisciano (Assassin [with two assistants]),
Richard C. Valanzulo (Assassin Assistant No. 1), Alvin Dunton (Assassin
Assistant no. 2), Alfred Goglia (Former disc jockey), Barbara Rieger
(Secretary, bi-lingual), Alan McKnight (Man whose wife doesn't under-
stand him), Rufus Eggeressy (Local politician), Fedor Bressack (Corvette
owner), Paulette Richter (Dietician), Arthur Arrington (Errand boy),
Helen R. Rice (Cleaning woman, retired), Huntington Huckel (Software
market research analyst), Dolores Horowitz (Worried mother), Fred Kan-
tor (Stock broker, just out of Harvard), Mona Lieberman (Former model),
Ling Sun Van (Asian diplomat), Edward Carlson (Actor, unemployed),
Prescott Anderson (Man returning from dentist), Dan Barnhardt (Manufacturer of plastic novelties), Jack Alpern (Short order cook), Mary Ann
Osterman (Jilted lover), Pearl Richardson (Secretary, black), Apostolos

Papas (Greek businessman), Liza Farnum (Woman in meditation), Joseph Pettrisini (Peanut salesman, Coney Island), John Pollock (FBI Agent), Nancy Gurda (Fat teenager with straw pocketbook), Max Cross (Fugitive, interstate), Frank Pleskunas (Union bassoon-player), William O'Connell (Suffolk County chess champion), Lee Moskovitz (Ghost writer), Frank A. Kuzynski (Student of the arts), Ralph Neylan (Man who just got out of the Air Force), Roger Sidenburg (Delicatessen owner), David W. Sherer (Man with migraine headache), Linda Rumsey (Yawning girl), Angelo Cassipento (New York State boxing commissioner), James Rubin (Man from Xerox), Sam Simmons (Pornographer), Louisa P. Adams (Assistant librarian), Peter Sidenberg (Sears and Roebuck shoe salesman), Richard C. Yang (Chinese physicist), Gary Werlein (Keypunch operator from Spokane), Dolores Yablonsky (YMCA director), James Storkland (Yalie, black), Kathleen O. Croogan (Woman with canker sore on inside of her left cheek), Arthur Zuckerman (Chief of Public Works, Fargo, ND) G. David Wheelwright (Luci Nugent's gynecologist), Anthony Martinelli (Pizza parlor proprietor), Murray Sampson (Embezzler (at large)), Susan Goldberg (Drum majorette), Jonathan Walker (Undertaker, retired), Daniel Babbage (Pederast), Mary Scheetman (Former mistress), Virginia Blaisdell (Tough girl with cigarette and white handbag), Miguel Regalado (Tourist from Mexico), Francine Mohlenkamp (Switchboard supervisor), Robert Mullins (Corporate Vice-President), Standish D. Lawder (Film-maker), Robert Osterweis (Man suffering from emphysema), Brenda M. Porter (Secretary, menstruating), George Linden (Man who looks very tired), Wanda McKinny (Divorcée), David Lyons (Glue sniffer), Terry Hadley (Movie and TV starlet), Lars Christensen (Egyptologist), Elizabeth Nichols (Girl who looks like Joan Baez), Nicholas Lamont, Jr. (Man with sideburns), Carolyn Schago (Social worker), Andrew B. Scott (Man picking his nose). Thank you, Audrey.

necrology n. 1: a list of the recently dead 2: obituary. | Webster's New Collegiate Dictionary.

Necrology is a dramatization of urban Americans caught unwillingly in their daily routine. The film is a continuous unedited study during which the camera was held steady in one position. Its reductive, essentialized form and technique link it to the minimalist tradition of modern painting and sculpture. | MARY MYERS, Film-Makers' Cooperative Catalogue.

In *Necrology*, a 12-minute film, in one continuous shot he films the faces of a 5:00 p.m. crowd descending via the PanAm building escalators. In old-fashioned black and white, these faces stare into the empty space, in the 5:00 p.m. tiredness and mechanical impersonality, like faces from the grave. It's hard to believe that these faces belong to people today. The film is one of the strongest and grimmest comments upon the contemporary society that cinema has ever produced. | JONAS MEKAS, *Film-Makers' Cooperative Catalogue.*

Several short films (at Ann Arbor Film Festival) seemed notably successful in the creation of special effects. Among these was *Necrology*, by Standish D. Lawder, an eleven-minute panning of the camera down what seemed an endless stairway, upon which people stood motionless and glum. These circumstances, plus the constant idea of the title, gave a haunting suggestion of people on their eventless way to hell. I was later told that the film was made with a stationary camera trained on down escalator, and then the film was run backwards. A long, "cast of characters" at the end . . . seemed to me to destroy a desirable mood, but it certainly pleased the crowd. | EDGAR DANIELS, *Film-Makers' Cooperative Catalogue.*

If *Necrology* were merely "one of the strongest and grimmest comments upon the contemporary society that cinema has produced," it would be pretty boring. Fortunately, it is considerably more (and less) than that. Without doubt, the sickest joke I've ever seen on film. | HOLLIS FRAMPTON, *Film-Makers' Cooperative Catalogue.*

It is first of all a satire of itself, and of pomposity in the underground film movement. I mean, sure this is a society of conformism and we're all going to die. So what? We all know that—Lawder hardly needs to take up eleven and a half minutes of our time to make such mundane points. Such a simplistic (not to mention depressing) reading of the film misses the point altogether: by listing the cast at the end Lawder makes this a celebration of life rather than submission to death.

He reminds us that the people we have seen do have identities, after all—sometimes mundane, sometimes humorous, sometimes fascinating, but all individual. If we have seen them as an indistinguishable mass, the problem isn't that people are dull and impersonal, but that we don't take the time to notice what is unique and interesting in each other. (Of course, the cast list is largely, if not wholly fictitious, but that's all right, too. If there wasn't actually a "fugitive, interstate" on this escalator at this time, there surely was on some other escalator at some other time.)

The end credits, then, in their denial of the rest of the film, constitute an attack on various trends toward formalism, and away from populism, in experimental cinema. Far more directly though Lawler is attacking the Hollywood star system and the media's tendency to single out spectacular events and individuals, thus creating unreasonable role models for their audience. This is a film of and about everyday people, depicted performing their everyday routines. Are they more important than they were before they were recorded on film? Is John Wayne more important than he was before he was recorded on film? Is Mark Spitz more important than he was before he was televised? Etc.?

STRUCTURAL ANALYSIS

The credits listed at the end of the film are woefully incomplete. The following is a complete breakdown of the relevant statistics regarding *Necrology*.

Total performers: 326 (191 male, 135 female)
Credited performers: 76 (53 male, 23 female)
Uncredited performers: 250 (138 male, 112 female)

Frames of darkness between escalator and cast: 329 (28½ black, 300½ grey). The order of appearance is also listed incorrectly. It is thus virtually impossible to identify any of the individuals. Following is a list in order of appearance, separated by sex (M = male, F = female):

MFFMFFFMFMMMMMMFFMMMMMMMFMMMFFMMFMMFFF
MMMMMFMFMFMFMFFMMFMMFFMMMFMFMFFMMMMMFMMFM
MMMFMMFFMMFMMMMFFFFMMFMFMMMFFFMMMMMF
MFFMFFFFMFFFMFMFFMMMFMMMFFMMMMFFFFFMFMMFM
MMMMMFFMMMMFFFFMFMFFMMMMFMFMMMMMMFMFM
MMFMMMMMMFFFMFFFFFFMMMFFMMMMMFFFFMMMFFMMMF
FMMMMMMMFMMMFMMFFFMMFFFFFMMMMMMFMMMMMFM
MMMMFMMMF(?)MMFMFMFMMMFFFFFMMFMFFFMFFMFM
MFMFFFMMMFMMFMM

In examining these statistics, certain patterns come immediately to mind, patterns which raise serious questions about Lawder's integrity. Most obvious is the implied sexism of the credits. Only 17.04% of the women in the film are credited, whereas fully 27.75% of the men receive credits. Furthermore, all but two of the women's credits reflect sexual stereotyping, and of these two, one is pejorative (fat teenager), and in the other instance, the woman is identified as working *for* men, as social director for a YMCA.

There are other disturbing structural patterns as well. If this is an unmanipulative film, how does it happen that there are so many round numbers (250, 300) and threes? Consider the following: 53 men credited, 23 women credited, 30 more men than women credited, 3 more uncredited men than total women, etc. Most disturbing is the fact that before the credits there are 3 more frames of darkness than total performers in the film. Why the discrepancy? Two of the extra frames can be accounted for. One may be the hand which reaches into the frame at one point; one could conceivably be Audrey who is thanked in the credits; last frame, however, is totally inexplicable, though it corresponds to the one frame which is half black and half grey. We must assume that this is a totally frivolous structural symbol, since Lawder provides no resolution to the mystery. Some people might argue that viewers would not generally notice such details. Perhaps this is true on a conscious level, but who can deny the powerful subconscious impact of such disturbing discrepancies.

—

NICK BARBARO

VOL. 18, NO. 3
APRIL 3, 1980

Five Easy Pieces (1970)

DIRECTED BY BOB RAFELSON

Five Easy Pieces wants to make us despair for the future of America, but actually it only made me despair for the future of American movies. Great, even good, filmmaking opens us up to the possibilities of the human and physical worlds about us. . . . A cunning little youth exploitation picture like *Five Easy Pieces*, with its pre-fabricated angst and Sunset Strip alienation, dulls the senses and blunts our perceptions—its manipulative single-mindedness limits the way we see. In some ways, the film is entertaining—after all, it panders to us with a brothel-derived insistence upon our own superiority and sanctity. But the audience I saw *Five Easy Pieces* with seemed to leave the film as one might a whorehouse—wondering whether one's easy satisfaction was worth enduring the falseness and relative debasement. | JOEL SIEGEL, *Film Heritage*, Winter 1970–1971.

"Alienated" people in real life, no matter what they're alienated from, are a bore, and in movies they're even more so, especially in movies as inadequately written (Adrien Joyce) and directed (Bob Rafelson) as this one. | EUNICE SINKLER, *Films in Review*, November 1970.

Five Easy Pieces received a great deal of critical acclaim when it was released in 1970. Director Bob Rafelson was applauded for investing an American topic (the road-as-panacea movie) with a European cinematic sensibility. But what contemporary critics find momentous in a film is given context years later and reevaluated, quite often to the detriment of the film's reputation. The easiest thing about *Five Easy Pieces*, was that it was easy to like; I found only two critics who didn't. Jack Nicholson is almost always likable, no matter how despicable his character's actions may be. And the picture's beautiful images, unconventional shooting and editing, and its slow pace endow the film with significance merely through its association with the European "art" movie. Few critics had the audacity to challenge a film so attuned to the critical establishment's prejudices against the typical American product. In fact, two critics liked the film for mutually-exclusive reasons. Richard Schickel thought the film unique, with "no convenient analogies between director Bob Rafelson's work and other movies." Robert Mundy liked it because it was "firmly entrenched in a tradition of American post-war cinema—a group of films involving a rootless, inarticulate hero"; the film's uniqueness was that it was so "un-American in style."

The film itself is as self-indulgent as the critics' reactions to it. Its heavy-handed identification with Bobby Dupea, its rejection of alternate points of view through one-dimensional characterizations, its lack of sympathy for women and laborers, and its rejection of a materially-oriented, occupationally-defined status quo all invest the film with only an apparent significance. Nicholson confers a multitude of insignificant gestures, mannerisms, and actions on his character, seemingly brought on by his retreat from mankind and all intended to impart depth and complexity to his portrayal. Laszlo Kovacs's cinematography is equally specious, beautiful in itself but by consequence inappropriate for the film's depiction of empty psyches.

The deceptive complexity of Nicholson's anxiety-ridden characterization bumps up against the one-dimensional straw (wo)men placed in his path throughout the film. As Dupea encounters and rejects the emotions and perceptions of these various "characters," the inability of American culture to provide a meaningful life for its citizens is proposed. Each character is no more than a cipher, though, an image of the working class, the intellectual, or the alienated. The film shows about as much sympathy for (and honesty about) its characters as Dupea does. Watching *Five Easy Pieces* ten years after its release and critical and popular acclaim one quickly notices how outdated and reactionary some of the film's notions are. The lesbian's hostilities and neuroses were apparently funny to most viewers in 1970, but today the complexity of sexual issues makes us uncomfortable to see this segment of the population abused in its characterization. The film is equally one-sided in its portrayals of the working class. Lacking absolutely any culture (bowling and country music notwithstanding), Dupea's friend Elton and girlfriends Rayette and Betty are too innocent and too ignorant to be credible. The movie would have us believe that Dupea is just too intelligent and too sensitive to his environment to find satisfaction or solace among the film's imbecilic working class.

The movie doesn't play any fairer on the other side of the tracks, either. Dupea's family and the visiting intellectuals are relatively lifeless and inhuman. The men have physical afflictions, a metaphorical rendering of their emotional and psychic decay. The women talk too much. When one woman intellectual invades their home spouting empty intellectual platitudes, Dupea and the audience are allowed to drain off some of their frustration through his equally vacuous emotional outburst. Susan Anspach's Catherine provides a short-lived relief from the film's (and Dupea's) attacks on the surrounding characters—that is until her uncontrollable sexual desire for Bobby overcomes her justifiable distaste for him.

Ultimately, the film spurns Bobby's attitude as well. His emotional detachment is undermined by his vulnerability to Catherine's rejection and his confession to his father. His last action is completely selfish, the film's final admission that the road offers no better alternative (morally or otherwise) to self-fulfillment than interpersonal relationships. It's a moment seemingly intended to salvage the film from its previous excesses and one-sidedness by undermining its focal point, Bobby Dupea, and the viewer's sympathies.

Like many other films released in the late sixties and early seventies, *Five Easy Pieces* attempted to plug into the youth generation's egalitarian set of values, while simultaneously appealing to the most self-indulgent aspects of its new sensibilities. *Easy Rider* (from the same producers) offered a relatively simple formula for escaping the malaise of the city and the previous generation, despite its catastrophic though superficial ending. *Little Big Man* presented a parable of the Vietnam War, and by extension all cultural aggression, by juxtaposing the comic ignorance and masked violence of the white world with their overt decimation of the Indian "counter-culture." *M*A*S*H** showed us how crummy white America can be for waging a war in the third world, but the demonstration didn't preclude the prospect of having a good time anyway. *Five Easy Pieces* follows the same pattern—at times more intelligently, at other times by more shallow and self-satisfied means. As Pauline Kael wrote at the time: "The few movies that the 'film generation' responds to intensely are the most sentimental (about youth) and the most despairing (about America). It's a bad combination."

It's not the only bad combination in these films either. The defensiveness of an entire generation's revolt against values and beliefs that eventually overtake them is compensated for by the protagonists' superiority and flexibility when faced with the numerous physical and moral onslaughts characteristic of the Establishment. *Easy Rider* is salvaged from Peter Fonda's egotistical figure of Christ only by Dennis Hopper's far superior characterization of a mumbling bumbling reject from the white status quo. In *Little Big Man*, Dustin Hoffman's Jack Crabbe spends his pubescence and adolescence wandering (and wondering) between two worlds—superior to the white world because he can't find a satisfying life with them and superior to the Indians—well, I guess because he's white. In *M*A*S*H*, our heroes are doctors, not just any doctors but the best surgeons in the whole war. And in *Five Easy Pieces*, Bobby Dupea crosses class boundaries like Jack Crabb crosses racial and cultural ones, and his viewpoint is consistently privileged.

Eventually, the heroes who lack the confidence and assuredness of John Wayne and Gary Cooper still manage to ride roughshod over their environment and its inhabitants because they are at least conscious enough to reject the ways and manners of all the belligerent, pathetic, and/or ignorant characters they encounter. In the sixties and early seventies, we tended to picture these protagonists as piteous examples of men (and that *is* the only sex involved here) unable to express their sentiments or find compassion in the world. By now, we realize the compassion they don't find is lacking mostly in themselves, and the one-sided characterization of their antagonists is painfully apparent.

Jack Nicholson has made a career portraying the typical seventies' protagonist, a man who makes only the most reluctant of emotional commitments. Each of his major roles was well-recognized and well-publicized following *Easy Rider*; almost every year he won an Oscar nomination until he won the award in 1975. However similar the roles may have been, though, there is an interesting and revealing progression from film to film. As the general population, and youth in particular, began to accept the world-as-is despite its flaws, Nicholson's rejection of commitments is increasingly colored by the surrounding environment. As the decade unfolded, Nicholson's characters found themselves alienated from a progressively restricted and restrictive milieu. In *Five Easy Pieces*, the whole world is an emotional and intellectual vacuum—workers and intellectuals, the uncultured and the cultured, lesbians and waitresses. In *The King of Marvin Gardens* (1972), the world is Atlantic City and consists of an assortment of screwballs and crazies, including his own brother. In *The Last Detail* (1973), the restrictions and duties of military service make emotional commitments impossible. In *Chinatown* (1974), the underside of urban America, where the father of the city rapes his daughter (both metaphorically and literally), undermines the integrity of personal attachments. And finally, in *One Flew Over the Cuckoo's Nest* (1975), Nicholson's personal commitments run up against the most circumscribed of all the environments in these films, a mental hospital.

What this tells me is that by 1975 the moviegoing public, still dominated by the young, was less likely to identify with Nicholson's rejection of and aggression toward an environment that wasn't severely circumscribed by its debilitating effect on one's emotions—like the military, the city, or a mental institution. No longer could films like *Alice's Restaurant*, *Easy Rider*, and *Five Easy Pieces* take pokes at all different segments of the population. If a character or a movie was to garner the viewer's sympathy they could no longer dump trash in rivers (*Alice's Restaurant*), ridicule women (*M*A*S*H*), or use homosexuality for an easy laugh (*Little Big Man*).

Seeing quite a few movies from around the turn of the last decade, one quickly notices how exceptionally they chronicle the outdated attitudes of America's Old Left. As the seventies became the eighties, we collectively lamented the loss of innocence, the "sell-out," that characterized those who participated in the "movement." We remember the undying adherence to principles no matter how violent the opposition, the camaraderie of the participants, and the openness about sexuality. We forget that women were still supposed to keep their shrill mouths shut, and that homosexuality was still good for a laugh or two. With the end of the Vietnam war, the relative acceptance of the civil rights movement, and the political enfranchisement of the young, the dominant issues of the left were defused and the media abandoned those whose civil liberties were yet to be granted, in particular women. Possibly the remaining issues no longer appealed to a liberal press, or maybe they just lacked the visual explosiveness of the older issues. But nonetheless, the emphasis was put on the youth generation's reintegration into the dominant social order.

By consequence, the attitude of the country in the seventies has been pictured as increasingly conservative. Undoubtedly, there has been an increase in both religious activity and right-wing organizations like the Ku Klux Klan. But these are merely aberrations brought on by a deteriorating economy; they are not characteristic of social attitudes in general.

The seventies have brought as many changes in cultural attitudes as the late sixties. Emotional and religious feelings still preclude total acceptance of the equality of women and homosexuals, but few expect them to work for less than equal pay, or assume that their attitude toward equality is illegitimate and presumptuous an intellectual level. If anything, the late seventies have proven to be more open to changes in social structure and cultural attitudes than the late sixties and early seventies. It's a rare occasion these days that we beat each other over the head for expressing opposing viewpoints on an issue. And women and homosexuals can give vent to their anger and frustration without much fear of a violent backlash.

We really shouldn't be surprised that the Old Left so easily reentered the mainstream of middle class society from whence they came. The issues that precipitated and carried "the movement" held little promise for any fundamental social changes. For the most part they were "selfish" issues— freedom from an involuntary draft and a dirty environment. And despite the rhetoric, there were very few concerned with the equality of women and even fewer concerned with changes in the basic social institutions and economic structures that perpetuated their alienation. What the movies from the late sixties and early seventies show us is the lack of vision characteristic of the counter-culture and its participants, the inability to envision another social order. These movies also inadvertently suggest how far we've come toward accepting various lifestyles and sets of beliefs without feeling the necessity to disarm their legitimacy in our popular culture.

———

MICHAEL SELIG

VOL. 13, NO. 4
DECEMBER 1, 1977

Nashville (1975)

PRODUCED AND DIRECTED BY ROBERT ALTMAN

Is there such a thing as an orgy for movie-lovers—but an orgy without excess? At Robert Altman's new, almost-three-hour film, *Nashville*, you don't get drunk on images, you're not overpowered—you get elated. I've never before seen a movie I loved in quite this way: I sat there smiling at the screen, in complete happiness. It's a pure emotional high, and you don't come down when the picture is over; you take it with you . . . You get it from the rhythms of the scenes. The picture is at once a *Grand Hotel*-style narrative, with twenty-four linked characters; a country-and-Western musical; a documentary essay on Nashville and American life; a meditation on the love affair between performers and audiences; and an Altman party . . . All of the allusions tell the story of the great American popularity contest. Godard was trying to achieve a synthesis of documentary and fiction and personal essay in the early sixties, but Godard's Calvinistic temperament was too cerebral. Altman, from a Catholic background, has what Joyce had: a love of the supreme juices of everyday life. | PAULINE KAEL, *The New Yorker*, March 3, 1975.

> There is no possible way to explain the WHY to the structure of *Nashville*. . . .
> Each actor gave freely of his or her histories, routes, connections, or non-
> connections and, stirred by Altman's extraordinary capacities in overview
> and technical skill, rounded out the *Rashomon* of the United States. . . . All
> you need to do is add yourself as the twenty-fifth character and you know
> that whatever you think about the film is right, even if you think the film is
> wrong. | JOAN TEWKESBURY, Introduction to her screenplay of *Nashville*,
> August, 1975.

> Fellow taxpayers and stockholders in America . . . | HAL PHILLIP WALKER.

Robert Altman's Bicentennial epic conveys his personal reflection on the
state of the nation and his political call to fellow Americans on the nature
of the state. Altman's success results from shaping uniquely American materials and sensibilities into a complex ideological network; but more importantly it depends on his formal structuring of a 1970's American way of
seeing. *Nashville* works better, perhaps, than any other Altman movie
because the message is delivered by calling attention to the film's formal
organization, an organization that mirrors an evolving American mode of
perception.

In a post–World War II modernist world where an individual is simultaneously assaulted by sights, sounds, motions, messages and events, one
must adapt and develop a way of coping with the overload or else become
overloaded. Altman opens his film with an example of informational overload, a commercial message for the film itself. Why? He is not trying to sell
the film to the audience; everyone has already paid for his or her ticket. But
his parody of the hyper-record sell, no longer having any commercial function, calls attention to the commercial message itself and to the familiarity
of its form. Altman's commercial assaults the viewer with a barrage of informational, visual and aural stimuli. Because we have seen such patterns
hundreds of times before, we accept the form easily but understand it as
parody because of its novel appearance as the introduction to a movie.

From the opening record album spin-out into the center of the frame,
Altman builds up to multiple layers of impression, creating constant movement on several levels. As the record album spins into focus, a voice-over
announcer begins his hyped-up sales pitch. As the album cover is centered
in the frame, the songs on the record begin playing loudly in the background. Altman continues his escalation of sensations by zooming into the

Nashville. From the core collection production photographs of the Margaret Herrick Library, Academy of Motion Picture Arts and Sciences.

group portrait framed on the album cover while other albums recorded by people in the portrait circle behind the "Nashville" album. As the announcer names each actor in the film, his or her face appears in the central album frame, and the names of the songs run down the right side of the screen while the cast names roll up the left side. Every time the announcer says, "Nashville," the letters flash (each time in a different color) across the bottom of the screen. The pattern continues, as Joan Tewkesbury has said, "until everything has whirled and spun and played through your senses." The interior framed group portrait zooms out to the larger group portrait, the album spins back away into the center, the songs and the announcer are cut off, and only the word *"Nashville"* appears in white at the top of the black screen.

Here, in one minute, Altman sets up the style and pacing for his entire film in a "package" with which we are all familiar. The commercial message not only indicates a way of seeing steeped in the economic terms of mass media packaging, but it provides a modernist text of simultaneous impressions out of which we can organize our experience, evaluate it and judge it.

In other words, Altman's multi-layered assault on the senses more directly corresponds to our everyday reality than a simpler linear sound-pictorial narrative.

> Let me go directly to the point: I'm for doing some replacing. I've discussed the Replacement Party with people all over this country, and I'm often confronted with the statement: "I don't want to get mixed up in politics," or "I'm tired of politics," or "I'm not interested." Almost as often, someone says, "I can't do anything about it anyway."
>   Let me point out two things: Number one: All of us are deeply involved with politics whether we know it or not, and whether we like it or not. And, number two, we can do something about it. When you pay more for an automobile than it cost Columbus to make his first voyage to America, that's politics. | HAL PHILLIP WALKER

Part of the problem of being able to perceive and take in simultaneous sensations involves learning how to organize them meaningfully in order to make evaluations and decisions. Through mass information and communication, one realizes that everything from the purchase of a six pack of beer to the nature of one's relationship with a member of the opposite sex to the choice of language necessitates a political decision. As Altman has structured the first sequence to set up the pattern for his modernist text, so the second sequence functions to set up a pattern for the necessity/impossibility of ascribing meaning to the complexity of issues that we see, hear and feel. In other words, as soon as Altman identifies an American mode for perception, he balances it with our American dilemma for interacting with that mode. When the record commercial assault dies down, the white letters of "Nashville" remain at the top of the black screen and a voice-over begins a new message. To the words of "Fellow taxpayers," the black fades in to a garage door. The white block print letters remain stationary, but turn to blue and become a sign on the garage door. This very neat perceptual trick—reversing black screen to white door and white letters to navy blue letters—subliminally, as well as structurally, contrasts the two sets of realities. In going from one element to the other, Altman uses the word "Nashville" as a continuity transition around which the viewer can help organize associations. "Nashville," identifiable as a city and film, provides a kind of perceptual image to hang onto during the transition from one reality to another, but it explains nothing about either experience. Our mental tendency to organize impressions into something meaningful is fulfilled while nothing meaningful is rendered; the word *Nashville* is too simple and superficial to explain the experience.

The necessity and impossibility of rendering meaning is further developed on another level by what the sign below "*Nashville*" suggests. "Walker-Talker-Sleeper," the central sign on the garage door, hints at a further inadequate defining process by sloganizing the garage, the place where the "Walker-Talker" (the campaign van) sleeps. As the van drives around with its P.A. system blaring out campaign messages, it expresses social criticisms and cultural comments that, while making sense, are turned into such facile statements that they no longer explain anything. As Pauline Kael has said, "There are valid observations made to seem fake by a slimy infection." The second sequence introduces a theme that goes hand in hand with acknowledgement of the modernist viewpoint: assignment of meaning to the complex array of impressions seems necessary, but the process itself reduces experience, sloganizes it and molds it into cliches. Thus, in the first few minutes of the film, Altman sets up the structural pattern for the remaining three hours of film.

> There is no question about being involved; the question is, "What to do?" It is the very nature of government to strain at a gnat and swallow a camel. As loyal citizens, we accept our take-home pay, understand most of the deductions and even to a degree, come to expect them. However, when a government begins to force its citizens to swallow the camel, it's time to pause and do some accounting. | HAL PHILLIP WALKER

After his introduction and prologue scenes, Altman opens *Nashville*'s dramatic section by contrasting events in two recording studios in the same building. He then introduces all twenty-four characters in one long sequence at the airport (only Karen Black/Connie White is not there, but her poster image represents her). The interweaving of characters, music, sights and sounds in the airport and freeway sequences establishes them and their lives within a modernist context, a barrage of sensory impressions which Altman choreographs into a bombardment of movement and timing. His use of continuously moving camera, rhythmic cuts between characters, background band music, a TV announcer both on screen and as off-screen voice-over commentator, airport noises, characters talking and overlapping each other, continues to build in momentum to the freeway sequence, where background banjo music adds a whimsical element to the frenetic cutting, the Walker van continues its droning commentary, the continuously moving camera incorporates wider perspectives in aerial and high angle shots, and freeway noises, conversations and arguments are juxtaposed until, once again, "everything has whirled and spun and played through your senses"—only this time it all occurs within the context of a dramatic, illusionary reality.

Following this barrage-like exposition, Altman departs from this style of sensational overload and moves to a "floating narrative," much like the style of TV soap operas in which the lives and events of many characters are presented by cutting back and forth between them. Altman periodically brings together and connects his twenty-four characters through devices of communication: telephones and telephone conversations, music and radio programs, music and taped songs, the PA announcements of the campaign van. He continuously presents events happening simultaneously, as in his cutting between Barbara Jean's hospital room, the highway, Sueleen's bedroom and the hospital hallway. At the same time he slowly introduces a time element: cutting between simultaneous events at the two bars, he moves to Del's telephone to one of the bars the and then follows Del's end of the telephone conversations to events that unfold at home with Lennea. In the same way, Altman begins by cutting between four simultaneous church scenes, offering us perspectives on as many characters as possible, then moves time forward by cutting to Opal walking through the junkyard as the ringing churchbells signal the end of Sunday morning. Slowly then, Altman begins cutting events into a progressive time pattern, from the stock car races to Mary and Bill's hotel room to Tom's room to evening events to the following morning. Fewer things occur simultaneously as the camera begins more and more to catch each character impressionistically rather than following them all at the same time.

Events continue to progress in this way until the last sequence of the film, the Parthenon rally, where Altman reunites and focuses again on all his characters in one place. Unlike the airport scene, here the characters are united by a single event on which their reactions and responses depend. The Parthenon rally and the subsequent assassination act as the narrative's culminating hub, while all the characters move like spokes of a wheel in relation to it. Altman moves from the barrage of simultaneous moments in many characters' lives to a progressively more linear pattern until he is once again able to present many perspectives simultaneously responding to one single unifying element.

Altman has slowly driven all his characters toward this one event and its aftermath. His post-assassination cuts between the characters keep returning to Winnifred/Albuquerque on stage and to her audience. Interspersed with the characters' reactions, the shots of Albuquerque are initially in close-up, but increasingly become more and more distant. At the same time, close-ups and medium-shots of the audience appear for longer periods of time. Finally, Albuquerque and the audience are united in one long shot that includes stage, crowd, Parthenon, campaign banner, American flag and sky; finally, the camera pans up to the white sky. Altman slowly moves from the variety of impressions of many simultaneous events and levels of sensations to a single, all-inclusive picture-sound reality. The dramatic narrative closes on white (in contrast to its opening in black), and while the credits roll by Albuquerque and the black gospel choir continue singing "It Don't Worry Me" in voice-over. After the credits conclude, the voice-over continues against the black screen for almost three minutes, ending the film with a single aural impression. In direct contrast to the introductory sensory assault, Altman ends by reducing all experience to one single impression.

> Let's consider our National Anthem. Nobody knows the words! Nobody can sing it! Nobody understands it! It doesn't arouse half as much patriotic emotion as "My Country 'Tis of Thee." . . . Read it through carefully—and I say read it because I know you can't sing it—read all four verses and you'll understand what I'm talking about. Yessir, I would support, work and vote for replacement. Change our National Anthem back to something people could understand, back to something that would make a light shine in their faces, back to something they could sing with their hearts, instead of humming and mumbling through a confused series of frowns. | HAL PHILLIP WALKER

Just as Altman structurally moves the film from a simple stimulus with a readily understood meaning, so the whole film explores a complex series of events and sensations for an order and meaning to the complexities of American culture. Cutting back and forth between the characters' gestures, reactions and responses, their dynamic personalities emerge, but nothing of their internal workings is hinted at. They remain the sum of their exposed surfaces as no psychological or narrative meaning is assigned to their existences. Barbara Jean comes the closest to exposing an internal emotional depth, but that is because her emotions have become her raw surface, both as a star and as a person, turning her into a fragile human being. The key narrative character, her fate and its meaning is more unresolved than anyone else's at the film's end.

Narcissistic Tom listens to his own music while he picks up and discards women with as little apparent concern as he changes the channels on his TV set. Yet, in contrast, he seems to care intensely about his music (songs that some might call "sensitive"). What motivates him? The loving and good Linnea, who needs Tom's love badly enough to be unfaithful to her husband, appears equally as subtle and complex. The Tricycle Man, the magician who without speaking moves through scenes and events, transporting characters to one another, remains the most shadowy of all. None of the exposed surfaces add up to any conclusions; no one's character is explained, perhaps, because it is impossible to do so.

Altman develops the events of the rally and assassination in the same way that he treats his characters. First, we see the shots from a distance, then the assassin's face, then the resulting chaos on stage as well as the way the event registers on the faces and triggers the reactions of all the characters. But, merely seeing does not make sense out of the event itself or explain why it happens. Earlier in the film, Opal explains a "truth" behind assassinations: "You see, I believe that people like Madame Pearl and all these people here in this country who carry guns are the real assassins. Because they stimulate the other innocent people who eventually are the ones who pull the trigger." Opal, who turns off her tape recorder to make the statement, makes her notion sound as fatuous as the platitudes of the Walker Talker. But Opal's point, despite the fact that she is affected and gushy and always missing the point, is really not as fatuous as she makes everything she says sound. Her observation, like the campaign van's speeches, rings true and is the closest the film comes to explaining the assassination. But the moment of Opal's observation is easily passed by, because her last shreds of credibility have disappeared by her "yellow school buses" speech. Again, the problem remains: how to sort out the complexities in order to evaluate and assign meaning.

What we need first and foremost is a common sense approach, nothing complicated. . . . No . . . all will not be easy but we will bask in the satisfaction of having done what we should have done . . . and if we don't get it done today . . . we may run out of tomorrows! | HAL PHILLIP WALKER

Hal Phillip Walker, the disembodied PA voice, the name on campaign posters and the reason for the rally, represents a network of issues which holds the film together. Walker's Replacement Party solution to the problems of American life promises "New Roots for an Old Nation," and believable roots or values elude all the characters. It is important that the text of Walker's speech is heard in the film out of its written, linear order, for Walker's cliches can be dropped into any context at almost any time and still mean the same things. Thus, the Walker Talker appears and reappears, randomly inserting social commentary throughout the movie. But the politician's double-talk platitudes offer no solutions; they only reaffirm what people already believe, offering appeasements that ease the frustrations and compensate for the contradictions of their lives.

In much the same way, *Nashville* serves as a prism for contemporary American life, suggesting our multi-perspective view of reality and developing our incomprehension of ultimate meanings. But by pushing toward an ordering, a simplification that culminates in one event and one song, Altman suggests that learning to live with cultural contradictions yields an affirmation and assignment of meaning to life in and of itself. Like the audience that sings, "You may say that I ain't free/But it don't worry me," we can live with the incomprehensibility of our world and its contradictions while still following our inclination to order, affirm and believe in the meaning of our collective existence.

———

LAUREN RABINOVITZ

PART II

Hollywood Auteurs

FORD, HAWKS, STURGES, MINNELLI, SIRK

As noted previously, in CinemaTexas's glory days, many writers were influenced by the *auteur* theory, and especially the version adapted by American critics from its French origins in the 1950s critical writings of Francois Truffaut, Jean-Luc Godard, Jacques Rivette, and others—themselves in thrall to the pioneering ideas of André Bazin and Roger Leenhardt. Broadly speaking, *auteurism* is based around the somewhat romantic notion that certain Hollywood directors of the classical era were able to make excellent movies *and* put their personal stamp on films produced on an otherwise impersonal industrial assembly line. The idea had different philosophical intonations in its French and American versions: whereas French critics tacitly (or overtly) were influenced by post–World War II European existentialism, critics in the United States mainly responded, not especially self-consciously, to the American myth of rugged individualism. (That these rugged individualists were men was taken as a given, the occasional Dorothy Arzner notwithstanding, whose marginalized presence is also symptomatic of early *auteurism*'s blind spot concerning LGBTQ filmmakers.)

In the American context, it is difficult to overstate the subsequent influence of Andrew Sarris's book *The American Cinema: Directors and Directions 1929–1968* on the 1970s generation of academic and journalistic film scholars and critics. Sarris's adaptation of French *auteurist* theory was pragmatic and personal rather than methodologically rigorous (to put it mildly), but it provided an instantly coherent and useful conceptual framework for making sense especially of the work of directors working on the assembly line of the classical Hollywood cinema. Sarris's hierarchical categorization of directors was idiosyncratic and unsystematic, but it provided every movie fan who read the book with both critical guidance and grist for ongoing arguments. Half a century later, the historical consensus seems to be that Sarris got more right than wrong, although there are some directors he may have underestimated (e.g., Billy Wilder, Douglas Sirk), and *auteurism* as a critical construct has become less relevant in the "post-Hollywood" context of blockbuster, tentpole, actuarial filmmaking (although it recurs in mutated form in some discussions of certain contemporary directors such as Christopher Nolan, Kathryn Bigelow, and David Fincher).

This section considers the careers of six major Hollywood directors who are highly regarded by critics, all clearly major *auteurs* in both traditional and contemporary senses, and whose work was often very commercially successful. These were not obscure artists, but major players in the classical Hollywood industry. Their careers span the history of American commercial filmmaking over the first half of the twentieth century, from midway through the silent era to the post–World War II collapse of the studio system, which marked the end of Hollywood's golden age.

These directors are core architects of the genres in which they most often worked. Ford and Hawks returned again and again to the Western and the war film, although the more eclectic Hawks, along with Preston Sturges, also contributed greatly to the development of the screwball comedy. The style and narrative structure of Hollyood musicals and melodramas were profoundly influenced by Minnelli, while Sirk was known especially for his melodramas (also known within the industry as "women's films").

Among this group, Sirk and Sturges were the most persistently and inventively subversive of conventional narrative structure and the dominant white middle-class thematic emphases of the Hollywood mainstream. Sirk was ahead of his time in addressing the hidden class structures of American society in *All That Heaven Allows* (1955) (remade and revised with an additional exploration of racial tensions by Todd Haynes in *Far from Heaven* [2002]) and the ever-present stain of racism in *Imitation of Life* (1959). Sturges was fascinated by the hypocrisy of social customs, creating lacerating and hilarious commentaries on marriage in *The Palm Beach Story* (1942) and America's obsession with celebrity (way ahead of his time here) in *The Miracle of Morgan's Creek* (1944) and *Hail the Conquering Hero* (1944). Sturges and Sirk were also not just masters of their medium but also— within the industrial constraints of Hollywood—genuinely radical stylists. Sturges, in love with the very sound of spoken language, drove the machine-gun dialogue characteristic of the screwball comedy to new heights of incisive observation and invention, and he was a vastly underrated director of ensemble casts. Meanwhile, in the 1950s, Sirk was one of the first major Hollywood innovators of widescreen composition, and his hypersaturated color palette was simultaneously excessive and achingly expressive.

These really are the talents that built the Hollywood film industry.

JOHN FORD (B. 1894, USA)

After beginning his directing career in 1917, Ford initially established his reputation as a maker of Westerns, but his varied and extensive filmography contains examples from almost every film genre. In 1914, he moved cross country from Maine to Hollywood, initially working as a stuntman and occasional actor. He would go on to direct over sixty films in the silent era, and achieved real prominence in the mid-1930s after winning an Academy Award for *The Informer* (1935).

Sarris describes his ascension to the pantheon of Hollywood: "Ford developed his craft in the twenties, achieved dramatic force in the thirties, epic sweep in the forties, and symbolic evocation in the fifties. His style has evolved almost miraculously into a double vision of an event in all its vital immediacy and yet also in its ultimate memory image on the horizon of history . . . A storyteller and a poet of images, he made his movies both move and be moving" (*The American Cinema*, 1968).

The Western, essentially out of vogue in the '30s, was revitalized by the success of *Stagecoach* in 1939. The genre would continue to evolve over the next half century, changes catalyzed by Ford in films like *The Searchers* (1956) and *The Man Who Shot Liberty Valance* (1962). If not the inventor of the myth of the American West, Ford was an important participant in the ongoing cultural discussions that defined the very meaning of our Western archetypes, generating an image of American history that, for better and worse, continues to resonate today. From Martin Scorsese and Peter Bogdanovich to Eagle Pennell and Pedro Costa, his influence has cut across multiple generations of filmmakers, leaving behind a legacy of near mythic proportions.

HOWARD HAWKS (B. 1896, USA)

Known for his ability to work in and master any genre, Hawks directed more than forty films during a lengthy career spanning the entire Hollywood studio era. Before becoming a director, Hawks was a race car driver, a pilot, and a flight instructor; perhaps not coincidentally, many of his films explore masculinity and professionalism. "A director of parts as well as a unified whole," Sarris explains, "Hawks has stamped his distinctively bitter view of life on adventure, gangster, and private-eye melodramas, Westerns, musicals, and screwball comedies, the kind of thing Americans do best and appreciate least" (*The American Cinema*, 1968).

His Westerns, including *Red River* (1948) and *Rio Bravo* (1959), and screwball comedies, such as *His Girl Friday* (1940) and *Bringing Up Baby* (1938), are among his best-known films. He contributed to the establishment standard *film noir* conventions with *The Big Sleep* (1946) and turned hard-boiled romance on its head with *To Have and Have Not* (1944). In *Dawn Patrol* (1930), *Only Angels Have Wings* (1939), and *Air Force* (1943), he brought a taut maturity to aerial films. In those films, as well as his Westerns and *Hatari!* (1962), he explored the group dynamics of men in a unit working together. Still, the gender politics of Hawks's films are very different from those of John Ford. The introduction of a woman into a typically male-centered Ford narrative inevitably represents a move toward domestication and civilization and away from adventure and the frontier. In Hawks's world, women are disruptive, less domesticating, and more erotic, and typically independent-minded and strong-willed. In films like *Ball of Fire* (1941), *Only Angels Have Wings*, and *His Girl Friday*, the lead female character becomes at least a codriver of the film's narrative. And Hawks also directed *Gentlemen Prefer Blondes* (1953), a ringing endorsement of proto-feminism, female bonding, and a major influence on Madonna's early career persona.

PRESTON STURGES (B. 1898, USA)

Sturges himself described his talents most succinctly: "I did all my directing when I wrote the screenplay. It was probably harder for a regular director. He probably had to read the script the night before shooting started" (*His Life in His Words*, 1991). Sturges refined the screwball comedy into its most mature form, blending the speedy wit of the elite with the slapstick of fools (or vice versa) in striking comedies of American error. The very concept of the screenplay as an art form arrived with Sturges. Already recognized as a go-to screenwriter of dramas and comedies in the 1930s, his list of achievements only begins with *The Great McGinty* winning the first Best Original Screenplay Oscar and Orson Welles lifting the structure of Sturges's *The Power and the Glory* (1933) for *Citizen Kane*. One of the first scriptwriters to use his talent to leverage a directing assignment, in a dazzling display of creative energy, Sturges turned out seven great films in a row between 1940 and 1944. He left a vital stamp on Hollywood's war years, apparently with the same effortless speed and finesse as his characters' dialogue. He's remembered largely for the five-year run beginning with *McGinty* in 1940, followed briskly that year by *Christmas in July*, then *The Lady Eve* (1941), *Sullivan's Travels* and *The Palm Beach Story* (1942), and finally *The Miracle of Morgan's Creek* and *Hail the Conquering Hero* (1944).

Sturges's films are essentially very witty and sharply observed satiric assaults on the most sacred American secular institutions: romance (*The Lady Eve*); politics (*The Great McGinty*); advertising and consumer culture (*Christmas in July*); marriage (*Palm Beach Story, Miracle of Morgan's Creek*); war, heroics, and celebrity culture (*Miracle of Morgan's Creek, Hail the Conquering Hero*); and even Hollywood and filmmaking (*Sullivan's Travels*). Sturges crafted his films with an ear for ornate dialogue, creating wildly talkative pictures that satirically portrayed Americans of various classes and backgrounds trying to achieve frequently conflicting versions of the American dream. One memorable exchange in *Sullivan's Travels* summarizes better than all of the many Hollywood satires made in the intervening decades the absurd contradictions and conflicted class consciousness of the industry itself. In the scene, an exceedingly earnest film director pitches an idea for his next project, and the studio head responds eagerly:

Sullivan: I want this picture to be a commentary on modern conditions, stark realism, the problems that confront the average man.
Lebrand: But with a little sex.

VINCENTE MINNELLI (B. 1903, USA)

Vincente Minnelli arrived in Hollywood after a successful career directing Broadway revues in the Ziegfeld style. Odd jobs before that included billboard painting, a dresser at a department store, and a short stint as an art student. That he was eventually labelled a "stylist" with little substance seems more a reflection of his past than the material of his films. Ed Lowry argues, "We must certainly categorize Minnelli as something more than a decorative artist, for the stylistic devices of his films are informed with a remarkably resilient intelligence. Even if we are finally to conclude that, throughout his work, there is a dominance of style over theme, it ultimately serves only to confirm his contribution to the refinement of those techniques by which Hollywood translates meanings into style and presents both as entertainment" (*International Dictionary of Films and Filmmakers,* 1991).

Sarris basically concurs, although his summary of Minnelli's talents comes off as a bit condescending and snooty: "Only Minnelli believes implicitly in the power of his camera to transform trash into art, and corn into caviar. Minnelli believes more in beauty than in art" (*The American Cinema,* 1968). Always attracted to and fascinated by artifice, Minnelli's stylistic language was rarely subversive but rather definitional of classic Hollywood form. Even when the films were more daring in content—*The Pirate* (1948), *The Band Wagon* (1953), *The Cobweb* (1955), *Home from the Hill* (1960) and *Two Weeks in Another Town* (1962)—their *mise-en-scènes* were the very paradigm of studio style.

Minnelli landed at MGM, a studio with an established stylistic tendency favoring conservative, soberly polished expression, which Minnelli tweaked with his flair for baroque visual and narrative extravagance. Spending the next two decades at MGM, he directed *Cabin in the Sky* (1943), the first Hollywood musical with an all-black cast, brought lavish beauty to the mundane in *Meet Me in St. Louis* (1944), and pushed the boundaries of Hollywood visual excess in musicals like *The Pirate, An American in Paris* (1951), and *The Band Wagon.* Often overlooked are his remarkable melodramas and dramas, including *The Bad and the Beautiful* (1952), *The Cobweb,* and *Some Came Running* (1958). As the Hollywood studio system progressively self-destructed in the 1950s, numerous French critics championed his work, noting both the lacerating commentary on American social values in his dramas and the literally spectacular color schemes of his musicals (Jean-Luc Godard subsequently name-checked *Some Came Running* in *Contempt* [1963]).

DOUGLAS SIRK (B. 1897, GERMANY)

"Time, if nothing else, will vindicate Douglas Sirk," prophesied Andrew Sarris in *The American Cinema*. A half century later, Sirk's name is bound together with the genre of melodrama and the affection of his creative progeny. Todd Haynes and Rainer Werner Fassbinder professed such love for his melodramas that their own legacies now come with a Sirkian addendum. Sirk's cinematic world is defined by a distinctive array of colors, themes, and symbols. Recurrently set in and around a 1950s suburban milieu littered with socially inflected material artifacts (television sets, most memorably), Sirk's films are full of images of married women finding and losing themselves in torrents of emotion and identity crisis. "Women think in Sirk's films," noted Fassbinder, "something which has never struck me with other directors. None of them." Sirk's thematic and stylistic propensities became the foundation of the 1950s Hollywood melodrama, a genre he so dominates that he is sometimes mistakenly taken to be the sole innovator of the form.

Sirk described his attraction to films with this peculiarly intense emotional electricity: "So slowly in my mind formed the idea of melodrama, a form I found to perfection in American pictures. They were naive, they were that something completely different. They were completely Art-less." He transformed this often denigrated genre into a very commercially successful connection with American audiences, in part because audiences also understood that Sirk's melodramas were exploring situations and emotions that were quite familiar to them. It took the less perceptive critical community at least a few years to recognize the complex exploration of racial tensions in *Imitation of Life* (1959) or the heroic struggle of the lonely suburban mother in *All That Heaven Allows* (1955). As with Minnelli, the French critics at *Cahiers du Cinéma* were some of his original champions, and later directors and scholars would recognize the strong queer inflections of Sirk films. As Jean-Luc Godard observed, "This, anyhow, is what enchants me about Sirk: this delirious mixture of medieval and modern, sentimentality and subtlety, tame compositions and frenzied Cinemascope."

———

STEVE FORE, LOUIS BLACK

VOL. 11, NO. 2
OCTOBER 14, 1976

Stagecoach (1939)

PRODUCED AND DIRECTED BY JOHN FORD

I found the story by reading it in *Collier*'s, I think it was. It wasn't too well developed, but the characters were good. "This is a great story," I thought, and I bought it for a small amount—I think it was $2,500.

I tried to sell it to the studios, but nobody was buying. After the studio heads read it, they said to me, "But this is a Western! People don't make Westerns any more!" | JOHN FORD, in Richard J. Anobile, ed., *John Ford's Stagecoach.*

In one superbly expansive gesture, which we (and the Music Hall) can call *Stagecoach*, John Ford has swept aside ten years of artifice and talkie compromise and has made a motion picture that sings a song of camera. It moves, and how beautifully it moves, across the plains of Arizona, skirting the sky-reaching mesas of Monument Valley, beneath the piled-up cloud banks which every photographer dreams about, and through all the old-fashioned, but never really outdated, periods of prairie travel in the scalp-raising seventies when Geronimo's Apaches were on the warpath. Here, in a sentence, is a movie of the grand old school, a genuine rib-thumper and a beautiful sight to see.

Mr. Ford is not one of your subtle directors, suspending sequences on the wink of an eye or the precisely calculated gleam of a candle in a mirror. He prefers the broadest canvas, the brightest colors, the wildest brush and the boldest possible strokes. He hews to the straight narrative line with the well-reasoned confidence of a man who has seen that narrative succeed before. He takes no shadings from his characters: either they play it straight or they don't play it at all. He likes his language simple and he doesn't want too much of it. When his redskins bite the dust, he expects to hear the thud and see the dirt spurt up. Above all, he likes to have things happen out in the open, where his camera can keep them in view.

He has had his way in *Stagecoach* with Walter Wanger's benison, the writing assistance of Dudley Nichols and the complete co-operation of a cast which had the sense to appreciate the protection of being stereotyped. You should know, almost without being told, the station in life (and in frontier melodrama) of the eight passengers on the Overland stage from Tonto to Lordsburg. . . .

Onward rolls the stage, nobly sped by its six stout-hearted bays, and out there, somewhere behind the buttes and the crags, Geronimo is lurking with his savage band, the United States Cavalry is biding its time to charge to the rescue and the Ringo Kid is impatiently awaiting his cue to stalk down the frontier-town street and blast it out with the three Plummer boys. But fore-knowledge doesn't cheat Mr. Ford of his thrills. His attitude, if it spoke its mind, would be: "All right, you know what's coming, but have you ever seen it done like this?" And once you've swallowed your heart again, you'll have to say: "No, Sir! Not like this!" | FRANK S. NUGENT, *New York Times*, March 3, 1939.[1]

Stagecoach (1939) is the ideal example of the maturity of a style brought to classic perfection. John Ford struck the ideal balance between social myth, historical reconstruction, psychological truth, and the traditional theme of the Western *mise en scène*. None of these elements dominated any other. *Stagecoach* is like a wheel, so perfectly made that it remains in equilibrium on its axis in any position. | ANDRÉ BAZIN, *What Is Cinema? II.*

---

1. Nugent was a regular reviewer for the *New York Times*. His effusive admiration of Ford, apparently expressed for the first time in this review of *Stagecoach*, led him eventually to Hollywood, where he worked on the screenplays of eleven John Ford films between 1948 and 1963.

Stagecoach. From the core collection production photographs of the Margaret Herrick Library, Academy of Motion Picture Arts and Sciences.

With a directorial career spanning almost fifty years and including around 130 films, John Ford stands as one of the foremost figures of the American cinema. The evidence of those of his films now available for viewing has established him also as one of the most expressive American film artists. Although Ford directed many types of films, he proudly called himself a director of Westerns; and it is within this genre that he did some of his richest and most expressive work, weaving stock genre characters, situations, and symbols into rich and complex tapestries which evoked some of the deepest conflicts within the Western itself.

The Western is perhaps the only truly American film genre, its roots buried deep in the American cultural experience: the expansion of the civilization of the Eastern United States across the wilderness to the Pacific coast. In its most simplified state, the Western concerns the conflicts between this civilization and the wilderness into which it thrust itself. As the genre developed, certain stylized elements representing these conflicts developed as well. Archetypal characters began to appear along with objects, motifs, plots and numerous other elements which became standard for the Western. These elements are recognizable to the Western audience largely through the consistency and frequency of their recurrence in different films within the genre. A Western filmmaker can depend on the fact that his audience will recognize certain genre elements and, in so doing, will impart to them values which he, as creator, need not explain. For example, to the Western audience, a Western town immediately suggests an outpost of civilization in a hostile wilderness, a community which has formed to provide both protection and the advantages of culture to its members. The desert landscape suggests a wilderness hostile to the white man. Its barrenness may deprive man of what he needs to survive; the rocks may hide Indians or badmen. A stagecoach in the desert represents a small convoy of civilized people who have pitted themselves against the probable dangers of the wilderness. The members of the genre audience carries with them these and many other preconceptions when they go to see a Western. The saloon, the jailhouse, the wagon train, the railroad, the showdown, the card game, the six-gun, the sheriff, the Indian scout, all have specific meanings for the audience of Western films. In employing any genre element, the filmmaker necessarily suggests more than he shows.

In his book *The Six Gun Mystique*, John Cawelti outlines three categories of characters in the Western: the "townspeople," the outlaw (or Indian), and the hero. The "townspeople" are the representatives of civilization, including public officials, Easterners, white women, and most of the citizenry of the Western town. These are the people who must be protected from savagery if the mission of civilization is to succeed. On the opposite side are the outlaws and the Indians, opponents of civilization who must be either killed or confined if the "townspeople" are to be kept safe. In the center stands the hero. He may come from either side, but he must possess some of the characteristics of both. He must have the skill and some of the savagery of the opponents of civilization, while maintaining a commitment to the mission of the "townspeople"; and, by the same token, he is somewhat isolated from both groups. Certain characters may cross the line from one side to the other (the army sutler who sells guns to the Indians, the Indian scout for the cavalry), and other characters may seem entirely unplaceable (e.g., the hero's sidekick). But on the whole, Cawelti's categories are helpful, especially in terms of the conflicts which underlie the genre.

Jim Kitses, in *Horizons West*, begins an examination of some of the structures of conflict which are central to the Western. He draws a table of genre antinomies under the large leadings of "The Wilderness" and "Civilization." Under "Wilderness," he lists the concepts of "The Individual," "Nature," and "The West" which stand in opposition to the "Civilization" concepts of "The Community," "Culture," and "The East," respectively. Kitses makes the point that each side of the opposition contains ambivalences. For example, the values of the Individual include both freedom and extreme self-interest. The Community opposes to these values both restriction and democracy. The purity of Nature is opposed to the corruption of Culture, but Nature's savagery is countered by Culture's humanity. The West, though valued as the hope of the future, represents a traditional agrarian life style; while the East, associated with established values, also reflects the new order of industrialization. Kitses demonstrates that both sides of the conflict embody some values which are dear and some which are repugnant to America's concept of itself. It is within the play of these values against one another that we must search to understand the genre's popularity and longevity with the American public.

Stagecoach provides a good point of departure for an examination of Ford's use of Western genre elements. It was Ford's first Western since the silent days, thirteen years before; and its success reopened to Ford his favorite genre in which he was still to do his finest work. The screenplay was written by Dudley Nichols from Ernest Haycox's story "Stage to Lordsburg." Nichols must be given credit for much of the film's dramatic structure and cohesion. Paul Jensen notes that Nichols's screenplays often tended toward a "*Grand Hotel* format of isolating a group of characters and then watching their interaction." This format is employed in *Stagecoach*, but the interaction of the characters takes on a significance outside the story line by his or her relationship to specific archetypal Western figures.

At first praised for rejuvenating the genre and then proclaimed by such critics as André Bazin as the classic Western, *Stagecoach* has recently suffered a decline in prestige. This is largely due to the discovery that many of Ford's later Westerns are more personally and expressively complex. In her book on Ford's Westerns, J. A. Place complains that Ford's themes in *Stagecoach* "are specifically stated and lack the rich complexity for them to become meaningful outside the context of the narrative." Each character, she says, "exists primarily as a foil for the others." I would argue that all Westerns, by virtue of their being Westerns, function in a context outside the narrative. Ford works largely with established character types, each of which contain specific meanings within the genre. The use of dramatic foils, a technique which Ford frequently employs, enables him to place in opposition these genre types and all they represent. The meaning of these foils is clear only in generic terms.

Stagecoach concerns the journey of nine people by stage across a stretch of wilderness under siege by Geronimo. Its characters are a kind of cross-section of genre types. The ordeals of the journey require the group to function as a community, and the characters emerge from the trip somewhat changed. Ford's interest is in depicting the elaborate structure of personal and social relationships which develops as the journey progresses. His method is to juxtapose each character with every other, thereby comparing and contrasting the various types and placing in opposition the values which they represent. The process at hand is the construction of an ideal America in the West, a metaphor for the birth of the United States out of Europe and a reinforcement and justification of the American culture. In its confrontation of values (possible alternatives for America), *Stagecoach* rejects certain attitudes in favor of others: it upholds the traditional family, but rejects inherited status; it encourages individualism, but disavows big business; it forwards a code of personal ethics, but denigrates the restrictions of narrowly enforced laws and public "morality." Thus, it conveys a positive image of the values dearest to America, not as it actually is, but as it ought to be.

Two characters in *Stagecoach* fit into Cawelti's category of the Western hero: Johnny Ringo and Curly Wilcox, each representing an opposite side of this Western type. Ringo, who has been sentenced to prison for attempting to defend his family against Luke Plummer and his brothers, has recently escaped in order to avenge the killing of his brother. Though he stands at odds with the law, Ringo is not an opponent of civilization but a wielder of justice and therefore not to be mistaken for a badman. Wilcox is a US Marshall returning Ringo to jail, the only safe place for him with the Plummers on the loose. Yet the rapport of these two men suggests that they have much in common. Both represent the ideal Western type: strong, silent, kind, simple. When Ringo manages to take his revenge by killing the Plummers, Wilcox allows him to escape to his ranch in Mexico. Both men understand that the laws of civilization are not always strictly applicable in the wilderness.

The two female passengers on the stagecoach embody the two main genre types of women: the good girl and the bad girl. In *Stagecoach*, the distinction is more social than actual, since both represent the finest virtues of womanhood. In Ford's Westerns, women tend to embody the most sacred values of civilization, functioning as carriers of culture and fulfilling the essential roles of mother and nurse. Men may win the West, but women civilize it.

The good girl is Lucy Mallory, just arrived from the East and on her way to meet her husband who is in the cavalry. Attractive, well dressed, and proper, Lucy displays a fragility which requires protection, but possesses a fortitude which pushes her on toward her husband regardless of personal danger. She is weak because she is pregnant, and on the journey she gives birth to a baby boy. As an instance of life born into the wilderness, the event requires little symbolic interpretation and becomes a paradigm of woman's significance in the West.

Dallas is the bad girl more as a result of bad luck than by choice. Orphaned as a child, she has been forced to make her living any way she can. She is the typical "prostitute with a heart of gold," taking quite naturally to her womanly roles when given the opportunity—nursing Mrs. Mallory and taking care of the newborn child. Dallas is unassuming and obviously considers herself inferior to Lucy, but Ford indicates that the difference between them is largely one of circumstance. Dallas aspires without hope to attain Lucy's status; but, if she is to survive in the West, Lucy must exhibit some of Dallas's strength.

Acting as Lucy's protector on the journey is Hatfield, a Southern gentleman who makes his living in the West as a gambler. When he sees Lucy boarding the stagecoach, he decides, without ulterior motives, to serve as her escort. To him she seems to be "an angel in the jungle," a lady (carrying with her the sacred values of civilization) requiring the protection of a gentlemen. But, Hatfield's idealized code of honor requires him to show elaborate courtesies to Lucy while displaying a scorn for women of Dallas's type. When the stagecoach seems sure to be captured by Indians, Hatfield is ready to shoot Lucy to preserve her honor. Fortunately, he is killed before he can do so. By exploiting our generic association of the Southern gentleman with an aristocratic code, Ford uses Hatfield to show that such a code is out of place in the West. Thus the idealized, democratic America being constructed in the wilderness is strictly separated from the decadence and elitism of European (via Southern) aristocracy—depicted most clearly in the scene where Hatfield offers Lucy a drink from a silver cup, but refuses to do the same for Dallas.

Though outcasts in terms of Eastern standards, Ringo and Dallas are the passengers best suited to survival in the West. Products of the frontier, their outcast status results from hardships imposed on them by the uncivilized wilderness. When the stagecoach stops at a way station for dinner, they seat themselves at the same end of the table as Lucy Mallory. Observing this, Hatfield escorts Lucy to the other end of the table. Both Dallas and Ringo assume that it is he/she who has driven the respectable folk away. Thus they are thrust together and made aware of their similarities by the social pressures of the group. By showing these social forces at work among established genre characters, Ford reflects conflicts in the West in general and, by extension, in the American culture itself.

Doc Boone is another outcast character. An Irish drunk, he represents a type more common to the films of John Ford than to the Western. Boone's career as a doctor has been ruined by his drinking, and is evicted from town, along with Dallas, as an undesirable person. Though Mitchell plays the role for comedy, we are bound to take him seriously as a result of his role as frontier healer. Ford forces this seriousness by calling on Boone to deliver Lucy Mallory's baby. Dousing his head with water and drinking scalding coffee, Boone is able to sober himself sufficiently to perform the delivery. During the Indian attack, Boone joins in the fight with Ringo, Wilcox, and Hatfield. All four of these characters assume the role of protectors of civilization on this occasion, although Hatfield's aristocracy and Boone's personal weakness prevent either from becoming true Western heroes.

In contrast to Boone, we are *not* asked to take seriously the comic stagedriver Buck. His constant talk of turning back serves as a comic foil to most of the other stage riders who wish to proceed. Buck's cowardice reflects the actual fears of all the passengers, but since Wilcox never allows him to shirk his duty, he never becomes a real threat to the group.

Representing the common genre type of the Easterner unable to contend with the savagery of the West is Peacock, the whiskey dealer from Kansas City, Kansas. Prim, shy, and cowardly, he represents, in comic extreme, the weaknesses of the Easterner as commonly depicted in the Western. Peacock is the only one of the passengers who consistently wants to turn back, and, when the passengers are asked to vote on whether to continue without their cavalry escort (democracy in the New Land, forwarded by Curley, the Western heroic type), Peacock reveals his inadequacy as a Westerner in one of the great Freudian slips of all times. "I want to reach the bosom of my family in Kansas City, Kansas as quick as possible," he says. "But I may never reach that bosom if we go on. Under the circumstances . . . you understand . . . I think we should go back with the bosoms . . . ahem . . . I mean, with the soldiers." The Easterner is "immature" in his unwillingness to thrust himself into the threat of danger. The easiness of Eastern (and, by extension, European) life has destroyed the "masculine" individualism required in the New Land. When the Indian attack comes, Peacock is never called on to defend the stagecoach, since he is the first one wounded. Although the wound is not fatal, it indicates his helplessness in facing the dangers of the West. At the same time, taking an arrow in the chest marks a kind of ritual initiation by pain into Western "manhood."

As soon as Doc Boone discovers that Peacock is a whiskey dealer, he appoints himself Peacock's protector, taking frequent samples of his client's wares. This protector/protected relationship is in ironic contrast to Hatfield's relationship with Lucy. Instead of functioning as protector, Boone becomes Peacock's greatest menace, (as Hatfield will become Lucy's when he attempts to "save" her by killing her) forcing him to continue the dangerous journey against his will and depleting his whiskey supply all the while. The Boone-Peacock relationship also reflects the banker Gatewood's parasitic relationship to the new Western community. On the other hand, Peacock makes his living from the vice (and ruination) of men like Boone; and, no matter how shy and retiring the victimizer, it is only fair that he be victimized. Ford is able to suggest the numerous ties between Peacock and Boone merely by seating them side by side in the coach and consistently framing them together during crucial scenes.

In transferring "Stage to Lordsburg" to the screen, Ford and Nichols combined and eliminated several of the characters who seemed to duplicate one another as genre types. A cattleman present in Haycox's story was eliminated, since the values he represented were already embodied by Ringo and Wilcox. An Englishman was omitted, because the fastidiousness and ingenuousness associated with the English in the Western already appeared in the character of Peacock, and the English aristocratic code and sense of propriety were reflected in the Southerner Hatfield. The whiskey dealer in Haycox's story is not named Peacock and in no way resembles Donald Meek, in fact, Haycox has him die along the way of a heart attack brought on by over-indulgence. Only two main characters were added to the film who do not appear in Haycox's story: Ford's Irish drunk Boone and the banker Gatewood.

Gatewood (Berton Churchill) is one of the most interesting characters of the film in terms of Ford's expression of genre and conflicts. He represents the worst aspects of civilization. He is fat and egocentric, and, as a banker, is associated with the business-industry mentality of the Northeast. "Don't let the government meddle with business," he is once heard to say. But in addition to Yankee industriousness, Gatewood brings to the West the corruption of the East, taking passage on the stagecoach to escape town after he has stolen the money from his own bank. While Ford allows us to like every other stagecoach passenger, he makes Gatewood entirely despicable: stuffy, scowling, sanctimonious, and entirely unconcerned for his fellow passengers. Gatewood frowns on Dallas in utter hypocrisy and demands that the stagecoach proceed even though Doc Boone says it would be unsafe to move Lucy so soon after having given birth. When the Indians attack the stagecoach, Gatewood not only fails to take up its defense, but becomes so hysterical that Doc Boone is forced to punch him out.

Gatewood embodies the corruption which necessarily travels with civilization and which has begun to contaminate the purity of the West; and Ford relates him to the Eastern moral order, which is also taking hold in the New Land, by making his wife a member of the Ladies of the Law and Order League, the group which is responsible for expelling Dallas and Doc Boone from town. The League is composed of hook-nosed and withered matrons, who represent, in Doc Boone's words, "a foul disease called social prejudice." Civilization has its own evils—corruption and prejudice—which stand to balance the savagery of the wilderness. "There are worse things than Apaches," says Dallas looking at the Ladies of the Law and Order League.

Gatewood's respectable corruption can be seen in direct contrast to the outcast purity of Ringo and Dallas. Society is unable to protect its citizens equally. It has provided no useful alternative to Dallas's prostitution, but stands ready to condemn it. Nor has it been able to protect Ringo's family from the savage Plummer brothers or to punish the Plummers for their crimes. But the law has punished Ringo for trying to obtain justice on his own. Justice requires that he escape from prison and kill the Plummers: to right the wrongs society is unable to right, Ringo must break the laws of society.

The dramatic structure of *Stagecoach* allows Ford to place in visual opposition the landscapes of the wilderness and the architecture of civilization. Sequences played in a town or frontier outpost are alternated with sequences of the stagecoach making its way through the desert. For the first time, Ford uses the setting of Monument Valley; and, with its barren plains and awesome stone monoliths, the location serves as a perfect visual expression of the Western wilderness in genre terms, both beautiful and forbidding, and somehow sacred. Dwarfed between the monuments of nature in Ford's long shots, the stagecoach becomes a visual correlative for the tenuous state of civilization in the wilderness.

The presence of the wilderness is essential to the meaning of *Stagecoach*. It provides a real setting for the dangers which threaten civilization and, as a land without societal restrictions, it serves as a place into which good people like Ringo and Dallas can flee for a new start. Once Ringo has settled his score with the Plummers and Dallas has confessed her past to him, they are cleansed and can be reborn in the promised land. Their flight is a replaying of the American myth of renewal in the Western expanse.

The optimistic tone of the film can be traced largely to the central fact that, as long as the wilderness exists, there remains the possibility of escape from societal restrictions. The paradox is, of course, that as man moves into the wilderness he transforms it and begins the process of civilization once again. By the mid-fifties, Ford has begun to question the openness of the metaphorical expanse; and in *The Man Who Shot Liberty Valance* (1962), its possibilities are locked in a flashback from a present time in which civilization has already closed the opportunities offered America by the West. But in *Stagecoach*, Ford is still hoping; and perhaps that is what makes the film one of the clearest and most beautiful expressions of the American ideal ever to emerge from the Western genre.

———

ED LOWRY

VOL. 19, NO. 3
DECEMBER 10, 1980

The Man Who Shot Liberty Valance (1962)

DIRECTED BY JOHN FORD

What gives [the Western] a particular thrust and centrality is its historical setting; its being placed at exactly that moment when options are still open, the dream of the primitivistic individualism, the ambivalence of at once benef-icent and threatening horizons, still tenable. | JIM KITSES, *Horizons West.*

Ironically, *The Man Who Shot Liberty Valance*, the film in which John Ford most directly confronts the contradictions inherent in the mythology of the Western, begins and ends in a time and place in which the options mentioned above are most certainly not open. The town of Shinbone, at least as it stands when the film begins, is truly a civilized community, and as for the wilderness beyond the town limits, as Hallie so proudly states, "Now it's a garden." "The dream of the primitivistic individualism," a potent myth in other Westerns and in the entire body of American cultural history, has been literally "railroaded," as Ford fills his pastoral opening shot with the billowing smoke of the incoming train. Then, to ensure that we don't miss his point, Ford has Link Appleyard, the retired marshall, attribute the changing nature of the town entirely to the railroad. However, the coming of the "iron

horse" was inevitable and was more of an effect than a cause of the relentless march of progress. Besides, as always, Ford is more interested in talking
about how changes affect people, not machines.

> Perhaps the single most significant conflict in the Western is between the
> community's demand for order through cooperation and compromise, and
> the physical environment's demand for rugged individualism and a survival-
> of-the-fittest mentality. | THOMAS SCHATZ, *Hollywood Film Genres.*

In *Horizons West*, Jim Kitses lays out a philosophical dialectic of what he
sees as the essence of the Western. He sees the basic conflict as that between
Civilization and the Wilderness, and believes that virtually all of the struggles found in the Western genre, be they internal or international, can be
at least loosely associated with this archetypal dichotomy. Some examples
are: Community vs. Individual, Restriction vs. Freedom, Culture vs. Nature,
Knowledge vs. Experience, Humanity vs. Savagery, East vs. West, Future
vs. Past, and many others. Granted, some of the pairings could be regarded
as arbitrary or at least questionable, but his basic argument is strong. Furthermore, Kitses provides us with a wonderful framework through which
to discuss the characters in *Liberty Valance*.

> The absence of extras and the lack of a persuasive atmosphere [in
> *The Man Who Shot Liberty Valance*] forces the spectator to concentrate
> on the archetypes of the characters. | ANDREW SARRIS, *Film Culture*, Sum-
> mer 1962.

Nowhere is the lack of "persuasive atmosphere" more evident in this film
than in the initial confrontation between Liberty Valance and Ransom Stoddard. As Tom Schatz points out, Valance and his henchmen step from behind
the papier mâché boulder wearing trenchcoats! Yet the archetypal (and stereotypical) characterizations and situation are such that we are willing to
"go along for the ride," so to speak. We have all seen this type of hold-up
countless times before in movies, yet never before has the villain been quite
this villainous nor the gentleman so adamant in his gentlemanliness.

It is quite obvious that neither Rance nor Liberty can remotely fathom
the other's way of life. The personality of each character is conveyed through
a representative material possession: Rance has his lawbooks, Liberty his
silver-knobbed whip. The respective implements, as well as the men who

carry them, fit perfectly into Kitses's model. And it is these "things," the possessions important to Rance and Liberty that evoke the most hostile reactions from each personified half of the Civilization/Wilderness dialectic. This in itself is a sign of the attitudinal changes that lie ahead (capitalist-based ideology), but more important at the moment of confrontation is the way in which the two men demonstrate their basic disgust with and mistrust of the other's worldview.

Of course, as Rance later notes, "When force threatens, talk's no good anymore." Liberty's Wilderness-based answer to the situation is to tear up the lawbooks and to flay at the Eastern attorney with his whip. At this point, Ford dollies quickly in for a closer shot of Valance just as the villain sneers, "Law?! I'll teach you law! Western law!" This blatant, attention-grabbing cinematic device, bordering on camp (as does the entire scene), works for two reasons: 1) The whip slashes across the frame, only to land off-screen; and 2) Ford has summed up the position of Valance, and by implicit extension, The Wilderness, in one dynamic shot.

Still another dichotomy which describes the opposing ideologies of Stoddard and Valance is Thought vs. Action. Whereas Valance (re)acted violently to the sight of books, his adversary reflects/thinks almost abstractly about the man who attacked him. He tells Tom and Hallie that he must seek revenge on "the man with the silver-knobbed whip," and later realizes that Liberty is in the restaurant when he spots the same whip on a table.

Despite the vast ideological differences between the two men, they can be discussed as a pair largely because of their *similarities*. Both are very strong in their convictions, and are therefore able to dominate other people. Still, Liberty is able to physically dominate Rance, which Ford continually expresses not only through the narrative action, but also with his pictorial composition. In virtually every confrontation with Liberty (and later with Tom Doniphon), Stoddard is on the ground, looking up at his adversary, whether they are out on the trail, in the cafe, or in the street. On the other hand, Ransom is able to intellectually dominate nearly everyone else in the community. An example of this is in the school, where Stoddard often condescendingly corrects his pupils for essentially unimportant grammatical errors. An even more blatant display of his penchant for domination is in his relationship with Hallie.

Whereas Stoddard and Valance might be seen as polar aberrations of the community, Hallie could be classified as a confused mediator. Her sympathies lie totally neither with the Wilderness nor Civilization, but somewhere in between. Of course, as can be expected in a Ford Western, her position is largely determined by her man; unfortunately for Hallie, she has two men, and therein lies much of her confusion. Although Tom Doniphon and Rance are very different types of men, their respective relationships with Hallie are again quite similar; each provides the relationship with a certain strength, one physical and the other mental, and these traits provide the foundation on which the potential relationships are based. Tom and Hallie exchange compliments on physical appearance, whereas Rance calls Hallie "a smart girl" as she brags that he's going to "learn" her to read and write. Ford further illustrates these conflicting views of the nature of love by contrasting the ways in which the two men admire Hallie. Stoddard generally focuses (through Ford's camera) on her face and his eyes follow her head when she walks away from him; Doniphon often compliments Hallie when she's bending over in front of him. The latter's attitude is firmly conveyed when, after hearing Hallie declare that she is independent, Tom can only say, "Like I said, Hallie, you sure are purty when you get mad."

> [The Western hero's] loneliness is organic, not imposed on him by his situation but belonging to him intimately and testifying to his completeness.... The Westerner is not thus compelled to seek love; he is prepared to accept it, perhaps, but he never asks of it more than it can give, and we see him constantly in situations where love is at best an irrelevance. | ROBERT WARSHOW, *The Immediate Experience.*

Tom Doniphon clearly straddles the line between the worlds of Wilderness and Civilization, and as such is the true mediator of the film. Furthermore, where does the character stop and the screen persona of the actor begin? John Wayne, in conjunction with John Ford, virtually defined the role of the Western hero; countless times we have seen him wander away at the end of the story, trapped in his role as lonely redeemer. In this particular case, he can easily out-Wilderness Liberty Valance, and one gets the sense that he is at least the intellectual equal of Ransom Stoddard. He *is* able to read, and he seems to understand and accept Rance's love for his lawbooks. Yet, he has lived in a time when the Wilderness was something that had to be tamed or shot, not "put into jail," as Rance wants to do with Liberty. Torn between two worlds, Tom is unable to exist fully in either one, and as a result he is continually frustrated. His code of honor will not allow him to start trouble with Liberty Valance, but as he clearly intimates at the election, if Valance is ready for some, Tom knows who'll win. Similarly, the smirking "just try it" he delivers to Liberty in the cafe is a straightforward challenge to the villain, who knows that he is just not the match for Doniphon, even with two henchmen to Tom's one.

Doniphon's frustration in the community is centered around his love for Hallie. Ransom's arrival in town is recognized instantly as a threat by Tom, who takes over the swabbing of Rance's wounds when he becomes uncomfortable with the closeness with which Hallie is working on the beaten pilgrim. He pegs Rance as a "ladies' man," which is said half-mockingly and half-admiringly. Tom is simply too independent to ever be extremely popular with the females, a point succinctly made through the perception by Hallie's parents of the implications of Rance's arrival and the potential conflicting interest for their daughter's attention. Mother is totally enamored with Rance, the nice young man, while Father is still waiting for Tom to pop the question.

Tom continually barges in on Hallie and Rance as they are touching one another for one reason or another. Although his love for Hallie is not an "irrelevance," he most certainly does not "ask more of it than it is prepared to give." He makes a bravado attempt to scare Rance off with both words and a trick, but he just ends up getting socked in the jaw, and *that* is what finally convinces him that Rance is worthy of carrying forth the flame of Civilization. From that point on, he is totally in Rance's corner, whether it be at the election or at the infamous (or is it legendary?) shootout.

> As the community's development poses an even greater threat to the Westerner's individual posture and worldview, his role as agent of civilizations grows increasingly ironic and ultimately even tragic. | THOMAS SCHATZ, *Hollywood Film Genres.*

Tom is acknowledged by all as the leader of the community, which is not surprising when we examine the alternatives. Ford has again presented us with a varied and interesting group of characters, all of whom are incompetent in his/her own unique way. One who does provide a certain type of leadership is Dutton Peabody, who as editor of the *Shinbone Star,* has the main local forum for his well-articulated, populist ideas. This character represents yet another facet of the face of Civilization, as he is really just, in

Schatz's words, "another one of Ford's philosophical drunks." Then there is the marshall, who appears to spend his time wolfing down steaks "on the cuff" and finding new excuses and means of avoiding Liberty Valance. The rest of the males in the town spend their time working and drinking, and are quite willing to let Tom (and later Rance) tell them what is the right way to think and act. The only characters who might have the strength to lead are Hallie and Pompey, but of course both are excluded from the important work of a white and male-dominated world.

When the going gets tough, everyone looks to Tom, and he finally decides everyone's fate for them. As was mentioned above, when Tom sees that Rance is flexible enough to at least acknowledge the physical side of life (Mind vs. Body), he is ready to turn over the reins of leadership, and does so quite blatantly at the election. Also, by turning down the nomination for delegate (and we must wonder what his "personal plans" are) he opens the gate for Peabody, who in fictional history will probably be discussed in the same breath as his hero Horace Greeley. Tom's verdict for Liberty Valance is of the spur-of-the-moment type, but it's a decision that "he can live with."

In the long run, Tom's most important decisions come at the territorial convention. There the two conflicting ideologies meet head-to-head. As Peabody states in his address to the convention, statehood represents "farms, fences, schools, and progress for the future." Opposing them are the ranchers who want the land to remain open so that they can continue to grow rich off it. The classical mediator would be ambivalent when presented with these two choices, but the look on Doniphon's now unshaven face as he watches from the stairs shows that he is disgusted with the hype and circus atmosphere that pervades the ranchers' camp. He is quite aware that the world is changing, and hands over the gauntlet to Rance, who is obviously more capable of leadership in the times ahead. This, of course, is not a painless decision, for in convincing his friend to go back inside and accept the nomination as territorial representative (in the same action relinquishing his claim on Hallie), Doniphon is "committing himself to a life of isolated uselessness" (Schatz).

The Man Who Shot Liberty Valance can never be fully appreciated except as a memory film, the last of its kind, perhaps, from one of the screen's old masters.... What he wishes to conserve are the memories of old values even if they have to be magnified into legends. The legends of which Ford is most deeply involved, however, are the legends of honorable failure of otherwise forgotten men and women who rode away from glory toward self-sacrifice. | ANDREW SARRIS

We were destined to follow a certain historical path in reaching our present cultural condition, and we necessarily have rewritten history to convince ourselves that indeed we have taken the "right" path, that our destiny represents the fulfillment of promises made and kept. | THOMAS SCHATZ, *Hollywood Film Genres.*

Ford eventually takes us to the other side of his narrative bookend, as Senator Stoddard finishes his tale-confession. By utilizing this unique (for him) narrative style, the director is better able to pinpoint the changes in values that have occurred through the passing of time. How has Shinbone changed? Well, there are more buildings and better streets, but most of the changes are matters of style and ideology. The pace has picked up, as is evidenced by the eager young reporter and the braggadocio of the man in the train who testifies that "she'll do 25 mph" the entire trip. However, Ford seems to be most intrigued/upset by these modern folks' obsession with money. The man in the train station calls after the cub reporter to pay for his phone call, and the mortician claims that he's not "made a nickel" on Doniphon's funeral, so has wisely absconded with the corpse's boots to help cover his overhead. Of course, this is just the type of pragmatic behavior that Tom Doniphon would have supported, but the political-minded/ image-conscious Stoddard insists that Tom wear all of the now antiquated accoutrements of the Western hero as he travels to his happy hunting ground. And to punctuate the fact that it is not just the proletariat who now must by necessity focus their lives on the capitalist ideology, Stoddard offers Pompey some "pork chop money" on his way out the door.

As Schatz states above, the conclusions are inevitable. To get from the world of *Stagecoach* and *The Searchers* to our present state, we had to pass through the town of Shinbone, in both its incarnations. But in comparing the two versions of the town, we see that the changes are largely superficial. The railroad was often robbed much like the stagecoach, albeit for bigger booty; also, the voluminous amounts of beef eaten by Link Appleyard in the cafe may have been "on the cuff," but they weren't necessarily "on the house," as each steak was resentfully marked down on the chalkboard, which is not dissimilar to the account to which the reporter charges his call.

It's all just a little more corporate and less personal now. However, subtle changes such as these grow in importance when one is "growing old and remembering through the thick haze of illusion," as Sarris believes that both Ford and his characters are doing here. And, in our culture's persistent interest in the myth of the West, they may be precisely what we as a culture have done and are doing.

——

DON HARTACK

VOL. 13, NO. 3
NOVEMBER 21, 1977

His Girl Friday (1940)

DIRECTED AND PRODUCED BY HOWARD HAWKS

His Girl Friday (1940) is one of the fastest of all movies, from line to line and gag to gag. Besides the dynamic, highly assertive pace, this *Front Page* remake with Rosalind Russell playing Pat O'Brien's role is a tour de force of choreographed action: bravado posturing with body, lucid Cubistic compos-ing with natty lapels and hat brims, as well as a very stylized discourse of short replies based on the idea of topping, out-maneuvering the other person with wit, cynicism, and verbal bravado. A line is never allowed to reverberate but is quickly attached to another, funnier line in a very underrated comedy that champions the sardonic and quick-witted over the plodding, sober citi-zens. | MANNY FARBER, *Artforum*, 1969.

His Girl Friday is Howard Hawks's best comedy, and quite possibly his best film. . . . Hawks's steady pace never gives us time to question the charac-ters' motives. Molly Malloy jumps out the window and is promptly forgotten; Walter kidnaps Bruce's mother and is promptly forgiven. Only in retrospect does this delightful comedy reveal itself as possibly the most subtly cynical film Hollywood has produced. | RICHARD CORLISS, *Talking Pictures*.

> I think that motion is far more interesting than just talking. Anybody can stand still and talk, and even in motion I've tried to make my dialogue too fast, probably twenty percent faster than most pictures. Sometimes we put a few unnecessary words on the front of a sentence and a few on the end, so that people can overlap in their talking and you still get everything they wanted to say. . . . We did it in a picture called *His Girl Friday*. And if you have actors who are good enough, it's a lot of fun to do. It gives you a sense of speed. . . . If you can get the sensation of speed, people can't just sit back and analyze how bad it is. | HOWARD HAWKS, *The Men Who Made the Movies.*

Howard Hawks claims he got the idea for *His Girl Friday* at a dinner party he was giving. He thought it would be a good idea for the guests to amuse themselves by doing a reading of *The Front Page*, the Ben Hecht and Charles MacArthur play. He handed the male reporter's part (Hildy Johnson) to one of the women while he took the managing editor's lines (Walter Burns). After a few pages of dialogue, Hawks grew excited and decided that the play was better with a girl playing Hildy Johnson. He called co-author Hecht and suggested changing the reporter's sex for a future film project. Hecht liked the idea but had other project commitments; so Hawks hired Charles Lederer to write additional dialogue for a new script. Lederer had scripted the 1931 movie version of *The Front Page*, directed by Lewis Milestone, and had helped Hecht on other Hollywood screenplays. On *His Girl Friday*, he worked with Hecht (who receives no screen credit) to revamp characters and dialogue while preserving the wit and style of the original.

When *His Girl Friday* premiered in New York City in January, 1940, it baffled and excited critics and public alike for just one reason—its speed. Hawks's actors overlapped their dialogue; they spoke in lower tones of voice; conversations ran almost simultaneously. Hawks reinforced the sensation of speed by keeping his characters in constant activity. For example, when Walter finds out that Hildy is getting married that day, he nervously reacts by rubbing his hand, touching the phone, picking up a carnation from a vase and slipping it into his buttonhole. All the while, he struggles to keep an impassive face. When he tries to convince Hildy to write the exclusive Earl Williams capture story, his impassioned, aggressive speech drives her around the room, first clockwise and then counter-clockwise. When Hawks can't rely on his characters' motions, he uses such techniques as the rapid cuts between the reporters talking into their phones or the searchlight sweeping across the room to keep the pace frenetic. Hawks's comedy clocks

His Girl Friday. From the core collection production photographs of the Margaret Herrick Library, Academy of Motion Picture Arts and Sciences.

in at 240 words per minute, about 100–140 wpm faster than the average speaking rate; but his timing, camerawork and editing make it seem faster still.

The film is so mannered, especially in its pacing, that the degree of stylization calls attention to itself. Hawks ultimately uses such self-consciousness to parody his actors/characters. When Louie asks Walter Burns what Bruce Baldwin (Ralph Bellamy) looks like, Burns replies, "Oh—like that actor—Ralph Bellamy." Burns later quips to the Sheriff, "The last man that said that to me was Archie Leach just a week before he cut his throat." Archie Leach was Cary Grant's real name. Such self-conscious references don't really disrupt the film, but merely add to the film's insane pacing by adding hilarious laughs at the absurdity of believing in the characters as real people. Coupled with the timing and character acting, the parodic elements contribute to the development of an essay on the absurdity of any kind of ethical or moral commitments—any commitment to "normal values"—in the modern world.

THE HAWKSIAN WORLD

Hawks's films celebrate the solidarity and validity of the exclusive all-male group, dedicated to the life of action and adventure, and a rigid professional ethic. When women intrude into their worlds, they represent a threat to the very existence of the group. However, women appear to possess "positive" qualities in Hawks's films: they are often career women and show signs of independence and aggression in the face of the male, particularly in his crazy comedies. Robin Wood has pointed out quite correctly that the crazy comedies portray an inverted version of Hawks's universe. The male is often humiliated or depicted as infantile or regressed.... For Hawks, there is only the male and the non-male: in order to be accepted into the male universe, the woman must *become* a man.... This disturbing quality in Hawks's films relates directly to the presence of woman; she is a traumatic presence which must be negated. | CLAIRE JOHNSTON, *Notes on Women's Cinema.*

[Rosalind] Russell does not become an imitation male; she remains true to the two sides—feminine and professional—of her nature, and as such promises to exercise a healthy influence on the hard-boiled, all-male world of criminal reporting. It is as newspaper reporter, rather than as wife and mother, that she discovers her true "womanliness," which is to say, simply, herself. | MOLLY HASKELL, *From Reverence to Rape.*

The flaw in *His Girl Friday* [is that] the choice offered Hildy is much too narrow to be acceptable, the surrender to irresponsibility too easily made, the alternative too glibly rendered ridiculous (given the alternatives the film offers, the only morally acceptable ending would be to have Hildy walk out on *both* men; or to present her capitulation to Walter as tragic). | ROBIN WOOD, *Howard Hawks.*

The pivotal issue of *His Girl Friday* is Hildy's decision whether to marry the tepid, dull Bruce Baldwin or to team with Walter Burns because of their mutual understanding, respect and love for professionalism. While Molly Haskell may praise the film's ability to allow a woman to find her "personhood" in a non-domestic sphere, that cannot negate the restrictive options that Hildy faces—marriage to home, children and a pallid Bruce or marriage to career and ego with a maniacal Walter. Hildy's choice remains an either/or decision, and Hawks's preference for the latter is hardly a less oppressive choice than the former.

The cynicism of the Hawksian world is apparent in the options Hildy faces before she makes her final decision. Mollie Malloy provides a striking contrast to Hildy's professional career woman, representing a caricature of what Hildy could be. Mollie's extreme devotion to one man (whom she claims she doesn't even know) seems to manifest itself chiefly through histrionics and whining. The reason her suicide is so quickly forgotten is that it provides only a physical extension of rather unattractive and unpleasant "feminine" hysterics. Hildy, who can view Mollie's hysterics with a cool and detached eye, still handles her with sympathy. Condemning the reporters for their callousness, she is the single person to register a concern and strong reaction to Mollie's suicide attempt.

If Mollie functions as a reminder of "feminine" inadequacies in comparison to Hildy, so, too, do the men function as reminders of "masculine" inadequacies. The sheriff, the warden, the doctor, the mayor, Joe Pettibone and even Earl Williams are largely incompetent and ineffectual when trying to yield power and dominate. The other men—the reporters—are secure only because they have no such power illusions—about their jobs, their beliefs or themselves. The one reporter who does, Bensinger, the butt of a number of running jokes, gets duped and suckered by Walter Burns. While Hildy tells Walter that she doesn't like his act (the by-product of a dog-eat-dog world view), she cannot quite suppress a giggle at the thought of Bensinger's disillusionment. The men of the press have each other, they have their ability to use words, and they have their cynicism. Interestingly enough, the reporters echo Walter's praise for Hildy's superior ability to use language (the symbol of her ability to survive in their world) after reading one of her pieces.

Whereas Walter mockingly tells Hildy he needs a piece that "only a woman could write," the story that the pressroom reporters read is at least one that none of them *could* have written. Hildy's sympathetic treatment (and exploitation) of Earl during the interview and her sense of melodrama in the piece itself retain human sympathies far beyond the capabilities of the pressroom boys. As a matter of fact, Hildy's story may seem pretty trashy and melodramatic, but we accept her as a topnotch reporter not only because everyone in the film says she is, but also because her sensitivity makes her seem capable of writing so much better than anyone else.

Ultimately, Hildy is the only character who can understand and walk in both the world of Mollie Malloy and that of the pressroom boys. Her choice to remain with the press seems less a decision to relinquish her "non-male" attributes than a commitment to continued excitement and frenetic activity. Hildy's decision for the active, motion filled life of the journalist is her only possible choice. As Hawks suggests in an interview, it is the only way she can work up enough sense of speed so that she won't have to think about how limited her options really are and how bad life really is.

To be a normal woman, you need normal men around you. | ROBERT GRAVES

Poet Robert Graves's statement on "normalcy" reflects Hildy Johnson's personal dilemma and points to the conflict arising in screwball comedies of the 1940s. *His Girl Friday* is the first screwball comedy to depart from the money-marriage-ego conflicts of *Holiday, My Man Godfrey*, and *The Philadelphia Story*, inserting into the same comic structure and pattern of action a conflict between career and marriage. Throughout the 1940s, career-marriage decisions for women provide the pivotal crisis point in screwball comedies, most notably in such films as *Woman of the Year* (1941), *Take a Letter, Darling* (1942), and *They All Kissed the Bride* (1942). Ultimately, in 1949, George Cukor's *Adam's Rib* was to take the marriage-career crisis (with the help of Garson Kanin and Ruth Gordon's script) to its logical conclusion— a comic study of sex role stereotyping and the validity of narrowly defined sex roles. *His Girl Friday*'s implicit understanding of the narrowness of sex roles provides the transition from the subversion of such statements in 1930's screwball comedies to the explicit statement of *Adam's Rib*.

———

LAUREN RABINOVITZ

VOLUME 8
SPECIAL EDITION
MARCH 12, 1975

Red River (1948)

DIRECTED AND PRODUCED BY HOWARD HAWKS

Howard Hawks . . . should be credited with having demonstrated that it had always been possible to turn out a genuine Western based on the old dramatic and spectacle themes, without distracting our attention with some social thesis, or, what would amount to the same thing, by the form given the production. *Red River* (1948) and *The Big Sky* (1952) are Western masterpieces but there is nothing baroque or decadent about them. The understanding and awareness of the means matches perfectly the sincerity of the story. | ANDRÉ BAZIN, *What Is Cinema*, vol. II

Red River (1948), as a comment on frontier courage, loyalty, and leadership, is a romantic, simple-minded mush, but an ingeniously lyrical film nonetheless. The story of the first trip from Texas to the Abilene stockyards is a feat of pragmatic engineering, working with weather, space, and physiognomy. The theme is how much misery and brutality can issue from a stubbornly obsessed bully (John Wayne, who barks his way through the film instead of moving), while carving an empire in the wilderness. Of the one-trait characters, Wayne is a sluggish mass being insensitive and cruel-minded on the front of the screen; Joanne Dru is a chatting joke, even more static than Wayne; but here is a small army of actors (Clift, John Ireland) keyed in lyrically with trees, cows, and ground. | MANNY FARBER, "Howard Hawks," *Focus on Howard Hawks*

Wayne had done, probably, 50 cheap Westerns where he didn't have to do anything. He read the script for *Red River* and said, "I don't know whether I want to play an old man." I said, "You're *gonna* be an old man pretty soon, and you ought to get used to it. And you also better start playing characters instead of that junk you've been playing." So he said, "How do I show that I'm old?" And I said, "Did you ever see me get up? Just do it that way." So he did it, and he saw the film and he said, "Lord, I'm *old*." He didn't have to do a lot of silly things, either. And Jack Ward said, "I never knew that big ox could act." | HOWARD HAWKS interviewed in *Take One*, November-December, 1971

In the first issue of *Movie*, published in May of 1962, that British magazine of cinematic criticism printed a chart which they said reflected in summary manner the editorial board's taste in directors. The categories listed were: Great, Brilliant, Talented, Competent or ambitious, and finally The Rest. Only two directors made their Pantheon: Alfred Hitchcock and Howard Hawks. They seem to be two very complementary figures to represent the best of cinematic *auteurs*. Hitchcock, who worked tirelessly away, exploring his slender niche, the murder/suspense/mystery; and Hawks, whose works are so variegated as to include examples from every major film genre, and then some—gangster, mystery, science fiction, Western, action adventure, comedy, musical, spectacle.

Probably the least literary and self-conscious of all major directors, Hawks's successes in so many differing types of movies probably reflect the straightforward approach he takes to any film—his main concern is to tell a good story. (He has said, "I think a director's a story-teller, and if he tells a story that people can't understand, then he shouldn't be a director.") Seeing his role in such a clear light, his method is centered on making the film story engaging, entertaining, and easy to follow. He would spend large amounts of time in the scripting stage, working and re-working the basic elements until they were lubricated and positioned exactly so that they fit together well, like the parts of a high-powered precision engine. On the set, one of his main concerns was to move the story along ("Get the scene the

Red River. From the core collection production photographs of the Margaret Herrick Library, Academy of Motion Picture Arts and Sciences.

hell over with as soon as possible," as he would put it). He would improvise with an actor so that his lines would not only impart information to the audience, but give the film a thrust. His performers would be on the move as they delivered their lines, they'd overlap their lines onto somebody else's, and interruptions were a matter of course. And whenever the sprinty dialogue failed to move the film along, he would add motion to stir things up a bit. This motion took the shape not of splendiferous camera moves (though a moving camera is a part of Hawks's visual grammatics), but rather in the form of exquisitely choreographed action on the screen. As Richard Schickel points out, "Whenever self-consciousness threatens, Hawks throws his characters into action."

Together with this emphasis on visual and aural thrust and pacing, is Hawks's flair for casting, which has seldom failed him, and the ability to get his actors to give just that extra amount which spells the difference between a walk-through and a performance. John Wayne is generally at his best in a Hawks Western; Walter Brennan never seemed so pesky nor so likable as in *To Have And Have Not, Red River,* or *Rio Bravo*; Humphrey Bogart and Lauren Bacall are defined by their work in *To Have And Have Not* and *The Big Sleep*; and Cary Grant, whether the mild-mannered and quiet professor of *Bringing Up Baby* or the whinnying, unscrupulous newspaper editor in *His Girl Friday*, has never shown comic timing so sharp, so right.

Red River is the first of five Westerns Hawks has made in the last three decades, and the Western form seems to have agreed with him, for his last two films, *El Dorado* (1967) and *Rio Lobo* (1970), are both Westerns, and are both variations on the theme delineated by *Rio Bravo* (1959). According to Hawks, there are only two basic Western stories: the winning of the west, and law and order after the land has been settled. *Red River* and Hawks's next Western, *The Big Sky*, belong to the first type. After Hawks had settled his west, his Westerns began to focus on smaller groups of men in action—in *Rio Bravo* there are only three men and a dried-up drunk who stand off the enemy—and as his focus narrows, and his groups become smaller, they address themselves to a different theme: law and order.

In his book on Howard Hawks, Robin Wood lists the stock characters of the Western genre:

1. Hero
2. Hero's friend
3. Woman of doubtful virtue
4. Nice girl, schoolteacher or farmer's daughter
5. Hero's comic assistant
6. Singing cowboy
7. Comic Mexican.

In *Red River*, the characters portrayed by John Wayne, Montgomery Clift, Joanne Dru, and Walter Brennan cover four of these types; two others, the singing cowboy and the comic Mexican can be filled in by members of the crew of drovers, with Quo, the Indian, substituting for the Mexican. Only the nice-spirited schoolteacher is missing. Looked at so analytically the types are obvious, but as evolved on the screen, the characters never seem so typical as to be types, and situations never force them to slide from the familiar to the cliché.

But there are other elements of the Western which are also imperatives of the genre, and we also find these in *Red River*. I am speaking of such things as:

1. *The Journey*. A long journey over a vast expanse of land, usually under the most dire circumstances. In *Red River*, both the wagon train and the cattle drive serve as examples.
2. *Revenge*. The revenge motive, one of the most basic emotional responses, is central to most Westerns, so much so that the "every-time you look over your shoulder" speech is a standard. In *Red River* Tom tells Matt: "I'll catch up with you. I don't know when, but I'll catch up. Everytime you turn around expect to see me, 'cuz one time you'll turn around and I'll be there. Gonna kill you, Matt."
3. *Sex*. There is a strong sensual current, which in the best Westerns flows nearly unnoticeably and manifests itself only by the slightest gestures—a pause, a look, a few jittery words—which give an important extra dimension to the film. In *Red River*, Fen's goodbye to Tom, begging him to take her along, is red hot and passionate, and Hawks gets this across by getting us to notice how she feels by the curious way she puts things. She has knives in her knees, and half of every day is dark and cold, she reminds him.
4. *The Railroad*. It is principally seen as the civilizing symbol, and it also reiterates the toughness of the vast land, which could only yield to the toughest men and the iron horse. The entire cattle drive in *Red River* is made simply to get to the railroad, so that besides being the sign of civilization, it represents a sort of salvation.
5. *The Territory*. It is in the form of a territorial imperative, and those characters who best know the boundaries of the territory and can use it to their advantage are called heroes. This notion of territory exists in two forms. One is literally The Territory as land, as *some-body's* land, as property. In this form, trespassers are the ultimate evil and are punished with death, unless, as in the early sequence in *Red River*, the trespasser is man enough to call the land his. The second form The Territory may take is a personal one, and involves the limits of dignity of the individual. When Matt takes the drive away from Tom, he is taking his cattle to be sure, but he is also stealing pride from within Tom's personal boundaries.

Both *Red River* and *The Big Sky* involve journeys. More than a mere easy plot device, the long trek usually has the effect of a trial by fire, whereby the principal characters are seen as improved, matured, after the ordeal. It serves this function in *Red River*. But the journey nearly sunders the very basis of the film's world, and one of the themes most dear to Hawks particularly, the loyalty of one man to another. It is this pitting of father and surrogate son against each other, in the absence of actual bad guys—save for the hundred or so faceless Indians—and Hawks's preoccupation with loyalty (which, depending on whose side you are on, is either saving the drive from ruination by a madman or a treacherous doublecross), that makes this Western a classic of the genre.

All through the film we are thrown false leads as to what the final showdown will be. From their earliest encounter, we expect it to be between Cherry and Matt. Hawks throws in a little marksmanship contest between the two and some muttered, over-the-shoulder dialogue by Groot which subtly leads us to expect just that. But when it comes down to it, and after we have been led to expect that confrontation all along, the character of Cherry is summarily brushed aside on the way to the real showdown. (Very noticeably, we never find out what happened to Cherry; it is unimportant to Hawks.) If we get an uneasy feeling when Tom and Matt finally face each other, it is a feeling Hawks worked to get: it is a tiny twist of the standard showdown, but, significantly, one in which no one is clearly in the right, and no one can come out ahead. And it is that queasy feeling which delimits this Western from all others, it is that feeling which marks that climactic scene as a classic, despite the inability of Joanne Dru to reach the heights of her part.

Even though she has problems with her role, Joanne Dru is almost right for it. She is comely enough to have that mysterious, slightly shady background that Hawks likes to give his women. She has enough of an edge about her to make her answers to Wayne's questions just enough of a mixture of humor and sensuality that so characterized so many rejoinders from Hawksian women. But, sadly, she doesn't have enough of an edge to go all the way, which is what the women in Hawks's films must do. By go all the way I mean this: the female character in a Hawks film must be a woman who can go straight to the limits of her dignity as a person for her man *without* losing that toughness that makes her unique. Fen, Tom's woman whom he loses in an Indian raid early in the picture, is that type of woman, one who could take hold of Wayne and tell him how she can make his nights warm and how she longs to go with him so much she feels as if she had knives "stickin'" in her. Joanne Dru's Tess has one big chance to show her truest colors, in that final scene, and she blows it. It is partly, to be sure, the fact that the scene is not an easy one to pull off. But it is also the fact that she goes shrill where she might have been acerbic, just slightly ludicrous where she should have been just this side of hysterical uncontrol. As it stands, her performance is an embarrassment; but the preeminence of the sequence in the history of the Western film, plus some help from Walter Brennan make it still quite formidable.

There are so many nice things that Hawks does in his films, it does one good to note that they are the very ones he took pride in, the ones he studied to make good and memorable. I'm speaking of the masterful way he can mix exterior shots with interior sets and still maintain the illusion of the vast expanse of the West. The early sequence with the wagon train as well as the stampede both contain carefully edited interior set shots, put together in such a way as to make it all appear exterior. And although he didn't have that intuitive eye for camera placement that makes John Ford's Westerns some of the most beautiful films ever, Hawks's camera serves the story he is telling admirably: panning dramatically at the beginning of the drive, or capturing the excitement of a river crossing, or simply holding his camera still as a hissing, flaming arrow announces the Indian raid by coming directly at it (and at us!).

Hawks has a simple story to tell, but that doesn't mean he will tell it simply, or either, that he thinks he is telling the story to a bunch of simpletons. We realize that a drive must be made, but aren't told right off just exactly why. We are told part of the reason in that first scene between Matt, Tom, and Groot. Then more after Tom leaves, in the scene between Groot and Matt. And later we are told more in the bunkhouse address Tom gives his men. Finally, in the gathering of the men that first evening of the drive, Cherry fills in the details by telling how rough things were in Texas after the war. Telling us a little at a time, Hawks is not merely teasing us, he is cleverly getting us interested in the story; it is yet another, subtler, method of thrusting the film along.

By virtue of Hawks exploring the genre with commanding force, of his respect for the simple narrative as well as his audience, of his complete fidelity to his craft, of his inclusion of most of the stock Western types without letting them appear stereotypical, of his tenacity to the elements of the genre without appearing derivative—by virtue of all of these, *Red River* deserves to be called one of the finest Westerns ever made.

—

CHARLES RAMÍREZ BERG

VOL. 23, NO. 1
SEPTEMBER 30, 1982

Sullivan's Travels (1941)

DIRECTED AND WRITTEN BY PRESTON STURGES

People always like what they don't know anything about. | *Sullivan's Travels*

John L. Sullivan is at a crossroad in his career; the successful director of such hits as *Ants in Your Pants* of 1939 and *Hey Hey in the Hayloft,* he now feels morally compelled to make a movie of the profound suffering of humanity "that ordinary people don't know anything about." Sensing that he has lost touch with the people, at least those who go to movies, Sullivan is caught between a naive notion of what the people need and his knowledge of what they want: a movie "that would realize the potentialities of film as the sociological and artistic medium that it is . . . with a little sex in it." It isn't in his proposed film project but in his travels that Sullivan finds the often absurd balance of life's comedy and pathos for which he is searching. *Sullivan's Travels* somehow contrives to be both *Hey Hey in the Hayloft* and *Oh Brother, Where Art Thou?*; Keystonesque chases, snappy dialogue, food fallout and panty shots are counterpoised with scenes of bread lines, flop-houses, cruelty, quiet despair.

The situation, like those in most of Preston Sturges's films, is more than a little bit ridiculous. Sturges was one of the greatest social satirists of his time and *Sullivan's Travels* reveals the almost systematic irony of life in America in general and, specifically, life as lived in Hollywood and in the movies by the rich and the middle-class. In this atmosphere of social satire endemic to all Sturges films, two particularly Sturgeon(?) themes are obviated in *Sullivan's Travels*: the rich versus the poor and what Andrew Sarris calls "the modesty of heroes who dread becoming little fish in the big pond." The wealthy and successful Sullivan's desire to sojourn into poverty and despair, however noble the motivation, is absurd: his valet helps him dress down (way down) with a costume of old clothes he has gotten from the studio's wardrobe; his initial attempt to join the down-trodden have-nots, accompanied by an entourage of physician, secretary, chauffeur, etc.; his valet and butler calling for detailed information on freight train schedules and the proper method of hopping a freight, driven to the rail yard in a limousine. Trouble in paradise.

Sullivan is almost totally unprepared for the hard knocks and is absurdly and delightfully out of place. His straining, clumsy boarding of the train car would seem to have little to do with the idea invoked by the phrase hopping a freight, and the more seasoned tramp who witnesses this utterly graceless exhibition disgustedly mutters "Amateurs!" Sullivan, undaunted (or unaware) sallies forth into a totally one-sided conversation with the tramps about the weather and the current labor situation. The tramps leave the car in dignified silence, obviously preferring to be alone.

> The poor know all about poverty and only the morbid rich would find their poverty glamorous. | The butler, in *Sullivan's Travels*

The trouble Sullivan encounters becomes increasingly less benign, and amidst the laughs and pratfalls which predominate at the beginnings of his travels, the shot of the crowd of hobos rushing the freight car, scrambling to find a place and keep up with the train, is very frightening and sad. His fortuitous meeting with the girl (Veronica Lake) provides him with a travelling companion who will enable Sullivan to stay just on the lighter side of poverty. Through the train yards and bread lines, they can still be comforted by each other's presence and warmth, mustering enough good humor to laugh at the bad food and bed bugs and wear a sign for some business advertising the loathsome and despicable position of looking like a tramp. Even when you have almost nothing it seems it is still possible to be exploited.

Though the two are sometimes met with charity, it often comes with a price-tag. Hot food and a shower necessitates a preacher's lecture of the unimaginable hellfire awaiting the sinful poor. At a flophouse a placard reads "Have you written your mother today?"; it is at once overwhelmingly pitiful in its incredible impropriety and maddeningly typical of the value systems attributed to and demanded of affluence, financial self-sufficiency or destitution. The imposition of middle-class morality seems inextricably linked to the institutions of justice and charity. When Sullivan emphatically states that a film director would never do six years hard labor for assault, it is clearly an inarguable statement: justice, charity and opportunity run on a sliding scale. It is significant that the greatest display of charity (and the one which affords Sullivan's moment of revelation) is the screening of the cartoons by the black congregation since they had been systematically excluded from the American middle-class and its attendant value system.

Sturges's ability to shift from broad humor to stark pragmatism is bound, thematically, to what Sarris describes as the "insane illogic of the American success story"; the irony is essentially a part of the American dream and not in whether or not that dream is realized.

This speed is very depressing. | THE DOCTOR, in Sullivan's Travels

Sturges employs differences in pacing, lighting, camera distance and dialogue to emphasize the disparity in the worlds Sullivan mediates. Fast-talking, clever dialogue, a predominance of a static camera and medium shots, and a flat lighting characterize the Hollywood and middle-class life. Sturges's impressive experience as a screenwriter shows in this film for the dialogue is apt and hilarious. The conversation between the two maiden ladies at the farm sets the pace and the standard:

—Did you notice his torso?
—I noticed you noticed it.
—Don't be vindictive, dear. Some people are just naturally more sensitive to some things in life than some people. Some are blind to beauty while others. . . . Even as a little girl you were more of the acid type, dear. While I, if you remember. . . .
—I remember better than you do.
—Well forget it.

The near-absence of dialogue in the traditional world of road and diner and its absence in the milieu of the Hoovervilles, soup kitchens, alleys and rail yards contrasts greatly with the flash of Hollywood: the absence of dialogue in the tramps' society metaphorically illustrates the absence of a voice in the society at large. Darkness is integrally related to the poverty of this other world, and the shots of the hobos take on a despairing and ominous tone. The shots are longer and the camera more fluid in these parts of the film; movement for a tramp is abbreviated or even abortive. The use of the montage of people's laughing faces with a superimposition of Sullivan and the girl at the film's end is literally a blending of the two worlds: how mighty are the fallen.

> There's nothing like a deep-dish movie to drive you out into the
> open. | VERONICA LAKE, in *Sullivan's Travels*

Sullivan's Travels wasn't the first movie about the art and business of making movies, but it has a special resonance. Sullivan's anticipation of finding good movie material in the *real* world stems not from his knowledge of life but his equation of life to a movie: "There's always a girl in the picture," he impatiently explains to a policeman, "haven't you ever been to the Movies?" For all his savvy about pictures, Sullivan doesn't understand his audience nearly as well. When he joins the maiden ladies at the local triple feature he at least sits with the audience which watches his films. Looking at and listening to the people crunching candy and popcorn, it becomes clear that Sullivan may have a very different relationship to movies than the ordinary Joe he is so fond of speculating about. It is later, while watching the cartoons that Sullivan really joins the audience. He incredulously asks the fellow next to him, "Hey, am I laughing?" Deciding finally against making *Oh Brother, Where Art Thou?*, he has realized it's not bad being just another fish in the big pond.

> There's a lot to be said for making people laugh. Did you know that's all some
> people have? It isn't much, but it's better than nothing in this cockeyed cara-
> van. | JOHN L. SULLIVAN, in *Sullivan's Travels*

———

ANN LAEMMLE

seminal work set a particular pattern of narrative development that served the genre through the Depression, in his own work as well as in others— Hawks's *Bringing Up Baby*, La Cava's *My Man Godfrey*, Leisen's *Easy Living*, notably scripted by Sturges. The formula was recognized by the mutual attraction (initially affliction) of the principal male and female character and their subsequent ramblings through, rantings on, and eventual restitution of the screwball world at large (usually the habitat of the very wealthy) and the institution of marriage. The final embrace became, albeit mistakenly, a defining characteristic.

Given time, though, a film genre in the hands of Hollywood masters begins to feel its way in the dark outer recesses surrounding its arbitrarily set boundaries. A Western comes to be defined/recognized by its iconography of open spaces and ramshackle towns with dirt streets, men who wear guns on their hips and horses under them—i.e., the visual elements of the American frontier between 1860 and 1890—rather than being recognized by the good guys in white running the bad in black out of town. *The Gunfight at the O.K. Corral* and *High Noon* take on elements of the social melodrama, *Oklahoma!* gives us a taste of the musical Western. With the screwball comedy, Capra was the first to explore the outer limits of the formula in a series of explicitly economic and political comedies (*Deeds*, *Smith*, *Doe*), while Hawks, moving in another direction, stressed the sexual implications of a genre one of whose major characteristics was the aggressiveness of the female character.

What must finally be asked is to what extent a film genre forms a coherent body of works, and how as critics, rather than as part of the audience, we begin to define, rather than just recognize, a particular formula. These are not two entirely separate actions, for to define a genre is to enumerate the reasons why we, the collective we of the audience, come to call a particular set of films by a particular name. This has both narrative and stylistic implications. Somehow we know that a film with a cowboy in an urban locale is less a Western (*Lonely Are the Brave*), just as a film with a cowboy who isn't aggressive with his fists and guns is also less a Western (*Destry Rides Again*). The history of popular film criticism is strewn with negative comments about films that stretch the boundaries of a formula too far. But these limits have less to do with expectations about the development and continuity of narrative action, than with expectations about certain static elements—a particular protagonist, antagonist, and constellation of characters, a particular setting, a style of acting (note that the star system often forms a recognizable genre all its own, i.e., John Wayne films), and the possibility of several particular narrative elements (e.g., the final shoot-out). In the hands of a good director, a genre is less a narrative formula, by which he travels from point A to point Z, than a blueprint from which he can either construct an edifice like all the others on the block or dazzle us with his own architectural genius, even if his building still has walls, windows, floors, ceilings, and doors.

Hail the Conquering Hero has a number of elements by which we've come to recognize the screwball comedy. Characteristically, there is a protagonist who reacts to the world acting on him, rather than acting on the world himself—compare Cary Grant in *Bringing Up Baby* and *Monkey Business*, and Gary Cooper in *Deeds* and *Doe*. A potential mate is (Libby) unhappily attached to a dull, husband-type (Forrest Noble)—compare Rosalind Russell and Ralph Bellamy, in *His Girl Friday* (a role Bellamy often repeated), Claudette Colbert and the character King Westley in *It Happened One Night*; or the inverse in *Bringing Up Baby* with Cary Grant and his fiance assistant who wants "no domestic entanglements" to interfere with their work. There is also a constellation of minor screwball characters ("humors" to Northrop Frye), often of the privileged classes (Mayor Noble and family)— comparisons abound, the wealthy family in *My Man Godfrey* and *Easy Living*, Hepburn's family in *Bringing Up Baby*, Cooper's Deeds and assorted entourage; or the inverse, Cary Grant bringing his screwball antics (cartwheels) into the staid home of Hepburn in Cukor's *Holiday*.

Hail the Conquering Hero also has a number of conventional narrative elements. Most examples of screwball comedy initiate the film's action with a mistaken and/or assumed identity on the part of either or both the male and female protagonists. Woodrow is mistakenly identified as a war hero, and it is his assumption of this role which moves the plot. In *Easy Living*, Edward Arnold throws his wife's mink off the roof, and it lands on Jean Arthur, who then becomes identified as a romantic adjunct to Arnold. In *My Man Godfrey*, William Powell plays a Boston blueblood who assumes the role of a butler to Eugene Pallette's screwball family. In both *Deeds* and *Doe*, Gary Cooper assumes that Jean Arthur and Barbara Stanwyck are anything but what they are, which is not innocent and naive. Another characteristic narrative element is the final assembly of characters for the protagonist's conversion and/or confession. In *Hail the Conquering Hero*, the political rally serves as Woodrow's moment of truth (!?). Compare almost all of Capra's films: Deed's victory at his sanity hearing, Doe's conversion when Stanwyck and company convince him not to commit suicide, Smith's victorious Senate filibuster, and Stewart's Christmas Eve conversion in *It's A Wonderful Life*. Finally, characteristic of almost all screwball comedies is the coupling of the male and female principals, even when tangential to the film's complications and eventual resolution. Again, this is the case not only in *Hail the Conquering Hero* but also in the Capra films just listed.

Stylistically, the screwball comedies represent what is possibly the pinnacle of sound film comedy. Often, like plays adapted to the screen, they are condemned for being talky, for lacking the "pure" cinema of moving cameras, shots from oblique angles, elaborate compositional texture, a profound editing strategy, all that is conventionally (that criticism has historically deemed) peculiarly cinematic. This is a rather short-sighted perspective, to say the least. Hitchcock does one thing, Renoir another; but no one condemns Hitchcock for not using longer takes, and no one condemns Renoir for lack of dynamic editing. Screwball comedies move, using not necessarily the same cinematic movement as Westerns or gangster films, but they are far from lacking the kind of energy that is peculiar to the movies. There is as much visual as verbal wit between Hepburn and Grant in their Hawks's comedies, and the talk itself, the banter, the wheedling, the pestering in all screwball comedies has a plastic quality all its own, exemplified by the genre's common use of overlapping dialogue. Hawks estimates the dialogue in his comedies is "probably twenty per cent faster than in most pictures."

Preston Sturges has been particularly vulnerable to the criticism that he lacks style. But his long takes and eye-level camera allow the movement to develop within the frame, between the characters or between the characters and their environment. Sturges's cutting may lack dynamism, it may even be a little choppy, but he is aware of how to cut between parallel lines of action for comedic effect (note the scene of the train pulling into the station and the ability to milk all he can from Franklin Pangborn's reactions throughout the film). He is even not without the ability to subtly counterpoint sound and image. Our first view of Libby and Forrest ends on a barely audible, low note from a tuba, followed by Libby informing Forrest that his father the mayor wants to talk to him.

What is particularly interesting about Sturges is the rather anarchic message that comes through his pictures. Equating heroism and what was to be later termed "mom-ism" with fraud, deceit, and politics, Sturges is able to poke fun at a multitude of sacred American institutions. The middle third of the film is possibly the most hilarious indictment of small-town politics in the history of American cinema. Yet these are small potatoes to Sturges. The closing is the most unlikely of "happyends," and I mean more unlikely than anything Capra perpetrated to keep his populist dogma intact, and in so being the ideology of the film is allowed to turn back on itself. The incongruities, the seams that hold the fabric of a film's world-view intact, are allowed all the play they need, and credibility, that "suspension of disbelief," no longer functions, is meant to no longer function. The good-natured satire of war heros, politics, and the Oedipus complex is subordinate to Sturges's anarchic story structure, his ability to make us accept the most unlikely happenings, and his confidence that the essence of the movies is that they can do anything they want as long as they keep moving.

———

MIKE SELIG

VOL. 1 NO. 15
MARCH 14, 1972

Meet Me in St. Louis (1944)

DIRECTED BY VINCENTE MINNELLI

The film (*I Dood It*) left one totally unprepared for *Meet Me in St. Louis* (1944), which has remained Minnelli's masterpiece in the lyrical evocation of an era. It is filled with an excitement that appears to have swept through MGM during the war; the film's director, cast and technicians seem to have given *Meet Me in St. Louis* a dedication, humor and charm that only a labor of love can evoke. To a public that was not quite prepared to accept Judy Garland as an adult, she suddenly became one and the songs by Hugh Martin and Ralph Blane were placed at her disposal like gifts before a shrine. No one else has ever been able to sing these songs as well. Judy Garland created a stylized portrayal of American adolescence that remains an object lesson in musical-comedy performance, a blend of the real and the idealized. Her singing of "The Trolley Song" is still a captivating romp, superbly arranged, but in "The Boy Next Door" and "Have Yourself a Merry Little Christmas," she made her Missouri teenger as mature as Duse. A few years ago, during an informal talk, Minnelli said that *Meet Me in St. Louis* was "full of inconsistencies of plot" and that the real reason why they wanted to do the picture in the first place was the Halloween sequence ... | ALBERT JOHNSON, "The Films of Vincente Minnelli: Part I," *Film Quarterly*, Winter, 1958

Her (Margaret O'Brien's) annihilation of the snowmen she can't take to New York would have been terrifying if only she had adequate support from the snowmen and if only the camera could have had the right to dare to move in close. Being only the well-meant best that adult professionals could design out of cornflakes or pulverized mothballs or heroin or whatever they are making snow out of just now, these statues were embarrassingly handicapped from their birth, and couldn't even reach you deeply by falling apart. Her walk on Halloween, away from the bonfire into the deepening dark of the street, her fear and excitement intensifying as she approaches her destination (the insulting of the most frightening man in the neighborhood) and follows the camera (which withdraws a few feet ahead of her in a long soft curve) are a piece of acting, of lovely, simple camera movement, and of color control which combined, while they lasted, to make my hair stand on end. If the rest of the picture's autumn section, which is by far its best, had lived up to the best things about that shot, and if the rest of the show, for all its prettiness, had been scrapped, *Meet Me in St. Louis* would have been, of all things on earth it can never have intended to be, a great moving picture—the first to be made in this country, so far as I can remember, since *Modern Times*. | JAMES AGEE, *The Nation*, November 25, 1944

Meet Me in St Louis (1944), made a good ten years after *Footlight Parade*, represents an important development which took place in musicals in the '40s: while the backstage musical—a staple of the '30s in many ways— continued to be made, the period musical, of which *Meet Me in St. Louis* is perhaps the most famous, developed as a genre in itself. Simultaneously realistic and stylized, a work like *Meet Me in St. Louis* presents people in situations of a believable, everyday quality, but made to look as sentimentally attractive and as ideally typical as possible. Songs are performed under the pretext of being spontaneous responses to human situations (apart from those performed, of course, at social dances) and the audience is made to dredge up appropriate feelings from its own collective memory in response to situations remarkably familiar rather than exceptional.

Thus, *Meet Me in St. Louis* is something of a stylistic exercise, the application of Minnelli's elaborate sense of *mise-en-scène* toward the evocation of an ordinary, half-remembered childhood and adolescence in the good-old-days. Interiors are lushed-up with dark mahogany woodwork and furniture, red plush chairs, and a constant parade of Victorian clutter and pattern never completely receding behind the foreground figures of the family that

Meet Me in St. Louis. From the Metro-Goldwyn-Mayer production and biography photographs of the Margaret Herrick Library, Academy of Motion Picture Arts and Sciences.

operates in them. No summertime exterior shot is complete without the darting image of a running, bicycling or playing child providing momentary motion in the background. Minnelli seems obsessed with light. The developing attraction between Esther and John is evoked in the scene between them in which Esther asks him to turn out the lights with her after the party because (supposedly) she is afraid of the dark. Houses during the autumn sequence glow from the inside at night with the same warm, yellow tones one associates (appropriately) with Jack O'Lanterns. The flaming of the bonfire as Tootie walks away from it is one of the most consciously beautiful touches in a movie climaxed, visually, by the bright lights of the St. Louis exposition. And throughout, there seems to be a concerted attempt to capture the eerie, unnatural colorations of gas-lighting as deliberately as in the cafe paintings of Toulouse-Lautrec.

The film's use of color is something else again, for it is difficult to tell how many of its stylizations are due to the limitations of color film at the time, and how many are intentionally mannerist. The picture takes on, at times, a flat, two-dimensional look (appropriate for a period piece), largely because the color values of distant or secondary objects tend to be as prominent as the narrative focal points of the frame. In the beginning of the film, say, our eyes are continually distracted by the red of the catsup being bottled, or of the tomato soup being eaten at dinner—and Minnelli may well have *wanted* bright red foods precisely to give us this questionable pleasure. As Wolcot Gibbs commented in his *New Yorker* review of the time, "In *Meet Me in St. Louis*, for instance, there is a scene featuring an enormous Christmas tree, or rather that would feature it if all the ladies on the set didn't look like Christmas trees, too."

Meet Me in St. Louis's surface pleasures, though, tend to make certain of its underlying implications a lot more palatable than they would otherwise be. Considered as a film made while America was at war, one can see a now almost insidious patriotism underlying the final scenes, in which the family, after copping out on going to New York, decides that St. Louis really is the greatest place in the world (apparently because it's the only one they've known). They have cultivated a middle American way of life—although probably one more related to the middle America of 1944 than 1903, "far from the America of sweat shops and steel jungles," as Charles Higham and Joel Greenberg write—and cherish it with almost smug self-satisfaction. The scenes are as affecting, for they play on a love for home and hearth that only the most cynical of us can ever reject completely, as the sentiments now can seem a bit dubious. Ultimately, *Meet Me in St. Louis* can be seen as subtle propaganda for the war effort, a commercial for the American way of life and the traditions which the country was striving to protect at the time, and as such it is considered by some to be one of the high points of the American cinema in general, being at once a work of great popular appeal, of pictorial and visual sophistication, and of outstanding cinematic know-how.

———

GEORGE LELLIS

VOL. 12, NO. 4
FEBRUARY 21, 1977

The Band Wagon (1953)

DIRECTED BY VINCENTE MINNELLI

Arthur Freed had discussed the idea of doing a picture based on the songs of Howard Dietz and Arthur Schwartz, and now he was ready to move. He even had a name for the new picture.

The team's most famous stage musical, in 1931, was *The Band Wagon*. Arthur thought it was still a great title. The stage production, however, had been a revue, and a plot would have to be concocted around the title.

Fred Astaire, who'd starred in the musical on Broadway with his sister Adele, was semi-committed to the project. His presence sparked an idea. It would be delicious to base the characters on actual people. Why not base his part on the Astaire of a few years back, who'd been in voluntary retirement? Why not develop the situation further by suggesting that fame had passed him by?

The subsequent brainstorm of patterning the role of a producer on such flamboyant types as Orson Welles and George S. Kaufman came easily to mind. The writers would be based on Betty Comden and Adolph Green. It was a great coup to get them to write the screenplay, and they proceeded to satisfy themselves. | VINCENTE MINNELLI, *I Remember It Well*.

The Band Wagon marks a subtle change in attitude for Minnelli toward the musical format. The narrative mode of the musical most closely resembles that of the fairy tale: the characters are clearly defined as archetypes, the expectation of the fantastic allows a high degree of stylization and abstraction and foreknowledge of a benevolent universe and a happy ending. Minnelli has always been conscious enough of his medium to set up a tension between these "fairy tale" elements and our more fundamental cinematic perceptions. For instance, most film-goers still relate to the cinema as primarily a "realistic" medium, confusing its power of illusionism with that of mimesis. The format of the musical (thought of as an "escapist" or "fantastic" medium) has allowed Minnelli to exploit this contradiction with a high degree of artistry.

Before Minnelli, the backstage musical always excluded itself by framing the musical action with the stage, even if from that island of dramatic safety it took off into the empyrean as with Busby Berkeley. In contrast, Minnelli has always accented the abstraction of the film image by framing it against a backdrop of artificiality in other mediums: the *trompe l'oeil* countryside of *Yolanda*, the little stage of *The Pirate*, again the stage and ultimately the ballet in *An American in Paris*. In this context, the action "off-stage," as it were, is always equally fantastic, or more so, than action on.

The question still remains, though, why are these actions possible, and even essential, if the cinema is thought to be a fundamentally "realist" medium. The answer is, of course, the star system and the musical actor. In the backstage musical, we know from the very first that all the kids are singers and dancers waiting for the chance to be stars. In the Minnelli musical, we know from the very first that the characters are stars and we wait in expectation for them to dance and sing. The concept of the non-actor as star is essential to the Minnelli musicals of the forties. In *The Pirate* for instance, the audience is not satisfied until Manuela is revealed as Judy Garland, it being unthinkable that Garland would be in a non-singing/dancing role, especially in a musical! Minnelli as always plays with the mythic capacity of the cinema, juggling the concepts of identity and appearance, character and actor, actor and identity, with a virtuoso flair.

This is precisely why *The Band Wagon* differs from the previous Minnelli musicals. Tony Hunter is introduced as a failing film actor in musicals who doubts his ability to entertain. Furthermore, *The Band Wagon* appears to have all the trappings of a backstage musical, especially in that all the characters are already actors. The primary differences between *The Band Wagon* and the formula backstage musical are that the characters are, from the start, proven, successful show people, and that we are given cause to doubt the ultimate success of their new show, normally an unthinkable supposition. In other words, *The Band Wagon* is an "after-the-musicals" musical; the triumph of the benevolent universe no longer seems to be a given, the fairy tale seems to be souring. In this regard we may venture to say that *The Band Wagon* may be the first existential musical.

As in all of his musicals, Minnelli toys in *The Band Wagon* with the subjects of illusionism, stylization and performance. But, in none of his other films do the simultaneous correlations and discrepancies between the cinema and life reverberate off one another with such frequency or profundity as they do in *The Band Wagon*. The most startling evidence of the film's heightened self-reflexiveness is in its Pirandellian inscription of its authors and stars into the characters and events it presents. Most obviously, Fred Astaire plays Fred Astaire (who, for the purposes of the film, is called Tony Hunter), a former song-and-dance man of the Broadway stage who has gone to Hollywood and attained widespread popularity in such films as *Swinging down to Panama* (an obvious reference to the 1933 Astaire-Ginger Rogers musical, *Flying Down to Rio*). Immediately it becomes all but impossible to distinguish Fred Astaire, the movie star, from the character he is playing in *The Band Wagon*. The top hat and cane, the trademarks of Astaire/Hunter which form the background for the film's opening credits, are arranged within a white frame. As the credits end, we are shown that these objects are an important part of the film's opening sequence, an auction of movie memorabilia. Thus the hat and cane are deprived of the functional significance they held in the Astaire-Rogers musicals so that they become icons of Astaire himself. Placed as they are within a picture frame, they suggest that the story we are about to see will be that of Astaire himself, framed within the Minnellian universe. Only through our knowledge of Fred Astaire, the movie star, will we fully understand Tony Hunter.

Similarly, the writers *in* the film (the Martins) correspond to the writers *of* the film (Betty Comden and Adolph Green). Like Comden and Green, the Martins are a couple who write musicals, the man most frequently writing the music while the woman writes the book and lyrics. In *The Band Wagon*, Comden and Green employ the already-composed songs of Howard Dietz and Arthur Schwartz; so, on a secondary level, they also stand in for the team of composers. This is further substantiated by the fact that the title of the film is simultaneously the title of the show within the film and of a

Dietz-Schwartz revue which had appeared on Broadway in 1931. Since Astaire had starred in this revue, his identification with the character of Hunter is once again stated. Finally, in the character played by Oscar Levant, a third inscription occurs. Les Martin, in his hypochondria and studied grouchiness, obviously refers to Levant himself, whose similar complaints had made him a well-known Hollywood "character."

Minnelli's recounting of the idea for *The Band Wagon* includes a provision for the inscription in the film of every major contributor except himself, suggesting that none of the characters represent the director. In fact, Minnelli is present in two characters, both of whom act as director of the play within the film: Jeffrey Cordova and Tony Hunter. In Cordova can be seen a self-critique of Minnelli's penchant for flamboyance and aspiration toward art and significance (the Astaire-Charisse dance which becomes a shambles amidst the explosions of Cordova's *mise-en-scène* is a superb lampooning of the fiery ballet in *The Pirate*). Cordova represents for Minnelli a pretentiousness and self self-importance which he can see in himself but finds repugnant to his own populist attitudes toward the movies and entertainment in general. In dialectic opposition to Cordova is Tony Hunter, whose average-guy manner and common-sense approach finally win out over Cordova's pomposity, restoring the "modern version of Faust," "the musical morality play of meaning and stature" to its original form, a light and easily accessible musical entertainment.

This conflict between the two auteurs (the two Minnellis) becomes the central opposition in *The Band Wagon*'s thematically dominant examination of "high art" vs. "low art." Almost every conflict in the film centers around this question: the struggle for control of the play between Cordova and Hunter; the animosity between Gabrielle Girard, the classical ballerina, and Hunter, the soft-shoe movie star; the split between the Martins which arises from their personal dissatisfaction at attempting to give their light-hearted entertainment "high art" significance; the break between Girard, when she wishes to remain in the show, and Paul Byrd, who is against her doing "insignificant" work. Not surprisingly, "low art" triumphs in the resolution of the question. After all, *The Band Wagon* is a movie and thus represents the "low art" pole of the legitimate theater/popular film dichotomy.

But what Minnelli strives for is a synthesis of the high/low distinction, a marriage of Hunter and Cordova in his own work, achieved in the final version of the revue in the number in which Fred Astaire and Jack Buchanan, dressed identically with the top hat and cane which had earlier been

has sold his soul to stylization and a personal mythology, only to suffer the damnation of economic failure as *The Band Wagon* lays an egg.

The answer, as Hunter comes to realize, is that entertainment is people: the kids in the chorus, the crowds on the street, and the customers of the arcade. Entertainment is communication; whether the language is dance, music, or cinema is unimportant. It is when the actors conquer the language, instead of allowing the language to conquer them, that they develop a successful show and establish a dialogue with the audience.

Within this attitude can be found the professional ethos of *The Band Wagon*. Someone, we are told, must be at the helm of any production (the director); and that person creates, not by studied attempts at significance, but through coordinating, participating in, and working with the talents of a group, all of whom share in the act of creation. Similar to the professional groups of Howard Hawks's adventure films, the characters of *The Band Wagon* are highly skilled and devoted to their work. It is an existentialist ethos in which self-commitment (to the show) becomes the *raison d'etre* and the moment (of performance) reigns supreme. This becomes beautifully clear in Hunter's theme song, "By Myself," which celebrates, with only a trace of melancholy, the solitude of the individual. Hunter's art need not have the sanction of critic or audience, since it is enough for him alone.

Hunter's song focuses the narrative on his search for his musical identity. The musical sequences in the train station and the arcade are initially startling because they disturb what appears to be "realist" space. Paradoxically, while Hunter is thought to be past his prime on the stage, he can still perform. What he has lost, in terms of the universe of the Minnelli musical, is the ability to relate to the stage as a world and the world as a stage. Hunter is suffering from a crisis in which actor and identity are an unresolvable contradiction. He can no longer view the artificial world of the film as the surface of a fictional reality; and, concomitantly, he can no longer equate appearance and character.

In this context, the importance of the "Shine on Your Shoes" number is that Hunter realizes the importance, and even the necessity of maintaining appearance; because, for the actor, especially the *film* actor, appearance is identity, and actor is character. The equation of these characteristics is essential to the phenomenology of the Minnelli musical, so that once Hunter has mastered his appearance as an actor/singer/dancer, he has mastered the cinematic space of the arcade and identified it as a filmic world.

Minnelli purposely sets the "Shine on Your Shoes" sequence in a garish arcade where Astaire performs unobserved by any other major character in the film. Astaire dances, not with the other middle-class patrons of the arcade, but with the black shoe-shine attendant, further isolating Hunter and underlining the performance as being totally for himself. Yet, in terms of the Minnellian world, this self-commitment holds a metaphysical signif- icance, and Hunter's performance literally electrifies the arcade, defying natural law and magically activating the mysterious "?" box into a joyous explosion of flags, horns and fireworks.

Similarly, Minnelli withholds the first scene of Hunter and Girard danc- ing together until they are alone in the park and without an audience. Their dance thus denotes the primarily personal significance it holds for the char- acters. It is simultaneously a graceful, perfectly coordinated performance by two talented professionals (both within the story and in actuality) and a beautifully stylized bit of love making. The importance of the performance to the characters in a Minnelli musical is indicated by the fact that, almost without exception, characters fall in love only after they have performed together, the performance substituting for a first sexual encounter which leads to personal involvement and affection.

Finally, the existentialism of *The Band Wagon* is probably most evident in the attitude of Tony Hunter at its conclusion. Assured that the show is a hit, Hunter is somewhat dismayed that no one has come to his dressing room to congratulate him; but stifling any tendency toward self-pity, he announces that, nonetheless, he will go out on the town to celebrate alone as he begins to hum a reprise of "By Myself." At this point, it is evident that Hunter is disappointed, but it is even more evident that he will be able to make it alone—without laurels, without Gabrielle's love—as long as he is satisfied with his performance. When he emerges from his dressing room, he discov- ers the entire cast and crew waiting to sing "For He's a Jolly Good Fellow" and Gabrielle waiting to give him a big kiss and her love.

It is significant that at the end of *The Band Wagon*, the benevolent world no longer seems to be a given provided for in the narrative format, but a creation of the community of characters in the film. The possibility of failure has always been present in both the show and the romance. Hunter sings the refrain of "By Myself" in a calm acceptance of his identity and is fully resigned to celebrating that discovery alone; but ultimately he is returned to his people, the community of actors he has nurtured who now thank him with a backstage celebration. The benevolent world is reinforced, perhaps with a greater poignance than ever before, for the happy ending literally comes from nowhere and, thus, is all the more happy in its fortuitousness. Lest we take it all too seriously, the five main players turn to the camera and sing a reprise of "That's Entertainment," both as a celebration of their success and as a Pirandellian farewell to the film spectator.

———

DAVE RODOWICK, ED LOWRY

VOL. 12, NO. 4
APRIL 11, 1977

All That Heaven Allows (1955)

DIRECTED BY DOUGLAS SIRK

Sirk, a European intellectual, captured as well as anyone the paradox—the energy, the vulgarity, the poverty of values, the gleaming surfaces and soulless lives, the sickness of delusion, the occasional healthy burst of desire—of America, of the fifties, of the cinema itself. Working for the most commercial of producers, Ross Hunter, whose America was one of picturesque landscapes, drowsy mornings, intrigue-ridden afternoons, and happy endings, Sirk managed to use these elements (to bring them, in fact, to a stylish apotheosis), in order to expose them from within. The staples of middle-class life—handsome houses, lavish decors, fast cars, busy social lives, spoiled, demanding children—were the bars of the prison. The mirrors and frames that are Sirk's visual trademark, reflect, among other things, both the frozen, artificial quality and the illusory nature of these creature comforts. Sirk's women all seem to come to us from some glossy-magazine spread, harried, but perfectly coiffed, housewives in a two-dimensional world from which some escape while others remain flattened and embalmed. | MOLLY HASKELL, *From Reverence to Rape* example of the first kind of melodrama are the films of Alfred Hitchcock which, while they may also be thrillers, are usually based on melodramatic conventions. The second kind of melodrama can be found in the work of Frank Borzage and, to a lesser extent, George Cukor.

Melodrama is too broad a concept to be accurately called a genre. Like tragedy, it implies a world view which can be found in many genres. Unlike tragedy, it does not ask us to explore our humanity, but to look at our humanity in relation to external forces. It is the great paranoid viewpoint, since it is usually the total society against one person. What we usually think of as melodrama is the purest manifestation of this view. There is nothing intrinsic in the form which causes it to fall into sentimentality and banality, it is just the fact that most people who use the form are content to remain stolidly within the conventions. Melodrama will never truly be appreciated until we begin to see it as a form and not as a pejorative term.

II

All That Heaven Allows is a sentimental melodrama. The plot is so familiar that most of us know it, having seen it in countless other films. An older, respectable woman falls in love with the younger, socially unacceptable man, who she then gives up when it threatens the security of her children. Her sacrifice, however, comes to nothing, and it is only through an external factor, such as an accident to one of the lovers, that she is able to regain her happiness. The woman is usually noble, if weak, the man strong and unruffled by anything, the children spoiled and difficult, while the townspeople are a bunch of priggish busybodies.

While Sirk keeps all these situations, the point he wishes to make has been changed by the details he fills in around the edges of the story and by his style. The film opens with a high angle shot of a peaceful looking town. A church steeple dominates the right side of the frame. As the camera pans from the steeple in order to follow a car in the background, the music changes from a lush, romantic sound to a more classic, and simpler, single piano. This opening shot sets up the thematic parameters of the film. Sirk shows us an idyllic-looking town in long shot which changes when he moves closer and we are able to see the social rigidity that lies beneath the surface. At the same time, the use of the church steeple to dominate the frame foreshadows the domination of social structure over the lives of the characters. He uses the conventional plot, but only in order to reveal what underlies the convention.

Cary is a widow who is trapped within the role that society has set out for her. Her life consists of waiting for her children to come home for the weekends and the occasional cocktail party or dinner that her circle gives. Early in the film Kay tells Cary that our society is not like that of ancient Egypt, where the wife was considered a possession and thus walled up when her husband died, and she says that that does not happen anymore, to which Cary replies, "Doesn't it?" The idea of social values which dehumanize the individual, make them an object, is developed here. Cary is socially trapped within her role of widow as to which men are available to her. Harvey is the socially acceptable mate, because he is too old to catch anything younger. He is silver-haired and continually recounts how fragile his health is. Kay can casually announce that she likes him because he acts his age, for after all, sex after a certain age is incongruous. Cary is being forced to fit a pattern whether she likes it or not. She is only a social object, for she lives only through the normal social relationships, each of which tends to reinforce the others. This is expressed visually through the use of mirrors in her house and Sara's. Within her society, she is continually reflected and observed, doubled, and trapped. She can never experience a wholeness because she is always finding only herself wherever she looks.

Her affair with Ron allows her to look beyond her closed circle. Both his and his friend's houses are dominated by windows which open out onto nature. Ron is a primitive who embodies the concept of the natural man from *Walden*. He offers Cary a new outlook on life, but she is afraid to take it because of the social pressures on her. Ron is, after all, beneath her socially and to marry him would be to degrade herself (and the memory of her husband, as her son tells her). She eventually proves to be not strong enough to break with the dictates of society (a fact shown visually when her son gives her a television set for Christmas which will alleviate her loneliness, and we see her reflection on the television screen as one mirror added to her life). Sirk then reunites the two because of Ron's accident, thus assuring the happy ending and maintaining the classic melodramatic formula. But it is precisely Sirk's point that a happy end is so mechanically given to us and to her, for only such a melodramatic incident as Ron's accident could shake Cary out of her conformity. Sirk's view is finally pessimistic despite the film's happy ending, for only such an extreme event as Ron's accident can cause a change in our society.

There are certain problems with the film, the main one being the fact that the alternative society is so sketchily depicted that we must depend on the surface for substance. That is, we must assume that the fact that Ron and his friends grow trees, and enjoy dancing and wine at their dinners is proof of the strength of their course. The alternative almost seems too pat. If the film is perhaps hollow at the center, it does show how Sirk is able to use the conventions of melodrama in order to document a social process. What Cary discovers through the course of the film is that she is only an object in the eyes of most of her society and family. Sirk, under the guise of telling a love story, doodles in a critique of bourgeois society. To say that he does not go far enough, while it should be pointed out, does not take into account the fact that he was working within a formula and that his critique could not be overt and total for he would otherwise lose his audience. To criticize him for not giving us a whole loaf, is to fail to understand just how miraculous the half loaf he gives us is.

—

VALENTIN ALMENDAREZ

VOL. 12, NO. 4
MAY 2, 1977

Imitation of Life (1959)

DIRECTED BY DOUGLAS SIRK

The dialectic of the melodramatic consciousness is only possible at this price:
this consciousness must be borrowed from outside (from the world of alibis,
sublimations, and lies of bourgeois morality), and it must still be lived as *the*
consciousness of a condition (that of the poor) even though this condition is
radically foreign to the consciousness.... The melodramatic consciousness
is not contradictory to these conditions: it is a quite different consciousness,
imposed from without on a determinate condition but without any dialectical
relation to it. That is why the melodramatic consciousness can only be dialectical if it ignores its real conditions and barricades itself inside its myth. Shel-
tered from the world, it unleashes all the fantastic form of a breathless conflict which can only ever find peace in the catastrophe of someone else's fall: it
takes this hullabaloo for destiny and its breathlessness for dialectic. | LOUIS
ALTHUSSER, *For Marx.*

I tried to make a picture of social consciousness—not only of white social
consciousness, but of a Negro one, too. Both white and black are leading imitated lives.... There is a wonderful expression: seeing through a glass darkly.

Everything, even life, is inevitably removed from you. If you try to grasp
happiness itself your fingers only meet glass. It's hopeless.... You don't
believe the happy end, and you're not really supposed to. | DOUGLAS SIRK,
Sirk on Sirk.

Douglas Sirk wields a double-edged sword. It's not that he has somehow
split the cinematic sign, causing it paradoxically to mean two things at once,
but that he endows it with the potential to draw upon two diverse but related
codes, each of which presents its own interpretation and mode of perception. This is why mirrors, windows, precise framing, and highly structured
mise-en-scène are so important to Sirk's style: they are barriers of expression, barriers of emotion, and barriers of social class. In the context of what
Stephen Heath has defined as the identification/separation dialectic of
cinematic perception—in that area where Godard or Straub would choose
to decode or destructure—Sirk has very democratically severed the poles
of interaction, forcing us to choose one side or the other: we either live inside
the characters' hearts or observe them from outside their glass case. Rous-
seau's paradox assumes a certain relevance here: do we cry because we are
unhappy, or are we unhappy because we cry?

The opening sequence of the film establishes an equivalency between
two sets of people: two husbandless women, each one a stranger to New
York, each with a young daughter; but since one is white and one is black,
a division becomes apparent and a realignment along class lines will be
solidified and determined by the narrative. Annie Johnson loses little time
settling herself into the role of a servant and, in doing so, edges Lora Meredith into the role of master. Neither one can be faulted for this; they are
immediate victims of appearance and expectations. If Sarah Jane looks
white, then Annie is her "mammie"; if a black woman answers Lora's phone,
then she has a maid; and, more importantly, if Lora has a maid, then she
must be upper middle class. As class lines become reaffirmed, the bustle
and chaos of the outside world (Coney Island) becomes excluded, its boundaries pushed off-screen as the middle-class world asserts itself and seals
itself over. It is easy to see how Sirk's *mise-en-scène* adapts itself to this
purpose. Lora and Annie's first meeting under the boardwalk is a first step
in closing off and internalizing the frame. Afterwards, as Lora begins her
material climb, the film concerns itself exclusively with middle-class envi-
rons and characters (until Sarah Jane begins her real revolt) as if no other
world existed.

Imitation of Life. From the core collection production photographs of the Margaret Herrick Library, Academy of Motion Picture Arts and Sciences.

Themes of ascent and descent, of class mobility, become readily apparent with their own correlatives of motion with the frame. Especially important is the use of stairs which act as a barometer indicating, in inverse proportion, material ascent and emotional loss, which is also to say, the elevation of form at the expense of psychological depth *à la Lola Montes*. During the first half of the film, ascent is the dominant code as Lora Meredith effects her climb toward the material and values of bourgeois existence. A first crisis point is reached when she must decide whether or not to marry Steve Archer. Their love scene is strategically interrupted, and a phone call from Loomis irrevocably separates them. There is simply no contest in the argument between a career on the stage and marriage. Their heated descent to the street (marking diacritically a sacrifice of psychological depth) is ironically counterpointed by Lora's claim that she is going to go "up and up and up." The argument over what is real—career or marriage—is double-edged in itself, for neither choice functions here as a reaffirmation of bourgeois values. Both Steve and Lora's careers are based on the primacy of illusion—acting and advertising—and both are thus equally unreal. And, though a ceremony of marriage might seem likely to function ritually as a reaffirmation, Lora's decision to marry Steve could only result in her losing dominance and depleting the energy of exclusion which makes the male characters of bourgeois melodrama subservient. Besides, no one ever gets married in a Sirk film.

In the second half of the film, however, the problem of class mobility shifts focus to Sarah Jane and the dominant code becomes descent. The material trappings of middle-class existence surround Sarah Jane, but they serve only to mark the class line which she may not cross. The satisfaction of all material needs eliminates economics from the politics of class apartheid, alienating the value system itself. It is Sarah Jane's inclusion in the bourgeois universe which defines her blackness, and hence the impossibility of class mobility. But since her material happiness may only be derived from the dominating class, she must descend from that universe in order to assert her whiteness and attain the possibility of class mobility. This is marked diacritically by her descent down the stairs as she goes repeatedly to meet her white boyfriend. Paradoxically, this theme of descent (a mirror image from the first half of the film) also marks the growth of psychological resonance in her character. Her revolt, signified by the scene in which she mocks an outlandish racial stereotype, can be read as an inexcusable sign of disrespect for her "betters"; but can she really be faulted for that disrespect, and can one disregard the reason and power of her discontent?

Previously I have written about the primacy of mirrors and windows in Sirk's *mise-en-scène* in the sense that they delineate borders of inclusion or exclusion among the characters and their class relationships, and that they mark the difference between appearances and their imitations. I say appearances because it is virtually impossible to penetrate beneath the superficiality of Sirk's characters. The two exceptions might be Sarah Jane and Annie, but for the fact that Sarah Jane is a split, ambiguous character and that Annie is a myth, a reflection of her function within Lora's bourgeois universe. In the first half of the film, mirrors are used to indicate a split between appearance and actuality: Lora acting as if all went well at her interview with Loomis, Lora practicing her script. This activates a code of performance among the bourgeois characters, whose endless role playing drains them of any psychological resonance—actors acting actors, as it were. In the second half of the film, this meaning is perpetuated with a deeper significance. It is as if the mirror images are no longer reflections but the source, the imitation itself becoming the deeper source of reality. Especially effective are the reflected scenes of the brutal attack on Sarah Jane by her white boyfriend (possibly one of the few unambiguous scenes of class struggle ever depicted in the American cinema) and Annie's realization that Sarah Jane is not working in the library.

In *Imitation of Life*, the mirror metaphor takes on a much larger significance than its use as a framing device—it is a paradigm for the entire film. As Sirk says, all the characters are leading imitated lives, searching their reflections for some vestige of real identity and finding only the pressure of cold glass. In the context of the film, the blacks' lives are derived from the whites and the whites' lives are derived from the stage—the source of the image is lost in its reflections.

The problem perhaps reaches its greatest intensity after Lora has achieved her material success and the focus shifts from mothers to daughters. A parallelism begins between Susie's Electra complex and search for love, and Sarah Jane's attempted passage into the white world, which, as Fassbinder has said, is not because white is prettier than black, but because life is better when you're white. It soon becomes evident in her search for love that Susie should have had Annie as a mother, and in her search for class mobility that Sarah Jane should have had Lora for a mother.

Lora Meredith becomes the master image for imitated lives and the totem animal for the bourgeois value system. Annie has no identity or existence outside of the economic context defined by Lora's career. Susie draws all of her fantasies and ideas of love from Steve, both because he is the only father figure she has ever known and because she is imitating her mother by competing with her. This developing three-sided relationship is summarized in one startling image: Lora, looking at Susie and Steve from a high angle shot is excluded by a pattern of rafters which from a white triangle in the frame, enclosing the two below; but too, Susie and Steve, are separated by the bar. This shot suggests the impossibility of their ever being united as a family. Soon after, she has confessed her love for Steve to Annie, Susie observes Steve and Lora kissing. Our perception of the relationship changes: Susie observes the couple in a high angle shot from behind her window, in Sirk's films always a signal of the politics of exclusion (or its converse, entrapment). Her own expectations of marriage to Steve are ruined by her mother's.

At this point we must keep in mind that Susie's problems are "banalized" by, and act as a counterpoint to, the more violent, emotional problem of

Sarah Jane's attempt to transcend class barriers. Once more Lora acts as a model, for Sarah Jane begins her efforts at class mobility on the "stage." Sirk, however, reasserts the impossibility of her break with her class. She is like a bird which nearly destroys itself by beating its wings against the bars of its cage. As I have stated the problem before, Sarah Jane must descend from the bourgeois world (where she is irrevocably defined as black) in order to make her transcendence of class possible; but each time she is followed by her mother, an agent of the middle-class who immediately throws her identity into focus. Sarah Jane may move from one club to a better one, but this does not mark her ascension to a better life—for if she is able to reach Lora's level of material existence, she will only discover how empty it is.

If we define the film's structural focus as Lora, what does this do to the position of the long-suffering Annie, who is an obvious point of sympathy in the film? Of all the characters, her position is the most ambiguous depending on which way one chooses to read the film. If one moves along the lines of identification (the way which should reaffirm class values) Annie obviously dies a martyr's death; but it should be evident that I personally find this tactic untenable, although this sort of ambiguity is the reason why Sirk was able to maintain his position in Hollywood. Sirk is amenable to the bourgeois melodrama because its core crisis is the family break-up. This enables him to dissect the institution of the family and not quite put it back together again.

Annie is a character who self-destructs out of political necessity. Her energy to sustain the narrative wears out in proportion to Lora's material gain, as her specific degree of servitude becomes unnecessary. As a preserver of familial values, her attitude is almost suicidal. She cannot bear to be parted from Sarah Jane, yet her every effort to interfere merely destroys Sarah Jane's slim chances at class transcendence. At every point she exists to preserve middle-class values which have no meaning for her, and to preserve the family unit which brings nothing but misery to her "families." She dies because she is no longer needed by anyone, which is to say, she is no longer needed by the narrative except to provide a point of resolution.

The funeral scene to *Imitation of Life* is perhaps one of the greatest tear-jerkers in the cinema's history, yet, perhaps because of this, it is important to ask for whom do we cry? As Sarah Jane pushes through the crowd to reach those with whom she belongs there is a sense of great tragedy, not because she acknowledges too late a mother's love, but because nothing has changed. Class lines have held firm and the family is still in a state of disintegration. Are we really given reason to believe that Lora and Steve will be married this time, that Susie is not still embittered and planning to return to Colorado, that Sarah Jane has any place in this reunion except to replace her mother as Lora's maid? Sirk's approach to the scene is full of ironies. Reflect on two odd cutaways in the funeral sequence: one is a shot of the funeral train from behind a store window which is lettered "Costume Rentals"; the other is a low-angle shot of a black child whose heads blocks off another sign causing it to read "AKERY" ("ache-ery"?). Draw your own conclusions. At any rate, no matter which way the scene is read, it is equally painful. In discussing another part of the film, Fassbinder notes that the real cruelty is that both readings are correct, the implication being that the paradox is irresolvable until the world has been transformed.

———

DAVID RODOWICK

PART III

Cinema-Fist: Renegade Talents

ULMER, RAY, ALDRICH, FULLER, WELLES, PECKINPAH

In 1987, George Morris and Richard Linklater curated a series of Sam Fuller and Robert Aldrich films in Austin. They called this series *Cinema-Fist,* a term the critic Peter Wollen used to describe Fuller's "muscular visual style." According to Morris, "his movies vividly portray the clash between personal interests and larger responsibilities. Fuller's men and women strive to hold on to their individuality in a world whose social and political institutions systemically depersonalize identity. In order to survive, they live along the twilit fringes of society. . . . In his greatest films . . . Fuller suggests that the inevitable result of such friction is violence and chaos. The events of the past three decades would seem to prove him right" (*The Austin Chronicle,* March 27, 1987).

This section focuses on directors who, despite working within the Hollywood studio system, were consistently, consciously, and proudly renegade. The drive of their work was a refusal to provide audiences with unearned happy endings, but rather to confront viewers with fictionalized analogues of the complexities and contradictions in the world they re-entered when the movie ended. This is not to imply that the directors whose work is analyzed in the previous sections were not, in their way, less provocative; however, the visual and narrative rhetoric of Ford, Hawks, et al., embraced a certain subtlety of expression that is not normally a significant part of the cinematic language embraced by the *Cinema-Fist* filmmakers.

The professional careers of the directors in this section were more sporadically successful, not surprising given the combative nature of their work. They actively sought to knock audiences off-balance. All had hits but were never long-term industry favorites. In their best work, you can feel their anger boiling over, spreading out from within the film's narrative to challenge not just genre conventions and Hollywood storytelling traditions, but the audience's understanding of the world itself, with regard to a whole range of hot-button issues—racism, masculinity, violence, violence against women, and the norms of heterosexual relationships.

Sam Fuller, Sam Peckinpah, Robert Aldrich, Edgar Ulmer, Nicholas Ray, and Orson Welles all worked within the industry whenever they had the opportunity. All fell out of favor with the studios at some point in their careers, with Fuller, Ulmer, Ray, and Welles ending up working well outside of Hollywood, often in Europe. A common thread here involves careers disrupted or truncated, combined with an apparently congenital inability to compromise in order to keep working within the mainstream.

Welles is unique here, as he is in any categorization of directors. No one else went so high; no one else fell so far. His career and life were so baroque that he becomes the architect of his own postmodern career. After *Citizen Kane* (1941), the ultimate Hollywood movie, he spent most of the rest of his career struggling to raise money for projects and wandering the world in pursuit of opportunities to work. Welles's career trajectory is indicative of another commonality among these directors, in that they were often their own worst enemies, causing so much friction for producers and studios that they recurrently put their own ability to keep working at risk. It's perhaps a stretch to propose that they wouldn't have had it any other way, but if you've ever watched an interview with Sam Fuller or Nick Ray, it's easy enough to reach that conclusion.

Cinema-Fist: Movies that punch you in your face.

EDGAR G. ULMER (B. 1904, AUSTRIA-HUNGARY)

Ulmer is unique. A remarkably prolific film director, almost always working with minuscule budgets, he seems to have approached almost all of his diverse productions with deadly seriousness. Often featuring protagonists struggling to transcend terrible situations brought on by a combination of their own intentions and some version of fate, Ulmer's films chased the status of Art with a captial A in low-budget productions that would seem to make even modest imaginative ambitions a fool's errand. This effort achieved maximum expressive impact with *Detour* (1946), which despite (or maybe because of) a stripped-down, sordid story, B-movie origins, and low budget, became perhaps the first American *Nouvelle Vague* film a decade before that movement began in France. Legendarily shooting as many as sixty setups in a day, Ulmer used his competence at the craft of filmmaking to push his projects farther than many of them deserved.

Although Ulmer emigrated to Hollywood to work on F. W. Murnau's *Sunrise* (1927), he never really broke into mainstream studio filmmaking, with the exception of *The Black Cat* (1934), starring Bela Lugosi and Boris Karloff. Usually handed the lowest of budgets, he produced more compelling images in his films than many directors working in much more extravagant circumstances. Working mostly with genre-based exploitation films and B movies, Ulmer also made films for niche minority markets. These included the first Ukrainian-language film produced in the United States (*Natalka Poltavka*, 1937), contributions to the semi-thriving Yiddish film industry (*Green Fields*, with Jacob Ben-Ami, 1937), and a musical with an all-black cast (*Moon over Harlem*, 1939).

Born in what is now the Czech Republic, Ulmer studied architecture and philosophy while working as a stage actor and a set designer for Max Reinhardt's theater. He was one of five directors on *People on Sunday* in Germany in 1930 (along with Curt and Robert Siodmak and Fred Zinnemann), from a script cowritten by Billy Wilder. Severely underappreciated for much of his career, Sarris provides a rather lovely assessment, noting that "the French call him un cinéaste maudit, and directors certainly don't come any more maudit. But yes, Virginia, there is an Edgar G. Ulmer, and he is no longer one of the private jokes shared by *auteur* critics, but one of the minor glories of the cinema. Here is a career, more subterranean than most, which bears the signature of a genuine artist" (*The American Cinema*, 1968). His inventive *mise-en-scènes* elevated what might have been lesser material to the upper echelon of Poverty Row's output. Many of his works, including *Bluebeard* (1944), *Ruthless* (1948), *St. Benny the Dip* (1951), and *The Naked Dawn* (1955), invite further study.

American culture. Ultimately, "Aldrich doesn't just ram his fist down our throats. He shoves in his whole arm" (George Morris, *The Austin Chronicle*, March 27, 1987).

SAMUEL FULLER (B. 1917, USA)

As myth would have it, "Hammer!" was the first word that came out of Fuller's mouth. An apt metaphor, considering the visceral, gut-punching films he would create over a forty-year career. Fuller's early life provides an indicative context for his sprawling filmography. At age twelve he began working as a copyboy for the local newspaper and by seventeen he was a full-time crime reporter. In his spare time, he wrote pulp novels before enlisting in the army during World War II, an experience that would inflect Fuller's style and themes with a distinctive "lyrical intensity" (*The Illustrated Who's Who of Cinema*, 1983).

"All of Fuller's movies are basically war movies," writes Morris. "The bleached terrains of *Forty Guns*, the stylized cityscapes of *Pickup on South Street* and *Underworld U.S.A.*, and the claustrophobic asylum of *Shock Corridor* are psychological battlefields. They're as treacherous and as lethal as their more immediately threatening equivalents in *The Steel Helmet*, *Fixed Bayonets!*, *Verboten!*, *Merrill's Marauders*, and *The Big Red One*. Violence and death stalk the people who lurch through these stories" (*The Austin Chronicle*, March 27, 1987). Always ahead of the curve in tackling controversial themes and ideas, Fuller made films about corruption, greed, racism, and interracial relationships that still feel more progressive than most films addressing those topics today. Sarris writes, "Fuller is an authentic American primitive whose works have to be seen to be understood. Seen, not heard or synopsized. . . . It is time the cinema followed the other arts in honoring its primitives. Fuller belongs to the cinema, and not to literature and sociology" (*The American Cinema*, 1968).

To put it mildly, the politics of Fuller's films are all over the ideological map. Fuller's determination to skewer, satirize, and expose was always intense and sincere, but his apparent point of view on specific issues could veer from progressive to reactionary and back again, sometimes over the course of a single film. As Sarris points out, at his best, his films are marvelously visual, visceral compositions that embody the contradictions of American society, works driven by Fuller's pulp sensibility, yellow journalism sensationalism, and aggressively physical manipulation of the camera. He used intense, almost frightening close-ups of emotionally tormented characters to create a kind of cinematic Beat poetry, and widescreen compositions stuffed to the gills with incongruous visual elements. The wild west "Ride of the Valkyries" opening of *Forty Guns* (1957), the psychological apocalypse that ends *Shock Corridor* (1963), or the subjective camera view (mostly from the perspective of the victim) used to show a prostitute beating up her pimp (her wig falls off, revealing a cue ball bald head) in the first scene of *The Naked Kiss* (1965) were as much an assault on Hollywood conventions as they were on audience sensibilities. "Fuller is fascinated with the contradictions of American life. He acknowledges the nastier implications of the energy that began to sour and curdle when there were no more frontiers left to forge" (George Morris, *The Austin Chronicle*, March 27, 1987).

ORSON WELLES (B. 1915, USA)

Both *Citizen Kane* (1941) and *Touch of Evil* (1958) present a warning in their final scenes, a caution to guard against the assumption that you can encapsulate the entire life of a person in a single story. And yet, Welles's legend remains as temptingly expansive as that of Charles Foster Kane, William Randolph Hearst, or Shakespeare's Falstaff. Whether the child prodigy or the drunken slob, the egomaniacal personas he translated to screen were often elaborately costumed, distorted reflections of identities he himself cultivated or found himself burdened with. The reality of Orson Welles as an embodied person is lost somewhere in the stories. Whether responding to myth or reality, Welles invented his answers cinematically, solving problems that may not have existed before he placed himself in some impossible situation, either behind or in front of the camera. This often involved crafting innovative effects from no budget at all; one, for example, involved smashing a mirror into a water-filled pan, whereupon the shards would reflect apparent waves onto Welles's face, conveying the impression that he was on the open sea, as he read a monologue from a never-finished adaptation of *Moby Dick* (Graver and Rausch, *Making Movies with Orson Welles*, 2011).

Obviously Welles transcends his categorization in this chapter. But rather than trying to reassess his career, placing him here is a testimony to his unique genius simply because of the wide range of categories that he fits into. Certainly he was a classic Hollywood director, responsible for both prestige pictures like *Citizen Kane* and *The Magnificent Ambersons* (1942) as well as less high-status projects like *Lady from Shanghai* (1948) and *Touch of Evil*. Other films took him geographically, logistically and/or conceptually far from Hollywood, including his Shakespeare films and *The Other Side of the Wind* (1972).

Welles's voice and his physical presence were themselves commanding phenomena capable of consuming the frames of his films, the stages of his theater productions, and the ears of listeners to his radio broadcasts. Most famously, he terrified millions of radio listeners by staging H. G. Wells's *War of the Worlds* as if it was a live news report. For Welles, rebellion against the system became just another facet of his mythology, but his work with actors, cinematographers, and increasingly limited budgets generated both a cautionary tale and a bravura role model for the ages.

SAM PECKINPAH (B. 1925, USA)

The whole underside of our society has always been violence and still is. Churches, laws—everybody seems to think that man is a noble savage. But he's only an animal. A meat-eating, talking animal. Recognize it. He also has grace and love and beauty. But don't say to me we're not violent. | SAM PECKINPAH

This quote encapsulates the philosophical foundation of Peckinpah's cinema. Violence, cynicism, fatalism, and nihilism have become the predominant descriptors of his work, and he remains to this day one of the most notorious renegade talents to emerge out of New Hollywood. The director's trademark themes of regeneration through violence, moral ambivalence, and the death and mythology of the American West are evident throughout his work, achieving their most eloquent expression in *The Wild Bunch* (1969). If *Bonnie and Clyde* (1967) opened the floodgates for graphic violence in Hollywood films, *The Wild Bunch*, two years later, ensured that those gates remained open forever. Peckinpah's film was the most extreme and the most articulate entry in the 1960s and 1970s cycle of revisionist Westerns that reappraised the conventional mythologies of America's expansionist history. In *The Wild Bunch*, Peckinpah employs and subverts, romanticizes and makes monstrous generic conventions to cast a fresh eye on rituals of violence, the toxic tendencies of masculinity, and legacies of racism and xenophobia.

Peckinpah established himself as an innovative director of Westerns with the classic *Ride the High Country* (1962). Influenced by the first generation of revisionist postwar Westerns by directors including Anthony Mann and Budd Boetticher, in which the standard cowboy hero starts to develop vintage Cold War neuroses and insecurities, Peckinpah found his directorial home in portrayals of a world in the throes of an increasingly painful and disturbing transition, a world that, for him, was descending into madness. From 1969 to 1974, Peckinpah directed a series of violent, downbeat, sometimes lyrical, sometimes deeply disturbing films, culminating with *Bring Me the Head of Alfredo Garcia* (1974), a simultaneously elegiac and apocalyptic work depicting an archaic society hurtling toward its imminent self-destruction. Anchored only by the director's belief that even in the midst of ruin and chaos, there is a need to search for a clear moral center, the film feels like the most fully realized of Peckinpah's raw aesthetic—a perfect synthesis of theme and style that is both self-indulgent and self-aware. The inherent nihilism of his later films seemed diametrically opposed to the newfound optimism coalescing in many mainstream Hollywood narratives of the late 1970s. Sam Peckinpah was not made for those times, and the combination of spiraling alcoholism and never-ending battles with the studios took him out of this world far too soon.

—

STEVE FORE, LOUIS BLACK

VOL. 15, NO. 3
NOVEMBER 22, 1978

Detour (1945)

DIRECTED BY EDGAR G. ULMER

Detour is an exercise in sustained perversity, a consistent demonstration of the absence of free will. . . . It is not even a question of fatalism any longer—the mechanisms of disaster have long overwhelmed any of our own intimations of morality. Ann Savage gives a performance which defies conventional credibility: ugly, unpleasant, a shrill unmodulated embodiment of the Yeats' dictum that only the unexplained is irresistible. | MYRON MEISEL, in *Kings of the Bs*.

Ulmer's world . . . is an irrational one governed by crazy nightmare more than by any coldly mechanical sense of fate. Ulmer's characters do not struggle against an externally imposed chain of events but rather are powerless prisoners of an irrational series of experiences which they can neither understand nor control. Ulmer's characters, deliberately inconsistent, act chaotically. They repeatedly surrender themselves to their intuitive but irrational impulses. Consequently, they lose control over their actions and their environment. Ultimately, they exist only as passive *reactors* to what happens to them. | JOHN BELTON, *Velvet Light Trap*, Summer 1972.

A system is a sort of damnation. | CHARLES BAUDELAIRE

Baudelaire's comment that "a system is a sort of damnation" could well have been Edgar G. Ulmer's personal motto. Throughout his long career he shunned both the production system of the big Hollywood studios and the systems of narrative and visual conventions which have come to typify the classic Hollywood cinema. Instead, he chose to carve out a career in the milieu of the Bs, often turning the limitations of their production methods to his advantage, while developing a style so highly personal as to border on the eccentricity. In this light, *Detour* is more than just the name of the film—it is the over-riding metaphor for the cinema of Edgar G. Ulmer.

Detour is often considered to be not only one of Ulmer's best works, but a classic of *film noir* as well. But, if we are to consider *noir* a genre, and therefore a recognizable set of visual and narrative conventions establishing a typology across a number of films, we would be forced to recognize *Detour* as a classic of the genre only in that it is the exception which proves the rule. The very title of the film defines it as a deviant, not only in its perverse denial of the conventions of genre and class, but also in its repeated over-turning of narrative logic. if there is a system to *Detour*, it lies in the demonic insistence of its own irrationality elevating its consistencies to a new realm of verisimilitude.

Detour is a *noir* deviant in many respects, especially in considerations of visual style, narrative mode and narrative thematics. *Noir*'s visual style is usually characterized by deformations of space (high-contrast lighting, compositions of either claustrophobic or indeterminate spaces, subjective alterations of the image) reflecting its themes of moral ambiguity and the labyrinthine, misleading nature of the urban milieu. In its points of visual departure, *Detour* is very *noir*-like. Its unrealistic, expressionistic lighting serves to distort and intensify its already disturbing angles and shadows. But unlike most *noir*, *Detour* does not insist on its urban locale; rather, it is the highway which is its obsession, and it is a road to nowhere. This idea is reinforced through Ulmer's preference for episodic sequences linked by a variety of optical effects, emphasizing the repetitiveness and the sameness of locales while undermining any notion of progression. Moreover, the

Detour. From the core collection production photographs of the Margaret Herrick Library, Academy of Motion Picture Arts and Sciences.

consistent, imaginative use of rear-projection also serves to undermine any notion of progress, adding a bizarre and disturbing quality to the naked illusion of movement. Lastly, Ulmer's camera movements may be the most outstanding and most unsettling element of his visual style. Nowhere has a moving camera been so deadly, reserving the possible exception of the cinema of Dario Argento (*Suspiria*, *Bird with the Crystal Plumage*); but if Argento's camera is deadly, it is also, at least, personable, immediately identifiable with the killer. Ulmer's camera is cold, distant, methodical, even sadistic in its revelation of *Detour*'s deformed universe. The camera wanders, but not aimlessly—each movement has a purpose, usually serving to accent the subjectivity of the story, focusing relentlessly on Al Roberts's tortured narration.

With respect to narrative mode, *Detour* adopts the *noir* convention of taking the point of view of the male protagonist, coded by a voice-over narration which keys the film to a subjective mode, generally in flashback structure. And if *noir* is able to dramatize its visual style in this manner, it is from the position of safety of a story told to someone, and therefore determined to end "happily," as in *Murder, My Sweet*. However, *Detour*'s narrative mode is almost exclusively an interior monologue, and Roberts's insistent narration snaking throughout the flashback sequences never lets us lose sight of the fact that the images are couched in the function of memory. Thus, there is no position of stability from which to judge the veracity of Roberts's story, already doubtful because of its paranoid edge. Moreover, the subjectivity of Roberts's discourse is further emphasized by the inclusion of dream and fantasy sequences as sub-texts of the flashbacks, ever-increasing our distance from the possibility of truth.

Detour's narrative structure is thus characterized by the constant undermining of logical positions by the inconsistency of actions, the preponderance of false trails and the incessant reversal of cause and effect. Roberts is even denied the *activity* of narration accorded the *noir* protagonist. He is completely victimized by *Detour*'s visual universe—his narration is condemned to a "remembering, repeating and working-through" of the totally irrational events to which he has been subjected. In other words, Roberts's narration in no way motivates the direction of the story; it appears, instead to be re-working its way back through the labyrinthine passages and blind alleys into which Ulmer's camera has drawn it. Nowhere is this idea more clear than in the segment after Vera's "murder," where, beginning with Roberts's face, Ulmer's camera begins a journey across the room focusing and unfocusing on a series of objects which effectively capsulize his past with Vera. Roberts's voice, however, seems to be completely dislocated from the progress of the camera, which traces with relentless logic an ironic counterpoint to his addled, frantic narration.

Detour takes its most significant departure from the conventions of *noir* in the context of theme. The thematic of the *noir* universe is wholly concerned with the betrayal of the male protagonist—betrayals by the law, betrayals by those outside his social class, and above all, betrayal by the *femme noir*—which he may overcome by a steadfast adherence to a personal code of action. *Detour*, on the other hand, is repeatedly concerned with the interaction of fate and circumstance which only occurs, of course, at the most inopportune moments and with the most perverse consequences. The law has no function here, really, except to reinforce Roberts's already paranoiac attitudes. In Vera, *Detour* substitutes a *femme monstre* for the *femme noir*, denying us even the moral duplicity which is part of the attractiveness of many *noir* heroines. Sue, the only potentially attractive character in the film, is almost immediately jettisoned and brought back only momentarily to counterpoint Vera's baseness. If the theme of betrayal returns to the text of *Detour* at all, it is in its refusal to provide Roberts with the classic form which would transform narrative as destiny, and thus give him a logical course of action. But the beauty of *Detour* is the pure absurdity of its progress, or rather its anti-progress, which paradoxically leads Roberts further and further away from his goal—marriage and the romantic ideal—the closer he appears to get to Hollywood, an icon not to be discounted.

In the final count, the idea of fate in *Detour* is concealed beneath the question of morality, which is revealed in the argument between Roberts and Vera toward the end of the film. Indeed, if Roberts's progress is to be measured at all, it is in the physical and moral deaths which structure his dark journey and mark the sum total of his "detours": Sue's absence may be considered as metaphorical death as she is forever excluded from his life; as Haskell dies Roberts accepts his identity; and, when Vera dies, "Haskell" becomes theoretically responsible for the murder, "Roberts" being dead by the highway. Thus, each successive death finds its double in Roberts's increasing moral alienation and loss of identity, until he is left a phantom in limbo, excluded both from his destination and point of departure.

In retrospect, *Detour* may be one of the great unrecognized works in the absurdist style, rivaling even Kafka in its determination to strip life of logic and stability. As if to prove that life is forever stranger than fiction, *Detour* proved to be Tom Neal's (Roberts) last film. He was soon afterwards convicted of murdering his wife in circumstances which strangely resembled those of the film.

———

DAVID RODOWICK

VOL. 17, NO. 2
NOVEMBER 5, 1979

They Live by Night (1948)

DIRECTED BY NICHOLAS RAY

There was theatre (Griffith), poetry (Murnau), painting (Rossellini), dance (Eisenstein), music (Renoir). Henceforth there is cinema. And the cinema is Nicholas Ray. | JEAN-LUC GODARD, *Godard on Godard*.

Of all American directors in the fifties, it was Ray—and, occasionally, Kazan—who most passionately portrayed the individual's rebellion against injustice. Passionately, but also intelligently. Ray's films are full of contempt for all forms of bigotry and oppression. They are critical, but rarely propagandistic, mixtures of pessimism and idealism. Their protagonists are usually "outsiders." And whether that outsider is a naive criminal (*They Live by Night*), a confused adolescent (*Rebel without a Cause*), a "primitive" (*The Savage Innocents*), or a Vietnam War protester (the Chicago Seven project), Ray devotes all his skill toward bringing them respect and sympathy. "Sympathy" is, perhaps, the key word. For, by forcing his audience to share in the emotions, sometimes highly alien, of these "outsiders," he is able to show more clearly the thin line between meaningful revolt and self-destruction, the exact moment when idealism plummets into paranoia. | Mike Wilmington, *Velvet Light Trap*, Fall 1973.

If Ray's nervous direction has no thematic meaning, he would be a minor director indeed. Fortunately, Ray does have a theme, and a very important one; namely, that every relationship establishes its own moral code and that there is no such thing as abstract morality. | ANDREW SARRIS, *The American Cinema.*

This boy . . . and this girl . . . were never properly introduced to the world we live in. | Preamble to *They Live by Night.*

Nicholas Ray's first feature film, *They Live by Night,* manifests a convergence of several artistic traditions welded together by an authoritative and distinct thematic and visual style. Although the film was made in 1947 and shot on a seven week schedule, *They Live by Night* was not commercially released in the United States until 1949. *A Woman's Secret* and *Knock On Any Door,* Ray's second and third features, had already been released by this time and had established his reputation as a director capable of evoking in his films both great sensitivity and hardened toughness.

It was Ray's experience in the theater and his association with Elia Kazan and John Houseman that led him on a path to Hollywood. While initiating his career as a stage actor Ray came to know Kazan, who directed him in his first New York play in 1935. Over the next ten years they collaborated on several theatrical projects and when Kazan went to Hollywood to make his first film, *A Tree Grows in Brooklyn* (1945), he brought Ray with him as his assistant director.

Ray's association with Houseman began in the late 1930s around the time Houseman and Orson Welles formed the Mercury Theatre. When Welles secured a directing contract at RKO Houseman followed him out to Hollywood. After Pearl Harbor Houseman was appointed chief of radio programming for the overseas branch of the US Office of War Information and he chose Ray to become his broadcast director. He also produced two successful Broadway plays directed by Ray, *Lute Song* (1943) and *Beggar's Holiday* (1946).

It was their collaboration on one of television's first big dramatic productions, *Sorry, Wrong Number,* in 1946 that brought Ray to the attention of Dore Schary who was then executive producer at RKO. During this postwar period, Schary was producing films with politically liberal leanings and was on the lookout for new talent to direct these low-budget films. He produced films such as Edward Dmytryk's *Crossfire* (1947) and Joseph Losey's *The*

Boy with Green Hair (1948). In 1947 Houseman agreed to produce a project titled *Your Red Wagon* for Schary on the condition that Ray be hired as its director.

Your Red Wagon was retitled *The Twisted Road* before it was finally released in 1949 as *They Live by Night*. It was previewed for the press in 1948 and received good reviews but the film unfortunately got caught in RKO management upheavals. Howard Hughes took control of the studio in May 1948 and Schary left in June. Although *They Live by Night* was scheduled for a July release, Hughes, for reasons unclear, chose to shelve it. After releasing the film in England in late 1948. Hughes decided to release it in America in October 1949. He accompanied its release with a flurry of sensational advertising designed to promote it as a "hot-red teen-age crime picture."

Typical of consumer advertising, Hughes's promotional slant, successful though it was, offered a deceptively inaccurate description of the movie's substance. Although there is some slight connection, the teenage exploitation market is a remote narrative influence on this film. What is immediately obvious, if only from the very title *They Live by Night*, is the film's relationship with the then-proliferating post-war stylistic movement that has come to be known as *film noir*. The cynical attitude and the expressionistic, shadow-laden visual style is most commonly invoked when describing the hard-boiled detective genre of the late forties but its presence can also be seen in such diverse genres as the gangster film (*Key Largo*, 1948; *White Heat*, 1949) and the melodrama (*Mildred Pierce*, 1945; *Sunset Boulevard*, 1950). *They Live by Night* is an amalgam of these generic and stylistic impulses.

Bowie and Keechie, the film's central characters, can only find refuge in the night. Not only does the night offer them the illusion of safety and thereby a fleeting chance for happiness, it functions as a backdrop for all their important decisions and actions. It is night when Bowie and Keechie first meet each other and when Keechie decides to leave with Bowie after the Zelton robbery. Their marriage, Bowie's decision to partake in one more bank robbery, and his death all occur at night.

While most of the narrative takes place at night and blankets all the decisive actions, this *noir* milieu is not conveyed as their natural habitat. Unlike the hardened gangsters, T-Dub and Chickamaw, who seem at ease in the dark, Bowie and Keechie seek and try to integrate themselves into the world of daylight, only to retreat into the seemingly viable refuge of night-time. The daylight world is the arena of normalcy, the world of non-criminals. It is only when they behave as blissful and carefree young newlyweds that they can exist in daylight. They only see the sun while traveling in the car after their marriage and when it spills into their honeymoon bungalow and their furnished room in New Orleans. It exhilarates them so that they decide to spend the day outdoors. Ultimately the excursion functions to disclose their darker identities, but it is the socially legitimizing act of getting married that allows them to briefly bask in the solar warmth of the daylight world.

Nighttime, however, does not offer them total solace; their night is fragmented and distorted by ominous shadows. When Keechie is nursing Bowie after his car accident in the scene in which she decides to leave with him, the focus is on the two of them as viewed through the bars of the brass bed, providing an image of literal and metaphorical confinement as well as casting heavy shadows across their frame of movement. At the close of the film, as Bowie walks across the yard to to look at Keechie once more before he leaves, he is surrounded and engulfed by shadows that suggest the imminence of his death. As Douglas Gomery points out, these shadows serve as the film's "antagonist." The police who are usually everpresent in *film noir* appear only three brief times in *They Live by Night*. They are unnecessary because the shadows fulfill their purpose. Thus when Bowie is killed the blow is emotionally struck by the encompassing shadows rather than the physical actions of the disembodied voices and hidden gunshots of the police.

Although *They Live by Night* does not evidence all the cardinal characteristics of *film noir*, (i.e., devices such as the investigative narrative structure which usually employs flashbacks and voiceovers, and the *femme fatale* stereotype), it does contain *noir*'s characteristic fatalism. As Jonathan Rosenbaum explains, the a priori fatalism is announced in the opening shots.

A romantic vision of the couple is immediately juxtaposed with anarchic movement erupting into violence; desperate action is treated as a spectacular form of choreography. Each element is intensely articulated, yet "distanced" into a sort of abstraction: the spatial-emotional continuity of the first shot set in relief by the underlining verbal montage that "explains" it, the speeding car turned into creeping insect by the deterministic overhead angles which circumscribe its apparent freedom, and the violence displaced by the cut to Bowie, bringing us full circle back to the romantic hero already condemned in the opening shot—a circle of pain defining the limits of Ray's universe. And the exhilarating plasticity of the flight across the field, pivoted around the imposing billboard, fastens all three characteristics to the pop iconography of a society that surrounds and ultimately crushes them, the social recognition that moulds their identities and makes them "real" at the same time that it signs their death warrants.

We must look also to the gangster film as one further tradition which informs this narrative. After all, this is a movie about people who rob banks. As such, *They Live by Night* is surely more related to the gangster tradition which includes films such as *I Am a Fugitive from a Chain Gang* (1932) and *Wild Boys of the Road* (1933), films which explore the fate of the unjustly accused and the societal factors which foment criminal activity among the economically and emotionally deprived; rather than the tradition of gangsters in films such as *The Public Enemy* (1931) and *Little Caesar* (1931), both of which feature criminals whose ambitions necessitated their destruction. *They Live by Night* contrasts the two types of criminality, Bowie belonging more to the former category and T-Dub and Chickamaw to the latter.

T-Dub and Chickamaw can exist comfortably in both the nighttime and daytime worlds. They know that their survival in the dark gangster underworld depends on their ability to pass innocuously through the daylight world of society. As Chickamaw advises Bowie, "One thing you got to learn, kid. You got to look and act like other people."

Bowie, however, is trapped between the two spheres, unable to accommodate himself adequately to either one. His presence in society will always be threatened with disclosure of his anti-social tendencies. Yet his existence in the gangster world is precarious at best. He is destined to be dominated by T-Dub and Chickamaw who through physical challenges bend him to their will. They abide by a gangster code that condones the use of force as a method of obtaining desired goals. Early in the film we witness Chickamaw's tendency to exhibit his penchant for violence. He throws a mirror across the room at Mattie when he feels he has been insulted, and his tailgating challenge to Bowie while they are driving causes Bowie to be chased into a collision.

When Chickamaw returns to Bowie's honeymoon hideaway to notify him of the need for another bank robbery, he answers Bowie's refusal by crushing the ornaments on the Christmas tree. Bowie offers to share his money with Chickamaw and T-Dub, still cherishing notions of the fraternal bonds among the three ex-cons. Bowie explains to Keechie his rationale for going along with the robbery as an obligation to stick by the men who befriended him in prison. Yet throughout the film, Chickamaw and T-Dub have pointed out that robbing banks is a three-man job. To them, Bowie is an investment. But Bowie harbors illusions that their bonds are grounded in camaraderie and shared experience. His naive view does not allow him to see that they are not concerned with his well-being but merely his performance as a functional piece of equipment.

In fact, Bowie and Keechie's ultimate flaw is their innocence. The film's initial suggestion of this is an intimate shot of Bowie and Keechie with subtitles reading "This boy. . . and this . . . girl . . . were never properly introduced to the world we live in." Bowie has been in prison since he was sixteen and Keechie has been isolated out at the gas station working for her alcoholic father. Both sets of parents had disturbed marriages. Keechie's mother ran off with a man who runs a medicine show and Bowie's mother married the man who killed her husband in a poolroom brawl. Like their mothers Bowie and Keechie both cherish the hope for something better in their lives. Ignoring the omnipresence of their destiny Keechie and Bowie express their hopes and plans for the future. Their plans are even expansive enough to include the addition of a child to their family.

Their innocence is conveyed rather succinctly through their exchange of watches. While involved with the Zelton robbery Bowie buys Keechie a watch that is displayed in a shop window with the tag "For Her." After he gives it to her he asks her what time it is and she replies that she has no clock to set it by. So they set by the time the hands say. As Wilmington states "It is their ultimate defense: their time is different from the world's."

Thus their innocence dooms them to stay on the run, never able to rest in either world. It is a dramatic situation, echoing the tragedy of Romeo and Juliet. They are doomed by forces beyond their comprehension. Although not related by the innocence of the lovers *They Live by Night* fits into a tradition of gangster lovers on the lam including Fritz Lang's *You Only Live Once* (1937), Joseph Lewis's *Gun Crazy* (1950), Jean-Luc Godard's *Pierrot Le Fou* (1966) and Arthur Penn's *Bonnie and Clyde* (1967). The lovers all take flight for a variety of reasons but their destinies are always determined from the start. Social outcasts all, but they all find momentary salvation in each others' arms.

MARJORIE BAUMGARTEN

VOL. 18, NO. 3
APRIL 21, 1980

In a Lonely Place (1950)

DIRECTED BY NICHOLAS RAY

After ten years of steadily shedding romantic conventions, the later *noir* films finally got down to the root causes of the period: the loss of public honor, heroic conventions, personal integrity, and finally, psychic stability. The ... films were painfully self-aware; they seemed to know they stood at the end of a long tradition based on despair and disintegration and did not shy away from that fact. | PAUL SCHRADER, "Notes on *Film Noir*," in *Awake in the Dark*.

I didn't say I was a gentleman—I said I was tired. | DIXON STEELE in *In a Lonely Place*.

One way of approaching *In a Lonely Place* would be to describe it as the ultimate *film noir*. Appearing in 1950, at the end of a decade of Hollywood *noir* films that began with *The Maltese Falcon* in 1941, *In a Lonely Place* refines the dark themes and excessive stylization of earlier *noir* cinema into a perfectly balanced, self-critical film. The disillusionment, distrust, and despair that plague Dixon Steele are much more subtle than the violent and passionate evils that confronted Sam Spade in *The Maltese Falcon*; and the style of

Nicholas Ray's film is more subdued than that of Huston's film and other pre-decessors. Nothing of the earlier *noir* films has been lost in *In a Lonely Place*, however: in fact, the film is what Paul Schrader describes as "painfully self-aware" of its cinematic lineage. The restrained *noir* themes and style of *Lonely Place* are evidence that the film knows and appreciates the limits, as well as the strength, of the *noir* tradition to which it belongs.

The psychological substructure of Ray's films is uncommonly rich and com-plex. No other filmmaker has rendered the basic American contradictions, both political and social, with Ray's insight and impact. His characters are the sons and daughters of the American dream—but it is a dream gone sour. At the heart of Ray's cinema lies the anguish of living from day to American day; his characters suffer not only their own personal agony, but the agony forced on them by a cruel and oppressive system. | MICHAEL GOODWIN and NAOMI WISE, "Nicholas Ray, Rebel!," in *Take One*, January 1977.

I was born when she kissed me; I died when she left me; and I lived a few weeks while she loved me. | DIX STEELE

As other *noir* films do, and as Nicholas Ray's best work does, *In a Lonely Place* critiques the values at the heart of the American dream. With two decades of roles as a tough loner behind him, Humphrey Bogart brought to the char-acter of Dix Steele (note the aural implications of the name) an archetypal masculinity that the film extends into psychotic violence. Laurel Gray proves herself to Dix at the police station by lying for him, and the pair negotiate a relationship with mutual cynicism. Dix and Laurel understand each other's defensiveness and build a positive relationship from their mutual isolation and estrangement. Like Bowie and Keechie in *They Live by Night*, Dix and Laurel share a love based on their opposition to conventional social values. It is one of the great ironies of *In a Lonely Place* that the success of Dix and Laurel's love makes them vulnerable to conventional mores. Their romance cannot escape socially acceptable forms: Laurel cooks and cleans up after Dix and types his screenplay, and he buys her gifts. When the representa-tives of social convention—Captain Lochner, Brub Nicolai, and Nicolai's wife Sheila—begin to dissuade Laurel from her love for Dix, Laurel con-fesses that she has always wanted a cottage by the sea. Dix makes a desper-ate attempt to combat Laurel's loss of faith by establishing material bonds between the pair: he buys Laurel an enormous diamond engagement ring, a trousseau, a car, and takes her to look at houses. This is the material security that Martha has been advocating for Laurel all along. These manic attempts to embrace the American dream only escalate the tension between the couple, however, and are consummated when Dix physically threatens Laurel. The basic blueprint of the American way of life—a strong man supporting a domestic woman—is projected as interpersonal violence in *Lonely Place*. "What can I say to him?" Laurel asks Mel, "I love you but I'm afraid of you?" It is the deep love between Dix and Laurel that convinces her to make herself physically vulnerable, and it is her vulnerability that eventually destroys the relationship.

> Thus *film noir*'s techniques emphasize loss, nostalgia, lack of clear priorities, insecurity; then submerge these self-doubts in mannerism and style. In such a world style becomes paramount; it is all that separates one from meaninglessness. | PAUL SCHRADER, "Notes on Film Noir," in *Awake in the Dark*.

> A good love scene should be about something else besides love. | DIX STEELE

Few love scenes in Hollywood films are more electrifying than the scene in the police department in *Lonely Place* when Laurel Gray demonstrates her blossoming love for Dix Steele by unexpectedly lying to provide him with an alibi. The lovers, if one can call them that, gaze at each other while Captain Lochner grills them about a murder. The pair never share a two-shot, and they never exchange one-shots: Lochner is in the background, first of Laurel's shots and then of Dix's, and fires the questions that keep the couple's conversation going. Stylistically as well as literally, this is a scene about something besides love; perhaps it is the ultimate *noir* love scene.

Noir films are usually about something besides love, about things like ambition, greed, lust, betrayal, and death. *In a Lonely Place* is remarkable because it presents us with a love that momentarily transcends greed, betrayal, and death; but in the *noir* world of the film even love eventually self-destructs. The moment when Laurel accedes to Dix's declaration of love is marked by the most extreme and most typically *noir* camerawork in the film. The camera looks up at Humphrey Bogart from an extremely low angle, and down at Gloria Grahame, who is seated on a low stool, as the pair coolly acknowledge their love. The disparity in the physical presences of the man and the woman is emphasized by a bizarre shot when Bogart steps into Grahame's frame to kiss her and the camera is at the level of his knee. Even the embrace continues the disparity in heights with Gloria Grahame's head

In a Lonely Place. From the core collection production photographs of the
Margaret Herrick Library, Academy of Motion Picture Arts and Sciences.

bent back at an incredible angle as she kisses Bogart standing above her.
Stylistically this love scene is about something besides love: the camera
suggests that Laurel has reason to be afraid of Dix from their first embrace.

> The *film noir*, although it was also a sociological reflection, went further than
> the gangster film. Toward the end *film noir* was engaged in a life-and-death
> struggle with the materials it reflected; it tried to make America accept a
> moral vision of life based on style. | **PAUL SCHRADER**, "Notes on *Film Noir*,"
> in *Awake in the Dark*.

> No sacrifice is too great for a chance for immortality. | **DIX STEELE**

Although *noir* lighting and camerawork are not as pronounced in *Lonely
Place* as they are in earlier *noir* films, throughout Ray's film they subtly
invoke the film's inheritance of disillusionment and despair. Dix Steele is a

noir hero, a guy who's tough enough to take it in a world of corruption and chaos by imaging murder too well. Dix has served his time in the traditional American male role of soldier, and there are stylistic suggestions that he learned the role too thoroughly. When he imagines a murder for Brub and Sheila, his face is in shadow; only his eyes are illuminated. He looks like a man obsessed with death. We "know" Dix is innocent, while the lighting insists that he is guilty. Like that of other *noir* heroes, Dix's guilt is an inseparable part of his American birthright. Unlike earlier and simpler *noir* heroes, however, Dix has a hand in creating his guilt, because he imaginatively understands the violence inherent in the American conception of masculinity. The style with which Dix has learned to deal with the *noir* world, the tough cynicism that distinguishes him from men like Lockner and Nicolai, ultimately brings about Dix's defeat.

In a Lonely Place is most basically a film about style, about Dix Steele's style, which is superior to everything else in the world of the film. This film believes in style, and believes in Dix Steele, but it understands that the American moral vision is determinedly opposed to style and that it is the moral vision that has to win. Dixon Steele's imaginative understanding of violence is socially unacceptable. Not since Lambert Strether sacrificed all his personal happiness in Henry James's *The Ambassadors* has an American suffered as much for his belief in style as Dix Steele does in *Lonely Place*. The style of the film is, as the style of James's novel is, exquisite. It is impossible to discount such style; and hence it is impossible to discount Dix Steele. It is ultimately the style of the film that makes Dix Steele a tragic hero, through its celebration of his distrust and cynicism. If Laurel Gray could just believe in Dix the way the film allows us to believe in him—if the American way of life didn't destroy the heroes it creates—there would be some hope for the future of the American dream. *In a Lonely Place* argues powerfully that the only hope is the self-reflexive circularity of style. In its exquisite condemnation of American ideology, *In a Lonely Place* offers us the solace of art. It creates what Paul Schrader terms "artistic solutions to sociological problems," and that is enough. It has to be. As Mel Lippman said in the film: He's Dix Steele, and if you want him, you have to take it all, the bad with the good.

———

ELLEN DRAPER

Kiss Me Deadly. From the United Artists photographs of the Margaret Herrick
Library, Academy of Motion Picture Arts and Sciences.

right-wing philosophy, as Bitsch intimated in his admiring description of Aldrich: "Disintegration of montage, explosion of the image; here is the first filmmaker of the atomic era." In a similarly effusive vein, when Francois Truffaut interviewed Aldrich for *Cahiers* in 1956, he said of *Kiss Me Deadly*: "It seems to me that you knew exactly how to transform the book by erasing everything that was bad, by replacing the law-and-order crudeness with poetic effects."

As the auteurist movement became entrenched on the American side of the Atlantic in the early sixties, the reputations of Robert Aldrich in general and of *Kiss Me Deadly* in particular grew in stature. As a result, for most of the last two decades the film has had no shortage of admirers among film historians and theoreticians of all persuasions. It has been appreciated and analyzed by Paul Schrader as "the masterpiece of *film noir* . . . at the end of a long sleazy tradition"; and by Jack Shadoian as "a movie that comes at you in a series of ferocious spasms [which] has captured the terror and fear behind the fifties' spurious calm." My intention here is to move in the direction of a more holistic reading of *Kiss Me Deadly* (though by no means a definitive one; analyzing this film is like leaping into a black hole of narrative, visual, and thematic images—that is to say, a task without end), guided largely by the insights offered by other critics and historians operating from a variety of cultural and aesthetic vantage points. This is, then, an attempt at synthesis, at building an analytical coalition of contexts.

II. THE SOCIOPOLITICAL CONTEXT

It should be common knowledge by now that Franklin D. Roosevelt's New Deal did not lift the United States out of the Great Depression; it took World War II to accomplish that bit of excavation. Historian Godfrey Hodgson has pointed out that:

> In 1945, the United States was bulging with an abundance of every resource that held the key to power in the modern world: with land, food, power, raw material, industrial plants, monetary reserves, scientific talent, and trained manpower. It was in the war years that the United States shot ahead of all its rivals economically. In four years, national income, national wealth, and industrial production all doubled or more than doubled. In the same period, the Soviet Union's initially

It was hard to see billions of dollars that came from the highest taxes Americans had ever paid in peacetime going in foreign aid, and harder still to see so little return and so little gratitude for it. It was hard to swallow the casualties and the humiliations of the Korean War, while knowing all the time that it lay within American power to erase the military strength of both North Korea and China in a single night. It was easier for many, in the end, to reach for simpler explanations than the tangle of technicality and complication which was all the government and the press seemed to offer to assuage their bewilderment. It was tempting to accept the logic of the conspiracy theory as Senator McCarthy offered it, two months after the fall of MacArthur:

> How can we account for our present situation unless we believe that men high in this government are concerting to deliver us to disaster? This must be the product of a great conspiracy, a conspiracy on a scale so immense as to dwarf any previous such venture in the history of men.

The frustration that American foreign policy encountered after 1948, then, gave McCarthyism its opportunity. | GODFREY HODGSON, *America in Our Time*

III. THE LITERARY CONTEXT

It seems appropriate at this point to discuss the Mickey Spillane phenomenon of the fifties in more detail. Spillane's first novel, *I, the Jury*, featuring private detective Mike Hammer, was published in 1947. In 1954, it was observed that in the intervening years some 24,000,000 copies of Spillane/Hammer mysteries had appeared in print. Spillane's basic style and narrative structure are characteristic of the hard-boiled detective formula developed and refined by Dashiell Hammett and Raymond Chandler, but Spillane's novels sold far better throughout the fifties than those of his spiritual forebears ever had.

Spillane's success first perplexed, then appalled the vast majority of fifties literary and cultural observers.

This is a phenomenon that merits examination, although part of that examination has been made before. What is phenomenal about it is that a series of books can be written in what is supposed to be the form of fiction, but is not truly fiction, but rather a wholly unadmirable kind of wish fulfillment on both an immature and a potentially destructive level, and be immediately successful on a scale far beyond average. | **CHRISTOPHER LA FARGE**, "Mickey Spillane and His Bloody Hammer," in Rosenberg and White, *Mass Culture*

Indeed it is true, as John Cawelti has noted, that

By most traditional literary or artistic standards, the works of Mickey Spillane are simply atrocious. His characters and situations not only strain credulity to its limits, they frequently turn the stomach as well. Spillane's narrative technique is so "hard hitting," as the reviewers say, that it has the expressiveness of a blackjack. His style and dialogue are awkward, stilted, and wooden. His idea of a theme consists of a primitive right-wing diatribe against some of the central principles of American democracy and English law.

Spillane's ability to portray female characters is also extremely limited; women in his novels are either vicious killers or utter innocents, and in either case their overriding ambition is to sleep with Mike Hammer. Nonetheless, despite his many aesthetic and ideological deficiencies, it is true that Spillane communicates with an almost unparalleled raw intensity; his scenes of violence are compulsive, bordering on the pornographic, as the final passage of *Kiss Me Deadly* indicates:

The smile never left her mouth and before it was on me I thumbed the lighter and in the moment of time before the scream blossoms into the wild cry of terror she was a mass of flame tumbling on the floor with the blue flames of alcohol turning the white of her hair into black char and her body convulsing under the agony of it. The flames were teeth that ate, ripping and tearing, into scars of other flames and her voice the shrill sound of death on the loose.

It looked, looked away. The door was closed and maybe I had enough left to make it.

Mickey Spillane did not emerge full-blown from a cultural vacuum, however; as was mentioned earlier, he is a descendant of Hammett and Chandler.

Since they are built up out of this texture of sexual provocation and masculine violence climaxed by the infliction of pain and death on the sexual object,

> Spillane's books are an extreme embodiment of the fear, hostility, and ambi-
> guity toward society and particularly toward women that are built into the
> hard-boiled detective formula. Where writers like Hammett and Chandler
> qualify the endemic aggression and sadism of this formula with a consid-
> erable degree of irony and complexity, Spillane's skill as a popular writer lies
> precisely in his ability to suppress characters and turns of plot that might con-
> fuse or enrich the essential emotional pattern, and in his capacity to invent
> incidents like the ritual striptease killing of *I, the Jury* that embody the central
> emotional themes of the hard-boiled formula with primitive and vivid direct-
> ness. | JOHN CAWELTI, *Adventure, Mystery, and Romance.*

Mike Hammer, then is the apotheosis of the McCarthyite hero, a combination lone avenger and grim reaper. He lives in a black-and-white world
untainted by neurosis-inducing ambiguities and constraints on behavior.
It is a world filled with evil individuals and conspiracies, yet one in which
that evil can be purged through the quick and efficient use of violence. John
Cawelti has compared the almost hysterical crusading tone of Spillane's
works with the popular evangelical religious tradition of America, and comments that his "brutal redeemer Mike Hammer is the agonized but final
outcry of the evangelistic subculture of rural America about to be swallowed
up in the pluralistic, cosmopolitan world of the cities."

IV. THE GENERIC/AUTEURIST CONTEXT

Of all the impassioned responses to the perceived fascistic tendencies of
Spillane's fiction and the world view to which it was linked, Robert Aldrich's
film version of *Kiss Me Deadly* is perhaps the most devastatingly deft. Part
satire, part critique of a McCarthy-suffused society, its under-appreciation
in its own time was a reflection of the inability of contemporary critics
(who for the most part were hamstrung by an aesthetically elitist point of
view privileging "high" culture at the expense of "popular" culture) to see
past the Spillane connection—the pulpy, formulaic, violent subject matter.
In addition, the film's status as a project of the commercial Hollywood
industry marked it, according to those same elitist critical standards, as
fundamentally "unserious." It is true enough that *Kiss Me Deadly* is, in
many ways, the culmination of the *film noir* tradition and of Hollywood's
version of the hard-boiled detective melodrama. This point of closure—or
self-immolation—is reached in this particular film because implicit in

Deadly's narrative and thematic thrust is the idea that the *noir* and hard-boiled traditions have become anachronisms in the schizoid, hyper-tense world of the fifties.

> The genre's standard equipment seems beside the point in an era of nuclear hazard. The explosions at the end of the film make all that has preceded—the "mystery," the tough action, the investigation, the gangster/crime and private eye film's entire sign system—meaningless. *Kiss Me Deadly* is a thesis film about the "great whatsit" and the human desperation it creates. | JACK SHADOIAN, *Dreams and Dead Ends.*

These traditions therefore serve as points of departure in *Kiss Me Deadly*, but it is the deliberate violation of the conventions of the *noir* and hard-boiled formulas. As George Robinson has suggested,

> Aldrich's best '50s films . . . present initially ordinary genre situations, guide the audience through the expected reactions that the genre has conditioned them to, and then exposes a new piece of information which destroys the set of assumptions under which the audience has been operating, reverses the moral field of the work, and tears the genre itself asunder. These revelations serve to hold a mirror to the audience, forcing them to see their darkest impulses, and shattering their most foolishly cherished beliefs.

As a result, *Kiss Me Deadly* is an incredibly angry, overheated film; the white-hot apocalypse that ends it is the only logical climax, given that *Deadly* was specifically intended by Aldrich and screenwriter A. I. Bezzcrides as a metaphorical (and very cynical) representation of what they saw as a society careening headlong toward its own destruction (and with the potential to take the rest of the world with it).

> I want to depict my utter contempt and loathing . . . for the cynical, fascistic private eye, Mike Hammer. . . . Perhaps that is why it did not do as well at the box-office as the other Mickey Spillane films, which made a sort of anti-hero out of him. The public probably wants that . . . people in this country chose not to take it seriously. They didn't think the parallels were pertinent. They didn't think we were embarked on a political/social course that says any ends justify the means. | RICHARD COMBS, *Robert Aldrich.*

An aura of romantic fatalism is of course central to the *noir*/hard-boiled ethos, reflecting a generally pessimistic view of the capability and likelihood of man to take control of his own destiny. In most *noir* films, this bleak outlook is tempered somewhat by a noble gesture on the part of the hero which enables him to affirm his ultimate humanity, to find, for a moment at least, his niche in the world. *Kiss Me Deadly*, though, contains no such affirmation; its pessimism is absolute and uncompromising and is supported by the film's constellation of characters and narrative situations, which again are derived from the *noir*/hard-boiled tradition but which here move to and beyond the outer limits of generic possibility.

Ralph Meeker's Mike Hammer is at the center of most of *Deadly*'s frenzied activity, but we as viewers do not necessarily view events from his perspective, a fairly audacious departure from the first-person norm of private eye fiction and films. Aldrich, in fact, encourages us very early in the proceedings to distance ourselves at least part of the time from Hammer, to view his character and actions (and their implications) *analytically*, and not to accept him at face value. When he grudgingly consents to give a ride to Christina (Cloris Leachman), a beautiful escapee from "the laughing house," she quickly establishes that she isn't crazy through enigmatic suggestions that "they" detained her at the asylum because she was in possession of certain "information," and by adroitly dissecting Hammer's personality.

Christina: You have only one real, lasting love.

Mike: Who could that be?

Christina: You. You're one of those self-indulgent males who thinks about nothing but his clothes, his car, himself. Bet you do pushups every morning just to keep your belly hard.

Mike: You against good health or something?

Christina: I could tolerate flabby muscles in a man if it would make him more friendly. . . . You're the kind of a person who never gives in a relationship, who only takes. Ah, woman—the incomplete sex. And what does she need to complete her? Why, man, of course. Wonderful man.

This brief exchange telegraphs to the audience a highly ambiguous image of Hammer that reverberates through and is fleshed out by the rest of the film. Hammer, it turns out, is precisely the "cheap bedroom dick" he (and every movie private detective) is accused of being. It turns out that he thrives on divorce business (which more hard-boiled detectives such as

Chandler's Philip Marlowe customarily reject as a violation of their personal integrity and the private eye's code of honor), turning his beautiful secretary Velda loose on adultery-minded husbands in order to get the goods on them. Aldrich also uses specific strategies of cutting and framing to emphasize the sadistic streak in Hammer's personality. After the detective beats the beejesus out of a thug who has been following him (finally throwing him down the longest flight of steps since *The Battleship Potemkin*), there is a cut to Hammer's approving leer as the bad guy bounces his way to oblivion. A similar strategy is used later in the film, when Hammer pries a key out of the possession of a sleazy morgue attendant by slamming the man's hand in a desk drawer. Aldrich cuts three times here from a close-up of the attendant's porcine features as he seems like, well, a stuck pig, to a three-quarter profile close-up of Hammer grinning at the man's pain. It therefore becomes increasingly difficult as the film progresses to identify with Hammer, as Aldrich relentlessly strips his character of all the conventional positive attributes of the hard-boiled hero.

Ironically, though, Hammer's amorality and physical ruthlessness has perversely enabled him to attain a much higher standard of living than is customary for movie detectives, who always seem to hole up in shabby offices located in run-down neighborhoods. Hammer drives an expensive sports car and lives in a plush contemporary apartment full of the trappings of the fifties' affluent consumer society. It is all very "tasteful," but it is also utterly sterile; we see no personal items lying around, nothing at all idiosyncratic that would indicate the presence of a sentient human being. He even has an electronic device to answer his telephone for him.

Aldrich here seems to be indicting the mindless middle-class materialism rampant in affluent postwar America; Hammer's total self-absorption simply marks him as the ultimate and ideal (for the needs of corporate interests) consumer. His lack of humanity is made even more apparent when we later see the now-dead Christina's apartment. "She fixed it up to suit herself," says the building superintendent, and the room we see is a bit dishevelled but definitely lived in, filled with books, older, representational paintings, classical music, and a bird cage (the bird too is ominously dead, however). Here as elsewhere in *Kiss Me Deadly* the garnishments of high culture represent a dissipated vision of a better world, a world trampled by greedy philistines like Mike Hammer, who at one point prods information out of a down-at-the-heels opera tenor by snapping in half one of the man's priceless recordings, and perverted by erudite gangsters like Dr. Soberin,

who offers a steady stream of references to classical mythology as he tortures and murders his way to the Great Whatsit, the film's unimaginably
lethal atomic McGuffin. It is as Jack Shadoian has suggested: "*Kiss Me Deadly*
is a sinister evocation of a leisured, acquisitive society that is cankered
beneath its show of cultured possessions, its hypocritical and skin-deep
appreciation of art and beauty."

In a generic sense, Lily Carver functions as the film's designated *femme
noir*: she is a ruthless, amoral black widow bent on snaring Mike Hammer
in her web. But again Aldrich ups the ante, as Carver is sicker, weirder, and
more deeply depraved than any of her formulaic antecedents. She is inca-
pable of passion or indeed any emotion; in this sense, of all the film's women
she is ironically the best match for Hammer. But Mike (and the viewer) is
instinctively repelled by her twitchily neurotic mannerisms and her whiney
voice. She is rootless, drifting from Christina's apartment to a furnished
room to Mike's apartment without so much as a toothbrush to anchor her
anywhere. She borrows clothes from Velda and, finally, even her supposed
identity is revealed as a sham. Her twin goals in life are an unfocused search
for the *Great Whatsit* (though she doesn't know what it is, when Dr. Soberin
tries to warn her of the consequences of opening this atomic age Pandora's
box, Carver's response is a terse "I want half" and a bullet in Soberin's belly)
and an apparently unconscious need to obliterate emotion, as is suggested
by this exchange in Carver's seedy flat:

Hammer: The bird in the cage—what happened to it?
Carver: It was a nice bird. It used to eat out of my hand.
Hammer: It died. Why'd you let it die?
Carver: It reminded me of her [Christina] every time it sang.

The world of *Kiss Me Deadly* is one in which emotion and personal commitment have been radically devolved. The characters move through the
film in a numb, greed-induced trance (the exceptions are Christina and
Nick, who, of course, don't last long); status and relative power are determined here in terms of physical muscle and animal cunning. Mike Hammer's inability to feel normal human emotions ultimately renders him vulnerable to the demons of the modern world, simply because he is neither
strong or cunning enough to effectively combat (or even comprehend) the
evil aligned against him. The cinematic and literary private detective ordinarily relies heavily on his own intuition as a behavioral guide, and those

intuitive decisions are arrived at through close personal contact with the people involved in the case in question. The range of Hammer's native private-eye intuition is extremely truncated, however, as his deliberate and total self-centeredness effectively deprives him of the ability to react properly to any situation with ramifications beyond his extremely narrow range of personal interests. As a result, *Kiss Me Deadly* works as a case history of Hammer's progressive impotence in the face of unimaginably (for him) sinister forces, until the detective's complacent, childish sneer is erased by worldly-wise cop Pat Chambers's invocation of the "magic" words: "Manhattan Project, Los Alamos, Trinity." As George Robinson says, "[T]wo-thirds of the way into the film, [Aldrich] cuts the ground out from under Hammer and the audience, revealing that Hammer has been manipulated by forces superior to him, beyond his comprehension." Hammer's only response is a lame "I didn't know," and the rest of the film details his complete inability to prevent the chain of events he has helped put in motion from dovetailing to a mind-boggling calamitous climax. There is no narrative closure in *Kiss Me Deadly*; rather, the literally explosive implications of its ending rain accusatory fallout over an entire society. This is, as usual in Aldrich films, a world of victims and victimizers, and good intentions are no defense against a bullet in the gut or nuclear obliteration.

Visually, Aldrich suggests Hammer's ultimately fatal vulnerability quite early in the film. Before he has become inextricably caught up in the film's net of conspiracy, Hammer receives a telephone call from Velda in his apartment in which she vaguely intimates the presence of danger. Aldrich cuts here from a medium shot of Hammer from a perspective inside the apartment to a longer shot in which Hammer is seen from the *outside* of his building, through his living room window. The impression of surveillance is unmistakable; Aldrich then cuts to an over-the-shoulder shot of Hammer looking down on the busy street below, where he sees nothing at all unusual. He senses the presence of something threatening, but its very intangibility renders Hammer powerless to defend himself against it. Paranoia thus quickly becomes a normal condition of existence in the world of *Kiss Me Deadly*. Velda later characterizes the nature of the film's evil, externalizing it as much as it is ever likely to be: "'They'—a wonderful word. And who are 'they'? 'They' are the nameless ones who kill people for the *Great Whatsit*. Does it exist? Who cares? Everyone everywhere is so involved in the fruitless search—for what?" Velda's last words here are doubly ambiguous: they are not necessarily phrased interrogatively, giving the apparently intangible "what" a spectral physicality. The suggestion seems to be that the true locus of evil floats freely between man's conscious and unconscious minds, and the evil we are able to see in the world is simply an externalized reflection of fundamentally internal forces.

Kiss Me Deadly is in general one of the most visually stylized films in the history of the American cinema. Its Wellesian visual hyperbole—including an extensive use of deep focus composition, dark, high-contrast *noir* lighting colliding from scene to scene with bright low-contrast, television-style lighting, exaggerated high and low camera angles, frequently bizarre point-of-view shots (including one from the inside of a body locker at the morgue, at the end of which the door slammed shut on the viewer's nose)— complements perfectly the film's chaotic narrative and overheated verbal imagery. It is a disturbingly accurate rendering of a society gone mad, a paradoxically "realistic" rendering of a surreal world.

Kiss Me Deadly, then, is a dark, savagely, bitterly funny film about the end of the world. The conventions of the *noir*/hard-boiled formulas provide the foundation for the narrative; Aldrich simply stretches those conventions to the breaking point and then beyond it, until they finally snap before our eyes. In its time, the film was a metaphorical reaction against both Eisenhower era materialism and complacency and McCarthyite paranoia; the film brilliantly conveys the idea that these apparently mutually exclusive world views are but opposite sides of the same grim coin.

——

STEVE FORE

VOL. 16, NO. 3
MAY 2, 1979

Ulzana's Raid (1972)

DIRECTED BY ROBERT ALDRICH

In the following discussion of *Ulzana's Raid*, plot details are revealed that are possibly more effective when encountered by surprise. Therefore, if you have not seen *Ulzana's Raid* before, we recommend you do not read these notes until after the film.

Like Godard's *Le Petit Soldat*, *Ulzana's Raid* is that rarest of birds: a film about an unpopular war (Indian or Vietnamese) which refuses simply to take the easy way out of crying injustice, but tries instead to unravel cause and effect. Shattering the long-established complacency of the Western, where Indians are almost invariably divided into pesky varmints or noble savages, Aldrich and Alan Sharp are decidedly uncomplacent in presenting them as both at the same time. Ulzana, whose raid is uncomfortably reminiscent in its military precision of a smaller-scale version of all those cavalry sorties which once cleared Indian lands for white settlers, is a barbarian who must undoubtedly be stopped; yet who are *we*, the film simultaneously wonders, to assume the absolute moral right to define barbarism? | TOM MILNE, *Robert Aldrich.*

Ulzana's Raid is, fundamentally, a Dark Ages Western. It is penetrated by mystery—the mystery, superstitions and rituals, both Christian and Apache, of two mutually hostile cultures—and by fear—the civilized fear of imminent death and torture at the hands of savages, and the lonely fear of solitude and defenselessness in the wilderness. It catches white-Indian relations at a retarded stage where the whites rested in 19th century Christian-missionary righteousness, and the dark skinned natives could be envisioned as manifesting the dark side, the subdued side, of civilization—the conquered inclination toward evil. Ruled by this obscurantist attitude, *Ulzana's Raid* turns into a sort of horror Western. | DUNCAN SHEPHERD, *Cinema*, Spring 1973.

The United States was not going into Vietnam merely for crass power objectives, but for the salvation of the Vietnamese, who, like the majority of mankind, lived in poverty and ignorance. The fight against Communism demanded not only military power and determination, but all the prowess of an advanced industrial society and the generosity of a nation that led the world in its search for peace, prosperity, and freedom. | FRANCES FITZGERALD, *Fire in the Lake*.

Nowadays, we don't want to be removed from our heritages, but we do view them differently. Whereas we used to be able to do camp and call it a homage or a goof on this or a spoof on that, you can't even use those words anymore. We need a new word for whatever we are doing now. It's a little more rebellious. It's like taking the old genres, the old horses, and baring all the nerves. It's different. It's angrier in a way. On the surface, it's lighter and funnier and crazier. People get off on it in so many ways. But really, underneath it all there's more anger than there was in the '60s preachy kind of, "here's the answer." Nobody's even trying to say, well here's the problem. | GEORGE ROMERO, Director (*Night of the Living Dead, Dawn of the Dead*).

Lieutenant: My father believes it's a lack of Christian feeling toward the Indian that's the root of our problem with them.
Major: From a pulpit in Philadelphia, that's an easy mistake to make. | From *Ulzana's Raid*

Just as the American dream exploded in the 1960s, as official US policy sunk incredible numbers of lives and dollars into the self-willed mire of Southeast Asia, and as American cities and campuses burned as a domestic reflection of that foreign war, so too did the Western film genre fragment into multiple ideological camps. This in itself is not particularly surprising—the Western is the American literary formula most directly concerned with interpreting and, until recently, with justifying the meaning and rationale of traditional American values. As John Cawelti has put it,

> The classic Westerns of the 1940s and 1950s depended on and reaffirmed for us the traditional American view that violence was the fault of evil and corrupt men; good men might be forced to use it in purging society of corruption, but this would lead to a regenerated social order. With the fading of this hope and the growing sense of danger from personal and collective violence in our society, Americans have had to come to some kind of emotional terms with an unregenerate world.

Thus, the American Western has, of late, made tentative movements in several different directions in an attempt to cope with current realities, and each of these mutant strains has as its basis the revision or complete disposal of conventional American beliefs. Most strikingly, there are Sam Peckinpah's nihilistic eulogies for the demise of the rugged individual in a bottomlessly corrupt society, in films like *The Wild Bunch, Junior Bonner, The Getaway* and *Convoy*. Other recent revisionist Westerns have offered drastically-altered interpretations of legendary Western heroes (*The Great Northfield Minnesota Raid, The Hour of the Gun, Doc,* and *Butch Cassidy and the Sundance Kid*) or more "realistic" pictures of the West than are found in the traditional mythology (*Will Penny, Bad Company,* and *McCabe and Mrs. Miller*). In *The Missouri Breaks* the genre itself (and by extension American society) is declared dead, a proposition that has yet to be proved or disproved. In any case, the operative strategy in most of these films is aimed at dragging the Western formula into line with the prevalent attitudes of the cynical, myth-denying seventies. There is a militant denial of generic convention; heroes become schlemiels and neurotics, traditional codes of honor are both anachronistic and a threat to life and limb, and civilization itself becomes the enemy.

Then there is Robert Aldrich's *Ulzana's Raid*, the only Western in recent memory that manages to construct a revisionist history almost totally within the framework of the traditional Western formula. It is unconcerned with applying a contemporary perspective to post-Civil War Arizona;

Indian society is not romantically celebrated as an alternative culture infinitely preferable to a terminally corrupt white civilization (as in *Little Big Man*), nor is the cavalry troop a collection of psychotic, bloodthirsty imperialists.

Instead, *Ulzana's Raid* functions both as a surprisingly subtle (considering Aldrich's alternately celebrated and vilified "hysterical" narrative and visual style) political parable, and as a visceral, at times horrific, adventure story. This is mainly because Robert Aldrich is one of the most adept and imaginative manipulators of genre in the history of American film. Aldrich never attempts to deny or negate generic convention. Rather, as George Robinson has pointed out, Aldrich's best films

> present initially ordinary genre situations, guide the audience through the expected reactions that the genre has conditioned them to, and then exposes a new piece of information which destroys the set of assumptions under which the audience has been operating, reverses the moral field of the work, and tears the genre itself asunder. These revelations serve to hold a mirror to the audience, forcing them to see their darkest impulses, and shattering their most foolishly cherished beliefs. As a result, Aldrich's best films . . . are among the most complete denunciations of the American Dream and its Dreamers ever committed to celluloid.

Thus, *Ulzana* at first looks almost like one of John Ford's cavalry Westerns, with stereotypical characters (the shavetail lieutenant on his way to a rite of passage; the careerist, by-the-bank sergeant; the grizzled, buckskin-clad scout) and an archetypal situation involving marauding Indians whose rebellious behavior must be curbed for the good of the encroaching white civilization. The cavalry troop departs the fort in pursuit of Ulzana's raiders to the strains of a jaunty military tune, and the settlers threatened by Ulzana display the properly stoic pioneer spirit and courage.

Beneath the surface of this conventional expository material, however, runs a current of disturbance brought on by the increasing obviousness that nobody really knows what Ulzana and his warriors might be up to. The young Lieutenant Debuin sees the pursuit of the Indians as an adventure, an opportunity to test himself as a man. The major reacts as the bureaucrat he is—he simply wants Ulzana arrested and punished according to the standards of white man's justice (once, of course, Ulzana's "probably intentions" are determined). The trail-wise scout McIntosh bluntly states that it is absurd to expect Ulzana to play by the white man's rules, that the raiding party's "probable intention is to burn, maim, torture, rape, and murder." This frightening premise is supported by a chorus of soldiers and settlers who scurry about the periphery of the narrative expressing a foreboding bordering on sheer terror at the possibility of an encounter with the Apaches.

This undercurrent explodes into the foreground of the film when Ulzana and his warriors come upon the settler woman and her son being escorted to the fort by a single trooper. The Indians attack, whooping and yelling in the great *Stagecoach* tradition, and the soldier starts to gallop away, abandoning the woman and child. She begins to scream, and the soldier turns and rides back toward the settlers' wagon. There is a close up of the woman expressing joy and relief at the return of her protector, but it is here that Aldrich puts in the zinger. All conventional patterns of behavior ever established in the Western formula are suddenly and irrevocably destroyed as the soldier puts a bullet through the woman's forehead. He then tries to escape with the boy, but failing that, given a last chance to defend himself, to die "honorably," opts instead to shoot himself. The Apaches then mutilate the trooper's body in a rivetingly gruesome fashion. This is an incredibly disturbing, terrifying sequence of events, both because of the extreme violence and because of the shattering of generic convention that has taken place. Then, when McIntosh subsequently and accurately reconstructs the scenario for the horrified Lt. Debuin and expresses his approval of the trooper's actions (the Indians would have tortured the woman and the soldier), it becomes completely clear that *Ulzana's Raid* is concerned not just with scrutinizing and criticizing the conventions of the Western genre but, even more importantly, with forcing the viewer to reconsider the viability of Western, Christian-oriented civilization itself in the totally alien and hostile—but recognizable and familiar—universe of the film.

Seen in this light, *Ulzana's Raid* is an obvious allegory of American experiences in Vietnam. Using the Western genre as the perfectly appropriate embodiment of traditional American values, Aldrich explores our most devastating cultural weaknesses, the xenophobia and the (often benign and unconscious) institutionalized racism that the Vietnamese war exposed like an open wound, and which movies like *The Deer Hunter* simply help to perpetuate. *Ulzana* demonstrates that America's cultural chauvinism is its tragic flaw and its Achilles's heel; as in Vietnam, *nobody* really wins, and the very concept of victory becomes provisional, illusory and inherently pyrrhic. As Ed Lowry has suggested,

> With *Ulzana's Raid*, the Western (and perhaps, with it, the American consciousness) seems ready to accept Western settlement as an act of colonization. The white man has moved his family and his army into a decidedly *foreign* country, and Ulzana's band conducts its own brand of guerrilla warfare which resolutely withstands West Point tactics and the attempts of the colonizers to understand it.

It is this sense of a totally alien presence that is at the heart of the film's narrative momentum, a growing dread of a sudden, total and devastatingly incomprehensible challenge to traditional American values. *Ulzana's Raid* makes an unexpected stylistic and thematic connection here with recent American "exploitation" horror films such as *The Texas Chainsaw Massacre*, *The Hills Have Eyes*, *Eaten Alive*, and *Night of the Living Dead*. Like these films, *Ulzana* is concerned with the implications of existence in an American society profoundly influenced and affected by a decade of escalating horror in Southeast Asia as witnessed by millions of us on the evening news. It is a suddenly and completely malevolent world that confronts the protagonists of both *Ulzana* and *Chainsaw*, a nightmare world dominated by the constant threat of unimaginably brutal and apparently senseless violence and death (for this reason, *Ulzana's Raid* has to be one of the few truly claustrophobic Westerns). The enemy in this world is not something or someone to be *faced* in a neatly-organized final showdown. He is instead scarcely seen at all, often not until the very moment he swoops down on an intended victim. This is an enemy whose motivations simply cannot be comprehended within a traditional Judeo-Christian value structure—he is both unknown and unknowable. Ulzana's steamrolling destruction of Rukeyser's farm vividly demonstrates this cultural gap. The frightened but admirably brave immigrant farmer shouts epithets at the Indians from his barricaded house: "All right, you drunk fellas! . . . You don't get this farm away from me!" But Ulzana and his warriors are not stereotypically comic drunken savages, nor do they care in the least about taking Rukeyser's farm. They simply want to kill and destroy for reasons unfathomable to the white mind, and in this case they do so by ironically adapting a white cultural symbol/cliché (the last-minute cavalry rescue) to their own uses.

Through the character of the scout McIntosh, Aldrich suggests that the only way to deal with this threat is to try to stay a jump ahead of it and to altogether abandon considerations of ideology. Asked why he doesn't hate the Apaches for their atrocities, McIntosh replies, "Be like hatin' the desert 'cause there ain't no water in it. I can get by just bein' plenty scared of them." This is a healthy attitude to assume because the violence promised and visited upon each of Ulzana's victims is, to the Apache's white pursuers, the most salient aspect of the alien, incomprehensible culture he represents. The violence in *Ulzana's Raid* is easily the most extreme, explicit and gruesomely suggestive ever depicted in an American film outside of that in the aforementioned "exploitation" horror films. But Robert Aldrich has rarely taken a romanticized view of violence in his films; the violence of *Ulzana* is heightened but not substantially different from its use in earlier Aldrich films such as *Kiss Me Deadly, Attack!, Ten Seconds to Hell* and *The Dirty Dozen*. There are no spiritual, slow motion dances of death here as in *The Wild Bunch* or *Bonnie and Clyde*, no cathartic vengeance as in *Dirty Harry*. There is is no sense of release in Aldrich's violence, only the absolute, irredeemable end. The violence is graphic, but it takes place in real time, and the reactions of living witnesses are as important as the violent acts themselves because these reactions represent the clash of culture against culture.

The chief witness and at-large representative of Western civilization in *Ulzana's Raid* is Lt. Debuin, whose exclamations of "Oh, my God!" and "Sweet Jesus!" upon the discovery of another of Ulzana's horribly mutilated victims, speak volumes, especially since Debuin's father is a minister. It is with bitter and unintended irony that Debuin takes the Lord's name in vain under these circumstances, as the Lieutenant is in the process of discovering that his carefully-ordered Christian system of ethics is being rapidly dismembered by this encounter with a culture that he simply cannot fathom. Debuin is a typical Aldrich liberal; he is intelligent and well-intentioned but hopelessly naive and inexperienced, which in this hostile world is a virtual death sentence for him and the men under his command. He sincerely tries to understand Ulzana's activities through his questioning of the enigmatic Apache scout Ke-ni-tay (no doubt so that he can restore order to his own value structure by pitying the poor savage), but the Indian is only able to speak from his side of the cultural barrier. He speaks of the smells of dogs and women and of killing in order to take a man's "power," but Debuin is just not able to expand his frame of reference to encompass Ke-ni-tay's Apache philosophy. The Lieutenant's world view is further scrambled when white troopers mutilate the body of a dead Apache (reflexive blood-lust and racist remarks are the only outlets available for the white soldiers—eventually, even for Debuin—frustrated and terrified by Ulzana's apparently senseless carnage). "What bothers you, Lieutenant," says McIntosh, "is that you don't like to think of white men behavin' like Indians. Kinda confuses the issue, don't it?"

Ulzana himself remains a shadowy figure right to the end of the film, in keeping with the totally alien otherness of the culture he represents. Aldrich successfully avoids judging the Apache culture both by balancing the Indians' atrocities with the blind racist brutality of the white, and by making Ke-ni-tay, whose own behavioral motivations are as mysterious as Ulzana's, the real hero of the film. Ke-ni-tay is much more visible than Ulzana, but he remains as culturally impenetrable as the renegade Apache. His reasons for remaining loyal to the white man's army are as vague as Ulzana's reasons for killing, and as a result Ke-ni-tay is at first patronized and then increasingly hated and feared by Lt. Debuin. Aldrich meanwhile manages to suggest, without becoming overly anthropological about it, that Ulzana's actions, brutal as they are by white standards, are nonetheless a valid means of expression within his own culture. There is, says Aldrich, a rational mind at work here; Ulzana goes out on his raid in order to regain the self-respect denied him by prolonged confinement on the white man's reservation. Even more surprisingly, familial ties are as important to Ulzana, it seems, as they are to the white civilization that considers him an anarchistic savage. He finally gives up his life upon receiving from Ke-ni-tay the news of his son's death. Ulzana dies as he lived, with dignity and isolated from the alien white man's society.

Ulzana's Raid ends with the suggestion that Lt. Debuin may yet live long enough to grow up in this dangerous world. The dying McIntosh has provided him with a suitable role model—the old scout has not survived the final battle, but, as Robert Aldrich himself has said, "Since it's impossible to 'win' everything in life, whether you're a football player, a soldier, or a politician, your interior self-esteem comes out of how hard you *try* to win— the degree of your struggle." Faced with McIntosh's refusal to make the long and painful journey back to the fort and his demand to be left to die in the way of his choosing (as Ulzana has done), Debuin takes a final stab at the old morality: "It's not Christian," he pleads. "That's right, Lieutenant," replies the weary McIntosh, "It's not."

———

STEVE FORE

HISTORICAL BACKGROUND

Films exist with only a casual connection to historical realities. Even contemporary stories are at best impressionistic. For one to get angry at a film for not being accurate is ludicrous. This is especially true in light of the arguments that historians will get into over an event. There have been numerous historical revisionist movements over many events from Custer to the causes of the Civil War, from the Depression to the American Revolution. The tides shift back and forth as interpretations of the facts change and as the "facts" themselves change. To expect films, because of their mimetic nature, to attain some kind of "truth" is not only foolish but utopian.

Often the best film *about* a subject is historically the least accurate. We need only Pirandello, Beckett, Sartre and John Ford to remind us that history does not speak with one voice but many. Still the history from which a film derives can be interesting, if only for the distance it displays from the event. *Ulzana's Raid* takes its name from an event that occurred in 1885. In terms of the specific actions within the film, it is a fiction woven around a title, but in almost every other way the film is exceptionally faithful to the history and the times that it is about.

In December 1884 a new Indian agent was appointed to the San Carlos Reservation. As the result of tensions between the agent, the army and the Indians, on May 17, 1885, Geronimo and four other chiefs left the reservation with thirty-two warriors, eight grown boys and ninety-two women and children. The Indians made their way to Mexico killing scores of whites and Mexicans as they travelled. In four months of campaigning against them, the army killed six warriors, two women, and a child.

One of the renegades, Ulzana, crossed back across the border in November, travelling with ten other Indians. As they made their way up through Arizona they were discovered, and the army was soon on their trail. Ulzana and his men, however, would disperse and fade into the night, regrouping later and leaving the army confused. In late November the band began an attack on Fort Apache. On the way there they killed two settlers. Two days after these killings, November 26, they descended on the White Mountain Apache village near the fort and killed 12 reservation Indians. One of their number was killed.

During the next four weeks, Ulzana and the remaining nine warriors travelled close to 1,200 miles through Arizona and New Mexico before slipping back over the border into Mexico. They killed 38 persons, they stole, rode and wore out over two hundred horses and mules, and they tied up thousands of soldiers in their pursuit. At least twice they were completely dismounted and they were always being chased. Yet they lost only the one man at the White Mountain Apache village and they caused General Crook to completely reorganize the whole system and strategy of his troops in the area.

It should be noted that the above is a summary of the events based on the writings of a historian from the 1930s. The historical attitudes toward the raid may well have changed since then. Regardless of dates, names and places, however, the feelings of conflict, tension and misunderstanding between two peoples, so clearly articulated in the film, is an historical reality that will not change.

———

LOUIS BLACK

VOL 9 NO. 2
OCTOBER 9, 1975

Forty Guns (1957)

DIRECTED AND PRODUCED BY SAMUEL FULLER

The themes of love and death, marriage and death, sex and violence, are given their most original and powerful treatment in *Forty Guns*. This is the Fuller movie about which it is hardest to write because more than any other it is pure experience, pure movie. From the opening sequence we are plunged into a world presented in terms of interacting images of animal energy and violation; the visual and aural rhythms of the opening sequence present the clash of two sexual drives, a mutual rape. As Jessica Drummond and her forty horsemen sweep past the Bonnell brothers in their wagon, hooves pound, dust swirls, horses rear and whinny, and the whole is tied together by a crucial phallic crane shot as the wagon appears to plunge up between the two lines of horses. Then the camera sinks until it is we, the audience, who are tearing straight into the turmoil. Out of this violent clash comes the intimate connection in Fuller's work, as in American society, between sex and violence, and in particular between sex and guns, the ultimate expression of frontier virility. | NICHOLAS GARNHAM, *Samuel Fuller*

I couldn't use my original ending. I was asked to change it, and I changed it. The ending I originally shot was a powerful ending. I had Sullivan facing the killer, the young brother of Stanwyck. I had him grab Stanwyck and hold her in front of him. He knew he had Sullivan in a spot. I had him defy Sullivan. And Sullivan kills Stanwyck. Then he kills the boy and walks away. That was the end of the picture.

I had to put in that line where Sullivan says that he aimed the bullet so that it wouldn't kill Stanwyck. She's alive in the end, and they're happy. A lot of people liked it, because they like to see the boy and the girl get together. I don't think that's important. . . .

It's a rough ending. I've seen so many pictures, from *High Noon* back, where the heavy grabs the girl and holds her in front of him, putting the hero in a hell of an embarrassing situation. Always, at the last minutes, she pushes him away, and the hero kills him. I don't like that in any Western. It doesn't make sense. That's why I wanted Sullivan not only to shoot Stanwyck, which the studio thought was enough, but to kill her. | SAMUEL FULLER, in *The Director's Event*

Samuel Fuller makes films like no other director. He may be the only living filmmaker who consciously and continually strives to speak to his audience first on a violently emotional, and only after that an intellectual level. Above all he wants the audience to react to what he is showing them. Fuller can never forget his audience, so every move is designed to gain a reaction, to shock the viewer into examining whatever relationship Fuller has put on the screen. Violence, put into a context where it is no longer conventionalized, is the tool he usually uses to shock us. Because of this strategy, he is often dismissed by critics for being crude and obvious in his thought and effects, of playing on our base emotions. In other words, Fuller is accused of being a reactionary hack who exploits, or at best fails to understand, the violent material he uses. His films are much more complex than his critics assume. Their simplicity, which the critics quarrel with, is an integral part of his artistic method.

Fuller's work is simple and straightforward because that is the most effective way that he can get his message across. His world and characters are structured so that only a predetermined reading is possible. His protagonists are never "alive" in the way characters in Renoir, Ozu, or Ford's works seem to live independently of the film. Fuller's characters have an obviously symbolic side which continually influences our reaction to them. He uses such a method because he is a moralist and consequently a polemicist. He once said in the *New York Times*, "I think I am personally more interested in what I have to say in my pictures, something I want to say and get it off my chest, not just in trying to make a buck." Most of what he wants to say concerns the treacherousness of life, society, people and the need to accept the fact that actions have real consequences.

In one of Sam Peckinpah's television shows, Brian Keith knees an Englishman in the groin. The Englishman gasps that that is against the rules, to which Keith yells back, "It's not a game!" Such a concept lies at the heart of all of Fuller's work. Many of his films are an attempt to break through the patina of falseness, the tone of unreality, which lies over the conventions of Hollywood genres. Both *The Steel Helmet* and *Fixed Bayonets* reveal the messiness of war which the standard war film has romanticized. *Dead Pigeon on Beethoven Street* revises the image of the private-eye *and* the way the genre was transformed by the New Wave films, particularly in *Breathless*. In *Forty Guns*, he attempts to de-romanticize the Western, but succeeds only to a certain extent.

Forty Guns is an inversion of the values which we have come to expect in the Western genre. Instead of riding into town on horses, the Bonnell brothers (obviously modeled on the Earps) travel in a buckboard. All through the film Griff rides in it, even when he is going to arrest his brother's killer. The connotations of such a choice (buckboard = town + civilization; horse = freedom + individuality + rootlessness) are subconsciously experienced by the audience so that we feel that something is wrong when Griff drives the buckboard. Events become even more dissonant for the audience when Griff goes into the Marshall's office and immediately has a gun stuck in his back. Chisum, the Marshall, a friend of Griff's who is losing his sight, is in trouble and expects Griff to help him. Instead Griff advises him to run, since it is better to be alive and blind than dead, and smilingly says he will not help because it is not his business. There are other such unconventional moments throughout the film, as when Griff has Wes cover him with a rifle whenever he is about to face anyone. They all contradict our idea of the Western hero.

If Griff does not act the way we have been led to expect a hero to act, then Jessica totally challenges our idea of the Western heroine. Traditionally women in Westerns are either whores or virgins. While they exercise some sexual control, that aspect is usually played down (if the virgin), or burlesqued (if the whore), e.g., compare Clementine and Chihuahua in *My*

Darling Clementine. Instead, women exert a moral, passive control over the men and woe to her who attempts to have an active voice, for she usually winds up dead. Jessica, though, is presented in an overtly domineering and sexual way. Dressed all in black on a white stallion, she comes sweeping across the countryside followed by her forty docile gunmen. Her domination of the men who surround her is based on a sexual domination, as with the Sheriff. Everyone desires her, but she has taken over the father's position (she wears the pants, sits at the head of the table, rides at the head of a column of men) and needs no other phallus.

It is not only the inversion of values which interests Fuller. He also examines the relationship between violence and sex in the Western. Jessica can be seen as a dead woman, dressed all in black. Later, she acknowledges her love for Griff (the bringer of violence), and can wear a white blouse. At the end she is totally dressed in white. It is the violence embodied in Griff which awakens Jessica's sexual nature (as is seen when she wants to handle his pistol and taunts him with being afraid when he will not let her). Then there is Brockie, who goes throughout the countryside impregnating all the women, while at the same time unable to control his violent impulses in town. A connection is made between his need to shoot off his pistols and his need for orgasm with a girl (a point made when Jessica takes his pistols away after he shoots the Marshall—while she is *also* talking about his illegitimate children). There seems little difference to Brockie between sperm and bullets. When he shoots the Marshall, his face takes on a look of sexual excitement. The most obvious marriage of sex and violence is seen in the relationship between Wes and Louvenia, the gunsmith. They each use the terminology of guns to connote a sexual meaning. The merging of the two emotions is expressed in the famous shot of Wes looking at Louvenia through the barrel of a rifle. The camera zooms in on her face, then there is an immediate cut to the two of them kissing. The signification of a gun barrel, the zoom, and the kiss is obvious.

The implication is that the Western is based on a ground of sex and violence, and that neither seems complete without the other. That is the legacy of the Western, a genre in which violence lurks behind chivalry and sexuality resides within the instruments of death. That is why the ending of the film is so effective, because we are brought face to face with the end of a dream. When Griff shoots Jessica as Brockie holds her captive, all Brockie can do is stand there stunned for he has believed in the legend of the West, and it is the legend which gave justification for the violence. All Brockie can do is stand there and yell "I'm killed" as Griff kills him piece by piece. Griff knows that his life is more important than any rules, and with his shot he destroys a certain conception of the West forever.

However, *Forty Guns* is not a complete critique of the Western, for it has no context in which to be grounded. The fact that Fuller has inverted the expected values is not enough, for the film still remains tied to those same values. Partly, this problem is the result of the production company, which made Fuller tack on a happy ending (and it is obviously tacked on since it follows the only fade in the movie). More precisely, though, it is in the aspect of individualism that the film remains firmly tied to the genre. Griff is the hero, and there is nothing he does in the film which turns the audience against him, not even the shooting of Jessica, for it is followed by proof of his love for her when he loses his temper and kills Brockie slowly. In the same way, Jessica is the heroine and despite her castrating manner she quickly gives up everything for the love of Griff. It will take Godard and *Wind from the East* to show just what the individualist ethos in the Western subsumes. Maybe that is why *Forty Guns* seems the most schizoid of all of Fuller's films. His intentions are at odds with his use of the genre. Despite the confusions lying at the heart of the film (and the incoherence of the plot is a reflection of them), *Forty Guns* retains its emotional power to make us, the audience, experience what lies underneath the conventions we so glibly accept.

—

VALENTIN ALMENDAREZ

VOL. 9, NO. 4
DECEMBER 4, 1975

The Naked Kiss (1964)

DIRECTED, WRITTEN, AND PRODUCED BY SAMUEL FULLER

The Naked Kiss has style to burn. It has been directed to a fare-thee-well by Samuel Fuller, one of the liveliest, most visual-minded and cinematically knowledgeable filmmakers now working in the low-budget Hollywood grist mill. And its subject is downright ridiculous. . . . Patently absurd as the plot may be, Mr. Fuller has filmed it with flair, and he has drawn a richly amusing performance from Miss Towers. Stylish handling of sensational nonsense. Mr. Fuller's wild little movie has a decided edge. | EUGENE ARCHER, *New York Times*, October 29, 1964

Sam Fuller has come up with another meatball. Mr. Fuller likes to deal with harsh realities. This time out it's a blow-by-blow account of a prostitute (right, she has that proverbial heart of——). . . . [*The Naked Kiss*] is a mixture of the ugly and the sticky, larded with blunt designed-to-shock lines and situations all adding up to a mess of pretentious insanity. | ROBERT SALMAGGI, *New York Herald Tribune*, April 29, 1965

The Naked Kiss is not only one of Fuller's most important films but one of the key films of the sixties. Needless to say, the critical reaction in Britain and America has been almost total rejection. . . .

   The Naked Kiss is Fuller's most difficult film to come to grips with. It demands, for instance, that we come to terms with a millionaire who owns a twenty-five dollar tape recorder, and with a song-and-dance routine involving crippled children somewhere on the far side of *The Sound of Music*, but most of all it demands that we take Fuller seriously. | PHIL HARDY, *Samuel Fuller*

That *Naked Kiss*. And let he who is not a ghost say he has felt nothing. | MICHEL DELAHAYE, *Cahiers du Cinéma*, March 1966

Sam Fuller is almost unique among American low-budget film directors in that he also writes and produces most of his films. He is, thus, one of the few American filmmakers who can be called an *auteur* in the strictest sense of that word: a creator with the degree of control to make his films entirely his own. Fuller's unconventional and uniquely strange films seem to inspire the most extreme reactions in his audience. Those who hate him and detest everything he does are balanced by a group of equally impassioned admirers who would canonize Fuller, seating him at the right hand of Orson Welles. It is easy enough to reject Fuller's films for their lack of naturalism, their gut-punch sensationalism, and their seeming ludicrousness. But they possess a raw power and a decided "otherness" which makes it worth the while of any film enthusiast to try and discover just what Fuller is up to—if not out of curiosity for his ardent admirers, then at least for the fact that Fuller seems consistently capable of astonishing and, sometimes, of downright offending us.

   Fuller came to films from journalism, where, as a reporter, he was in first-hand contact with the seaminess, amorality, and weirdness which infest his films. In the first issue of *American Film*, Fuller writes about his experience in the news business:

Covering an execution . . . Told by a man who hacked his family to death with a meat cleaver on a Hudson River barge that he was sorry if he hurt them . . . Listening to a leaper's sex problems on a 30-foot ledge before he squashed a luckless passerby like a gnat . . . Accompanying a rookie cop from the 24th Precinct on a routine complaint to stumble over a slain body in a subterranean office . . . Successfully interviewing J. P. Morgan only to watch my copy destroyed by the City Editor because he knew J. P. never granted interviews . . . Using Sunday editions as bedsheets and blankets riding the rods with Depression displaced persons . . . Every newspaperman has such a Hellbox to draw from. Every newspaperman is a potential filmmaker.

And, of course, the implication is that those without such experiences can never make films about what life is "really" like.

Fuller's films have the impact, the immediacy, and the lack of subtlety of newspaper headlines (which, by the way, he uses frequently and strikingly throughout his films). Every word rings with importance, his characters speaking in terse colorful phrases or sometimes slipping into ridiculously flowery prose. In those areas in which most filmmakers would strive for flowery prose. In those areas in which most filmmakers would strive for verisimilitude, Fuller tends to schematize—to literalize abstractions and to bluntly state what others frequently work at keeping subtle. Characters are almost always known by single names: Kelly, Griff, Grant, Candy, Mac, Buff, Peanuts, Hatrack (just to name a few from *The Naked Kiss*). Fuller uses them as representative types, symbols, or objects, drawing us away from them while involving us in the action and emotion of the film with exciting and flamboyant images and bizarre camera setups and cutting techniques. Fuller is the cinema at its most visceral, appealing to our gut-level reactions to such things as the brutalization of women, the innocence of children, patriotism, perversion, sex, violence, and death. As Godard has Fuller say in *Pierrot Le Fou*, "The cinema is like a battleground. Love . . . hate . . . action . . . violence . . . death. In a word: emotion." Fuller demands only that we react—that we become excited or astonished, that we laugh uneasily, that we take offense. So, if you want to coast along with *The Naked Kiss*, to allow Fuller to shock and astonish you, perhaps you should wait until after the film to read the remainder of these notes in which I engage in still another reaction: an attempt at analysis.

I am not doing a sermon, but this picture is about a hooker who attacks, face to face, pious people. The naked kiss is the kiss of a perverted being. This is a picture about hypocrisy, falsity, and bigotry. | SAM FULLER, *New York Times Magazine*, February 28, 1965

I thought it would be very effective if a girl kills a saint and no one believes that the saint is really guilty of a horrible crime. That's the premise I wanted. | FULLER, in *The Director's Event*

Fuller infuses the objects, characters, and situations of *The Naked Kiss* with unique and personal significance, weaving them into a dense and frequently confusing complex of meanings. He seems to be creating new archetypal situations or at least revamping old archetypes to give them newly charged implications: the reformed prostitute who kills the perverted "saint"; the debauched, but still innocent, child who redeems the whore; the cohabitation of prostitute and "town virgin." The Naked Kiss is a signifier of Grant's perversion, a literalization of his psychological state; but it is a unique signifier which has value only within this particular film.

Fuller ascribes this kind of unique significance to a number of common objects and types. Playing children, everywhere present in the film, are blatantly symbolic, but Fuller gives them more significance than the simple innocence they usually represent. The children are redeemers (Kelly gains respectability by working with them; the little girl's testimony prevents Kelly from being charged with murder) and love objects (Kelly's work in the children's hospital is an outlet for her repressed compassion; Grant's pedophilia is an outlet for his repressed lusts). Miss Josephine's dress form, decorated with battle ribbons and topped with a helmet, is personified as "Charlie," a substitute for her fiancé killed in the war. "Charlie" later becomes Kelly's silent confidant as she makes her fateful decision to marry Grant, and, still later, serves in its original function as a fitting form for Kelly's wedding dress. The telephone, by which Kelly is to inform Grant she is leaving town, is transformed into the instrument by which she humiliates Griff, and later becomes the weapon with which she bludgeons Grant to death. There is also a kind of Oriental feeling of obligation between the men who fought together in Korea (a key to the Grant-Griff friendship, and the reason Griff gives money to the trouble-making brother of a fellow soldier), and the Oriental nature of the characters' obligations is underlined in Griff's statement that Kelly will be his *ichiban* ("Number One").

Each of these elements seems to be charged with meanings which contribute to the significance of the film. But it is as if Fuller is creating his own iconography which we must learn at the same time we are "reading" it. John Ford frequently creates complexes of meaning which are as rich and interesting, but within the established iconography and archetypes of the

Western, utilizing a kind of generic "shorthand" which is familiar to us. With Fuller, I frequently get the feeling I am watching a film in a genre with which I am unfamiliar, whose "shorthand" I am unable to understand. And, as confusing as the experience may be, it is also invigorating. Fuller seems to be creating from a source so personal that he often seems obscure. (Dare I compare it to *Finnegans Wake*?) It remains for some Fuller enthusiast to examine in detail this level of his films, as Nicholas Garnham has done rather generally in his book on Fuller by lumping all the director's films together.

> When I started the film as a shocker, the original impression I wanted was of a wonderful, almost dull, very, very ordinary love story: the poor girl from the wrong side of the tracks, the rich man who falls in love with her. Well I hate those kinds of stories. So I knew I was going to have fun the minute she finds him molesting the child. | FULLER, in *The Director's Event*

If there is a best way into the "meaning" of *The Naked Kiss*, it is probably through its dominant theme of illusion and reality. Opening with a direct cut into the middle of a violent, highly emotional fight, the film immediately captivates while challenging and astonishing us. We see Kelly overpower her pimp in a most "unfeminine" display of strength as her wig falls off to reveal her shining bald head. The credits appear across a closeup of her face as she replaces her wig and repairs her makeup, restoring her mask and reconstructing before our eyes the first shattered illusion (her "femininity") in a film devoted to shattered illusions.

Every character in the film hides behind such masks. Beneath Kelly's feminine attractions ("Enough to make a bulldog bust his chain," Griff comments) is a cold, tough, and violent human being, the result of her life as a prostitute. But Kelly's hardness is just another mask, a shield to protect her soft, compassionate, and romantic side. And even this is not the end, for Kelly's compassionate attitude toward the children at the hospital provides a cover for her sordid past, an opportunity to fulfill her dreams, and an escape from the work she decides to quit when she notices, in Griff's mirror, that her mask of feminine beauty has begun to crack. Griff is a respected police officer who runs a "clean" town, but he is anxious to pay Kelly for her services and happy to refer her to Candy's whorehouse across the river, where he seems to be a regular customer. There is even a suggestion that Griff regularly hangs around the bus stop to sample and refer to Candy the incoming beauties (as he does with Kelly) in a scene in which Hatrack, one of Candy's "bon-bon girls," reminds him that he met her under similar circumstances. Grant, Fuller's "saint," is spoken of as "society's most eligible bachelor," "a hard worker," whose "name is synonymous with charity," who saved Griff's life in Korea, and for whose great-grandfather the town is named Grantsville. Yet beneath this mask of culture hero lurks the most socially despicable of types—the child molester.

The characters are driven by drastically opposed impulses within themselves, which coexist without causing them too much anguish. Griff seems undisturbed by the conflict between his passion for sex and his repressive attitudes about keeping the town "clean." He is friendly to Kelly as long as she is a prostitute, but is enraged by her attempts to become something else, accusing her of being an evil influence on the children she works with. Kelly's first customer in Grantsville and the last "trick" of her career, Grant becomes her worst enemy. But Kelly is more than the bad girl with a heart of gold. She is a tough professional with a violent nature, slapping or physically assaulting almost every major character at some point during the film. At the same time, she is gently with the children and openly sincere with Grant. Both aspects of her character exist and function simultaneously (in order to save her friend Buff from prostitution, she furiously attacks Candy, the madame). Finally, there is no indication that Grant is not sincerely charitable, that he is not a hard worker, or that he was not a war hero. There is simply the fact that he is also a sexual deviant.

Kelly's real mistake is trusting in illusions when she should know better, surrendering so totally to her dreams that she is willing to forget the dirt that she (and Fuller) knows lies beneath all attractive surfaces. As a prostitute, she has been unable to remove her protective mask of hardness, to enjoy the romantic aspects of sex, to find expression for her love of Beethoven, Byron and Goethe (which she pronounces "Go-tha," indicating she has never discussed him with a fellow enthusiast). Kelly's attempts at respectability are surrounded with illusions: her sincere, but absurdly saccharine, conversation with Miss Josephine about the four angels who guard us when we sleep; the story she tells the crippled children in which they are able to walk and run; her romantic dream-vision inspired by Grant's films of Venice and his Beethoven recording. She is so captivated by the illusion and determined to grasp it ("Girls are always chasing dreams. Why shouldn't I have the right to catch mine?") that she refuses to acknowledge the sign of Grant's perversion: his Naked Kiss. At the end of the scene in which Grant first kisses her, Fuller pans to the still running projector which has been showing the scenes of Venice. Its lamp glares into the camera and we hear the flapping of the film on the finished reel as it continues to revolve, reminding us that those things which Kelly is reaching out for (and what we, in the movie theater, are watching) are merely illusions which, of course, cannot last forever.

When Kelly begins to follow in Miss Josephine's steps by confiding in "Charlie," we ought to recognize (as should Kelly) that she is withdrawing further and further from what she knows is real. But Fuller allows us to become so involved in Kelly's illusions that we share a good deal of her shock when she discovers Grant fondling the little girl. Fuller draws us in so effectively that we ignore the danger signs just as Kelly ignored the Naked Kiss. Kelly's fault is in knowing just how sick and dirty the world actually is and then allowing herself to begin living as if she did not. The false hope she conveys to the crippled children in her story expresses her own illusion— that if she believes hard enough her dreams will come true.

> When she does find out this man's secret, and she realizes that he has given her a Naked Kiss, she's shocked, and he's shocked that she's shocked. Since she's a hooker, he thought that she would understand why he likes little girls. Why should she be surprised? He just hit the wrong girl. I thought that was good copy. | FULLER, in The Director's Event

Discovered with the little girl, Grant becomes as open and honest with Kelly as she was with him in confessing her past. He confesses his deviance, and, furthermore, offers her a place in his dreams: "You live in my world and it will be an exciting world. My darling, our marriage will be a paradise. Because we're both abnormal." But Grant's dream of a life filled with delicious perversions is as illusory as Kelly's dreams of romance and normality. He assumes that her experience as a prostitute makes her receptive to his desires. "That's why I love you," he tells her. "You understand my sickness. You've been conditioned to people like me." Grant and Kelly view one another in accordance with their own dreams, casting themselves in fantasy roles and attributing qualities to one another which have no basis in fact. In her blindness, Kelly is moved by the fact that Grant proposes marriage even though she has confessed her past to him, when, in fact, it is her confession which motivates his proposal. Grant's misunderstanding of Kelly is just as severe. The kind of orgiastic "paradise" he offers her is exactly the kind of life she wishes to escape. Counselling Buff against prostitution, Kelly tells her, "You'll become a block of ice. Your world will become so warped that you'll hate all men—and you'll hate yourself. . . . " For Kelly, a normal life with a normal man seems just as exotic and attractive as Grant's dreams of perpetual orgy with a prostitute.

Kelly kills Grant, not because he is a menace to society, but because he has shattered her illusions. (She later admits to Griff that she had not thought of protecting the little girl.) It seems strictly a matter of chance that, when her violence erupted into murder, it was directed against a socially despicable character. Once the charges against her have been dropped, Kelly is told that she has become something of a town heroine. She bemusedly replies that they certainly put up monuments quickly in Grantsville. Suffering from its own shattered illusions about Grant, the community is eager to replace their fallen idol with a new figure to admire. But Kelly no more fits this role than she did the one imagined for her by Grant. It is Kelly's recognition of this fact that marks her progression in the film—not from bad girl to good girl, but form a woman of dreams to a woman almost without hope. Kelly walks coldly through her crowd of admirers and out of the town, away from attempts at respectability, away from illusions of romance and security, and away from those men on whom she would be forced to depend. Passing down the sidewalk, she stops to caress an infant in a baby carriage, repeating a similar gesture she performed on her first day in town. Certain in her knowledge of the seaminess and self-interest which motivates all adults, Kelly (like Fuller) still maintains a blind and almost absurd faith in children.

Children are redemptive figures because they are the only true innocents. By its corruption and destruction of this innocence, Grant's pedophilia strikes Kelly at the tenderest spot of her deepest belief, and at a time when she is most vulnerable. By placing all her hopes for redemption and fulfillment in the hands of Grant, Kelly lays herself open to just the kind of blow she receives. The most disturbing implication of the situation is that she is unable to let down her defense even once, to trust even a man who seems to embody perfection. It confirms what she should already have learned: that she is totally alone to take care of herself. *The Naked Kiss* is Sam Fuller's claim that he's been there and he knows.

———

ED LOWRY

VOL. 12, NO. 1
JANUARY 25, 1977

Touch of Evil (1958)

DIRECTED AND WRITTEN BY ORSON WELLES

The subject matter of *Touch of Evil* is so banal and its story line so confusing, that, as crime melodrama, it is fit only for theaters which grind out "Bs" fifteen hours or more a day. However . . . Welles has furbished it with photographic, directorial and acting touches which compensate for the irrationality of the picture itself. . . . The role Welles wrote for himself . . . is a synthetic assemblage of negative characteristics which appeal to Welles, one surmises, for private rather than professional reasons. | JEREMY BROWNE, *Films in Review*, April 1958.

Confusing, somewhat "artsy" film. . . . Smacks of brilliance but ultimately flounders in it. . . . Welles establishes his creative talent with pomp, but unfortunately the circumstances of the story suffer. There is insufficient orientation and far too little exposition, with the result that much of the action is confusing and difficult to relate to the plot. Taken scene by scene, there is much to be said for this film . . . but *Touch of Evil* proves it takes more than good scenes to make a good picture. | "RON," *Variety*, March 19, 1958.

Q.—The movement of the actors and the camera in relation to each other in your films is very beautiful.

Welles—That is a visual obsession. I believe, thinking about my films, that they are based not so much on pursuit as a search. If we are looking for something, the labyrinth is the most favorable location for a search. I do not know why, but my films are all for the most part a physical search. . . .

Q.—That is why your mise-en-scène is lively: it is the meeting to two movements, that of the actors and that of the camera. Out of this flows an anguish that reflects modern life very well. . . .

Welles—I believe that that corresponds to my vision of the world; it reflects that sort of vertigo, uncertainty, lack of stability, that *mélange* of movement and tension that is our universe. And the cinema should express that. Since cinema has the pretension of being art, it should be, above all, film, and not the sequel to another, more literary, medium of expression. | Interview with Welles by JUAN COBOS MIGUEL RUBIO, and JOSÉ ANTONIO PRUNEDA, *Cahiers du Cinéma*, April 1965.

In Welles's *oeuvre*, *Touch of Evil* is perhaps the one film which is most consistently misunderstood. It is commonly criticised for not working in either the narrative format of the detective story or even as *film noir*, where a certain moral ambiguity is to be expected. On one level it is easy to see that the film is thematically wrapped up in the idea of pursuit, or the search; yet there is never any real doubt as to the culprits or their culpability, and the notion of suspense does not play a prominent part in the story development. Within this realization, it is easy to see that the focus of *Touch of Evil* is on the process of the search itself; and, if there is no resolution, this is merely a defining aspect of the search.

In a cogent and concise analysis of the film in *Film Comment,* Terry Comito develops a reading based on the Welles quotes above. He proposes that once we relate to Welles's border town, not as a geographical space, but as a visual space, we read the film as being inseparable from Welles's "phenomenology of cinematic style." As Comito defines it,

Welles' habitual deep focus means that any place that a character may for an instant inhabit is only the edge of the depth that opens dizzily behind him, receding along the arcades of Venice, California, like some baroque hallucination. The violence of the motion Welles sets plunging through these depths means that "foreground" and "background" no longer serve as static games for a comfortable middle distance (a "middle" both optically and ethically). Instead, all three are points on a single system, through which, just beyond the circle closed about any given moment's awareness, the assassin pursues his prey, and through whose sinuous passages the investigator must seek out an unknown evil. . . .

We may best understand the perceptual world of *Touch of Evil* as labyrinth, in which the viewer too is invited to lose himself. . . . The middle shot, as André Bazin has written, appeals to the "natural point of balance of the viewer's mental adjustment." The intention of Welles' style is precisely to subvert this balance: by opening upon the vertiginous ambiguities of space to deny us the safety of the frame of reference through which we habitually contemplate the world.

A number of other examples support this paradoxical notion of a closed system and open space. For instance, through deep-focus composition, Welles establishes a limited set of visual reference points (on the American side: the oil derricks and the Ritz Hotel; on the Mexican side: Grandi's Rancho Grande, the brothel, and the St. Mark's Hotel) which are placed, at various times tangentially in the frame to suggest that the characters are moving in a closed space, and that their pursuit is marked by a continuous return to the same points. This further establishes the labyrinth motif: that the characters are moving in a closed space, aware of boundaries, but unaware of their position in respect to those boundaries. The exceptions which prove the rule are located in the sequences marked by tight framing and well defined space (the interrogation of Sanchez; the meeting in Vargas's hotel room; the hall of records et al.) in which the characters develop a conceptual and moral framework that, although it is somewhat arbitrary, orders their understanding of events and our understanding of them.

If we reconsider the opening sequence of the film, we can establish the transition between the labyrinth motif and the other primary thematic concerns of the film in relation to it. This sequence, a three-minute take, begins with a close-up of someone setting a time bomb, which, incidentally, will explode at the end of the take. The purpose of this exposition, in my reading, is to establish this series of thematic concerns in the narrative system of the film: 1) that the characters move in a fixed, ultimately destructive temporal continuum (delimited by the time bomb); 2a) the spatial character of the composition is labyrinthine and equally fixed (as seen in the initial establishing segment); 2b) the characters are unaware of the limitations of this spatio-temporal closure (as seen in the opposition of camera to character movement); 3) the concept of a border which arbitrarily establishes a set of rules and norms which are actually meaningless and transgressable; and 4) the act of violence (the explosion) whose purpose is to displace balanced relationships (Vargas/Susan), establish a central event where the various circles of pursuit intersect, and to rationalize acts of transgression.

At this point, we must keep in mind that the nature of the search is movement in a closed system. The act of violence causes a displacement (loss) in the system which initiates the search cycle. The dialectic of the search never reaches full synthesis; rather, it resolves/resumes at its point of departure as a surrogate is found to cover the immediate loss. By using the case of Hank Quinlan as a model, we can also demonstrate that the nature of this closure is Oedipal and destructive. The analogies are obvious. Quinlan walks with a limp, his defect provides him with an intuitive understanding, and he exhibits a series of symbols of phallic compensation: his cane, cigars, compulsive eating, etc. Quinlan's search begins with the strangulation of his wife and his inability to catch the murderer. As a result, he regards all of his suspects as guilty and sees that justice is done by systematically framing them. In this respect, he compensates for his loss through revenge. The act of violence has displaced him from the system of justice and moral accountability from which he derives both his sexual and official power. Rather than accept exclusion and an identity as an outsider, he establishes an alternative system which morally rationalizes his transgressive acts (e.g., crossing the border into Mexico to investigate the bombing). Furthermore, he finds surrogates for his wife which are sexually transgressive: Tanya, the prostitute, and Menzies, his "partner" (Tanya remarks, "That cop—he loved him").

It is also revealing to note the opposition inherent between the surrogates. Tanya, on the Mexican side of the border, is associated with the eternal return: the closure which defines a time and distance that, paradoxically, is both recovered and lost. This is symbolized by the player piano, "so old that it's new," whose song continues despite the displacement of the player. Pete Menzies is on the American side of the border and is associated with the unknowing acceptance of Quinlan's alternative moral system from which he derives respect. Inclusion in one set necessitates exclusion from the other, and since Quinlan is drawn to both his need of women (love of mother) and need for respect among his male peers (love of father), at any moment he is an outsider to one system. In this respect, the boundary concept delimits the polarity between the two systems, both of which are morally reprehensible to the viewer.

It is the tendency of most critics of *Touch of Evil*, to view the relationship between Quinlan and Vargas as being antithetical, but in the analysis I have just established, it is easy to see them as equivalent and parallel. The explosion, and the ensuing investigation, serves to separate Vargas and Susan. From the very first, Vargas confuses the search for his wife with the search for the bomber, and, ultimately, the search for evidence to discredit Quinlan. He describes the bombing incident as being bad for "us," ambiguously referring to both his country and his wife. Since the bomb was planted in Mexico, but detonated in the United States, his jurisdiction is placed in question making him an "observer," an outsider. At one point, Vargas is framed against a billboard which reads: *"Welcome Stranger to Picturesque Los Nobles, Paris on the Border."* As a Mexican, he is implicated in an alternate system of justice, on the American side, in which he has no authority; and, by the time his wife has been abducted, he is "acting as a husband" (i.e., on the Mexican side, in the fight at Rancho Grande), not as a police officer. Vargas is essentially caught in the same polarity as Quinlan. In the case of Vargas, it is also easy to see that Schwartz, the local D.A., takes the place of Menzies in relation to Quinlan. In this light, we can establish the following homologies: Vargas/Susan: :Quinlan/Tanya, and Vargas/Schwartz: :Quinlan/Menzies.

Following our paradigm which accounts for the pursuit theme through its transformations in a general Oedipal pattern, we can see that Vargas's search for his wife necessitates the removal of Quinlan, the father figure who has placed the power of Vargas's authority (phallic adequacy) into question. And Quinlan, through his association with Grandi, has tainted the entire narrative system with a touch of evil (reconsider the Night Man: "It stinks in here! Let's get some air in here! It's a mess, a stinkin' mess!"), so that he must be displaced in order to bring the system to a coherent closure. The turning point in Quinlan's fate occurs when he strangles Grandi. At one stroke, he brings his pursuit full circle by avenging his wife's murder and fixing himself in a moral framework by establishing Vargas as an outsider (creating evidence showing Susan to be a drug addict and a murderess). The dissipation of his Oedipal energy is represented by the loss of his cane (note the sign on the hotel door as he leaves).

As Vargas is reunited with Susan, Quinlan is reunited with Tanya, so that the last opposition involves the restoration of the moral system that Quinlan has tainted. Menzies turns on Quinlan (presenting the cane to

Vargas) because he is first displaced by Grandi, and eventually Tanya. It becomes his duty to lure Quinlan from the safety of closure within the brothel, where the sound of the piano masks his words. Quinlan's peripeteia is objectified in a startling sequence which begins with a low-angle, full shot of him walking out on the porch of the brothel, cutting to a reverse shot which immediately cranes up, diminishing his size in the frame in a high-angle shot dominated by an arch above the porch.

At this point, the frame positions of Quinlan and Vargas are set in complete opposition (where previously they were equated through establishing low-angle shots), as Vargas snakes his way through the labyrinthine catwalks above Quinlan and Menzies. It is significant that these positions come to be reversed as Vargas must pass under the bridge that Quinlan crosses. Essentially, he is committing a frame-up on the same order as Quinlan's: condemning the man by misrepresenting the evidence against him. As Quinlan's voice echoes beneath the bridge, we begin to realize that the words which will be used against him will have a meaning which is discontinuous with his self-defense. It is in this knowledge that he shoots Menzies with Vargas's gun. Quinlan goes to wash Menzies's blood off his hands in the river, and, confronting Vargas, claims that it was he who killed Pete. In a symbolic sense, Quinlan is correct; however, Menzies shoots Quinlan in the back, as Quinlan refused to do to Vargas. In appealing to his old partner, Quinlan is once more marked by the blood as if he cannot escape the system of guilt (loss of innocence) and compensation. He finally dies, falling into the quagmire of the river, and, after 24 hours of narrative time, brings the circle to a close.

The ultimate value of *Touch of Evil* is its refusal to place any of the characters in an unambiguous position, either as a function of the visual dynamics, or, concomitantly, as a function of the visual dynamics, or, concomitantly, as a function of character development. At the end we assume that Sanchez was, ironically, guilty all along, because he has confessed. But much is made of the scare tactics of interrogation, so Sanchez may just as easily have confessed under duress. Given the preponderance of personal, moral, and psychological labyrinths we weave about ourselves, it is no wonder that we are all, in some degree, outsiders. A guilty party will always be found to expiate our own guilt, and to account for our loss of innocence within our arbitrary moral systems, whether he be a Quinlan or a Sanchez. In the filmic system, the only apparent endpoint is death. It is this implicit existential assumption that establishes misrepresentation as a fact of human nature: the circle always closes on the self at the exclusion of the other. Or, as Tanya says at the end of the film, "What does it matter what you say about people?"

———

DAVID RODOWICK

A NOTE ABOUT THE NOTEWRITER:

David Rodowick is a mythologician and textual tactician who is thinly disguised as a graduate student in film theory and criticism. Rampant rumors that say he ignores everything on the left-hand side of the Atlantic are patently untrue. His most fervent ambition in life is to rewrite JR entirely without dialogue.

VOL. 9, NO. 1
SEPTEMBER 8, 1975

The Wild Bunch (1969)

DIRECTED BY SAM PECKINPAH

Peckinpah's theme is not a preoccupation with losers, with men who are out of their time—the one to which his beneficent critics subscribe—nor is it the celebration of violence, as others would have us believe. In fact, violence is merely the most visible manifestation of Peckinpah's obsession with the effects of a continuing loss of individual freedom and singular human identity to the collective power system which has come to be known as society. Peckinpah's statement is as old as civilization itself and it goes like this: the more we, as individuals, seek safety and protection within society, the less free we shall become; and as the power of that society grows ever greater, the smaller and less identifiable we will be as singular human beings. And if in our fear of facing up to a few violently sick people we keep selling our freedom to society for protection, who will protect us when that society itself becomes sick? The scorpion has a poisonous sting; but the collective violence of the ant army is infinitely more deadly. | RICH SASSONE, *Filmmakers Newsletter*, March 1973

I would prefer to believe that Sam Peckinpah was sincere when he stated that he wanted to make a picture so strong, so stomach-churning, so detailed in its catalogue of horrors that all the glamour, all the attraction of violence for its own sake would promptly disappear.... But there is a law of diminishing return even in movie violence. As faces explode repeatedly into pools of gore, as hands clutch convulsively at perforated bellies, as men tumble from their horses in a writhing mass under machine gun fire, the film begins to lose its effectiveness. | ARTHUR KNIGHT, *Saturday Review,* July 5, 1969

Sam Peckinpah's directorial hallmark seems to me to be incoherence of narrative amid buckets of blood. *The Wild Bunch* is a bit of Western nostalgia about a gang of over-age bad guys operating north and south of the border circa 1913, fleeing from Texas railroad-employed bounty hunters and dealing in guns with Mexican bandit generals. The films starts off with a bloody shoot-up in a Texas town and winds up with a shoot-down of the good bad guys and the bad ones in a Mexican town that is the bloodiest and most sickening display of slaughter that I can recall seeing in a theatrical film. And quotes attributed to Mr. Holden that this sort of ultra-violence is a healthy purgative for viewers are just about as sick. If you must see *The Wild Bunch,* be sure to take along a barf bag. | JUDITH CRIST, *New York Magazine,* June 30, 1969

For the past fifteen years, Sam Peckinpah has been perhaps the most flamboyant figure on the American film scene. In the early 1960s, he earned a reputation as a top director and writer of Westerns both in TV and film. His second film, *Ride the High Country,* a low budget picture in which he first teamed up with Lucien Ballard, his superb photographer, won the grand prize at the Brussels film festival over Fellini's *8½.* His next film, *Major Dundee* was hailed as a masterpiece even though 55 minutes were cut without his approval, including a twenty-minute opening scene which introduces the characters and their situation. Peckinpah was outraged and demanded that from then on he would retain the rights to the final cut himself. This, among other things, earned him a reputation in Hollywood as a troublemaker. He was fired after four days of directing *The Cincinnati Kid,* and as a victim of an unofficial blacklist, could get no work for four years. He describes the period as "like dying," and admits that, in order to work, he was willing to accept some compromises to his freedom. Finally, a friend hired him for a TV production and soon thereafter he got the call for *The Wild Bunch.* Luckily, he and his producer, Phil Feldman, saw eye to eye on most matters and though 8 minutes were cut from the original version of the film, Peckinpah only regrets one cut, a flashback showing Deke's capture.

The Wild Bunch. From the Sam Peckinpah papers of the Margaret Herrick Library, Academy of Motion Picture Arts and Sciences.

The obvious thing about *The Wild Bunch* that sets it apart from previous films is the violence, and it is around the morality of screen violence that the initial critical debate revolved. The familiar argument raged over whether the viewer would be inclined to leave the movie theater and go out and commit mayhem or else be repulsed at the thought. Peckinpah has said that he dislikes violence and wanted his movie to reflect that distaste; he obviously wanted *The Wild Bunch* to be more than a simple treatise on violence. However, though the slaughter is grotesque, the revulsion the film produces is on a physical rather than moral level. Most of the victims are simply bodies whose sole function in the film is to die in an explosion of gore. We never get to know them as people, so it is the gore we react to rather than the death of human beings.

Nevertheless, there is a sense of fatality in *The Wild Bunch* that puts death into perspective. Peckinpah tells us this near the opening of the film when Pike kills his wounded comrade who can no longer ride. The man realizes

VOL. 19, NO. 2
OCTOBER 28, 1980

Bring Me the Head of Alfredo Garcia (1974)

DIRECTED BY SAM PECKINPAH

Once you have given up the ghost, everything follows with dead certainty, even in the midst of chaos. From the beginning it was never anything but chaos: it was a fluid which enveloped me, which I breathed in through the gills. . . . In everything I quickly saw the opposite, the contradiction, and between the real and the unreal the irony, the paradox. I was my own worst enemy. | HENRY MILLER, *Tropic of Capricorn*

No one loses all the time. | BENNIE, in *Bring Me the Head of Alfredo Garcia*

In an increasingly liberal era, many American movies have underwritten the notion that evil resides not in our stars, nor ourselves, but in our environment. Peckinpah insists that men can be animals, that fate is inside us, that evil exists; that America's posture in the world, her power and menace, owe not a little to the existence of that evil. | JIM KITSES, *Horizons West*

Bring Me the Head of Alfredo Garcia, a remarkable film whose submerged sexual tensions and guilts have no precedent in American films but are surely not unfamiliar to any reader up on his Hawthorne (or Faulkner, specifically *Sanctuary*, which once especially struck Peckinpah's fancy). | PAUL SEYDOR, *Peckinpah: The Western Films*

Peckinpah swallowed Robert Ardrey whole; it suited his emotional needs—he *wants* to believe that all men are whores and killers. | PAULINE KAEL, "Notes on the Nihilist Poetry of Sam Peckinpah"

Peckinpah's theme is not a preoccupation with losers, with men who are out of their time—the one to which his beneficent critics subscribe—nor is it the celebration of violence, as others would have us believe. In fact violence is merely the most visible manifestation of Peckinpah's obsession with the effects of a continuing loss of individual freedom and singular human identity to the collective power system which has come to be known as society. Peckinpah's statement is as old as civilization itself and it goes like this: the more we, as individuals, seek safety and protection within society, the less free we shall become; and as the power of the society grows ever greater, the smaller and less identifiable we will be as singular human beings. And if in our fear of facing up to a few violently sick people we keep selling our freedom to society for protection, who will protect us when that society itself becomes sick? The scorpion has a poisonous sting; but the collective violence of the ant army is infinitely more deadly. | RICH SASSONE, *Filmmakers Newsletter*, March 1973

Everything that happens, when it has significance, is in the nature of a contradiction. Until the one for whom this was written came along I imagined that somewhere outside in life, as they say, lay the solution to all things. I thought, when I came upon her, that I was seizing hold of life, seizing hold of something which I could bite into. Instead I lost hold of life completely. I reached out for something to attach myself, left high and dry as I was, I nevertheless found something I had not looked for—*myself.* | HENRY MILLER, *The Tropic of Capricorn*

It seems somewhat odd that, next to Alfred Hitchcock, though for radically different reasons, one of the best-known directors to the general public may well be Sam Peckinpah. Even George Lucas, Francis Coppola, William Friedkin, and Steven Spielberg, directors of the megabuck spectaculars, probably don't have cinematic personalities so clearly defined in the eyes of the general audience. Mention Hitchcock and people think of suspense and horror;

mention Peckinpah and they think of blood and violence. Since stirring up controversy over a decade ago with the ballet-like genocide of *The Wild Bunch*, Peckinpah has had a rocky, tumultuous and extremely public career. His exploits and opinions have made good copy, generating large amounts of press and earning him a certain amount of notoriety. Unfortunately, at the same time, the brilliance of his cinema has largely been ignored or misunderstood.

The controversy surrounding his career began long before his celebrity status. With roots in the theater, Peckinpah got his start in films by working with director Don Siegel on such projects as *Invasion of the Body Snatchers*. He soon graduated to writing and directing television Westerns and was responsible for the creation of two series, *The Westerner* and *The Rifleman*. In 1961, he directed his first feature film, *The Deadly Companions*, which also led to his first fight with a producer. As a result of the controversy, he lost control over the final editing of the film and wasn't very pleased with the result.

In 1962 he directed Randolph Scott and Joel McCrea in the low-budget Western *Ride the High Country*. The film immediately earned an enormous critical reputation in Europe and is now regarded as one of the masterpieces of the genre. The film's success produced his next assignment, directing Charlton Heston in the big-budget Western *Major Dundee*. It was on this project that most of the elements of the Peckinpah myth began to gel. He shot over schedule, went over budget, fought with the producer and ended up with a film that satisfied him but which the studio found too long. Without his approval, almost an hour was cut from the final release version. Despite certain critical raves for the film, Peckinpah's reputation within the film industry was shaky. After he was fired as director of *The Cincinnati Kid* following four days of shooting, he found himself unofficially blacklisted. It was almost half a decade before he directed his next film, and that only after a friend hired him to do a television version of Katherine Anne Porter's *Noon Wine*. The show received rave critical reviews and led to Peckinpah's hiring as director of *The Wild Bunch*. After that film his reputation was established.

Unfortunately, that reputation usually misses the range and genius of Peckinpah's cinema. A 1973 *Esquire* article on Peckinpah concentrated mostly, and in a negative way, on the violence and bloodletting in his films. The article acknowledged him as the director of *The Wild Bunch*, *Straw Dogs*, and *The Getaway*. It ignored the film he made after *The Wild Bunch*, *The*

Bring Me the Head of Alfredo Garcia. From the Sam Peckinpah papers of the Margaret Herrick Library, Academy of Motion Picture Arts and Sciences.

Ballad of Cable Hogue, as well as *Junior Bonner,* which followed *Straw Dogs.* Both of these films contain almost no violence at all; they are funny, leisurely narratives that examine the themes and issues Peckinpah finds so challenging and important—the death of the West, the role of the individual in society, and the nature of civilization. This illustrates the irony of Peckinpah's career; lambasted when his films feature violence, he finds his work totally ignored when they don't.

The issues of violence and of his media personality have tended to block any deep understanding of Peckinpah's cinema. *Bring Me the Head of Alfredo Garcia,* in particular, seems to have suffered. Generally regarded as a failure when it was released, the film's critical stature has only slightly improved over the years.

To set the record straight: *Bring Me the Head of Alfredo Garcia* is one of the most important and brilliant of Peckinpah's films. In many ways it represents the culmination of the first (and so far greatest) period of his work. It is an ugly, vicious film about not very glamourous people engaged in ugly, vicious activities. In retrospect, the lack of recognition of its importance to Peckinpah's canon is not so great an oversight as is the underestimation of

Alfredo Garcia's role in seventies American cinema in general. Released at a time when coy, self-serving liberal sweetmeats such as *The Long Goodbye, California Split, Save The Tiger, Carnal Knowledge,* and *One Flew over the Cuckoo's Nest* were the critical rave, its atmosphere of paranoia and desperation prefigured (and less glibly so) *Taxi Driver* and its ilk. What is important about the cinema of Sam Peckinpah is that when it was first recognized in the liberal critical climate of the late sixties and early seventies, it seemed reactionary and idiosyncratic. Now in the late seventies and early eighties, as the new right dominates, it seems equally reactionary and idiosyncratic. Not tied to any particular ideology, Peckinpah's films represent a strong and comprehensive personal vision.

The focal point of all Peckinpah films is the role of the individual in society, especially the individual who doesn't fit. This is especially true in *Alfredo Garcia*, in which Warren Oates's Bennie is a not very bright hustler/ loser. The film deals with the world of the misfit in very real and brutal terms. At times it seems as though the film is an almost conscious response to the anti-hero personified by Bogart in *Casablanca*, where the iconoclast is draped in mystery and romance and a hint of poetry. Oates's character has none of that grace or romantic aura. It is Peckinpah's peculiarly skewed vanity that allows him to see himself as very much like Bennie, as his constant public references to himself as a "good whore" illustrate. On that basis he will in no way glamorize the life of the outcast and misfit, a strategy that provides a romantic repository for impulses and emotion repressed by the society. Oates's Bennie is neither hero nor anti-hero—he is just a loser who struggles to survive. Shed of the trappings of conventional characterization, the essence of Bennie's role as outsider illustrates the corruption of the American cinematic mythologizing of this kind of character. Richard Lester's *Cuba* is one of the few other films that has tackled those myths; Lester's concern was the implicit legitimization of imperialism at their core.

Alfredo Garcia is structured such that the film's climax occurs sufficiently early to defuse the violent ending's potential for catharsis and heroism. The beginning is a deception, the exposure of which again removes the film from traditional "romantic adventure" terms. The middle of the film finds Oates and Isela Vega involved in an idyllic journey (interrupted by a rape) that seems almost awkward within the context of the film. Part of the problem is that Peckinpah has no idea on how to handle women, but this shifting of gears is also partly intentional, another attempt to ground the film in a kind of mundane realism. This is not the swelling cinematic romance of classic films but the awkward emotional interactions of two small-time hustlers.

The nature of romance and ritual is as important to Peckinpah as it is to John Ford, but whereas Ford's films are about the establishment and preservation of civilization, Peckinpah's are about its corruption and end. *Alfredo Garcia* is not only centered around the above romance, which defies all cinematic codes, but it contains rituals as well. The funerals and baptism of the film, as with the weddings, military parades, and marches in Peckinpah's other films, are not culture-affirming events, but are instead hollow activities that expose the rotting underside of a symbolic structure that is crumbling from within.

What is central to all of this is that Peckinpah never points fingers, saying "*They* are doing this." He always implicates himself and his characters in the dissolution of society. Whenever Bennie catalogs outrages, he always mentions himself. About Alfredo Garcia he says that he was "trying to beat this rap all his life, so have I, so have you." Peckinpah's outsiders are not romantic anti-heroes removed from the proceedings but *as* outsiders they are necessarily part of the all-encompassing civilization, serving as symptoms of its disease.

The sequence in which Oates ends up in a grave, as does Alfredo Garcia, as does Isela Vega, as will most of the other characters in the film, is the climax of the story. In a sense, after the grave sequence Oates is already dead in the same way that all of Peckinpah's heroes are already as good as dead in the worlds they inhabit. And this is how Peckinpah views himself. But none of them, neither Peckinpah nor his heroes, will lie down in the grave; they stride out and do what they have to do. The last part of the film is the rant of a madman and the vision of a madman, but it is also a last desperate attempt to accomplish something, to live by one's own standards and to bring a certain amount of dignity into one's life. It is in these attempts that the cinematic vision of Peckinpah is defined, a vision that is lived out in the films he makes and through the battles he fights to make them.

———

LOUIS BLACK

PART IV

America's Shadow Cinema

B MOVIES, EXPLOITATION FILMS, AND THE AVANT-GARDE

The Program Notes that follow on "Hollywood's Shadow Cinema" begin to address the idea of an eclectic alternative American film tradition that didn't just exist but flourished as a refraction of Hollywood. It was not a repudiation of mainstream commercial cinema, but a sometimes self-conscious, sometimes pragmatic (and sometimes both) response to specific industrial and creative circumstances, and a response that was always constructed *in relation to* Hollywood. The Notes initially locate the shadow cinema in the world of B movies that played as the bottom half of double bills in American movie theaters of the 1930s and 1940s, but the metaphor is extended in this section to incorporate both the exploitation films of the drive-in era and, seemingly incongruously, the experimental avant-garde cinema of Maya Deren and Kenneth Anger. The latter filmmakers were very much disconnected from Hollywood's industrial assembly line, but their work still showed a fascination with Tinseltown iconography and mythologies, and their radical stylistic experiments used the shared cinematic language to different expressive ends. Cumulatively, these filmmakers bent studio style all out of shape as they explored new ideas of form and narrative, ranging from the surreal to the baroque.

The argument is that these cinemas articulate, if not exactly a shared sensibility, at least a common language, though the audiovisual dialects incorporated within these works often seem rather at odds with the mother tongue. They do not constitute a separate culture from Hollywood studio filmmaking but rather a shadow, a variant, subversive in intent and/or effect. There is a certain unity among these filmmakers, despite their radically different production resources and ambitions.

What is shared is a mutual passion for filmmaking, translated as a certain intuitively critical and reflexively inquisitive sensibility through which each unique cinematic world is processed, coupled with a complete inability to make films that are not absolutely personal statements. Considering the disparity of films and filmmakers offered in this section, the cognitive and emotional connector among them is a love of watching, a passion for making, a near religious devotion to the battle to translate ideas from the imagination to the screen.

The first essay in this section, written for a CinemaTexas double bill of *My Name Is Julia Ross* (1945) and *Gun Crazy* (1950), nails the passion of the filmmakers and the integrity of their work, but is far too parochial in the range of filmmakers and films considered. Focusing mostly on low-budget Hollywood productions, it considers how they are Hollywood products but still somehow driven by ambition and vision to be so much more than was expected by the film companies that produced them.

Consequently, within the more expansive definition offered above, there are four distinct groups collected in this section:

There are films made within the Hollywood system, straightforwardly produced as commercial products. These include B movies and exploitation films, both industry-specific terms of production protocols (budget, shooting schedule, cast) and intention (they were almost guaranteed to make money, regardless of quality, as they played an established theatrical circuit). *My Name Is Julia Ross* and *Gun Crazy* are B movies; *Caged Heat* (1974) is an exploitation film.

There are films made outside of the Hollywood system, but which mimic at least the appearance of studio productions. Often, these works pushed the boundaries of horror, sex, and violence. Included here are *Two Thousand Maniacs!* (1964), *Assault on Precinct 13* (1976), and *Texas Chainsaw Massacre* (1974).

There are narrative feature films broaching content and style that were (and are) too radical for mainstream productions. Paradoxically, these are often studio-funded productions, but they fall into the category of "troubled" works (i.e., over budget, usually) in which filmmakers run so completely off the rails that the result is filmmaking gone mad. *The Last Movie* (1971) is one classic example of this kind of glorious trainwreck.

Finally, there are avant-garde and experimental films, driven by aesthetic rather than commercial concerns. These films often make meaning by ignoring, distorting, or reimagining conventional film language. While diverse stylistically and in terms of cognitive and emotional resonance, they remain clearly interrelated. Included here are the films of Maya Deren (1943–1958) and *Scorpio Rising* (1964).

This section features filmmakers in love with filmmaking.

———

STEVE FORE, LOUIS BLACK

VOL. 15, NO. 3
NOVEMBER 29, 1978

Hollywood's Shadow Cinema

One wonders where [certain B picture directors] . . . find the energy and
the inspiration to do such fine work, when native critics are so fantastically
indifferent. | ANDREW SARRIS, *The American Cinema.*

Any day now, Americans may realize that scrambling after the obvious in art
is a losing game. The sharpest work of the last thirty years is to be found by
studying the most unlikely, self-destroying, uncompromising, roundabout
artists. | MANNY FARBER, "Underground Films," *Negative Space.*

The above quote by Andrew Sarris has graced at least a half dozen sets of
CinemaTexas Notes in the past several years (and is even included in the
companion notes to these on *Gun Crazy*). The reason is obvious: it is an
articulate cry in the wilderness pointing at a neglect which is almost criminal. For several decades, with an incredible energy and intelligence, low-
budget Hollywood directors turned out interesting films only to be ignored.
This same situation still exists for, ironically enough, as the low-budget

works of Ulmer, Lewis, Fuller, Siegel and others from the thirties through
the fifties are being examined, the current B movies—exploitation films—
are being overlooked.

The most fascinating work among the low-budget directors didn't actually
occur until after World War II. The later war years were a reasonably stable
time. The economy of the country was healthy and, after more than a decade
of depression, getting healthier. By 1943–44 the Allies were winning the war
both in Europe and in Asia. The patriarchal leadership of Franklin D. Roosevelt gave way to the more manic, but not so obvious, presidency of Harry
Truman, proving once again how smoothly the democratic system worked.
And Hollywood had a succession of the best years in its history.

But the seeds of the coming madness were there. As well as the United
States was doing in the war, our Communist allies were also doing well. The
United States would get the bomb first, establishing both a supremacy of
power and scientific ability. The Bomb would bring with it, however, a terrible guilt that would subtly work itself into the fiber of the scientific community, the political establishment and finally the nation itself.

During the forties a united front with the Communists was desirable. But
the old red baiters and their younger allies were getting ready to crank up
the machinery of loyalty oaths, spy trials, and general suspicion of everything not "100% American."

The economy was extremely healthy, but part of this was due to the large
number of women in the work force. Many of them were holding positions
of responsibility previously held by men. The scene was being set for a new
order of sexual politics. Added to this economic imperative were the obvious
romantic confusions and hostilities that grow out of war. Many women had
left their husbands or boyfriends either for men who had stayed behind or
because time and distance became too great a burden. Many men found
women overseas and forgot about the ones at home. Of the relationships
that survived, some would be plagued by suspicion of infidelity and most
would go through crises as readjustments were made.

Hollywood was in the courts fighting the anti-trust action that would
finally dismember it financially. Meanwhile television was being perfected
in the laboratories, and by 1945 the first commercial stations would be on
the air.

All these factors would come together in the immediate postwar years.
America, used to thinking of itself as the tough arrogant underdog on the

side of right and justice, would finally begin to face up to its position as a dominant world power. Unlike the post–World War I period, when the United States refused to accept any responsibility in the world community, it now had no other option if it wanted to combat the Communist "threat."

It was the time of a certain amount of craziness in the land. The differences for returning soldiers, for women, for minority groups, between what was supposed to be and what there actually was, had finally become obvious. The great expectations of returning combat heroes/veterans were channeled into 9 to 5 desk jobs and growing responsibilities. A national psychosis seemed to be evolving.

For much of this century Hollywood has been one of the prime chroniclers of the nation's mood. It would be ludicrous to argue that mainstream Hollywood did not speak to these problems. In forms as diverse as the melodrama and musical, the problems and obsessions of American society began creeping in. In disparate genres, however, these problems are often dealt with in terms of narrative tensions or subtexts. In mainstream films made to "confront the issues" there is a certain glibness that belies the pervasiveness and profusion of the problems: witness *Pinky*, *Gentleman's Agreement*, and *The Best Years of Our Lives*.

It is in the work of a handful of low-budget directors that the madness is chronicled, depicted and challenged. A cinema of the perverse, dominated by an almost existential intelligence, began to grow up on the backlots of Hollywood. Certainly it was a cinema that did not take itself that seriously and one whose main concerns were always dominated by the commercial and not the intellectual.

Directors who had been around for a long time, such as Joseph Lewis, Edgar Ulmer, Jacques Tourneur and Anthony Mann, and newcomers like Phil Karlson (first directed 1944), Don Siegel (1946) and Sam Fuller (1949) began making films that embodied the current American mood. Many of their finest films do not confront the issues in the narrative, but in the very form and feeling of the film. The mood of Americans was not being articulated as much as felt, and in these films it was not being pronounced but created through the *mise-en-scène*.

These films fit into no genre; they are not even all *film noir*. They are the products of a variety of approaches and methods. In looking back at such films as *Phantom Lady* (1944), *Detour* (1945), *The Killers* (1946), *Out of the Past* (1947), *Ruthless* (1948), *Steel Helmet* (1950), *Gun Crazy* (1950), *Pickup on South Street* (1953), *Riot in Cell Block 11* (1954), *The Big Combo* (1955),

Johnny Guitar (1955), *Kiss Me Deadly* (1955) and numerous other films made within a decade or so of each other, we can begin to discuss this alternative Hollywood cinema, these shadows of the commercial big-budget blockbusters.

JOSEPH H. LEWIS

Lewis has a complex visual style, as intricate as Fuller's is direct, and fully as beautiful and effective. His subject specialty is neurotic sexuality, often given poetically provocative presentation. . . . As with Fuller, there is probably not a single film of Lewis's that does not contain within it at least a few minutes of classic filmmaking. | JOHN GABREE, *Gangsters: From Little Caesar to The Godfather.*

Joseph H. Lewis had been a Hollywood director since 1937, but it was during the time period just discussed that he did his most memorable work: *My Name Is Julia Ross* (1945), *The Undercover Man* (1949), *Gun Crazy* (1950), *Lady Without a Passport* (1950), *The Big Combo* (1955). Born in New York in 1900, he began his Hollywood career as a camera boy at M-G-M, soon graduating to the position of editor. During the 1930s he edited films at Mascot; and when the studio merged with Liberty and Monogram to become Republic Pictures in late 1935, he went along and was promoted to second unit director. In 1937 he received his first directing credit on Grand National's *Navy Spy*, which he co-directed with Crane Wilbur.

Lewis was to spend the next 21 years directing low-budget films for a variety of companies including Universal, Columbia, PRC, Monogram, United Artists and M-G-M. In all he was to receive credit for directing forty films, working in almost every commercially viable genre, but always with a low budget. Edward Dmytryk has said that Lewis was offered several A projects but was never able to make a go of it as a big-budget director. In 1958, he directed his last film, the Western *Terror in a Texas Town*, which took ten days to shoot at a cost of $80,000. He also did some television work, directing episodes of "The Rifleman," "Gunsmoke" and "The Big Valley."

Lewis is that anomaly—a director with one acknowledged masterpiece, *Gun Crazy*, several very good films and a slough of run-of-the-mill movies. His best films work more because of *mise-en-scène* rather than his direction of actors or development of the narrative. Lewis's world view is purely visual. He is a director with a consistent *vision*, but no discernible personality except an obsession with "neurotic sexuality."

Gun Crazy is an undeniably brilliant film, a true gift of the American cinema. Lewis's direction is gorgeous and the film is a tone poem of camera movements. It works better than most of Lewis's films largely because, for once, there is a strong narrative to wrap the visuals around. In this case the narrative, based on a story by MacKinley Kantor, was authored by probably the best screenwriter Lewis was to work with, Dalton Trumbo.

Trumbo, a victim of the anti-Communist blacklist, was working anonymously for the King Brothers (the producers) for a slim fraction of his former fee. As a result of this political accident, Lewis was able to get a first-rate screenplay to shoot.

Most of the time Lewis was not that lucky, and whereas such films as *My Name Is Julia Ross* and *The Big Combo* work and are interesting, they are not on the level with *Gun Crazy*.

—

LOUIS BLACK

**VOL. 15, NO. 3
(REPRINTED FROM VOL. 10, NO. 4)
NOVEMBER 29, 1978**

My Name Is Julia Ross (1945)

DIRECTED BY JOSEPH H. LEWIS

The director and scenarist of . . . *My Name Is Julia Ross* deserve a B-Plus for effort at least. It is quite evident that they strived earnestly to whip up excitement and suspense, but somehow that electrifying quality which distinguishes good melodrama is lacking. . . .

While Joseph Lewis, the director, succeeds in creating an effectively ominous atmosphere, he has not been as adept in handling the players, and that, we suspect, is why *My Name Is Julia Ross* misses. | THOMAS M. PRYOR, *New York Times*, November 9, 1945.

[*My Name Is Julia Ross*] is well planned, mostly well photographed—all around, a likable, unpretentious, generally successful attempt to turn good trash into decently artful entertainment. | JAMES AGEE, *The Nation*, November 24, 1945.

Lewis emerged with the success of *My Name Is Julia Ross* (1945), an ambitious baroque exercise that excited critics and audiences alike. Although of programmer length, the film was clearly budget beyond the normal restrictions attendant on a sixty-five-minute running time, and Lewis responded with flourish to his expanded resources | MYRON MEISEL, in *Kings of the Bs*.

My Name Is Julia Ross is an example of both Lewis's strengths and weaknesses. Most of the film is beautiful to look at, the atmosphere of paranoia and confusion created as much by camera movement and lighting as by the story. The story itself is surprisingly good, although the ending is awkward and hurried; yet there is something lacking.

The narrative mines the same vein as Hitchcock, and though Lewis is an effective stylist he gets nowhere near the mileage out of his material. It is a tribute to him that despite the low-budget and short shooting schedule he is able to get some of the same feel as *Rebecca*. The stories are even vaguely similar, though *My Name Is Julia Ross* has far more obvious sinister overtones.

By examining this film, one of Lewis's acknowledged best, we can begin to define his lack of cinematic personality. The conflicts within the narrative are not similar to his other films, nor do they share the same world. The only consistent tension is that of the functions of a sexual neurotic in a "normal" world. Lewis continually comes back to that topic, building *Gun Crazy* around it, as well as many of the finer scenes in his other movies: Richard Conte going down on Jean Wallace in *The Big Combo*, or in *My Name Is Julia Ross* that character of Ralph Hughes and his obsession not only with knives but with stabbing. The most perverse scene in *Julia Ross* has him rather manically shredding Nina Foch's underwear with a knife. This level of obsession is not only a foreshadowing of things to come, but it establishes a level of perversity to which the film will rarely venture again.

Possibly the most interesting part of the film is the character of Julia Ross. In a period when the *femme noir/fatale* was beginning to dominate, Lewis's women take on a special interest. They are by no means independent, but neither are they evil nor completely servile. There is something unusual going on with them. Cummins in *Gun Crazy* would seem to fulfill all the requirements of the bitch goddess until it becomes obvious that *she does love Dall*. There is a layer of interaction and tension added by her emotion that removes her character from the simplicity of most of the *femme noir*. Nina Foch's character also has a toughness and an independence not usually found in helpless feminine victims in suspense stories.

The final interest in the film is that it is a suspense story. Bs were not just Westerns, horror films and comedies, but included virtually every genre.

The variety of Bs gives individual efforts an even more interesting context. In this standard B suspense film programmer, we can again see the hints of Lewis's talents for visually portraying a claustrophobic, sexually hostile and dangerous world.

—

LOUIS BLACK

VOL. 15, NO. 3
(REPRINTED FROM VOL. 10, NO. 4)
NOVEMBER 29, 1978

Gun Crazy (Deadly is the Female) (1950)

DIRECTED BY JOSEPH H. LEWIS

One wonders where [certain B-Picture] directors . . . find the energy and the inspiration to do such fine work, when native critics are so fantastically indifferent . . . | ANDREW SARRIS, *The American Cinema*

Even with some adroit camouflaging, the Palace's new picture, starring Peggy Cummins and John Dall, is pretty cheap stuff. "Gun crazy" just about covers it. Handsomely produced by the King Brothers, from an original story by MacKinlay Kantor, this spurious concoction is basically on par with the most humdrum pulp fiction. . . .

In all fairness to Mr. Kantor's idea, the actual script, which he wrote with Millard Kaufman, is a fairly literate business. Even if the young desperadoes aren't motivated, apparently beyond Miss Cummins's grim appreciation of money and her partner's general restlessness, neither are they sentimentalized or offered as luckless tools of society. The dialogue is quite good and the photography is first rate. In fact, director Joseph H. Lewis has kept the whole thing zipping at a colorful tempo which deserves a much better outlet. | HOWARD THOMPSON, *New York Times*, August 25, 1950

> *Gun Crazy* . . . establishes conclusively that the minor artist [Joseph H. Lewis]
> is a major talent. It hurtles along with the mad energy of its protagonists, the
> personification of "youth run wild," the drive of vitality run amok. Unwavering
> intelligence with forms of mania has always been a hallmark of Lewis; here
> he deals with its most unbridled exemplar, without sacrificing any directorial
> sensibleness. Few films are more singularly preoccupied with externals to the
> exclusion of attention to interior states. In *Gun Crazy*, there are no interior
> states to be ignored. No psychological explanations are implied—John Dall
> is merely an intelligent, gentle man who (sigh) "just likes guns." This makes
> for good visceral cinema, wherein characters express themselves exclusively
> through their actions, and it is particularly appropriate to a central relation-
> ship such as the one between Dall and Peggy Cummins: their competition at
> marksmanship and their robberies become their means of expressing their
> feelings toward one another. Lewis . . . centers his narrative around sexual
> tensions; he has said that he wanted to show that "their love for each other
> was more fatal than their love for guns." Freed of the analytical baggage of
> abnormal psychology, Lewis fashions a direct cinema in which action and emo-
> tion are inseparable. | MYRON MEISEL, in *Kings of the Bs*

You might sit through *Gun Crazy* on the late night movie and let it slip right
by. It doesn't scream for attention like a film in the same vein by Sam Fuller
or Orson Welles is likely to. Yet the movie reveals a number of wonders to
anyone willing to watch it with the kind of care they would give a film by
Welles. In fact, its repetitive motifs, attention to detail, penchant for lengthy
single shots, creation of "content" through form, and even visual style
resemble Welles. But what is utterly amazing about *Gun Crazy* is that it was
produced very quickly on a low budget and made by a director whose careful artistry was never mentioned in his own time. Even now the name of
Joseph H. Lewis is almost unknown, though *Gun Crazy* is stacking up a
small but devoted following which will hopefully win for the film its
well-deserved place among the classics of *film noir.*

Perhaps the most impressive thing about the film is that it is so thoroughly cinematic, by which I mean that its conflicts, the emotions and attitudes of the characters, and the plot itself are conveyed, not through the
scripted dialogue, but through visual and aural imagery. If the conversations between the characters sound sometimes silly or obvious, it is at least
in part because the *mise-en-scéne* makes the talk unnecessary. The characters are viewed from the outside and we are never presented with their

Gun Crazy. From the core collection production photographs of the Margaret Herrick Library, Academy of Motion Picture Arts and Sciences.

motivations. We sympathize with them, but never really understand them. This stylistic attitude seems almost perfect for the film's subject. For *Gun Crazy* concerns itself with a man obsessed with guns, a woman with a passionate desire for action, movement and "things"—"lots of things, big things"—and their acts of self-assertion which take the form of physical assault on the world around them. The film's style embodies its content, conveying a world of feelings, emotions, and physical action through the most visual-visceral methods available.

There is perhaps a danger in "interpreting" such a film, but this cinema of feeling, of form equated with content—in which objects, costumes, framing and movement are used to convey concepts—lends itself quite obviously to the creation of (no doubt instinctive) symbols. The first scene of the film contains as literal a rendering of Freudian conflicts as any given scene of the surrealist *Un Chien Andalou*. *Gun Crazy* opens on a shot of a dark, deserted, rainy street over which pass the film's credits. At their conclusion, a young boy appears from around the corner and moves toward us as the camera pulls back to reveal that we are watching him from inside a store window.

The second shot quickly moves into closeup on his face as he peers through the glass; the third, from his point of view, moves in the opposite direction, into a similar closeup of a revolver in the display window. We return to the first camera position and see the boy break the glass by throwing a rock toward us, turn to the street to make sure he is alone, and then reach through the broken window and pull out the gun. Making his escape the boy stumbles and drops the revolver. A quick panning shot follows it in medium closeup as it skids across the wet pavement, stopping directly at the feet of the sheriff, who bends down to pick it up. Next comes a shot of the boy prostrate on the wet pavement, followed by an ominous low-angle closeup of the sheriff's face. The sequence illustrates Lewis's skill at cinematic conciseness. The first three shots establish the single driving characteristic of his protagonist. The two shots which move in opposite directions (first toward the boy's face, then toward the gun) draw them together and establish the boy's fascination with the object. That he is alone on a deserted street at night suggests that his fascination is very personal and perhaps secret; that he has come out in the rain suggest that the fascination is an obsession.

The Freudian reverberations are quite obvious, but contained brilliantly in the way the events are shown. If it seems overwrought to identify every gun as a phallus, it is at least clear that to the boy the gun represents something closely akin to it: maturity and power or (to be more Freudian) masculinity and potency. To gain it he must commit a forbidden act by breaking the window and stealing property. But his youth, his inexperience in these matters, and his resulting nervousness make him clumsy, and the evidence of his guilt seems to seek the feet of an imposing adult figure. The resemblances to the adolescent's initiation to sexuality are painfully evident, and the boy is left on the ground defeated beneath the ominous gaze of a father figure, the fear of castration realized in the man's possession of the symbol of potency which the boy has lost, and which will result in the boy's punishment. Yet, despite the psychological implications of this scene, the film never leaves the realm of Freudian universals or attempts to explain Bart's particular obsession with guns. The complex of conflicts established in this scene, however, runs through the film: guns are clearly related to sex, both are repressed by a benevolently castrating authority, and the individual's exercise of the power they represent takes the form of clearly anti-social acts.

This complex is further developed in the courtroom scenes, where a flashback establishes a business-like, sexless woman teacher as a sort of Oedipal mother who chastises Bart for showing his gun off in class and demands he give it to her. Other flashbacks contrast the boy's skill with the gun and his guilt-imposed impotence—his inability to kill. Bart's testimony that shooting makes him "feel good inside, like something important"; the teacher's statement that all boys seem to want to carry such phallic objects as jackknives, harmonicas, and baseball bats; and the judge's lecture—"We all want things, but our possession of them must be regulated by law"—establish on the verbal level an equation between property, guns and sexuality which Lewis has already achieved in the film's first sequence and which he will continue to explore through his *mise-en-scène*.

When Bart returns to town after a hitch in the army, we first see him with his two best friends, shooting bottles off a tree branch in the foreground of the frame which arches ominously over the trio. As his friends examine his set of dueling pistols, he tells them he taught marksmanship in the army and hopes to get a job demonstrating for Remington, and it seems that perhaps the somewhat frightening ambition he revealed as a child ("Shooting's what I'm good at—it's what I want to do when I grow up") may find a "constructive" outlet. But his introduction to Laurie Starr, which occurs in the sequence immediately following, turns his ambition in a more violent direction. As the men enter the carnival where they will encounter her in a sharp-shooting act, the camera tracks alongside them until they reach a couple of belly dancers which they stop to inspect. Lewis's high angle camera movement allows us to see the dancers in the foreground only from behind and from about the shoulders down (thus emphasizing their undulating hips), while letting us watch the pleased expressions on the faces of the three buddies as they look at the act. For the first time in the film, female sensuality is introduced, and appropriately precedes by only a couple of shots Bart's first sight of Laurie.

Their meeting is literally explosive. Spotting Bart in the audience Laurie points the gun toward him and fires. Bart flinches slightly, but his face immediately beams with even greater pleasure. Laurie's act is a curious meld of sex and guns ("So appealing—so dangerous—so lovely to look at"), and each time she fires her pistol, she presents to Lewis's camera (and Bart's point of view) her tightly clad, shapely profile. The attraction between her and Bart seems natural, and they "fall in love" while matching their marksmanship. Laurie seems willing to submit to him only because he proves himself better than her, but she wants him (he becomes worth more to her than a mere gun) in order to increase her worldly goods. She thus appeals to him by offering money—that is, a job with the carnival—but it is the combined appeal of sex and guns that wins him. Still he must be goaded by her into asserting himself, into defying the paternal authority of the social system by "kicking back." Only breaking the law to take what you want seems to resolve the stifling Oedipal complex which is equated with the authoritarian social pressures. That the film's emphasis is more Oedipal than social makes particularly disturbing the impotency Bart exhibits in his inability to kill. "Normal" living means never defying the paternal authority; but self-assertion becomes deadly. Each time Bart seems unwilling to continue their life of crime, Laurie coos her love for him and seduces him into another act of self-assertion. Deadly is the female because she makes one gun crazy.

The real marvel of the film is that it pursues these complexities for the most part by the repetition of carefully conceived visual motifs, rather than on the more literary, scripted level. The face of Bart as a young boy is framed in extreme closeup to the right of the frame as he takes careful aim at a baby chick he will kill with his BB gun, after which he vows never to kill again. In the scene where, as an adolescent, he is unable to make himself kill a mountain lion, his face assumes the same position in the frame and to the left his friends are seen in deep focus, goading him on to kill. We are referred to the earlier killing by the soundtrack as well, for the sounds of the birds in the trees around the boys are identical to the chirping of the chicks. The visual motif occurs for the third time when, escaping from a robbery, Bart leans over the back seat to aim his gun at a pursuing police car and his face is once again positioned on the right in the closeup. When he hesitates, Laurie, at the steering wheel in deep focus to the left of the frame, assumes the position of his young friends, yelling at him to kill the pursuers when he knows he cannot. The motif emphasizes how the scenes are related while at the same time conveying the development and increasing significance of Bart's hatred of killing. A similar composition emphasizes the relationship of two otherwise very different scenes. In the mountain lion scene, Bart's two friends, seated on the ground in the same position as in the shot described earlier, shoot at the lion while Bart, having refused to shoot, stands in left profile on their right. We see him only from the shoulders down and watch as his left hand clenches into a fist with each shot his friends fire, expressing his frustration and fear through physical action. A much later scene recalls this setup, when Laurie threatens to leave Bart if he refuses to rob banks with her. She delivers the ultimatum as she lies on the bed in left midground. Bart once again stands, left profile in the right foreground, visible only from the shoulders down, and we again see his hand form a fist in frustration and fear, linking the two scenes on the level of their similar effects and their similar origin in Bart's refusal to assert himself violently.

Another important motif employed by Lewis is the use of mirrors and reflecting glass. Breaking glass becomes a physical expression of violent self-assertion: the broken window in the film's first scene, the glass gum ball dispenser, shot to pieces in closeup, which opens the series of tableaux showing the couple beginning their life of crime. When Bart comes to take Laurie away from Packett, the carnival owner she is living with, the spurned lover grabs a mirror from the wall to throw at Bart; but before he is able to take it in his hands, Bart shoots it to pieces and Packett is left staring at his own image in the shattered mirror, reflecting his shattered self-image springing from his inability to prove "man enough" for Laurie. And in the next shot, where Packett tells them both they are fired and the two leave together, the leaves of a plant seen in extreme closeup in the upper right corner of the frame suggest for a moment that we are viewing the scene in the broken mirror. The significance of glass as a reflecting surface is reiterated on the level of dialogue when Bart tells Laurie, "I don't want to look in that mirror and see nothing but a stick-up man staring back at me." And shots of the couple standing before the reflecting glass of a shop window open and close the montage of the early part of their marriage. At first it is the glass of a jeweler's where they seem to be going to buy a ring; in the latter they stand before a pawn shop apparently preparing to hock the ring. Glass stands repeatedly between them and the things they want, and it must be broken if those things are to be had. But it also reflects the self-image as it is changed and distorted. Significantly, the fleeing couple is seen reflected in a window as they escape from their last job, the robbery of the Armour plant, and it is the image of which Bart is most ashamed: a stick-up man and his moll, always running.

Lewis finds a visual correlative to the constant distortion and wariness of the couple in the variety of costumes they wear: rodeo outfits, very conservative suits and glasses, a military uniform, a butcher's apron, a slacks suit, a fur, a beret. Their need to constantly move, their inability to find stability, and the physical danger in maintaining one "self" too long is made much clearer in this way than through all Bart's pained speeches to that effect. Most interesting is the Western garb which fills a position in still another visual motif of the film. As a child, Bart is seen straddling a wooden horse and playing with his BB gun in a young boy's rendition of movie cowboy. When he first sees Laurie and is attracted to her, she is wearing Western clothing, and once he joins the show Bart also assumes the costume of a Hollywood gunfighter. It is in this costume that he shoots at Packett, in his most forceful act of self-assertion by which he wins Laurie. Later, the couple use the costumes in performing a bank robbery. The importance of the Western motif is in the fact that it reflects both Laurie's glamorized conception of outlawry and Bart's attitude about the noble use of guns, concepts which are undercut by the action of the film.

A number of other striking visuals appear throughout the film. The pair's first killings occur during their robbery of the Armour meat packing plant, which involves a number of shots showing row after row of hanging animal carcasses, surrounding the murders with an almost sickening vision of real carnage (while at the same time presenting a vision of the casual butchery by which the corporate structure, that the pair attacks, survives). Another striking scene occurs toward the end of the film where the couple is fleeing the law in the woods of a national park. At dark Bart suggests they stop for the night since he knows the area and in the daylight will be able to lead them safely out; but, when daylight comes, a thick, ominously white fog surrounds them and they are worse off than before. In the *film noir* world, not even the sun can be taken for granted. Also interesting is Lewis's use of the bottom of the frame for the entrance and exit of images, a device which seems extremely rare in the left-to-right logic of most Hollywood films. Most noteworthy in this respect is the first appearance of Laurie, who enters from the bottom of the left side of a low-angle shot of Packett announcing her act, guns blazing over her head so that we first see the fire from her pistols and then the pistols themselves moving into the frame before Laurie herself comes into full view. The reverse occurs in the scene in which Bart refuses to turn himself over to his friends. Framed in a low-angle closeup, he begins to back away from them toward his sister's doorway while the camera remains stable, giving the effect of his literally slipping out the bottom of the picture.

But the most outstanding sequence in the whole film is the single shot bank robbery; for, if nothing else about the film were notable, this shot would make it all worthwhile and in a better known film would likely be touted the world round. Lewis sets his camera in the back seat of the car the couple is driving to a bank robbery. We see only the backs of their heads as they drive down several streets toward the bank and talk nervously to one another. Once they park the car, we watch Bart get out and go into the bank, leaving Laurie at the wheel. When a policeman appears near the bank Laurie slips out of the car and begins to talk with him in order to divert his attention from Bart's activities, the camera moving up over the front seat and watching her through the open car door. When Bart emerges from the bank they both jump into the car, the camera returns to its position in the back seat, and we ride with the couple as they make their getaway. The shot lasts almost three and a half minutes and is fraught with tension and suspense. By refusing to cut to another angle, Lewis forces us to assume a constricted position similar to that of the couple, dependent as much as they on the location of the car. Like them, we are committed to play out the scene in actual time once the robbery has begun, and we become tensely aware of the interrelation of the actions of the two because there is no cut to destroy the ticking away of seconds. As they escape, we are forced to ride with them, to share their exhilarating sense of flight after having sat for what seemed an eternity in front of that bank, and to share as well their fearful suspense as to whether they are being chased; and by keeping the camera pointed always forward, Lewis denies us the tension-releasing effect of being able to look backward to check for ourselves. Fourteen years later, in *Bande à part*, Godard was to "innovatively" place his camera in the back seat of a car, watching only the backs of the heads of the couple in the front seat as they drove and talked. It is interesting to speculate whether he borrowed the idea from *Gun Crazy*, but even more interesting to compare Godard's use of the shot as a disruption of filmic syntax, a rather dead-end critique of the cinema, with Lewis's integral and suspenseful utilization of the same technique to make more eloquent, rather than to disrupt, his *mise-en-scène*.

To say that *Gun Crazy* has not received the attention it should have is a gross understatement. But, to say it has been entirely ignored is not true, since the film seems now to have a rather enthusiastic following and its rediscovery has opened up a new but limited interest in the career of Joseph H. Lewis. Those rare critics who have had the opportunity to study a number of Lewis's films seem to unanimously agree that *Gun Crazy* is his masterpiece, but the quality of this film leaves room for a number of very good films "beneath" it. Lewis's work here seems a strong reaffirmation of the director's cinema, for *Gun Crazy* proclaims the cinematic superiority of a well constructed *mise-en-scène* over the most literate dialogue or brilliant delivery of lines, and suggests that such a marvel may come from almost anywhere.

———

ED LOWRY

VOL. 14 NO. 2
FEBRUARY 27, 1978

Films of Maya Deren (1943–1958)

DIRECTED BY MAYA DEREN

Meshes of the Afternoon (1943)
A film by Maya Deren and Alexander Hammid. Music by Teiji Ito. Running time: 18 minutes. With Maya Deren and Alexander Hammid.

At Land (1944)
Conceived and directed by Maya Deren. Assisted by Hella Hamon and Alexander Hammid. Running time: 15 minutes. With Maya Deren.

Study in Choreography for Camera (1945)
A film by Maya Deren and Talley Beatty. Running time: 4 minutes. With Talley Beatty.

Ritual in Transfigured Time (1946)
Conceived and directed by Maya Deren. Photographed by Hella Heyman. Choreographic collaboration: Frank Westbrook. Running time: 15 minutes. With Rita Christiani, Frank Westbrook, Maya Deren, Anaïs Nin, and Maya Deren's friends.

Meditation on Violence (1948)
A film by Maya Deren. Based on traditional training movements of the
Wu-tang and Shaolin schools of Chinese boxing. Flute: Chinese classi-
cal music. Drums: Recorded in Haiti by Maya Deren. Performance by
Ch'ao-li chi. Dedicated to J.M. Running time: 12 minutes.

Cinema—and by this is understood the entire body of technique including camera, lighting, acting, editing, etc.—is a time-space art with a unique capacity
for creating new temporal-spatial relationships and projecting them with an
incontrovertible impact of reality—the reality of show-it-to-me. It emerges
in a period marked, simultaneously, by the development of radio in communication, the airplane and the rocketship in transportation, and the theory of
relativity in physics. To ignore the implications of this simultaneity, or to consider it a historical coincidence, would constitute not only a failure to understand the basic nature of these contributions to our civilization; it would also
make us guilty of an even more profound failure, that of recognizing the rela-
tionships of human ideology to material development. | MAYA DEREN, *New
Directions*, 1946.

Maya Deren approached the New York City Greenwich Village scene for the
first time in 1937 as a well-educated girl of twenty who was acquainted with
many of the prevailing intellectual, psychological and philosophical concerns of the time. Deren's father, a Russian-Jewish psychiatrist who headed
a mental institution in Syracuse, New York, had grounded his daughter in
the issues of a relativistic world view and Freudian psychoanalysis. Her high
school education abroad in Switzerland, her undergraduate college education at Syracuse University and New York University, and her graduate work
at Smith College reenforced and developed her attitudes. She studied twentieth century developments in science, philosophy and ethics; she learned
current psychological theories, and she wrote her Master of Arts thesis on
the French Symbolists' influence on the Imagist poets.

Following receipt of her MA and her return to Greenwich Village, Deren
applied her theoretical knowledge to her interests in modern poetry and
modern dance. She wrote experimental poetry and she began a book on
modern dance theory in collaboration with black dancer-choreographer
Catherine Dunham. The mother of an emerging black modern dance movement, Dunham introduced Deren to other young black dancers as well as to
black tribal objects and artifacts, rituals and music. A growing interest in

Films of Maya Deren. Courtesy of the film still department of Anthology Film Archives.

African, Haitian and other black tribal music and customs infected other young New York artists, too, since they believed such primitive art and myths served as universal symbols of the inner mind, thus reflecting their belief in Jungian psychology and concepts of the archetype and the collective unconscious. Deren, who had rejected the Freudian psychology of her father's influence, found a compatible atmosphere for her creative development amongst these New York avant-gardists.

In late 1941, Deren left New York and toured with Dunham and her dance company. While in Los Angeles, Deren met Czech documentary filmmaker Alexander Hammid, whom she subsequently married. Hammid taught Deren the elements of filmmaking and he helped her make her first film, *Meshes of the Afternoon* (1943).

In *Meshes*, Deren sets up the formal elements and patterns which she will follow in all her films by cutting across traditional notions of time and space so as to blur the distinction between phenomenal experience and imagined experience. For example, when the first Maya climbs the staircase within the house in slow motion, Deren uses camera angle and placement to extend the concept of the stairs' length and the actual time it takes to climb. She further breaks traditional time and space orientation by combining camera angle and cutting on a motion when the second Maya figure falls backward onto the stairs, catches herself in mid-fall and then remains at the top of the stair-way. In each of these instances, Deren illustrates her concept that "the abso-lute differentiation between *here* and *there* loses meaning as *here* and *there*, being so mutually accessible, [they] become, in effect almost identical."

Deren applies the same logic to time chronologies and allows past and future to exist only as extensions of a continuous present moment. She ties these ideas together in the four-stride sequence that the Maya persona with knife in hand takes toward the sleeper in the chair. Her first foot lifts from a beach and falls in grass, the second foot falls onto a different grassy area, the first steps onto a sidewalk and then, finally, the second falls onto a car-pet, thereby unifying geographically separate events into one continuous movement. By further using cutting techniques to establish a fluid, linear space rather than moving the camera into or out of the space of the images, Deren negates any feeling of depth that would lead to a sense of dramatic illusion or depiction of realistic space. The shifting sense of time and space, the resulting confusion and mixture of identities, reality and unreality sug-gest an alienated sense of self and experience, both real and imagined.

Several critics have called Deren a descendant of the European Surrealist filmmaking tradition of the 1920s and 1930s. Although no evidence cur-rently exists to indicate that Deren actually viewed any of these European films before she made *Meshes*, she lived among many artists responding to the surrealist tradition and it thus seems likely that she would have been well acquainted with Surrealist concerns. Deren always insisted that *Meshes* was not a Surrealist film, and she rejected any psychoanalytic interpreta-tions of it. Her use of subjective camera, her creation of a linear space with little sense of depth and her repetitive use of symbol-motifs are significant breaks with Surrealist style; but her use of mirror, knife, key and flower within a dream experience lends itself to psychoanalytic interpretation.

Deren's next film project, *The Witch's Cradle*, points more specifically toward her increasing inability to work within a Surrealist tradition. She had employed the artists Marcel Duchamp and Pajarito Matta as actors in this unrealized work which was filmed in the Surrealist "Art of This Cen-tury" Gallery. The film's concept was inspired by the architectural structure of the gallery and the paintings and objects on display. Deren wrote that in making this film she was "concerned with the impression that Surrealistic objects were, in a sense, the cabalistic symbols of the twentieth century." She equated Surrealist artists with feudal magicians and witches as they all defied "normal" attitudes of time and space, discarding the validity of surface appearances and conventional causality. For reasons unknown, Deren abandoned work on this project; but as the rest of her films reveal very little evidence of classically Surrealist interests, it is probable that Deren reasonably saw no further creative potentials in pursuing a Surrealistic-psychoanalytic approach. Her films become much more Jungian in her attempts to be more universally comprehensible on metaphysical planes.

In her next film, *At Land* (1944), Deren sought an expression of a collective subconscious process without the use of metaphor. She again uses the quest for personal and sexual identity, but this time she conveys it without resorting to dream experience or imagery. Time and space are fluidly manipulated so that there is a continual present which incorporates past and future and a smooth blending of disconsonant geographical locales. For example, the figure climbs a tree until her head continues beyond the upper parameter of the frame. Deren cuts to a shot showing her head and torso stretched snake-like along the length of a banquet table. The figure continues to crawl down the table until another shot shows her legs still among the branches pushing themselves up out of the frame along the same path as the rest of her body. Editing in this fashion engenders a spatial and temporal contiguity between disparate times and physical locations. The smoothness of the cuts unites the shots in a plausible connectivity, the dislocation of the time-space dimensions being not as important as the dislocation of the subject. In her program notes on *At Land* Deren wrote, "This concern with time and space is not purely technical and one is not aware of the devices of the camera because the emotional rarification of this concern—namely, the curious dislocation of the individual in a suddenly and actually relativistic world, and her inability to cope with its fluidity or to achieve a stable, adjusted relationship to its elements—is the main element which was to be projected."

Deren's constant cutting during her subjects' movements provided a spatial continuity that led her to appreciate the possibilities of the camera as a choreographic element. Combining her dance insights with her film experience, she elaborated on the expressing of continuous movement through space by shifting from any narrative structure to isolation of a single dance movement in *A Study in Choreography for the Camera* (1945). P. Adams Sitney calls *Choreography* the first "imagist film" for its application of poetic principles to cinematic production. By layering fragmentary images of the dancer's movements in a variety of spatial areas, Deren creates a "dance, which is to natural movement what poetry is to conversational prose." Like the four stride sequence in *Meshes*, Deren's extension of her dancer's movement from the Metropolitan Museum to the woods to an apartment interior captures an idealized, floating gesture while commenting on the quality of motion.

Deren's artistic efforts peaked in 1946 with her film *Ritual in Transfigured Time*. In *Ritual*, she develops her dance movement-gesture by combining the motions among several people in the same way she joined movements in *Choreography*. In the two women winding yarn, at the party and in the statue-making dance sequence, one person begins a movement while another continues it and another completes it. Fluid activity results not from the identity of a performer or from the narrative context of the movement, but from the combined movements themselves.

In a film that centers on women, Deren explores a universal ritual—courtship and marriage—from a female point of view. As the widow in black moves through the ritual, she looks to a reappearing female figure (Deren) for guidance; and she ultimately weds, not the present male figure, but the sea, the Freudian and Jungian symbol for the eternal female principle. Deren, who had earlier used the sea in the conclusions of both *Meshes* and *At Land*, here finally suggests a joining of the female figure and her search for personal and sexual identity. As in her expression of the movements themselves, Deren again uses cinematic means to convey her resolution; through negative photographic processing the widow's black weeds become a flowing, white bridal gown.

Deren frequently referred to *Meshes of the Afternoon* as her "point of departure." In other words, she viewed her film work as a developmental process which centered around the same basic concerns. Her interest in the manipulation of time and space through purely cinematic means can be seen throughout her work culminating in *Ritual in Transfigured Time*. In *Meditation on Violence* (1948), Deren intellectualizes this process so completely that the artistic effort becomes a somewhat sterile application of her theories. Prior to production, Deren sketched several charts outlining in precise detail all aspects of time and movement contained in the film. She considered these charts to be an illustration of what is meant by conceiving the form as a whole and creating a non-literary continuity for film. In *Meditation on Violence* she claims to have tried to "abstract the principle of ongoing metamorphosis and change." Although she felt that the film required re-editing and a shortening of its length, she never had the opportunity to do so. Eleven years later Deren made one more film, *The Very Eye of Night* (1959), another choreographed dance and camera application that also employed a great deal of optical printing. (This is the only completed Deren film not included in tonight's program.)

Deren first stepped from the role of filmmaker to distributor and promoter early in 1946, when she offered the first American theatrical showing of a privately made 16mm film. At a time when little interest in film as an art form existed, Deren attracted a large audience for the screening of her first two films in the Provincetown Playhouse in New York City. One person in the crowd stressed the importance of the event for the artistic community when he told an investigating policeman at the door, "It is not a demonstration. It is a revolution in filmmaking."

Deren's success at becoming a public figure among the New York City artistic community may be due as much to her personal presence as to her ideas and work. All the descriptions of Deren published by her contemporaries attest to her ability to dominate groups of people with her dramatic appearance and her charismatic personality. In the mid and late 1940s, when she hosted one party after another for the New York intellectual crowd, Deren surfaced each time as the center of attention, though her personality eventually alienated as many as it attracted. In their descriptions of Deren, Rudolf Arnheim, Anaïs Nin and James Agee have labelled her everything from strong-willed, commanding, seductive and hypnotic to dogmatic, obstinate, restless, unsatisfied and energetic to the point of violence.

Deren completed the break from her initial creative period in 1947 with her receipt of the first Guggenheim Fellowship for filmmaking. With the advice of anthropologists Margaret Mead and Gregory Bateson, Deren went to Haiti to prepare a film that would more fully develop her concepts on myth and ritual. When the initial grant money ran out and Deren did not get a renewal, she put more effort into promoting film as an art form in order to solicit financial support for independent filmmaking. As a result, she never adapted the material from her Haitian trip into a film although she did publish an anthropological study of Haitian tribal rituals, *The Divine Horseman*, in 1953.

In conjunction with her public and administrative efforts to create an atmosphere for personal experimental filmmaking in New York City, Deren increasingly articulated her aesthetic ideas into a cogent theoretical framework. In 1946, she published *An Anagram of Ideas on Art, Form and Film*, her first and fullest elaboration of her aesthetic theories. Her other major publications, "Cinema As An Art Form" and "Cinematography: The Creative Uses of Reality," restate the ideas set forth in *An Anagram*. Aside from these written documents of her theories, Deren circulated her aesthetic ideals on her many lecture tours, college appearances and short-term teaching assignments throughout the 1950s.

Deren recognized that, since the Renaissance, man's belief in the realistic reproduction of experience had directed and promoted the concept of realism in the arts. She also noted that, whereas in painting "the image must always be an abstraction of the aspect, in photography the abstraction of an idea produces the archetypal image." Because of the indexical relationship between the world and the photographic image early filmmakers and photographers believed that they were representing reality. Deren maintains that because documentary filmmakers believed in the image as an end product of their art and because they assumed the image faithfully reproduced reality. She asserted that only when filmmakers conceived of the image as a basic material of creative action and understood the creative process as the primary act could they see the futility of attempting to document reality objectively. By failing to understand the subjective and selective nature and bias of camera placement, length of shots and editing of footage, early documentary filmmakers missed the point that any "documentary" must be a selective and subjective reality because of the subjectivity of the filming process.

Deren also criticized the history of animated film and Hollywood narrative film. She chastised the former for its failure to accept the realistic authority of the photographic image and for its ignorance of the unique properties of the art form; she criticized the latter for its imitation of literary modes and its reliance on nineteenth century assumptions for creating a realistic artificial illusion.

Deren argued for a filmic art that uses its basic property, the realistic nature of the photographic image, as a part of the creative process. Deren based her position on her assumption that form characterizes the quality and nature of artistic expression and that form must be derived from the unique properties of the artistic medium itself. Like the Abstract Expressionist painters who celebrated the two-dimensionality of the canvas and the quality and texture of paint as elemental materials in their creative actions, Deren insisted upon manipulation of the photographic image as part of the creative process of filmmaking.

Deren also found in the capability within the filmmaking process for synthetic constructions across time and space a creative method that could directly reflect concern of the age of the theory of relativity. Filmmaking, she said, has an obligation to work with these elements of the medium in order to "discover its own structural modes, explore the new realms and dimensions accessible to it and so enrich our culture artistically as science has done in its own province."

Her obsession with locating structures, reflected even in her organization of *An Anagram*, led Deren to a definition of a dualistic nature in the filmmaking process. She argued against the "horizontal" or linear narrative tendency in cinema and defended the "vertical" or "lyrical" style in film in which only a layering of images without time or spatial references exist. Deren illustrated her concept by stating that poetry is to literature what the vertical film is to cinema. Only by concentrating on the "vertical" can filmmakers break from linear and illusionistic spatial-time frames and emphasize the process depicting the felt reality, the only possible true reflection of a modernist world. As film critic Annette Michelson pointed out, Deren's claim for stylistic polarities parallels linguistic Roman Jakobson's formulation of structural modes in speech, and Jakobson's model provided the basis for Structuralists' application of "metonymic"/"metaphoric," "syntagmatic"/"paradigmatic" or "horizontal"/"vertical" modes to a variety of forms.

Deren died of successive cerebral hemorrhages in 1961 at the age of 44. Her theories on the structural aspects of the creative process and cinematic form anticipated Structuralist theories and trends in painting, sculpture and film, while the rich heritage of her film *oeuvre* has provided a model and inspiration for American independent filmmakers and for the further development of poetic film form. Her promotional and organizational efforts helped make wide-scale American independent filmmaking a reality.

———

LAUREN RABINOVITZ, MARJORIE BAUMGARTEN

VOL. 15, NO. 3
NOVEMBER 29, 1978

Scorpio Rising (1964)

DIRECTED BY KENNETH ANGER

Conceived, directed, photographed and edited by Kenneth Anger. Dedicated to Jack Parsons, Victor Childe, Jim Powers, James Dean, T. E. Lawrence, Hart Crane, Kurt Mann, The Society of Spartans, The Hell's Angels, and all overgrown boys who will ever follow the whistle of Love's brother.

"Scorpio Rising"
In my motorcycle jacket
the leather creaks as I turn
but boy I know I'm tough
wow the jacket feels strong around my slim body
and gee the zippers and snaps and buckles look swell
but when I ride o daddy
long hair flowing behind
Love

JOHN FLES, *Film Culture*, Spring 1964.

To be born under the sign of Scorpio, to be a Scorpio, is to have certain characteristics. Astrologically speaking, Scorpios attract those they want to attract; are centered on the inner self; are ruled by Pluto (god of the underworld); are associated with death, regeneration, violence, brutality, coercion. So it becomes extra-apparent that not only are Brando and Hitler analogies of the character Scorpio, but so is Christ. He is not just meant as a contrast. Christ, like (a) Scorpio, is a Rebel Rouser, with charismatic powers, and is associated with brutality and with regeneration. Hitler is another charismatic Rouser associated with violence, brutality and coercion, and arguably self-centered. Brando (Wild One) again is a Rebel Rouser, an attracter, centered on the inner self, associated with violence. They do not have all Scorpio's qualities, but they share many, and several overlapping ones.

So the "high" view (overman's view?) of the Myth of the American Motorcyclist is a "gay" view too, in all three meanings of that word—and is not. I have touched on the humor and the homosexuality. The other "gaiety" is the Nietzschean. And it is precisely in the confusion of role (hero, villain, stooge, overman, herd-man, decadent, nihilist, antichrist, fanatic), among the three counterparts of Scorpio (Brando, Hitler, Christ), that the parody becomes completely ambiguous. Hitler, for instance, is neither a villain nor an overman, quite; he has too much of all the rest. Nor is Christ merely the antithesis of Hitler or Brando (though he does appear "so pale, so weak, so decadent"—Neitzsche: The Antichrist). For the very act of paralleling Christ to Scorpio, as Hitler and Brando are paralleled to him, puts Christ to that extent on their level; and they on his. And, most important, as I have horoscopically shown, all four are Scorpios. Such is the scope of Anger's horror. All become, not overman, but Superman, the cheap, comic-strip version (Anger's restraint shows here; he has funnies in the film, but no Superman). All values are equated, negated; all emotions are cheapened; and the result is the most deeply nihilistic film I know. Nowhere is life so intently sterilized. Nowhere else is death made such a mockery: as a chic decorative skull; as the emblem on the pennant of a queer sports club. And yet, it is more terrible that way, becoming the ultimate reduction of ultimate experience to brilliant chromatic surface; Thanatos in chrome— artificial death, to round a vision of barren unreality. It is decadence decayed to a vapor, the exhaustion of even despair. | KEN KELMAN, Film Culture, Winter 1963–1964.

Man's authoritarian structure . . . is basically produced by the embedding
of sexual inhibitions and fear in the living substance of sexual impulses.

. . . When sexuality is prevented from attaining natural gratification, owing
to the process of sexual repression, what happens is that it seeks various
kinds of substitute gratifications. Thus, for instance, natural aggression is
distorted into brutal sadism, which constitutes an essential part of the mass-
psychological basis of those imperialistic wars that are instigated by a few. To
give another instance: From the point of view of mass psychology, the effect of
militarism, is based essentially on a libidinous mechanism. The sexual effect of
a uniform, the erotically provocative effect of rhythmically executed goose-
stepping, the exhibitionistic nature of militaristic procedures, have been
more practically comprehended by a salesgirl or an average secretary than
by our most erudite politicians. On the other hand it is political repression
that consciously exploits these sexual interests. It not only designs flashy
uniforms for the men, it puts the recruiting into the hands of attractive
women. . . . And why are these [things] effective? Because our youth has
become sexually starved owing to sexual suppression. | WILHELM REICH,
The Mass Psychology of Fascism.

Scorpio Rising is perhaps the most popular and widely renowned film of the
American avant-garde. Its release confirmed Anger's reputation as one of
the major underground filmmakers in this country and generated a stir
which reached from the pages of New York's *Film Culture* (which devoted
no less than five articles to *Scorpio Rising* in the first two issues following
its premiere) to the law courts of California. In the spring of 1964, soon after
Anger had received a grant from the Ford Foundation to enable him to continue his work, the Los Angeles vice squad busted a Hollywood art film
house and its manager for showing *Scorpio Rising.* At the subsequent obscenity trial, the prosecuting attorney refused to seat any juror who answered
in the affirmative to the question of whether they enjoyed movies. In retaliation, the defense recused all male jurors, contending that the film's homo-
erotic undertones might threaten such jurors' masculinity and adversely
affect their judgement. Following the testimony of numerous witnesses,
none of whom could make the film conform to the State of California's definition of obscenity, the all-female, movie-hating jury found *Scorpio Rising*
obscene nonetheless.

If such a judgement seems absurd by current standards, it must be admit-
ted that the film is still powerful enough to offend a great many people. Its

Scorpio Rising. Courtesy of the film still department of Anthology Film Archives.

power derives largely from its unique juxtaposition of found popular artifacts and cultural icons (motorcycles, children's toys, old movie clips, cops,
swastikas, rock music, etc.) which demands a reading of them in a radically
new and disturbing context. Anger's associations work almost subliminally
at points, building with a terrifying logic from the mundane to the cosmic.
The strata of sexuality violence and perversity he uncovers in seemingly
innocent, popular material corresponds closely to the kind of re-reading of
old rock songs by such New Wave poet-musicians as Patti Smith (in her Patty
Hearst version of "Hey Joe," the sadistic horse-fantasy of "Land of a Thousand Dances," and the overtly lesbian rendering of Van Morrison's "Gloria")
and the Sex Pistols (in their "sociology lecture" rendition of Iggy and the
Stooges' "No Fun").

Unlike most avant-garde filmmakers (e.g., Maya Deren, Stan Brakhage,
Hollis Frampton, Michael Snow), Anger seems less interested in film form
than film sense. This preference for proposing ways of understanding as
opposed to ways of seeing distinguishes Anger from his avant-garde contemporaries and relates him more closely to the traditions of the Hollywood

narrative film. It is no accident that Anger's tendency has been toward progressively larger budgets, nor that his book, *Hollywood Babylon* (first published in 1960), concerns the secret scandals of Tinsel Town (where Anger
grew up as a child actor). This fascination with Hollywood corresponds
closely to *Scorpio Rising*'s obsession with popular culture artifacts and suggests the extent to which the film addresses itself to an audience in a way
that Snow's formal rigors and Brakhage's formal distortions never attempt.
And though juxtapositions occur which radically violate Hollywood conceptions of narrative, *Scorpio Rising* does contain identifiable characters,
settings and narrative sequences; in addition, it is shot and edited to pop
music with a slickness and sense of humor familiar to Hollywood, but rarely
seen in the American avant-garde.

Anger's ironic sense infuses *Scorpio Rising* much as it does *Hollywood
Babylon*. Each proposes a deliberately sensational reading of tensions and
perversions beneath a glossy surface. In *Scorpio Rising*, Anger structures
his reading around a series of thirteen popular songs from the period 1961
to 1964. The level of punning and ironic association is evident in Anger's
description of the film as

> A conjuration of the presiding Princes, Angels and Spirits of the Sphere
> of MARS, formed as a "high" view of the Myth of the American Motor-
> cyclist. The Power Machine seen as tribal totem, from toy to terror.
> Thanatos in chrome and black leather and bursting jeans.

He speaks of the film in four parts:

> Part I. Boys and Bolts (masculine fascination with the Thing that Goes)
> [the first four song sequences].
> Part II. Image Maker (getting high on heroes: Dean's Rebel and Brando's
> Johnny: The True View of J. C.) [the following four song segments].
> Part III. Walpurgis Party (J. C. wallflower at cycler's Sabbath) [the next
> two song segments].
> Party IV. Rebel Rouser (The Gathering of the Dark Legions, with a Mes-
> sage from Our Sponsor [the final three song segments].

For the purpose of analysis it will be advantageous to discuss each of the
thirteen song segments individually.

1. "FOOLS RUSH IN"—RICK NELSON (1964)

An emblem for Puck Films begins the film. Puck is the prankish imp of Shakespeare's *A Midsummer Night's Dream*, a dangerously mischievous adolescent. "Puck" also suggests the word "fuck," though for the time being the implications of both this association and the adolescent boy remain covert. The slogan on the emblem, "What fools these mortals be," a quote from Shakespeare's Puck, establishes a position of ironic distance from the events which are to follow.

We are then introduced to the film's milieu—a garage full of machine parts and tools, a boy working on his motorcycle. The sequence begins with the kid uncovering the cycle, followed by a series of loving shots of chromium, tail lights, exhaust pipes, and ending with a shot of leather boots next to a chain. All the objects in this sequence are legitimate found artifacts which can realistically be associated with the cyclist. The loving pans and closeups, however, suggest an almost erotic attachment to the physical trappings themselves. The Rick Nelson song which accompanies the sequence enhances this feeling.

> Fools rush in
> Where wise men never go.
> But wise men never fall in love,
> So how are they to know?
> When we met
> I felt my life begin
> So open up your heart and let
> This fool rush in.

The fools who rush in are the same fools that mortals be. The song concerns this romantic *amour fou*, a mad love which wise men could never appreciate, but which every cyclist finds in his obsession with his chopper. The song may be the machine's love song to the cyclist or it may be the cyclist's to his machine.

A scorpion in a white oval rushes toward the camera, introducing us to the icon of the title. A husky, leather-clad back rises into an orange frame. The steel studs spelling out the film's title across the back of the leather jacket and Anger's name along the belt are both comic and suggestive of fetishism and sadomasochism. The cyclist turns his faceless torso toward the camera and we see his bare chest beneath the jacket. He walks forward and the camera seems to disappear into his stomach, as Rick Nelson sings, "Open up your heart and let/This fool rush in."

The foundation is laid. We've been introduced to the trappings of the cyclist, the romantic/obsessive language of pop music, and the male physique. All are presented erotically, but eroticism has not yet emerged as an overt subject.

2. "WIND-UP DOLL"—THE RON-DELLS

With the cyclist's leather hat perched atop its handlebars, the cycle takes on a life of its own. The fetishized object (the cycle) is personified, while the female singer defines herself as a mechanized object: "I guess I'm kind of a wind-up dolly, too." Women and cycles become equivalent: both are toys to be played with.

Shots of the cyclist using a wrench are intercut with those of a child winding up a toy motorcycle cop. The cyclist's obsession with his machine is comically compared to adolescent play, locating the cyclist in a pre-heterosexual stage of development. The masculine symbol of the motorcycle replaces women in the cyclist's affection, and is implicit in the lyrics of the song: "Wind me up, I'll fall in love with you." Objects of love become objects of possession for manipulation.

Seen clearly for the first time, the cyclist is wearing jeans, smoking a cigarette and has his hair slicked back. At the end of the sequence the camera comes to rest on a mirror which frames boy and cycle together, introducing the element of the cyclist's narcissistic attitude about physical appearances.

3. "MY BOYFRIEND'S BACK"—THE ANGELS (1963)

This sequence begins and ends with a closeup of a skull which leers down at the cyclist from the corner of the room throughout the song. It is the cyclist's song. Death is his boyfriend.

The song itself is up-tempo and cute, but beneath its playful and seemingly innocent lyrics is a disturbing equation of love and violence.

My boyfriend's back
And there's gonna be trouble. . . .

When you see him coming
You better cut out on the double.

Love is a contract of male possession which must be defended by violence.
With a boyfriend like Death or Danger, the cyclist's *amour fou* can be
defended in defiance of the rest of the world. The arena is male to male
conflict: "You're a big man now/But he'll cut you down to size." Addressing
lines like "You're gonna be sorry you were ever born" and "Hey, you're gonna
get a beating" to the audience and the world at large, the sequence outlines
a violently self-centered, narcissistic consciousness clearly defined in the
sequence where the cyclist looks into the mirror and Anger intercuts an
almost subliminal shot of four frames (one-sixth of a second) showing the
boy staring into the face of the skeleton. Death and his reflected image are
juxtaposed.

4. "BLUE VELVET"—BOBBY VINTON (1963)

The camera tilts lovingly up the legs of a man's torn blue jeans, arriving at
his crotch just as he is zipping his fly; Bobby Vinton croons, "She wore blue
velvet." The shot is risque and titillating after the fashion of Hollywood films
which coyly caress the body of a scantily-clad starlet. The juxtaposition proposes sexual role reversal, finalizing the homosexual shift only hinted at in
the previous sequences. The effect is not one of feminizing the cyclists, but
of making them overtly sexual. The camera voyeuristically watches as a
tattooed man pulls on a t-shirt, and pans slowly across the reclining body
of another bare-chested cyclist.

Repressed sexuality emerges in the form of fetishism. The cloth fetish of
the song is replaced by the denim and leather fetishes of the cyclists. The
masculine fetish of the cycle gives way to the fetishes of super-masculine
clothing and finally to the male physique itself. In this context, "blue" takes
on connotations of pornography (as in "blue movie")—repressed sexuality
finding expression in the generation of masturbatory images. The first overt
substitute phallus appears at the end of this sequence in the form of the
highway cone standing between the spread legs of the cyclist who strides
toward the camera.

Dressed and ready, a boy takes his cycle by the handlebars and begins to
roll it out of the garage.

5. "(YOU'RE THE) DEVIL IN DISGUISE"—ELVIS PRESLEY (1963)

"Blue Velvet" posits the male body as an object of admiration. Elvis concurs, singing, "You look like an angel" to Scorpio, reclining on his bed as he reads the comics, but adds: "You're the devil in disguise." In this context, "angel" clearly refers to the Hell's Angels motorcycle gang, to which the film is dedicated.

Suppressed sexuality pervades the images which hang on the walls surrounding Scorpio, and Anger draws these images from popular artifacts, thereby implicating all of American culture: photos of James Dean on a motorcycle, television images of Brando in *The Wild One*, the seemingly innocent Sunday comics. The first comic strip insert is of "Freckles and His Friends," showing a young man working on his motorcycle, reaffirming (as do the images of Dean and Brando) the role models of the cyclist. The ped-erastic undercurrent of "Dondi" seems shockingly overt in this context: Dondi invites an attractive older man to share his room with him. The cartoon of two boys with their arms around one another from the "Li'l Abner" comic strip is clearly to be read as homosexual; and the title of the strip, "The Sons Also Rise," suggests the boys' arousal to erection. "Dick Tracy" begins with a landscape of human skulls and bones. Even Charles Schultz is not immune to the critique, as Anger inserts a few frames of Lucy deliv-ering a sound "whop" to another of the "Peanuts" characters. It is not just that there are homosexual readings available for the objects Anger holds up for our attention, but that the sexual repression of an entire culture seems to be expressing itself in violent and anti-heterosexual images.

Each of these images proposes the role model of the tough guy as an expression of male sexuality. Scorpio conforms to this rebellious, dangerous pose, wearing dark shades and a Mafia t-shirt. Pulling out a cigarette he has stuck beneath the earpiece of his glasses, he attempts to light a match between his teeth. Here there is a moment when the illusion of toughness is shattered, as the actor burns his lip; yet it only serves to remind us of how tenuous and inhuman the image of toughness actually is.

6. "HIT THE ROAD, JACK"—RAY CHARLES (1961)

Scorpio rises from the bed and begins to put on his boots and a leather wrist band. Washed-out images of a muscular boy on a very souped-up motorcycle riding around an amusement park are intercut with Scorpio's preparations to hit the road. The road is dead end, leading straight to death: "And don't you come back no more." The camera pans past a clipping about a motorcycle accident: "Cycle Hits Hole and Kills Two." Death by fetish. Cats lick at a pile of bones on the floor.

7. "HEAT WAVE"—MARTHA AND THE VANDELLAS (1963)

The ritual of foredoomed rebellion and death begins as Scorpio slips several steel, skull's head rings onto his fingers. He sticks his finger into a bottle of cocaine and lifts it to his nostril. A noose hangs prominently behind him.

> Whenever I'm with him
> Something inside
> Starts to burning
> And I'm filled with desire.
> Could this be a devil in me
> Or is this the way love's supposed to be?
> It's like a heat wave. . . .

While Martha and the Vandellas sing about the hot flash of sexual desire, Scorpio gets his own hot flash from the coke. A barrage of images immediately ensues: flash frames of the orange background behind the credits; closeups of the wind-up cop, reasserting the adolescent quality of the outlet for repressed sexuality; a television picture of pigeons being liberated from a cage (literally "coming out," with its gay implications); wax museum figures of Bela Lugosi as Dracula (sexuality as total possession and killing) and Gary Cooper from *High Noon* (once again, male to male conflict seen in terms of the great American myth, the Western, fought with the phallic substitute of the revolver); rows of shining cycle trophies (phallic prizes affirming masculine superiority); a pirate flag (skull and crossbones).

Heat is the central metaphor, closely related to the phallic images of fire and light in *Fireworks*. Limited, high-key lighting emphasizes the feeling of intense fire amidst a vast darkness. Scorpio finds another phallus—a pistol (firearms, a "heater"). He aims it carelessly around the room, then at the image of a menorah on television (the anti-Semitic implications of which will become clear in sequence #10), and finally at the TV image of a crucifix.

Scorpio holds a glowing oval with a scorpion in the center, then presses it to his lips. Anger flash cuts to an image of the bare torso of the burly man in the credit sequence, as though it is he whom Scorpio is kissing. He puts on a helmet and picks up a large flashlight, which he holds between his legs like a giant penis (a mechanized equivalent to the roman candle in *Fireworks*).

8. "HE'S A REBEL"—THE CRYSTALS (1962)

Anger intercuts shots of the leather clad Scorpio (whom we now realize is a cop) walking along the sidewalk, with film clips from Cecil B. DeMille's 1927 *King of Kings*, showing Christ walking along a road followed by his disciples. The Crystals sing, "See the way he walks down the street," clearly equating Scorpio, Christ and the rebel of the song (which could be Dean or Brando).

> He's a rebel
> And he's never, never been any good.
> He's a rebel
> And he never, ever does what he should.

The no-good rebel is the ideal role model for the repressed. Scorpio assumes both the pose and the trappings of the modern rebel (without a cause, the Leader of the Pack). He has replaced the rebel Jesus. Anger's cross-cutting emphasizes both the similarities and differences between the two rebels. Scorpio's (sexual) aggressiveness is contrasted to Jesus's (sexually suppressed) benevolence. Jesus stops to minister to a blind man/Scorpio kicks the tire of an illegally parked motorcycle. Christ restores the man's sight/Scorpio gives the cycle a ticket. As a blind man opens his eyes to see the world for the first time, Anger intercuts a photo of naked men; and when the healed man kneels before Jesus to thank him, Anger inserts a closeup of an erect penis pointing at the camera then cuts back to the man rising from his knees, as though he has just administered a blow job. Anger emphasizes the attitude of subjugation necessary for the favors of the heroic rebel, while the Crystals sing about how proud it makes them to hold their rebel's hand.

Christ represents two thousand years of repression by the Christian church. Viewed in his own time as a rebel, he has become a supreme authority figure, imposing his own asexuality upon the entire Western world. Similarly, Scorpio assumes the image of the rebel, but finds a place only in the most authoritarian of social roles, that of the cop. Both Christ and Scorpio uphold and enforce the law. Rebellion is absorbed and made useful by the dominant ideology.

The surrender of the self to an attractive figure of rebellion equated with subjugation by an oppressive authoritarianism. The words to the song define the masochistic urge in romantic (and culturally acceptable) terms:

Just because he doesn't do what
Everybody else does,
That's no reason that
I can't give him all my love.

The Age of Christianity is finished and Anger makes no apologies for his joy at the dawning of the Age of Scorpio. Yet clearly the New Age represents only the rejection of one authoritarian code for another.

9. "PARTY LIGHTS"—CLAUDINE CLARK (1962)

To film this scene Anger threw a party in Brooklyn for a local motorcycle gang. He tried as best he could to keep wives and girlfriends off camera in order to emphasize the brutality of the all male group. This sequence continues the Christ comparison, intercutting the arrival of the cyclists with shots of the disciples filing into a room. The activities at the cyclists' party involve nudity and simulated homosexual acts, yet Anger somehow manages to keep it all within the realm of the kind of degrading rites of initiation administered by such all male groups as fraternities, lodges and the military, where repressed sexuality expresses itself in ritual acts of brutality and degradation. Significantly the brutalized man is referred to as the Pledge.

Apparently one of the cyclists Anger invited to the party thought it would be a good joke to attach a rubber dildo to the skeleton cut-out he was bringing with him. This object became one of the major points of contention in *Scorpio Rising*'s obscenity trial and resulted in the defense calculating that a "penis-like object" appeared in only nine frames (a total of about one-third of a second) out of the film's 44,500.

Of course, "penis-like objects" are everywhere in the film and the conga drum in this sequence is only one in a long series; but once the dildo appears there is no need for Anger to employ clever symbolic penises. One shot shows a man dancing with his seemingly erect penis poking into his partner's full skirt. At another point one of the men bares his buttocks and bends over as another leap-frogs toward him from behind, holding the dildo between his legs. Anger wryly cuts to a shot of Scorpio passing a sign with the word "greased" prominently displayed. Before the sequence ends we see Scorpio at the party.

10. "TORTURE"—KRIS JENSEN (1962)

While the cruel initiation rites continue, Scorpio enters a darkened church which he illuminates with his phallic flashlight. The New Age is to be born upon the altar of the Old. We see a portrait of Christ within a plaster white oval resembling the one containing the scorpion. A Nazi flag appears, placing the image of the menorah target in its proper perspective.

The images of super-masculinity have developed through a progression from physical aggressiveness to homoeroticism to ritual torture. The fact that a popular song states the trials and tribulations of romantic love in such anal-sadistic terms once again elevates the sequence's implications to apply to the entirety of American culture. The Pledge is attacked by the other men and the squealing of pigs is heard on the soundtrack. One of the film's most jarring and briefest flash cuts occurs here: a closeup of a man's scarred buttocks. The iconography of brutality is juxtaposed with an image of real suffering: the aftermath of a brutal S/M session, placed next to the images of Christ in his crown of thorns and Brando in his leather jacket, defines the embattled rebel as a willing masochist whose sexuality is satisfied only in his own abuse.

11. "POINT OF NO RETURN"—GENE MCDANIELS (1962)

Scorpio mounts the altar in a virtual coup d'etat. The oval icon of Christ is intercut with the oval Scorpio icon. Scorpio raises his pirate flag and Anger cuts to a line of motorcycle racers at the starting line. Intercut with images of DeMille's Christ riding an ass (a pun of which Anger was no doubt aware) into Jerusalem on Palm Sunday, journeying toward his own crucifixion, the cyclists' race is placed in the context of a conscious death trip. The song reinforces the reading: "I'm at the point of no return/And for me there'll be no turning back."

Scorpio starts the race by waving the skull and crossbones. The final trip to self-destruction has begun. The racers are intercut with stills of Hitler and helmeted Nazi troops at the very moment the song says, "No matter what the future brings/I've got to see it through." Scorpio shouts orders and waves a Luger. The Age of Scorpio, the sadism growing out of a repressive culture, the death wish, and fascism become roughly equivalent. The cyclists ride into the New Age and toward their deaths. Anger superimposes the Scorpio icon and the skull and crossbones.

12. "I WILL FOLLOW HIM"—LITTLE PEGGY MARCH (1963)

Two thousand years ago (as depicted in a 37-year-old movie) Christ rides into Jerusalem on a jackass. In 1964 a jackass in "Li'l Abner" kicks someone off a cliff while the two boys walk happily away, arm in arm. Clad only in a loincloth, a very young Mickey Rooney as Puck from the 1935 Max Reinhardt version of *A Midsummer Night's Dream* (a film in which Anger himself appeared as the Child Prince) spreads his arms in joyous acceptance. Little Peggy March belts out a song which celebrates her subjugation to male domination:

> I will follow him
> No Matter where he may go.
> There isn't an ocean so deep,
> A mountain so high it can keep me away. . . .
> I love him, I love him, I love him,
> And where he goes
> I'll follow, I'll follow, I'll follow. . . .

The world seems ready, in fact anxious, for the Age of Scorpio. Meeting the New Age is as simple as surrendering oneself to the Christ or to Hitler, as simple as surrendering oneself to death—and, as Charles Manson taught his followers, once one has lost his fear of death, any action becomes possible.

But at the very moment it seems obvious that Anger is advocating a joyous acceptance of domination and oppression, he jars us with further images of terror and repression. The images become overtly anal, scatalogical. Scorpio removes his helmet and turns away from the camera. Anger intercuts shots of a TV screen showing a liquid being poured into a cup, and of a man holding a coffee can full of liquid between his legs. It becomes clear that Scorpio is urinating into his helmet. He turns, now wearing a horrific Batman-like mask, offering up his urine from the altar. Anger intercuts shots of Hitler, a Nazi rally, and Scorpio raising a machine gun and kicking books off a stage. Little Peggy March wails, "He's my destiny."

13. "WIPE OUT"—THE SURFARIS (1963)

Sequence number thirteen (with all its evil implications) begins with the hollow, demented laughter which begins the Surfaris' greatest hit. The laughter rings out over a drawing of a skull wearing a long, blonde (feminine?) wig and smoking a cigarette called "Youth." In each of the eye sockets appear identical drawings of Christ pointing the way for an adolescent boy. The picture could have come from a Baptist Sunday School quarterly, but in this context is bursting with implications of pederasty. The cigarette (identified in segment #5 as a symbol of masculinity) clinched between the teeth of the skull becomes overtly sexual. Youth is literally being sucked off by Death ("My boyfriend's back and there's gonna be trouble"). The image recurs in a flash cut later in the sequence, when the burly cyclist of the credits is shown with a similar, "Youth"-imprinted cigarette in his mouth. Death has become the prophet of Scorpio.

The images and icons of Nazism, cycle racing, war and sadism swirl to a climax in which one of the racers "wipes out." Closeups, medium shots and long shots of the spinning red light of a police car alternate with shots of people leaping into the air, of racing trophies, and of a spinning cycle on display. The effect is orgasmic; the orgasm is death. The ritual death signals Scorpio's ascension.

The radically alternative reading of American pop culture, the unearthing of layer after layer of perversity just beneath the surface, is both stimulating and disturbing. The amoral attitude Anger assumes in delivering his attacks makes the film even more powerful. Most impressively, *Scorpio Rising* somehow manages to walk that precarious line between stating the equation between sexual repression and fascism, and becoming itself a fascist work growing out of that repression.

———

ED LOWRY

VOL. 15, NO. 3
DECEMBER 6, 1978

Two Thousand Maniacs! (1964)

WRITTEN, DIRECTED, AND PHOTOGRAPHED BY HERSCHELL GORDON LEWIS

I've been into seeing a lot of B movies and a lot of science fiction movies of the fifties, you know, the McCarthy type movies. And I've discovered that's the type of movie that really appeals to me much more than any so-called masterpiece because there are flaws in them, you can cross them, you can sleep if you want to and then come back and that's another story. That's a good thing. *Tout va bien* is like that.

I really discovered nice films like *Two Thousand Maniacs!* and *Pussycat Kill Kill*. | JEAN-PIERRE GORIN, Interviewed by Martin Walsh, *Take One*, Vol. 5, No. 1.

If I ever make a picture and take myself seriously, I'm gonna be in trouble. P. T. Barnum was wrong, there is more than one sucker born every minute. | DAVID FRIEDMAN, Producer of *Two Thousand Maniacs!*

It would be nice, for the sake of historians, if historical periods occurred in neat and orderly packages. Unfortunately, they don't. With the collapse of the Hollywood studio system beginning around 1947–1948, the system of distribution and programming that had evolved crumbled as well. The whole A picture/B picture method of double billing ceased to exist. Hollywood began to pour more of its energy into gimmicks (3-D, Smell-o-vision) into changing the method of projection and thus "improving" the film (CinemaScope, Cinerama) and especially into bigger budgeted films that would hopefully attract a waning audience.

It would therefore seem logical that old minor Hollywood products—B movies, cartoons, newsreels and serials—would no longer be made as the new system of distribution didn't require them. Eventually this would happen, but the change would take more than a decade. The fifties were a confused time for the motion picture industry. Cartoons would continue to be turned out for theatrical distribution until around 1962–63, when the last of the major studio's animation branches were shut down (only temporarily; they were soon revived for television). With the advent of television news, there was no longer any need for newsreels and most of them disappeared during the fifties. As historian Leonard Maltin points out, "Fox, Movietone and Universal lasted the longest, but their newsreels of the 1960s were sorry affairs." Although the form was long dead, the last official newsreel was released in 1967. The last real series of short comedies was the "Joe McDoakes" series which ended in 1956. The last serial was probably Columbia's *Blazing the Overland Trail*, also released in 1956. Thus we see the fifties as a time for dying off of the old Hollywood forms.

The one form not discussed above is the B movie. This was the product most dependent on the old system of distribution. A newsreel, a comedy or a cartoon could just as easily be shown before a big budget A feature as they could before a double bill, and they were until their expense proved to be too much. The Bs only made sense in terms of a specific distribution system.

Yet the Bs neither died off nor changed that radically right away. The mutation began, but it wasn't until the late fifties and early sixties that the product recognizable as the exploitation film fully emerged. The Bs of the early and mid-fifties are an old lot, some standard, some slightly more ambitious than the older ones in terms of cast and/or cost. A number of factors changed the Bs.

One of the main ones was the old "exploitation" film. Since *Traffic in Souls* in 1913 there had always been "exploitation" films. They took their material from the current headlines, societal obsessions and fears. They treated such taboo topics as drugs, sex, birth control, giving birth, etc. Some, like *Mom and Dad*, were enormously successful. Most managed to make a little money. As Hollywood changed and the production code began to break down, the topics these films had treated began to show up in the new low-budget movie. Along these same lines there had always been certain bastard children of the Hollywood system. The exploitation films as well as an independent black cinema during the teens through the forties. The markets covered by these black movies became the province of the new low-budget Hollywood films as well, especially in the mid sixties.

Outside of these systems the most important effects on the changing Bs were the individual styles of a number of film producers. Herschell Gordon Lewis, David Friedman, Russ Meyer, Samuel Arkoff and Roger Corman made the most significant contributions. Russ Meyer began making films in 1959 with *The Immoral Mr. Teas*. What he did was liberate the nudie film from the pseudo-documentary form it had been tied to and give it a narrative structure instead. The descendants of this change cover everything from hard core porn films to Hollywood mainstream films containing sex scenes. The fact that Meyer has both a brilliant sense of cinema and a bizarre self-reflexive humor only added more depth to this change. It would not be until the mid to late sixties that the low-budget Hollywood product would pick up on overt nudity and sexuality.

Lewis and Friedman began as partners mining the same soft core vein as Meyer. When they realized that it would soon play itself out, they decided to move into gore films. In 1963 they produced a film with a four day shooting schedule and a $20,000 budget entitled *Blood Feast*. It proved to be incredibly successful and they followed it with *Two Thousand Maniacs!* in 1964 and *Color Me Blood Red* also in 1965. Dismemberment, torture, ample blood letting and nudity were crammed into all three of these films, once again to be adopted by numerous other low-budget Hollywood films in the mid to late sixties.

LOUIS BLACK

Just as patrons of sex films pay their money to see the graphic sequences that pop up every ten or fifteen minutes, Lewis's public comes for the scenes featuring the gouging of eyes, the pulling out of tongues, and driving of stakes through heads that inevitably punctuate his films. So well known is "the Lewis touch" that he is frequently asked to direct others' films anonymously, thus making it impossible to determine exactly how many films comprise the Lewis canon. | CHARLES FLYNN and TODD MCCARTHY, *Kings of the Bs.*

Of course it's okay to like sordid sensationalism . . . but what does it all mean? | Psychology major.

People in the commercial film business equate technical ability with an ability to entertain people. There is no correlation at all. None. | HERSCHELL GORDON LEWIS

I really felt I should, for once, put my integrity on the line. | HERSCHELL GORDON LEWIS

There are many appeals for salvation of maligned and ignored (s)exploitation films—films, it is said, which, while denied the luxury of lavish productions values and six-digit star(lets)s, are coincidentally spared the insipid, castrated commentaries on socio-economic realities that ooze out of many first-run films. It is thought that producers and directors populating this ugly niche in the carnivorous film hierarchy may tread on subjects which avail themselves more to gut-level emotions, conflicts and characterizations, than do those craftsmen in the major studios. Relegated to skimpy exposure mostly in dilapidated third-run houses, drive-ins and rural theaters, bootstrap films provide enough violent action and profiles to sustain an undemanding audience's attention and to keep the independent filmmakers busy with reactant.

There has been little effort or willingness on the part of film critics or reviewers to consider films which are *obviously* not intent on adhering to "reasonable" production values or "civilized" subject matter. So-called sophisticated viewers are not amused about being short-changed by films which avoid even paying lip service to conventional (expected) methods of limiting disclosure. If one pays for a full price ticket, one expects that in the final balance, an appropriate equilibrium between a film-worthy subject and the efforts to suspend one's disbelief about that subject's own fictiveness, will be reached. If a flick isn't up to par, the audience feels cheated.

However, better production values ride a logarithmic conveyer that denies all but the most heavily financed productions the luxury of technical frills. Moderately budgeted studio films rely on scripting and often blockbuster subsidization to pull them out of the red, but independents' micro-budget endeavors receive no such support. They must invest their own sweat *and* money. Fifty-to hundred-thousand-dollar films are being made today, profitably, but these independents do not attempt to rival spit-shine studio work; instead, they rely on the long term, small gate receipts of films based on brutally explicit or "quick 'n' dirty" sex, or fantastically contrived gore. Theirs is not an area for adventures in theoretical strategies; they must ignore any slick pretensions and push out the product according to pragmatic economy. Case in point—*Two Thousand Maniacs!*

Herschell Gordon Lewis managed to break new ground in nudies and gore films in the early sixties (with *BOIN-N-G!* And *Blood Feast*, respectively), proving with two-men crews and self-slated actors that production values had absolutely nothing to do with consumption, that there is an audience (though relatively undemanding) that will continually seek out sensational titillation at the expense of high falutin' aesthetics. Lewis fashions his stories around basic human attentiveness to violence, blood and flesh, pointing out that large investments in a film do not guarantee success unless the film incorporates elements of storytelling that provide unavoidable, explicit stimuli. Because he had to pull his pictures together himself, economic viability was the necessary concern for Lewis; his gamble that subversion of the industry's standards of violence could successfully supplant his mass of technical shortcomings became the crux of the matter.

> The only film that an independent can make and survive with is a film that the major producers cannot or will not make. I regard that as a physical law, I don't regard it as a theory. It's been proven so many hundreds of times that it's no longer in question. . . . if you cannot titillate them with production value, you titillate with something else. | HERSCHELL GORDON LEWIS

Lewis understands what we all are afraid of seeing, but crave anyway. We are all aware of what gore is without seeing it, but Lewis reestablishes the manner in which we sense life and death intruding upon one another. He supplants our boredom with an idealized world of horror where anything can and does happen. The problem is that he accomplishes this identification through violence and mutilation, while the big boys plug away with multi-million dollar fiascos that wallow in their tepid concerns for artiness or popular liberal bias. It is not at all clear whether his portentous "art" is deliberate or not. While the townsfolk appear clumsy and disproportioned enough (Carol Mason was the June 1963 *Playboy* centerfold), it may be that

Lewis's scavenger-style shooting (though he claims *Two Thousand Maniacs!* was *heavily* produced in comparison to his other films) is lent more credence in its super-reality, inadvertently rather than as a deliberation. After all, here is a director whose prime motivation is to provide a product he knows genuinely appeals to an element he himself can't identify with.

> [*Blood Feast*] started an entire new category of filmmaking. Everyone was surprised at the business this picture did, including myself. There were many people who would not see it. There were a great many who wanted their money back. There were others who saw it five or six times, which bewilders me. | HERSCHELL GORDON LEWIS

> The discerning viewer will find Lewis' films to be much more than superficial gore; rather an eerie reflection of the repressed sado-masochism in us all that even the smallest voice inside seldom admits to. From *Bonnie and Clyde* to *The Exorcist*, from *The Wild Bunch* to *Jaws*, fragments of Lewis' kaleido-scope radiate. | ANTON SZANDOR LA VEY, High Priest, Church of Satan.

While contemporary (s)exploitation films are merely following the path to the gold which Lewis helped pioneer, many have garnered critical atten-tion due to subtle social commentaries which lay behind the brazenness like a hidden texture. It becomes a matter for an intelligent filmmaker to reveal that he is not serious about exploitation, that he is pandering to the neces-sary excesses of a genre in an effort to sell while he sneaks tongue-in-cheek one liners and off-beat characterizations into the script (e.g., Russ Meyer). The tendency of drive-in circuit films to reveal little-seen filmmakers' sar-donic exposés on American culture can only lead to broader categorizations of what "society" as an inclusive term implies.

Even in 1964, Lewis was on the ball. He quickly but neatly isolates malig-nant marital infidelities in a situation in which the social codes reinforcing individual insecurity are undermined. This allows us to witness the almost kinky (non-sexual) willingness of people to abandon their vowed alle-giances in the midst of chaos. As Bea Miller commits adultery willy-nilly, she is rewarded by "feeling the blade." When her husband submits to the intoxicating pleasures of white lightening, he is "entered" in the horse race. The punishments doled out are not consequential to any amorality the Mill-ers exhibit, as they are based on an abstracted vengeance motivation and not on that of atonement. Thus we see "normal" Americans flippantly (defiantly) exhibiting hedonistic impulses without the usually compensating second thoughts of feelings or guilt. Odd.

The step-by-step analysis of the predicament by the astute and heroic teacher Tom White is a demonstration of how rationalizations, though correct and logical, can easily be thwarted and overpowered by a relatively simple, though out-of-the-blue power: in this case, the two thousand maniacs of Pleasant Valley; but on another correlate, that of any indeterminacy.

When at one point the townsfolk appear to have lost their appetite for blood vengeance, Rufe maintains the centennial's fervor with authoritarian threats. He is a backwoods scalawag, a good ol' Southern boy, prone to drooling flashes of perversity, but he is capable of garnering respect for any project simply through his exuberance. Zealots are capable of temporarily seizing the day (this day in particular), but Rufe is an examination of a mob's focal point. His lack of verbal coherence is made up for by the tenets of patriotism, loyalty and heroism—a troubling analogy, for it establishes the easy compliance by society for authority, whatever its basis for command is.

Then the incredibly brilliant auteur touch—Lewis's own pickin' banjo score, as played by the Pleasant Valley boys, sardonically counterpointing the major acts of violence—violent acts so creative they were jerked off the market when Lewis set the precedent for gristle gore the previous year with *Blood Feast*. Noteworthy is that this stylization or signature of melodic, easy listenin' music with the bizarre became an industry standard, perhaps culminating with Arthur Penn's *Bonnie and Clyde*. Lewis's penchant for explicitness in violence also broke ground in that the same effects found their way into the films of more and more big-time directors, though in many ways his effects still, though cheaply executed, are unparalleled in the frankness of their exposure. It is this edging from sensationalism to frank "amateurishness" that permits his films to erupt realistically, rather than grotesquely.

———

BRIAN HANSEN

Todd McCarthy and Charles Flynn: You know, you were also included in the *Cahiers du Cinéma* issue 150, the big issue of the American cinema. You were classified as a subject for further research....

Herschell Gordon Lewis: Well, they also say that about cancer.

If Edgar Allen Poe had written *Brigadoon*, it might have come out looking like *Two Thousand Maniacs!* Herschell Gordon Lewis's film is a fairy tale gone wrong. It's a film of startling perversity from it's blood red credits to its innocuous yet chilling closing song. Before it's finished, *Two Thousand Maniacs!* calls into question our ideas about sanity/insanity, civilization/wilderness, justice/revenge, community/outsiders, reality/fantasy and just about everything else people tend to take for granted. The very nature of the horror film is turned inside out. By reversing the conventions of the genre, *Two Thousand Maniacs!* forces an awareness (at least on the part of a critic) of the possibilities for manipulation of those conventions.

The film opens in a fairly conventional manner—conventional in the sense of the following *generic* conventions, not in the sense of the unimaginative. Six Northerners are tricked into going to the Southern town of Pleasant Valley. There they are told they are to be guests of honor at a mysterious centennial celebration. They are led to the town by "Detour" signs which look like they were painted by a mongoloid idiot—which they may have been. The point is the six "chosen" people are ruled by signs. The signs are obviously unofficial, yet they are obeyed. The outsiders arrive in the town and get talked into participating, against their will, in a local celebration. As the film goes on, they find themselves increasingly isolated from each other by the townspeople as they are led to their own slaughter. In each of these actions (or lack of actions) they give up a bit of control over their own lives. Loss of control over the animal side of human nature is at the root of the werewolf legend, among others. Loss of freedom of choice and, by extension, of humanity is at the root of such films as *Invasion of the Body Snatchers* and *Night of the Living Dead*. More directly related to the loss of freedom in *Two Thousand Maniacs!* is the predicament of Joan Crawford in *Whatever Happened to Baby Jane?*. Crawford, a cripple, is totally at the mercy of her insane sister, played by Bette Davis. She doesn't ask for anything that happens to her; she can't change anything about her surroundings; she can't stop the cruel "jokes" played by her sister. The protagonists in *Two Thousand Maniacs!* find themselves in much the same situation.

Lewis, having established this conventional situation, wastes little time in subverting all audience expectations. The horror is brought outdoors, in the wilderness—often in broad daylight. Think of most horror films: *Dracula*'s horror arises, at least in part, from Dracula's appearance in London. The horror comes to the city, moves in next door and eventually enters the protagonist's house. *Night of the Living Dead* begins outdoors in daylight, but much of its horror comes at night and depends on our fear of horror coming inside, entering the home, the place of safety. In *Two Thousand Maniacs!* there is no place of safety to be violated.

The horror film is a film of darkness. It deals with our fears about what lurks in the shadows. Again, *Two Thousand Maniacs!* refuses to play the game. There are no shadows. There is nowhere to hide. Everything is out in the open—the protagonists, the townspeople overcome by the bloodlust, the violence. In yet another reversal, *Two Thousand Maniacs!* deals with fear of the known, instead of the conventional.

In *Two Thousand Maniacs!* even the means of death are unconventional (in every sense of the word). Horror films usually deal with a very personal sort of violence. Fangs, claws, strangulation—these are the means of death in films like *Dracula*, *The Wolfman* and *Night of the Living Dead*. *Two Thousand Maniacs!* is dominated by axes, stones, horses, knives and spiked barrels. The characters in the film are distanced from the violence by their weapons. The viewer isn't so lucky. Lewis dwells on the effects of these weapons. Long, lingering closeups of stumps (no, not tree stumps), punctured and mutilated human bodies, unattached body parts dominate the screen for much of the film's running time. Still, if this isn't too wild a contradiction, the film never oversteps the bounds of, at least, fair taste.

Perhaps the violence is acceptable because it is explained and, within the film, justified. In this, *Two Thousand Maniacs!* is more like Tod Browning's *Freaks* than this past year's horror hit, *The Hills Have Eyes* (both films which embody the outsider/community conflict). In *Freaks*, circus misfits are insulted and ridiculed by a "normal" man and woman. The peculiar (to us) code of the circus people demands revenge. *The Hills Have Eyes* makes no effort to justify its violence; there may be a method to the desert family/tribe violence but the viewer is not privy to it.

"This is our centennial. You've got to play by our rules."

This line is spoken by the mayor of Pleasant Valley. It is crucial to the understanding of *Two Thousand Maniacs!* It brings one of the major issues in the film into clear focus: how do we recognize and define "civilization." If we define civilization as a system of rules which order life, then Pleasant Valley represents civilization. The people in the town live by a set of rules. It may be different from our own (and that of the Northerners trapped in the town) but it certainly exists. According to the rules of the centennial (based on the need for vengeance against the North which had destroyed the town during the Civil War) violence is not only justified but necessary.

In fact, Pleasant Valley may not be as different from our own society as we would like to think. The townsfolk participate in a form of ritualized violence. We have our own distanced, ritualized forms—football, boxing, wrestling, supermarket sweep. In fact, this film itself is a form of ritualized violence.

(BE WARNED. *Two Thousand Maniacs!* has something of a twist ending, so if you want it to be a surprise, don't read any further until after you've seen the movie!)

The ending of *Two Thousand Maniacs!* is problematic. In a sense, it's a cop-out, a "well, we've got to get out of this somehow, so we might as well do it this way and just end it" kind of ending. It turns out that Pleasant Valley is an American Brigadoon, a town which appears but once every 100 years, on the anniversary of its destruction by Union soldiers in 1865. Using this dodge allows Lewis to avoid facing a major potential problem: Is this violence to be condoned and are the townspeople to be punished? By turning the film into a fantasy, Lewis avoids answering some of the moral issues raised. Had the film been shot a few years later, the ending might have been different. Films like *Night of the Living Dead, Rosemary's Baby,* and *The Omen* provide no escape for the characters in the film *or* the audience. Fairy tale endings in which evil is vanquished or explained away as fantasy or delusion are things of the past.

To call the ending of the film a cop-out, to say it is simply tacked on, may be to do an injustice to Herschell Gordon Lewis and his film. Lewis, while answering none of the questions raised, asks several more. The possibility exists that what took place was a dream or delusion, although there is one piece of tangible evidence which works against this idea. It certainly calls into question our notions of sanity and insanity. Who in the film can definitely be called sane. Were the townspeople (assuming they existed at all) sane? They lived by their own shared set of laws. Some of them seem to fit our criteria for insanity, but are our criteria appropriate in a setting as different from our own as Pleasant Valley? And what of the Northerners? Are they sane? What about the husband and wife who live to torment and cheat on one another? What about the husband and wife who seem inseparable and incomplete without each other? What about the two survivors, the two people with whom we identify most in the film? Their sanity (and their sobriety) are called into question by the state trooper whose aid they enlist after their escape. Lewis implies that no one in the film can be said to be truly sane. For that matter, what of the audience?

The context of the film's ending may even bring us to theological questions. Why is the resurrection of the dead, in this film and in others, a fitting subject for a horror film. The same idea is at the root of Christianity. Why is resurrection a horror instead of a Christ-like miracle? I won't even try to answer this question. It is enough to know that it is there, implicit in the film's "cop-out," "tacked-on" ending.

One final word. Think about the song which opens and closes *Two Thousand Maniacs!*, "The South's Gonna Rise Again." By the end of the film, the song has taken on a totally new, totally unexpected meaning. Think about it. The mind boggles!

—

WARREN SPECTOR

VOL. 13, NO. 4
DECEMBER 8, 1977

The Last Movie (1971)

DIRECTED BY DENNIS HOPPER

At 34, [Dennis Hopper] is known in Hollywood as a sullen renegade who talks revolution, settles arguments with karate, goes to bed with groups and has taken trips on everything you can swallow or shoot.

On the other hand, in the salons and galleries of Los Angeles and New York he is recognized as a talented poet, painter, sculptor, photographer and as a leading collector of pop art. He is also, after eight years on the movie industry's blacklists, the hottest director in Hollywood. *Easy Rider*, which cost only $370,000, is rapidly approaching a projected $50 million gross. In the process it has polarized a new film audience of under-30s, generated a new school of talented young directors such as Jack Nicholson, Peter Bogdanovich, Richard Rush and Melvin Van Peebles, and established the style of a New Hollywood in which producers wear love beads instead of diamond stick pins and blow grass when they used to chew Coronas. Yet to Dennis Hopper, *Easy Rider* was just a childish toddle in the direction he intends his movies to take. "My next picture," he has promised friends, "is really going to be heavy, man."

To make it, he solicited $850,000 from Universal, the studio that not so long ago gave us *Tammy and the Doctor* and *Ma and Pa Kettle at Waikiki*. Then he hired a cast that included some of the most conspicuous individualists in Hollywood, among them Peter Fonda, Dean Stockwell, Jim Mitchum, Russ Tamblyn, John Phillip Law and Michelle Phillips of the Mamas and the Papas. He hired Dennis Hopper as the movie's leading man, and he invited everybody to a location 14,000 feet above sea level in the backlands of Peru, a country where all the major drugs—cocaine, speed, heroin, hallucinogens—are restricted but can in fact be purchased over the counter without a prescription. "Get all those cats together down there," said one Hollywood reporter, "and you'll have the wildest scene in the history of the movies." | BRAD DARRACH, *Life*, June 19, 1970.

The curious problem with [*The Last Movie*] is that it is unlikely to speak directly or congenially to any particular audience. Its network of religious and literary symbol and its hectically non-linear structure push the film altogether out of bounds for the mass popular audience, while its almost gleeful preoccupation with Pirandellian puzzles of appearance and reality and its studied concept of life imitating art are likely to seem undigested and sophomoric to informed audiences. | FORSTER HIRSCH, *New York Times*, October 24, 1971.

I

At dinner the other night I told my friend Steve that he had to see this movie. I told him he would hate it more than any other film he would ever see. He would hate it so completely because it violated every one of his conceptions as to what a movie should be. He might be here in the audience tonight.

I liked it. I'm not quite sure yet how much.

It came like a legend, like a crazy man from the mountains, like a woman little met but much talked of, like a crucial document on our immediate past. It casts a six year shadow. We've heard of it from *Life* magazine and *Rolling Stone* and confused reviewers almost everywhere. The word on it was rarely good, but no matter how dull reviewers claimed it was, they always made it sound interesting.

My friend Ed was knocked out of his seat. It worked much better than either he or I had ever imagined it could. This was mostly because the only people who seem to take it completely seriously are the ones who hate it.

II

Tonight on television I watched *Hollywood on Trial*, which is a documentary about the Hollywood Ten, HUAC and blacklisting. Somehow what that film was talking about seemed a lot more important than whether this film is good or not. This film seems silly in comparison. It is silly. It is a film that has needed to be made since the birth of movies. Thank God it's done.

Dennis Hopper, after years of knocking around Hollywood and appearing in film after film, was one of the hottest commercial properties (dynamite word for a human being) in 1970, as a result of *Easy Rider*. After this film and because of his reputation for drug use and his politics, he was virtually unhireable in this country. The blacklist ain't dead, to paraphrase Frank Zappa, it just smells funny.

III

Clinton woke up after watching the film and snorted. He told me that he more than hated it, that he was angry. He was tired of filmmakers making films about filmmaking. It seemed to him a self-indulgent, circular activity which resulted in texts that made almost no sense outside of a certain circle of viewers.

I told Clinton that the other night a friend had watched Ken Jacobs's virtually unwatchable, almost staggeringly uninteresting film, *Tom, Tom, the Piper's Son*. It is a 100-minute experimental film which begins by showing a six-minute 1905 movie and then proceeds to show the movie speeded up, slowed down, speeded up slightly, etc., etc., and ends by showing the original six minutes over again. After the showing there was a discussion and my friend mentioned that she had found the film boring. She was quickly attacked by the other participants and told that if she didn't like the film she didn't understand movies.

Clinton looked at me, waited awhile, smiled as only he can smile, and said, "I may not understand movies, but I sure like them a lot."

Understand movies? How? In some vast theoretical way? The person I know who has read and understood the most cinematic theory almost never never goes to the movies. He is home reading books. He might like *Tom, Tom, the Piper's Son*. I'm not sure he would like *The Last Movie*.

Movies are themselves. They are not books or plays, television shows or holograms. To make the claim that we can understand all films by watching

Dennis Hopper in *The Last Movie*. From the core collection production photographs of the Margaret Herrick Library, Academy of Motion Picture Arts and Sciences.

one film in the same way we can understand all literature if we understand one sentence is to make a claim that boasts of a cinematic illiteracy almost terrifying in its arrogance and its ignorance.

Movies are entertainment before they are art. You can make movies that ignore this fact, but then your audience is limited to the already convinced, it is limited to an audience that we are told is the most discriminating, most cinematically literate, and most intelligent. They will tell you that about themselves any time you ask. I'm not quite sure if they would like *The Last Movie*.

Experimental films can become new cinematic grammatical texts, they can create new forms of narrative, they can show us new thematic approaches, they can redefine cinematic texture. They can also be a lot more interesting to read about (Warhol's early work, Jacobs's film) than to watch. They can also be incredibly exciting to see; they can be beautiful and they can be thought provoking. There is just this embarrassing tendency on the part of some writers and some viewers to give them way too much credit, to insist that they *are* cinema. Jonas Mekas has said, "There is a cinema of Antonioni, of Rivette and of Snow. The idea of *one* cinema is a fascist idea." Among the many other things it is, *The Last Movie* is an answer to the "one cinema" fascists.

IV

It comes on like the hero of a Peckinpah movie, determined, despite everything, to survive. And there it is at the end, bent and bleeding, torn and wounded, but somehow it is still alive, and somehow its sense of humor is still intact.

V

I'm not sure where to begin with this movie. There is a whole lot I want to say, but I'm not sure that it deserves it. Actually I am sure it does deserve discussion, but I am not sure if I can do it. And if I can, I'm not sure I should. This is the kind of movie people hate film graduate students over. The parts of it that work are so delightfully funny, often in such a moronic way, that to talk about them too long shows me up for a cripple involved in a race with a horse. Almost in spite of itself, this film moves gracefully to exactly where it's going and (to get completely outrageous) to exactly where it is intended to go.

VI

The Last Movie demands a variety of views. It is not enough of a piece to merit a long coherent essay describing what it is doing because that would be forcing an order where none exists. This film is not coherent or even very cohesive, and to pretend it is becomes lunacy.

To pretend that watching 100 minutes of *Tom, Tom, the Piper's Son* somehow leads us to understand movies transcends lunacy and approaches the worst kind of elitist bullshit. We are creating signifiers where there is nothing signified. We are deconstructing texts for no apparent reason and with no end in mind. We are binding the feet of film in the same way the feet of literature have already been bound, as if *we* know what is pretty and what is meaningful, and if it takes ten million words we will show why this film is it.

VII

Duck Amuck, which is a Chuck Jones cartoon being shown before *The Last Movie,* does almost all the same things and is funnier.

VIII

I'm not sure but I think Daffy Duck might like this movie. It fits his universe.

IX

At the very least this film can be a lot of fun, and if you don't try to understand it, and if you accept the fact that it is a very expensive home movie, and if you can even comprehend that it is one of the least dignified and least serious art films ever made, you just might make it through. I, hopefully, am not sounding too condescending. I'm just not sure what to say or even how to talk about this movie.

At a friend's house one night, we saw *The Last Movie* followed by *Texas Chainsaw Massacre.* At the end of *Chainsaw,* my friend Pam looked up clutching a pillow, barely able to speak, still shaking with fright, and said that she absolutely hated *The Last Movie.*

My friend Marge pointed out that usually when filmmakers went south of the border to make a film it was because labor was cheaper. On this film she said it was undoubtedly because drugs were cheaper. If the film had been shot in Los Angeles the budget would probably have doubled just paying for dope.

X

In order to discuss this film I feel that I should describe my bathroom habits and bedroom and what I had for breakfast and what shows I watch on television and who my friends are.

This is being typed on an old grey Smith-Corona portable that was lent to me by friends.

The Last Movie is about just that. It is about film and reality. It's along the lines of Pirandello's *Six Characters in Search of an Author.* It is a film about itself more than anything else.

When Godard deconstructs his text, when he takes his film apart and reconstructs it as we watch, he is doing it to talk about society and about people's interactions. Hopper is only talking about films and filmmaking. The points being made are about acting and directing and productions. The people are not real, the relationships do not materialize, the society is not looked at.

I read an unpublished manuscript several years ago in which the author was talking about what was going on around him as he wrote. At one point he mentioned that his wife was in the kitchen making meat loaf for dinner. Of course, I believed him, since there was no reason not to and who really cared or even noticed. Several lines later he confessed that he had lied and that she was actually making hamburgers.

Of course, I again believed him, but now I think that his wife really might have been making meat loaf, or she might not have been cooking at all, or she might not have even been at home. The nature of small fictions is fascinating because they lead us to the nature of large fictions. We tend to believe what we read or at least accept it. We react to film even more strongly because we think we can see exactly what is happening.

The Last Movie plays with that notion in every way possible. The form of the film matches the context of the story. The Indians become so enamored of the filming that they think the process itself is the movie. The film refers back to itself all the time. It is a film about a group of filmmakers making a film and then it is a film about a group of Indians imitating filmmakers making a film. Beyond this it is at times a film that attempts to fictionalize its own making. We see the party occurring. It is occurring "within" the film, but maybe the party actually occurred and Hopper just went and filmed some of it. It is a film with certain major stars (Fonda and Phillips) gracing, but barely noticeable in, the background. The filming becomes, maybe because of the concept of the film and maybe because of all the drugs, part of the film. There are obviously no clear lines drawn between, behind and in front of the cameras. No lines are drawn between the lives of the actors on screen and off. The film becomes a jumble with numerous layers of filmic reality and layers of filming reality meshed. The story in *Life* magazine served to introduce the American public into this jumble and make the audience aware that there were none of the conventional lines we have come to expect separating the film from what is going on outside and around it.

Because of its very incompetence, because of Hopper's overwhelming self-indulgence, because the film is almost incoherent at places and badly crafted, it succeeds in a way that *Last Year at Marienbad*, *Hiroshima Mon Amour* and most other films that ask these questions and raise these issues never could. What I wonder most about is what the Indians really thought of the filmmakers and the film.

XI

This film is like punk rock in that it is angry and inarticulate, in that it is excessive and does not pay attention to form, in that it is brutal without compassion, in that it is self-indulgent and undisciplined, in that you can pogo to it far easier than you can watch it.

XII

Most importantly, *The Last Movie* is not coherent, though there is an overwhelming temptation to try and make it coherent, a temptation for the mind to organize it in some way. It is not coherent even though Hopper might want us to believe that in some strange way it is.

XIII

The movie, all else aside, is occasionally brilliant. Movies are a religion. Movie-going is devotional and based on faith and the need for catharsis, and movie making is ritualistic and grounded in ceremony. Movie-making is also mythic and movies are magic and they have been studied by their devotees since the early days of Hollywood. Fan magazines, newspaper interviews, films on stars and on filmmaking and on Hollywood have all resulted in young men and women making the pilgrimage to Tinsel Town.

When Uncle Carl Laemmle made a star out of Florence Lawrence by staging a phony suicide, he created one of the first mimetic gods of the modern era (warriors were often mimetic gods)—a god so powerful that it assumes several identities at once and is constantly changing the range of those identities. Sounds like garbage? It probably is. The film talks about this a lot, though I'm not quite sure I know exactly what it is saying.

XIV

We always know it is Dennis Hopper and not Kansas and that Hopper is directing the film, that it is Dennis Hopper directing Samuel Fuller directing Dennis Hopper as Kansas. There is no way, given the structure of the film and the information revealed, that any kind of completely fictional narrative could be believed. More than ever believing any of the "story," I think we watch *The Last Movie* out of a fascination to try and see what it is going to do and where it is going to take us. We are always aware of the story-telling/movie-making that is going on.

XV

The only time the film becomes as dull and as stupid and as offensive and as insipid as the reviewers have hinted is when it slips into traditional narrative for about thirty minutes, roughly one third of the way into the movie. Hopper seems intent on displaying every sexist attitude one man can have. He almost succeeds.

XVI

I am twenty-seven and still alive and still angry and I have not stopped caring and in some bizarre way films like this feed me.

———

LOUIS BLACK

By midafternoon the games became more serious. Somebody made a cocaine connection and a number of actors laid in a large supply at bargain prices— $7 for a packet that costs $70 in the States. By 10 p.m. almost 30 members of the company were sniffing coke or had turned on with grass, acid, or speed. By midnight, much of the cast had drifted off to bed by twos and threes. At 2 a.m. I was awakened by screams. A young actress had taken LSD and was "having a bummer." At 3 a.m., I heard a rapping on the window beside my bed. A young woman I hadn't met was standing on a wide ledge that ran along the side of the hotel just below the windowsill. It was raining and her nightgown was drenched. "Do you mind if I come in?" She asked vaguely.

The scenes got wilder as the days went by. One clique threw whipping parties. An actor chained a girl to a porch post and, inspired by the notion that she looked like Joan of Arc, lit a crackling fire at her feet. Another actor swallowed five peyote buds in too rapid succession and almost died.

Dennis and most of his friends had some explanation or other for why they use drugs, but in fact most of them use drugs because the others use drugs.

In the New Hollywood it's the hip thing to do. It's also the hip thing not to get addicted, but some of the people I saw in Peru were nibbling godawful close to the hook. | BRAD DARRACH, *Life*, June 19, 1970

Hopper has a very small vocabulary as a filmmaker, and his thoughts here have all of the impact of revelations written down during an acid trip. | VINCENT CANBY, *New York Times*, September 30, 1971.

The Last Movie is a mad attempt to break through conventions and film—not just the Western film, the intellectual film or the mass "with it" film—but all commercial film.... The attack is at your neighborhood theater—and rather than acknowledge the attack, the public and its spokesmen prefer to say, "But indeed the man is mad." ... Hopper forces the assault, even attacks the film itself. We see black leader, scratches, notice that inserts are missing (clearly they are not), and at one point we hear the camera. For those who think these, and the crudity of the city scenes, are simply attempts to cover up the flaws, I point to the supreme technical skill, the near-perfection of the sequences of the Fuller movie and the Indian movie....

   The very title of the film, *The Last Movie*, is destructive, the expression of no place to go. If Hopper alienates the viewer, then he has succeeded. He has forced us to question what we see. In a sense it is an act of artistic suicide. No wonder audiences react against it, refuse to acknowledge the attack, the prefer to dismiss Hopper by saying, "I read about him in *Life*. He was on some drug when he made the film." | STUART M. KAMINSKY, *Take One*, June 1972.

The Last Movie is a film composed of a number of interesting, exciting, even dramatic shots; the syntax—the linking and ordering principle—is missing. Of course, there is that center portion of the film which seems to tell some kind of story in a semi-coherent fashion, but maybe that's a mistake—or maybe, that's the real movie and the forty minutes which precede it is a long, drawn-out exposition. It gives us lots of information, but it doesn't take us anywhere, or perhaps we should say it lets us wander anywhere.

   Whether this is the result of Hopper's search for a revolutionary new film form à la Godard or simply the outcome of Hopper's inability to order anything under the influence of mescaline is entirely irrelevant. In the final analysis, such a question can be answered only by conjecture. What we have is a film which challenges us to make some sense (or no sense) of it.

Whether seen as an enigmatic work full of mysteries or a pompously pretentious film full of shallow truths, *The Last Movie* refuses to reveal itself easily. It is subject to an unlimited number of readings, revealing as many meanings as there are people in the audience to pick them out. I don't know what it means. You don't know what it means. And, most of all, Dennis Hopper doesn't know what it means.

———

ED LOWRY

It's called *The Last Movie* and it's a story about America and how it's destroying itself. The hero is a stunt man in a lousy Western. When his movie unit goes back to the States, he stays on in Peru to develop a location for other Westerns. He's Mr. Middle America. He dreams of big cars, swimming pools, gorgeous girls. He's so innocent. He doesn't realize he's living out a myth, nailing himself to a cross of gold. But the Indians realize it. They stand for the world as it really is, and they see the lousy Western for what it really was, a tragic legend of greed and violence in which everybody dies at the end. So they build a camera out of junk and re-enact the movie as a religious rite. To play the victim in the ceremony, they pick the stunt man. The end is far-out. | DENNIS HOPPER, *Life*, June 19, 1970.

Billy the Kid is one of the most colorful figures in the mythology of the Old West. A deadly, cold-blooded killing machine, he reputedly gunned down scores of men ("not counting Indians and Mexicans") in his short lifetime, and would think nothing of murdering defenseless men if he took offense to their idle barroom talk. Eventually, civilization came to the Old West and Billy's reign of terror ended one night when a courageous lawman, Pat Garrett, tracked Billy to his hideout, went in alone, and killed the young desperado in a brief gunfight.

William Bonney is almost as well known in Western legends. After a tough childhood in New York's Bowery, he moved with his mother to Kansas, where at the age of 12 he killed a drunk blacksmith who had insulted his mother. Thus this mild-mannered and shy young boy was forced to live the rest of his life as an outlaw. A friend to the Mexicans and poor Anglos in New Mexico, he made many enemies among the wealthy cattle ranchers who ran the frontier territory. A skilled and cool-headed gunman and rider, he had killed 21 men before he was cut down shortly before his twenty-first birthday—shot twice, in the dark, from ambush, by a former friend now in the employ of the land barons.

William McCarty was a minor historical figure in the "Lincoln County War," a pawn in a socio-political struggle between two rival factions determined to rule the New Mexican territory. An itinerant ranch hand, McCarty was considered an outlaw once his side lost the war and his enemies ruled the territory. McCarty was eventually hunted down and killed by the Lincoln County sheriff. In all, he is known to have killed 4 men all of them unarmed.

All the above characters are the same man, of course, in his various mytho-historical reincarnations; The Last Movie, a film about Billy the Kid, has nothing to do with any of them.

*   *   *

The Last Movie is a study of the role of myth and ritual in the modern world. Specifically, it examines the role film has played in propagating the great myth of the century: the American dream. First Hopper takes us onto the set of a conventional Western about Billy the Kid; we see the deceptions inherent in the medium, both theatrically and commercially. All the action is faked, yet the director repeatedly pleads for more "realism." His vision of realism is summed up in an instruction to his star: "This is the death of Billy the Kid. I want it legitimate and different and better than it's ever been done before." No one notices the contradictions in this statement, because the movie makers are totally immersed in such unreality.

But if a film is an unrealistic replica of reality, reality can become an all too real replica of the filmic world. The Peruvians form their own film company, using fake equipment and techniques, but real action. The townsfolk begin to act out the ritualistic violence they have seen. Hopper tries to show them how to stage a fight scene, informing them that "It's all fake in the movies." But they ignore him, protesting, "But that's not real," and proceed to beat each other up. Hopper is amused at their naiveté, but in a real sense they are closer to the essence of movies than he is. In a conventional movie such as the one being shot in The Last Movie, the script reads "man is beaten up," and the audience sees a man being beaten up. It is a story of a real beating, perceived as a real beating; only the cinematic techniques are fake.

Peru is seen throughout as real in comparison to the superficiality of Hollywood and America. The casual acceptance of death in the society is shocking to Hopper (and to us, the audience), but it is merely an indication of our alienation from basic realities. Yet the film refuses to simplify, to portray the Peruvians as noble savages defending their traditions. "It don't mean we don't like nice things, Gringo," says Hopper's girlfriend. After her first taste of luxury, she is far more ambitious and greedy than he. Clearly progress is coming to Peru as it came to the Old West.

Civilization has its advantages and disadvantages, but it is certainly inevitable. Hopper and his friend continue the advance into the frontier at the end. In *Easy Rider*, two years earlier, Hopper portrayed the disastrous consequences of the American frontier turning inward on itself as its Western heroes travelled back East. In *The Last Movie*, America has found a new West and, in the frontier spirit, Hopper vows in his last line to "Keep heading West." This colonial spirit is damaging to the natives, but it is difficult to blame Hopper for trying to stay ahead of the frontier.

Of course, throughout the film there is confusion between Hopper the character and Hopper the director. The search for the gold mine, in its similarity to the quest of the Spanish conquistadors, underlines the exploitive nature of the director and the character. On another level the gold symbolizes Hopper's search for cinematic excellence and truth. The statement "It's not commercial. You can't make back your investment" applies as well to *The Last Movie*, a film which almost ruined Hopper's career, as to the gold mine to which it is referring. The partners' determination and dedication reinforce our admiration for their continued westering, even if the end result is the spread of the kind of American "culture" represented by the broom manufacturer.

As the film progresses, however, the various levels of reality become hopelessly intertwined and it becomes harder to see anything as real, pure, and free from mythic connotations. The actions of the village filmmakers are clearly patterned after cinematic cliches, but another powerful theatrical influence is the evidence—the Church. The film comes to resemble a religious pageant, and Hopper becomes a Christ figure. When Hopper is arrested by the villagers "for stealing our sets," the stage is set for a classic finale—but to which movie? Kansas is accused of interfering with the villagers in their "filming." As a member of the crew of the Billy the Kid movie, he has stolen their town for a set, giving them in return an education in violence. As an American living off Peru, he is guilty of prostituting

Peruvian culture. Moreover, Hopper the director may be doubly guilty of these things for making *The Last Movie*. Kansas fears for his life at this point, and we are encouraged to ask ourselves, "Will they really kill him?" And thus forced to determine what is meant by "real." Surely Dennis Hopper will not be killed. But will Kansas? Since he is Dennis Hopper, can he, in fact, die? Or is he to play a character who dies—Christ, or Billy the Kid, or Dean, the actor who played Billy the Kid? All of these possibilities are available on the simple plot level, without even considering the symbolic implications. Finally, Hopper is shot and killed, but rises and walks away when the scene is over. Again, the question may be "Who survives?" Hopper shows us several slow motion instant replays, but they serve only to emphasize, not answer, the question.

This last sequence probably symbolizes the story of Christ's death, complete with resurrection. But the story has been totally perverted: the priest is drunk, the atmosphere carnival-like and the hero a questionable character. The new mythology has supplanted the old. Billy the Kid has defeated Christ. But there is little discernable difference between the two systems of illusions. The resurrection is a movie stunt and leads nowhere—Kansas goes West to look for gold that he now knows he cannot find. This quixotic search, inspired by *The Treasure of the Sierra Madre*, seems every bit as ritualistic and unrealistic as everything else in the film. Ultimately, that's what is so unsettling about *The Last Movie*—people's options are limited and predetermined, like moves on Kansas's checkerboard; there's very little room for humanity. Thus the natives have eliminated the only unrealistic link, the equipment and technique, and are left with a pure, real cinema.

———

NICK BARBARO

VOL. 14, NO. 3
APRIL 3, 1978

Caged Heat (1974)

WRITTEN AND DIRECTED BY JONATHAN DEMME

When we made *Caged Heat*, there was a strong collective feeling that we were making a very important statement about an extraordinary phenomenon, i.e., the performing of brain operations on inmates for disciplinary reasons, which has gone on everywhere in the world including America. It still goes on. | JONATHAN DEMME

Caged Heat . . . is a typical New World release: fast, funky, loaded with sex, perversion and sadism, alternatively sleazy and sophisticated—and underneath it all, a subtle, in-group satire on the whole thing. The plot is little more than a throw-away framework for the secret gags, and an excuse for lots of little delights: A bluesy musical score by John Cale. An outrageous supporting performance by Barbara Steele. . . . A surprise cameo appearance by George Armitage and his whole family. . . .

   Jonathan Demme directs with a weird, nightmare continuity that makes the film oddly powerful, despite its essential shallowness. | MICHAEL GOODWIN, *Take One*.

I was glad to get *Caged Heat* in particular. I was ecstatic to be in a film that wasn't X-rated and to have the lead. I was still apprehensive about taking just any sexploitation film and I almost turned down this one because it required that I do some nudity. But I liked the action-packed script and Jonathan told me that the nudity would be matter-of-fact and not exploitive. No bizarre-angle closeups of my left breast, or things like that. I had very good feelings about Jonathan and felt that he wouldn't take advantage of me. So I agreed to do the film, and, as I had hoped, the women weren't treated as sex objects and I was given a chance to really act. | ERICA GAVIN, *Velvet Light Trap*, Fall 1976.

This film doesn't exist in a void. No film does. Films are of a time and a place. They are spoken in the language of their generation. *Caged Heat* is a film made in 1974 to be shown on the exploitation circuit (drive-in theaters, small rural theaters, and inner city ghetto theaters). As most exploitation films do, it exploits women's bodies and violence. Yet in this first film by Jonathan Demme there is something more going on.

The exploitation field is a pressure cooker for generic evolution, where genres are formed, mature, parody themselves and die in remarkably short periods of time. In 1970 Roger Corman's New World Pictures released *The Big Doll House*, a film which began a whole cycle of women-in-prison pictures. Where Hollywood had occasionally turned out films in this vein (*Caged*, 1950; *Women's Prison*, 1955), they were largely a variation on the standard (men's) prison genre. *Big Doll House*, however, generated several films which followed many of the conventions it had established: woman warden/male doctor, integrated cellmates, acceptance of lesbian relationships and, especially, women armed and dangerous at the end. There is no argument that *Big Doll House* is a predominantly sexist movie. "They plot an escape, survive torture, break out with guns blazing, and die like James Cagneys with Breasts," said William Wolfe in *Cue Magazine*.

Caged Heat is at once the best of the films in this genre and the ultimate send-up of them. In a good natured, but politically self-conscious context, Demme, working with his wife, producer Evelyn Purcell, presents female characters in traditionally male roles, imprisoned but rebelling against the authority which oppresses them and, most importantly, evolving toward a sisterhood in the process of that rebellion. As much as this film is exploitive, or funny, or violent, it is also about women together and women supporting women in a way that mainstream movies like *The Turning Point* or *Alice Doesn't Live Here Any More* have yet to touch.

Solidarity Forever!
Solidarity Forever!
Solidarity Forever!
The Union makes us strong!
    In 1909 the International Ladies Garment Workers Union struck the Triangle Shirt-waist Company. Company guards assaulted and beat picketing strikers. Twenty thousand garment workers then joined the "girls' strike" which the union won in 1910. | **HARVEY WASSERMAN's** *History of the United States.*

I don't consider myself sexist at all. I dig chicks probably as much as, if not more than, the next guy. . . . And you probably call *that* sexist because I said "chicks," but I grew up where the guys in my neighborhood said that. The other day a female journalist asked me if I was intimidated by women, and I said, "No, I had a great relationship with my mother. . . . I think she's marvelous." | **CLINT EASTWOOD.**

The Female equally with the Male I sing. | **WALT WHITMAN.**

We spent a lot of time in women's prisons, we read everything we could find about prisons and psychosurgery and lobotomy, and tried to put it all in there. Since we felt that this kind of thing is wrong, we decided that at the end, everyone should get away.
    The people who put up the money for the movie—not Roger, he just developed the script and distributed, and Evelyn got the private financing back fast—they wanted us to shoot another ending for the movie where the inmates either got killed or captured or whatever, so that the film could be shown in South Africa, which is a huge movie market which expressly forbids any scenes about black people successfully going against white people, especially by force. Of course we didn't shoot any such thing. | **JONATHAN DEMME.**

Jonathan Demme began in the exploitation film field working with Joe Viola. Together they wrote, with Demme producing and Viola directing, *Angels Hard as They Come* (1972) and *The Hot Box* (1972). In 1973, they wrote the story for Eddie Romero's *Black Mama, White Mama*, a women's prison picture. In 1974 Demme decided to try his hand at directing, landing

Caged Heat. Courtesy of Jonathan Demme.

a distribution deal with Roger Corman's New World Films. Demme's wife Evelyn Purcell, who had a long background in the film business, produced the film *Caged Heat*, which was shot in four weeks at a cost of $160,000. Within three weeks of its release, according to *Variety*'s figures, the film had made between $300,000 and $400,000. It is still in release today, appearing periodically as second feature on exploitation circuit double bills.

After *Caged Heat*, Demme directed *Crazy Mama* for New World and then went to work for the major Hollywood studios, making *Fighting Mad*, produced by Corman for Twentieth Century-Fox. In 1977 he made a film for Paramount called *Citizens Band*, a box office disaster about the CB craze. The film was retitled *Handle with Care* and shown at The New York Film Festival, where it created quite a stir. By the end of last year it had appeared on numerous ten best lists across the country and Demme was being seriously discussed for the first time.

Demme is an incredibly exciting director who has made some of the most interesting movies of the last decade. Working on modest budgets away from the big money/big star Hollywood syndrome, he has displayed a remarkable technical ability with an eye for composition and decor, a sensitivity toward character action and gesture, and a sensibility which might even be called *Renoirian*. At the same time he has consistently adopted political attitudes and taken chances that other filmmakers wouldn't dare. This is the advantage of working in exploitation films, where a modest budget and limited audience give freer reign to a filmmaker than the big budget Hollywood product which must not offend anyone. Part of the reason *Caged Heat* works so well is Demme's ability to continually shift gears between radically different tones and somehow make it work. The film moves from scenes of burlesque to scenes of satire to scenes of violence, and each seems to work both on its own terms and within the context of the film.

In a recent argument over Fascism and Anti-fascism in films, someone pointed out that *every* film by Jean Renoir was inherently anti-fascist because of its overwhelming humanism. Demme's films similarly demonstrate a love and respect for people, and his characters seem to transcend the exploitation form of which they are a product.

CREW AS CAST, ACTRESS AS ARCHETYPE

Caged Heat was a joint effort with many of the people behind the cameras making appearances before it. Tak Fujimoto, the cameraman, appears in the massage parlor sequence; the mechanic at the gas station is the camera assistant; the production manager is the plain clothes cop at the beginning; the prop man and unit manager are his partners; the guard who gets his ear shot off was also the grip, and so on. The man driving the sports car is Demme's former partner Joe Viola, and one of the women he picks up is his own wife; the family in the car is that of one of Demme's exploitation director colleagues, George Armitage (*Hit Man*, *Private Duty Nurses*, *Vigilante Force*).

> My film about women would be about struggles and loneliness. The woman would have to decide whether to conform or fight and whether she wanted to be accepted and loved or be an individual with her own thoughts and own brain. I don't even want to speak for other women in the movie. All I know is the struggles I feel inside myself lots of times. | ERICA GAVIN

Prior to her role in this film Erica Gavin had starred in *Vixen!*, an extremely popular sexploitation film by the king of soft-core porn, Russ Meyer. In *Caged Heat* Gavin's sexual vibrancy and acting naivete combine to create an

intense presence. She projects an exciting tension between character expectation (the passive, big breasted sex goddess) and performance (her Patty
Hearst stance in the raid on the prison). It is the kind of tension that only
exists because the actor is more than the role. It is the kind of performance
which passes beyond acting and into the realm of archetype. Erica Gavin
could stand next to John Wayne and have nothing to worry about.

DRIVE-IN REDNECK RADICALISM: AMERICAN POPULISM RESHAPED AND SHOWN OUTDOORS

From dissent to resistance; from resistance to revolution. | Popular saying
of the radical movement in the late sixties.

Not all of the films being made in the exploitation field are technically well
made and politically admirable. For the most part they exploit women, show
gratuitous violence, have little plot and lots of nudity. Yet surprisingly, here
in the most commercial field of Hollywood, there is an opportunity for
young directors like Demme to make films which address issues in extreme
ways which would be unfeasible in big budget Hollywood products. Perhaps
because these films generally play to a young working class-to-lower middle
class audience, they are prone to address social issues with a level of anger
and discontent rarely appearing in standard Hollywood fare. Many exploitation films take an almost radical stance regarding police brutality, homosexuality, women's rights, big business and the environment. They deal with
the politics of people and concrete events as opposed to espousing dogma
or polemics.

Caged Heat is about women on their own. There are no positive male
characters portrayed in the film. Boyfriends are constantly talked about
but never seen *or* needed. Men are consistently shown exploiting the women
with whom we are encouraged to sympathize. In a sense the film speaks to
the myth that women are dependent on men for survival, because it constantly shows that not to be true. The women start out the beginning of the
film isolated and even hostile toward one another, but by the end they have
built a community, a sisterhood.

At crucial points the film requires the characters to make choices between
self-preservation and helping the other women. The decision is almost
always for the other women. Jacqueline Wilson goes back to save Pandora
and Belle, Pandora cuts her hand to help Belle, Belle risks everything to help

Pandora. Two crucial scenes in this vein are Crazy Alice's decision (mostly for money) to help Wilson go back to the prison, and Layelle getting involved in something that doesn't concern her one time when she tells Pandora what is about to happen to Belle.

The images one is left with at the end of *Caged Heat* depend upon one's outlook. Unarguably most of the drive-in audience will probably remember the naked bodies and the funny bank robbery. I remember the pained look on Pandora's face as the warden shows her the picture that indicates her privacy has been violated. I remember the screaming faces on the electro-shock table where Wilson makes the political/oppressive connection—"this is rape"—followed by Maggie's violent ode to resistance—"You ball-less wonder." I remember the escapees returning to the prison to help their sisters, and I especially remember Lavelle's slow motion jump into space, gun in hand, her personal destiny under her personal control, caught in her movement from passive acceptance to active resistance, the only motion open for a person in an oppressive society. The film sings the song of resistance. Despite its exploitive nature, despite the tits and ass, despite the blood, there is the moment when the individual transcends society and takes her own life into her own hands.

> I have become friends with avant-garde singer-poet Patti Smith and her band. Through them, I think I am beginning to understand "where I am" as an actress/person and what I would like my direction to be. . . . I am an artist, underground now . . . but for me winter is ending, the ice is melting, and it is time that I peak above ground. | ERICA GAVIN

———

LOUIS BLACK

VOL. 14, NO. 3
APRIL 3, 1978

Caged Heat: Second Thoughts

Caged Heat is a movie composed of contradictions. Jonathan Demme addresses the victimizations specific to women because of their sex (voyeuristic objectification, gynecological brutality, and rape in the form of shock treatments and psychosurgery) as well as the need for active, self-reliant, aggressive heroines who exist in a world without men (the need having been created by our society's overwhelming lack of culture heroines: female characters who display qualities suited to epic adventure rather than limited array of stereotyped attributes that serve to reflect and promote our notions of the Eternal Feminine qualities). Ordinarily such sensitivity to women's issues is applauded as a cinematic and therefore cultural advancement. And in a sense it is. Yet both Jonathan Demme and *Caged Heat* are products of the exploitation film industry which, guided by its functional production and marketing motives, also capitalizes on tendencies which undercut, if not contradict, these pro-women sensitivities.

The exploitation industry frequently yields fascinating products since its output of formulaic films with sufficient amounts of violence and R-rated female nudity is set in a curious tension with vast directorial freedom that allows ample room for idiosyncratic manipulations within the confines of the pre-determined formula. Demme, who wrote and directed *Caged Heat*, stands out as an extremely talented and technically masterful filmmaker who is willing to make ideological leaps from the strictures of his women-in-prison genre story to deliberate cultural connections that expand the scope and impact of the film past the realm of simple and familiar prurient sensations. Nevertheless, *Caged Heat* seems to blend an uneasy mixture of sexual exploitation with radical and untypical character attributes and behaviors. It then becomes important for us to examine whether these apparent contradictions can co-exist without one subsuming the other and if so, how.

The overt political statements in the film are handled in such a deliberate fashion that their articulation cannot be overlooked. Demme carefully parallels the Doctor's use of gynecological speculum and the lobotomy drill so that these instruments become obvious phallic substitutes used to brutalize, invade and rape women. Not mincing words, Jacqueline tells him that his shock treatments constitute rape, an apt term since the overwhelming majority of psychosurgery victims come from the ranks of the most legally vulnerable in our society: women, children, gays, incarcerated prisoners and the aged. The sense of community that develops amongst the women is also a rare cinematic example of loyal and heroic interactions amongst women. At some point in the film each one of the escapees puts her life on the line to aid another. In the dream sequence Warden McQueen tells the women that their sexual relationships with men have put them behind bars in the first place and she cites their conviction records of stealing in order to look nice for men, streetwalking to make pimps rich, and killing other women as rivals for men's affections. It is only the escapees' eventual acceptance of their need to band together in rebellious combat that provides them with the concerted power necessary to free themselves.

Caged Heat's direct and positive political assertions have been dealt with extensively in the *Program Notes* by Louis Black and my further elaboration of the radical qualities of the film would prove superfluous. Thus, I wish to focus my attention on the disparity caused by the simultaneous depiction of (1) self-defined heroic women as subjects of their own story and (2) culturally and generically defined women as objects for audience gratification. Although the thrust of my attention focuses on the inherent exploitative elements that contradict the deliberate radicalism, I do so with the assumption of the reader's familiarity with the preceding *Program Notes*. My intention is not to assign greater value or significance to one aspect over the other or to determine which side of the balance the scales ultimately tip. The balance may prove unequal and uneasy at times, but it is the paradox of their mutual coexistence that makes *Caged Heat* such an intriguing work. The paradoxical blend of Demme's personal expression of concerns about social oppression in a format that capitalizes on and co-opts female nudity and popular issues for profit is a phenomenon deserving our attention. It serves as a model of the classic paradox faced by a personally committed director when working in the mass entertainment business as well as an example of one potentially viable solution to that dilemma.

From the title onward *Caged Heat* emphasizes exploitative titillation. Whereas the film could be a very direct political observation of the conditions imposed on women in prison, its title generates expectations of repressed and incendiary sexuality (which, although certainly a feature of prison life, is far from being its sole explosive characteristic). The sensationalism of the *Caged Heat* title focuses attention on sexual repression as the primary reason for breaking out of prison rather than a more complex system of personal and political abuse.

Film titles, whether used denotatively and/or connotatively, are descriptive tools which are designed to fulfill purposes broader than simple utilitarian naming functions. They provide succinct definitions, descriptions or commentaries on a movie's essential characteristic and also serve as key promotional and advertising aids. Just as we know that the heat in titles such as Raoul Walsh's *White Heat* and Fritz Lang's *Big Heat* indicate notions of intense emotional energy and police pressure, we know that the heat in the R-rated exploitation film *Caged Heat* places special emphasis on the word's sexual implications.

Even though *Caged Heat*'s title also carries connotations of suppressed and contained anger, the opening shots inside the prison temporarily disavow this interpretation. The first prison sequence is Lavelle's dream fantasy. She and an unidentified man are engaged in sexual activity through the cell bars while she brandishes a huge butcher knife which she guides forcefully in mock thrusts in the air above and behind her. The dream is sharply interrupted by the dissonant blare of the morning wake-up buzzer. As the sequence concludes with shots of Lavelle and the other prisoners waking, we come to associate Lavelle's frustrated heterosexual tensions and her potential capacity for violent but unfocused aggression with the general condition of women in prison.

Our familiar expectations for the linear narrative conventions of the women-in-prison action genre are disrupted by the jolting surrealism and rapidity of the dream sequence which also involves an abrupt shift in time, location and characters. In contrast to these disorienting sequences, Demme begins the next sequence with an almost cartoon-like image which manages to succinctly express one of the genre's most formulaic themes: that women in prison, although actively involved in lesbian relationships, are nevertheless sexually unsatiated and in need of heterosexual sex. The shot opens on a tight closeup of the seat of an inmate's shorts on which is written "KISS ME QUICK." Once the advertisement is read by the audience the woman walks into the recess of the frame opening up the shot to a wider view of the other inmates gathered in the prisonyard. Her proposition is not directed at any of the women prisoners since the eye level closeup point of view would be impossible for any of the characters present. It is a privileged camera angle and Demme uses its unique point of view to offer a gratuitous sexual come-on aimed exclusively at the theater audience and not at any of the potential lesbian lovers in her immediate environment. As such, the shot provides an affirmative reassurance to the heterosexual status quo.

Many cultural assumptions are operant here. The first is that women are primarily defined by their sexuality and, when incarcerated, the main deprivation endured is the loss of their heterosexual outlets. "Caged heat" becomes the dominant characteristic of prison life and thus lesbian relationships are formed as substitutive outlets for the inmates' overwhelming heterosexual frustrations. It is implicitly assumed that women are predominantly sexual beings and, when denied access to preferred sexual activity with men, will seek out makeshift alliances, since it is unthinkable for young women to be healthily portrayed as nonsexual, celibate, or homosexual. In our culture a woman is defined by her sexual relationship to a male Other.

The women-in-prison film genre is a narrative form which allows us to observe illicit sexual liaisons overtly and in a quasi-legitimate sphere. Thus these two initial sequences in the prison assure the audience that despite an abundance of lesbian activity, imprisoned women do not abandon their primary interest in heterosexual sex. While *Caged Heat* never portrays lesbianism in a derogatory light it implicitly asserts that these relationships are merely temporary substitutes for the imposed impossibility of relationships with men. By keeping the women's lesbian interests makeshift and subordinate to their primary interest in sex with men (as evidenced in the sexual dream, fantasies, conversational remarks about boyfriends, the phallic obsession of Belle and Pandora's stage skit, and Pandora's stash of nude photos of her boyfriend), the viewer is provided with lesbian images that are titillating yet never threatening to phallic superiority.

The demands of the exploitation film require that major emphasis be placed on soft-core sexuality. The fact that only attractive women who do not wear bras are imprisoned allows the viewer to suspend the world of realistic believability and approach the realm of wet-dream. The necessary titillation is provided by the female body, whether garbed in tight and revealing clothing or naked in lingering shower shots. Pandering to the audience's desires to see naked women is not a situation endemic to the exploitation market. Comparing the shower sequences in *Caged Heat* with the opening shower sequence in a more mainstream film such as Brian De Palma's *Carrie* we begin to see that female body exploitation is an axiom of the cinema (cheap thrills for the costuming department). Whereas the shower sequence in *Caged Heat* are stark shots of women waiting in line to wash their hair and brush their teeth, the camerawork in *Carrie* leisurely pans the locker room while gazing at the half-dressed teenaged girls through a soft focus lens. Is it any longer possible to make distinctions between exploitation and art?

One of the most interesting aspects of *Caged Heat* is that it portrays active women protagonists who exist in a milieu devoid of men. Conventionally in movies women are given more passive roles and when they are moved to action it is in response to their relationships with men. *Caged Heat* deals with women who can be moved to action on their own self-motivated terms. They have become the subjects rather than the objects in what resembles, in many aspects, a typical male-oriented action (specifically, jailbreak) story. The women in *Caged Heat* have subsumed the traditionally male qualities of courage, self-reliance and the capacity for violence—all qualities necessary for heroic struggles.

Yet their unquestioning adoption of traditionally identified male attributes and models of behavior further twists the phenomenon of exploitative voyeurism. Women with these male activist capacities are still threatening in our society, although we do have an ironic fascination with "ballsy" women. Thus *Caged Heat* works on two levels in that it allows women to function as the subjects of an action story while catering to our desires to observe these threatening women at a safe and secure distance. Concurrently, the women function as both subject protagonists and fetishistic objects. It is one of the paradoxes of *Caged Heat* that it can operate within the parameters of the exploitation film while pushing its objects of exploitation toward possibilities of subjectivity.

An intrinsic contradiction nevertheless exists between the characters' emotional commitment to other women and their absorption of male character traits and behavior patterns. *Caged Heat* offers hope for a future artistic tradition of women as heroic subjects, but it does nothing to encourage them to forge their own traditions and stories based on self-definition. These women achieve heroic status only because their actions conform to pre-existing, male-defined behavior codes and narrative structures. The transference of female characters into protagonists in male action stories amounts to emotional transvestism. Not that role reversal isn't interesting, instructive and valuable, but it is merely a transposition of elements within the same structure. It does not forge new roles, narratives and structures. New protagonists must shape new stories evolved from their own necessities.

——

MARJORIE BAUMGARTEN

VOL. 13, NO. 4
DECEMBER 7, 1977

The Texas Chainsaw Massacre (1974)

PRODUCED AND DIRECTED BY TOBE HOOPER

What's it like to have a nightmare from which you can't wake up? There have been films that explored nightmares (*The Manchurian Candidate*, for one), but they always let up when things get rough. *Texas Chainsaw* does not let up—it just keeps on getting worse. What's more, it captures nightmare syntax with astonishing fidelity. Fine photography and editing, and an amazing electronic score, add to the impact. Last year the Museum of Modern Art Film Library put on a special screening of *Texas Chainsaw*. They were right. | MICHAEL GOODWIN, *Take One*, Vol. V, No.1

TWENTY-FIVE REASONS WHY I DON'T WANT TO SEE TEXAS CHAINSAW MASSACRE

1. Avoidance of pain has always been one of my major priorities. *Massacre* is not so much gross as terrifying and not so much horrible as agonizing. It may not be the quintessence of pain, but it comes real close.

2. The great existential struggle of living in a universe that constantly reminds me that I'm going to die tends to sap my courage and weaken my sanity. The idea of my dying quietly at eighty surrounded by my grandchildren is a macabre enough contemplation for me. But dying young after being subjected to all manner of physical and emotional tortures is an idea to be avoided at all costs.

3. Like one of the characters in the film, I like meat.

4. Like the gas station attendant, killing is not something I get much pleasure from.

5. I like films to scare me, not make me hysterical.

6. The thread of my sanity is sometimes thin; all too often insane people frighten me because I have too much in common with them.

7. All too often insane people frighten me because I have so little in common with them.

8. It is really hard to fight a man who is holding an operating chainsaw.

9. I'm afraid of the dark. Sometimes it's intelligent to be afraid of the dark. You can't see very well and unfortunately not everyone sleeps as well as you would have them do in the best of all possible worlds.

10. I dislike cutting myself. There's just something about the sight of my own life's blood that makes me feel rather vulnerable to the vicissitudes of reality.

11. Dead bodies bother me. It sort of reminds me I might be dead someday too.

12. It's hard to reason with a homicidal maniac, especially when he has several cohorts who seem bent on laughing every time someone screams.

13. I don't know for sure what goes into sausage and I'm not sure I want to know what some people might accidently or purposefully put there.

14. I take comfort in the illusion that there is such a thing as normality—in filmmakers as well as in regular people.

15. I have a very vivid imagination. I can think up all manner of weird things to have nightmares about and I don't need fresh material. I can ruin a perfectly good night's sleep all by myself.

16. After about ten minutes of screen time I got a little tired of hearing a girl scream hysterically.

17. I'm starving and would really like to have a nice greasy hamburger for dinner.

18. I grew up in a Texas farm community. I once got stuck in a farmer's field and had to knock on his door to get him to help me get my car out of the sand. If you think I'm ever going to do that again, you're crazy.

19. I like people. And I prefer people who also like people.

20. I have written Program Notes for nine horror movies this semester and I'm beginning to wonder if any film means anything.

21. I like things that are somewhat subtle just so I can think about them for a while; there is nothing subtle about a chainsaw.

22. I'm still not sure that movies don't give some rather imbalanced people ideas about how to go about reeking mayhem. I'm not sure that they do either, of course, but the possibility could exist.

23. No one will convince me that "it's just a movie" is any kind of real comfort. People make movies, People also kill people. (No, I do not deduce that movies kill people; I've still preserved that much perspective.)

24. I'm worried that just because I don't want to die right now God has some sort of particularly disagreeable end planned for me. Crazy? Sure, but just in case you haven't realized it by now, I have actually seen this film and it does everything in its power to reinforce my paranoia.

25. I'm a social worker by profession and I know there are crazy people in the world. As much as I'd like to set your mind at ease, it just isn't the case that people don't do weird things.

———

RITA THEBERGE

*   *   *

So, once it was monsters and now it is maniacs. Horror novels and films used to create terrifying images of our innermost fears. Vampires, the Frankenstein monster, werewolves, mummies, and zombies represented terrors, which we were scared we might meet in the dark. In films certain actors, especially Karloff, Lugosi, and Lorre, came to be horror archetypes themselves. They transcend any role they played and when people went to see them in a movie like *The Black Cat, Mad Love,* or *White Zombie* they knew

Texas Chainsaw Massacre. Courtesy of Tobe Hooper.

exactly what they were getting. People screamed and fainted and continued to go to the theaters. Part of the advertising campaign for the original *Frankenstein* (1931) announced that there would be a nurse in the lobby. Having oneself scared half to death can be a surprisingly pleasurable experience.

The society changed and the film form with it. There was World War II and Nazis and ovens with people mass-murdering other people. The ritualization of war that allowed us to cope with disguised genocide broke down and we were forced to confront a new kind of horror. Still there is the scene in Roger Corman's *Bloody Mama* where the crowd arrives with picnic baskets to watch the police slaughter the Barker family. It is an image replicating the scene at the first battle of Bull Run, where the Washington DC elite drove out from the city with picnic baskets to watch the anonymous boys in blue slaughter the anonymous boys in grey. But when the tables were turned the elite hurried home. They didn't really want to be involved; they only wanted to watch. Audiences are allowed such privileges.

We *are* the audience with those privileges, fascinated by watching humans slaughtering humans. We are the audience watching Alain

Resnais's short *Night and Fog* about the Nazi concentration camps as he shows us modern day footage of tourists posing in the doorways of the ovens to have their photographs taken. It is Bermuda shorts and straw hats and Nikons and corpses and blood and mountains of hair and teeth.

Val Lewton came along during World War II and made a series of horror films that did not have lumbering monsters, sleek monsters or ugly monsters—films that tried to create psychological horror. Terror derived from mood and setting. The very recognizable world that people lived in— parks, swimming pools, and suburban backyards—became the setting. Horror was no longer confined to castles, small Bavarian towns, and spooky old haunted houses. It was moving into our neighborhoods.

The War ended and the Cold War began and Lewton essentially stopped making films. America and Truman and the bomb and Eisenhower and John Foster Dulles and Sen. Joe McCarthy and communists who lived down the block and who were undoubtedly going to move next door and try to change *us* in the middle of the night. Hollywood made a few science-fiction films but not many horror films.

The Korean War happened and it wasn't as easy to understand as other wars and we didn't win it as clearly or completely as we thought we had always won wars. But of course since we were right, and in the fifties we were almost always right—right to black list, right to ask any question of or about communists, right to sit by during the Hungarian revolt of 1956, right to support the French colonial invasion of Indochina—we did win it. God was very specifically on our side. Hollywood gave us *House of Wax* and *The Beast from 20,000 Fathoms* and even *The Creature from the Black Lagoon* in 3-D. 1956 saw *Invasion of the Body Snatchers*, a meeting of the horror film, the science-fiction film, and political allegory.

Then, in the late fifties, the monster film was reborn with Hammer Studios in England and American International Pictures in the United States leading the way. American society continued to change and movies with it. In 1960 Alfred Hitchcock made *Psycho* and the monster this time looked like you and me, and the terror came at a typically American motel, and the car and the clothes and the people were not alien at all but very real, and by 1960 close to 80% of the support for the French involvement in Indochina was coming from the United States.

Psycho pointed the way and a change slowly came to horror films. There were still movies with monsters and movies celebrating the grotesque and the unreal, but the horrors in society were changing. It had never been uncommon for Americans to have their neighbors brutalized or murdered. There had always been lynchings, but they were mostly of blacks; there had been wives beaten—some fatally—by their husbands, but they had probably done something wrong; there were the young girls and the not so young whose stomachs were torn up by illegal abortions, many mangled for life and many who died, but after all they had been immoral; there was Sacco and Vanzetti, Joe Hill, the murdered strikers at Republic Steel in 1936, the woman and children butchered at Homestead, and the Rosenbergs, but the government said that these people were all right to kill.

Almost single handedly a quiet man named George Metesky changed all this by setting off a series of bombs in New York City and earning himself the title The Mad Bomber. He didn't kill anybody in his private war with a major corporation, but he used our world, and not the celluloid world or the world over there where so many wars had been fought, as his battleground. Some of the many who enthusiastically followed in his footsteps were not so careful and people began to die. Some who came later only wanted to kill. Metesky was not the first, but he became the most famous and the crazies who committed random acts of violence in the day to day world became news. Suddenly it was no longer *them*—the blacks, the communists, immoral women—but it was *anyone* who might suddenly be killed, and usually for no apparent reason. Charles Whitman, Richard Speck, Charlie Manson, and others became famous. But they were just the very visible tip of the iceberg that seemed to keep growing: anonymous brothers who murdered sisters, children who murdered their families, handymen who killed their employers, people who slaughtered people they never met. The real horror has now become that some night your next-door neighbor might knock on your door and, when you answer it, blow your head off. The real horror is that, when walking to class or driving to work or watching a football game or picnicking in the countryside, someone may murder you. The real horror is snipers with guns and maniacs with knives and lunatics with bombs and very calm, normal-appearing people who suddenly turn deadly. It is *Targets*, *Two-Minute Warning*, *Dirty Harry*, and *The Texas Chainsaw Massacre*.

Whereas most horror movies trade on the ghosts of the dead or the supernatural transformation of the living, *Chainsaw* explores the almost unimaginable horror of those real events which appear in the headlines. When corpses rise from the grave in *Chainsaw* they are not resurrected by an other-worldly power, but dug up by real life ghouls. Lots of blood is not a real horror. Gore has become a S. Clay Wilson comic book release or a hysterical, screaming catharsis. The vast quantities of blood in certain movies allow us to deal with them as over-indulgent fantasies. *Chainsaw* is not that gory. It is its complete lack of humanity that is terrifying. More blood would have allowed us to look at the screen less. It is not a film about blood like *Blood Feast* or *Two Thousand Maniacs!* It is not even a grotesque and gross film like *Night of the Living Dead* or *Pink Flamingos*. It is not a voyeur's feast of violence like *El Topo*. For the most part it is a cold and sterile film about a nihilistic world, with no values, no caring and no compassion. Even the love relationships within the film seem unreal. It is a film that has grown out of our very real fears about the nature of American life.

We are forced by the film to realize that we live and play an active part in a world where someone's (and not just one, but several people's) pleasure can be torturing other people. We watch it and we scream at it or, even more perversely (but no less appropriately), we laugh at it. We watch it and we react to it in record numbers and thus we become part of it. We can call the butchering family horrible and inhuman, but if we weren't interested they would never have been brought to the screen.

The horror film is no longer an analogy of sexual fantasies or fears. Its strength no longer comes from our memory-association with our parents' creaking bed springs in the dark. Its beauty (and all horror films have a beauty) no longer comes from our first traumatic nocturnal encounters with our own sexuality. Horror films seem to be more and more an all-too-accurate statement about our own loss of humanity. Our sometimes-hysterical reaction of laughter seems to give a grotesque emphasis to that loss. We have met the inhumans and they are sitting all around. In a very terrifying way, because we all understand this film completely, we have become this film and when we laugh at it and in some way enjoy it we are endorsing our own dehumanization.

But, there is a calm after the polemic, because horror movies and even *Texas Chainsaw Massacre* are more than that. Horror movies are, in a sense, an exorcism. We cleanse our soul of the horror. The movie is a talisman. If we watch it then those events won't happen in our lives. In the same way we know that cinematic reality is not our reality, which we will never sleep with Al Pacino or Lindsay Crouse, we can begin to believe, in an almost unconscious way, that when we view these horrors we have somehow prevented them from entering our existence.

Texas chain saw massacre
They took my baby away from me
But she'll never get out of there
They chop her up and I don't care
I don't care, wo oh.

THE RAMONES, "Chain Saw."

The chainsaw is operated by a family of Texas-style lunatics, all veterans of a local meat plant, who have decorated their rural home with fragments of human corpses taken from graves at a nearby cemetery or from passersby unfortunate enough to wander too near. The victims in the film are a group of young Houstonites, skylarking in their van across the rural Texas countryside. The first half of the film follows the roving group as they encounter a series of minor horrors—a graveyard where corpses have been unearthed, an insanely sadistic hitchhiker—and end up at a deserted house, which used to belong to one of their families. The tension in this part of the film is almost unbearable. Shots of Franklin in his wheelchair amidst the ruins of the deserted house evoke terror by merely framing him with his back to several menacingly open doorways. His sister's high-pitched giggle, heard in the distance off-screen, is so shrill that each time we hear it we cringe with the fear that the murders have begun. Each moment we are expecting to hear the roar of the chainsaw, and each moment that it is delayed only serves to heighten our suspense. When the murders do begin, however, the film rushes headlong into a sheer nightmare that lasts for forty-five minutes without interruption.

Chainsaw undoubtedly offers one of the most intense and physically exhausting movie experiences available. There is a relentlessness to its pacing, its unendurably protracted scenes of horror and its intolerably mounting suspense which has less to do with entertainment than with catharsis, and less to do with catharsis than with pain. It is a film which generates horror, not through the liberation of demons from the psyche, but by confronting directly the reality of human pain. Not only are we forced to contemplate the horror of being held captive by a group of crazies who intend to torture you to death or the feeling of being skewered alive on a massive meat hook; we are also forced to face the pain of frustration (Franklin left downstairs by his sister and friends), of being confined to the wheelchair, of enduring the oppressive Texas summer heat.

The universe of *Texas Chainsaw Massacre* is unrelentingly hostile. "The world has gone crazy," one of the victims observes early in the film, and we are constantly reminded that the chainsaw massacre is neither isolated nor comprehensible. Following the report of the grave robbing, the radio continues to drone on during the credits, reporting the deaths of 29 people in the collapse of a building in Atlanta, fourteen cases of an infectious and fatal disease in San Francisco, the explosion of three storage tanks at a Texaco refinery, a suicide in Houston, as if all these events somehow were linked in a cosmic scheme to torment mankind.

Is there some grand explanation? The film itself seems to ridicule such an idea by making fun of Pam, the girl who is "into" astrology, as she searches for reasons in the fact that Saturn is in retrograde. At the same time, however, *Chainsaw* establishes its own cosmic context, constantly connecting scenes with shots of the sun or moon and projecting its opening credits across astronomical photographs of million-mile-long flames leaping from the sun's surface. By connecting the world's real social and physical brutalities with the conventional signifiers of nature that contribute the metaphysical dimension to the standard horror film (a hazy sun, the full moon, a dark forest) *Chainsaw* implicates the entire universe in its pain.

Are the killers crazy because their father is crazy? And is their father crazy because his father worked in a slaughterhouse? Are we all crazy because we eat meat? Do buildings collapse in Atlanta because graves are dug up in Texas? Or is the world in general crazy due to the total arbitrariness of the universe? Is pain the human condition? And, if so, what kind of a universe is this which torments us without reason? Is God the ultimate sadist?

All of these modern, almost Sartrean questions are raised and implicitly linked by the film, but no solution is even proposed. The universe seems to function according to Manson's Law: "No sense makes sense." Logic is no defense for it fails to take into consideration the total arbitrariness of lunacy. But our poor victims can only operate according to the rules they're familiar with. If your friends go off and don't come back, you should go looking for them. If your friend's jacket is on the front porch, your friend must be inside the house. And if, by some horrible chance, someone should try to kill you in that house, you run for safety to another one.

Logically, the characters have nothing to fear in the deserted house. Stories about haunted houses are for kids and, after all, those are only spiders in the corner of the room. But when Franklin discovers the bizarre bone and feather altar he cannot logically deduce its implications. Similarly, the numerous cars which the couple discovers seem weird but not terrifying. There is no way a rational person could assume that each car represents several hundred pounds of human barbeque.

Who we are at movies and during movies and after movies and what movies do to us is a question that many have talked to and about but no one has really answered. Because of the subject matter and the brilliant pacing at certain moments during *Chainsaw*, when we are alone, the world being just ourselves and the movie, we confront that question in a very real way on an absolute gut level. Some of us scream and some of us laugh and some of us pretend to be bored but because of our interaction with the screen and the importance in our life of that finite amount of celluloid at that moment, it all, somehow, becomes terribly important and completely unimportant. Movies, we are so tempted to say, are after all only movies, but then of course, are they?

Texas Chainsaw Massacre was produced independent of any major production company and was shot in a small town near Austin, drawing most of its actors and crew from local talent. In its numerous paradoxes the film represents the system of independent production at both its best and its worst. Most importantly *Chainsaw* provides an outstanding example of the kind of film which can be produced by a group of dedicated people working with very limited money, but lots of ingenuity and fortitude. The low budget/independent/exploitation status of the film allows it to confront modern horrors in a way no big budget Hollywood film (with its necessity to appeal to a broad audience in order to make back its investment) has ever attempted. By no means, however, was the film without restrictions—when it was completed, the distributor was distressed by the lack of gore and the total absence of sex, returning the film to its makers with orders to reshoot once scene putting Marilyn Burns in a wet T-shirt which would cling to her nipples. But the film was a labor of love for those involved, and the degree of their dedication is apparent in the minutely detailed, unspeakably grotesque sets and props of art director Robert Burns, the inventive and accomplished cinematography of Daniel Pearl and the creatively manipulative, expressionistically suggestive editing of Sallye Richardson and Larry Carroll.

Simultaneous to its demonstration of the capabilities of its creators, and the possibilities of the independent production, *Texas Chainsaw Massacre* also represents the fulfillment of the worst connotations of "exploitation film" in its exploitation of those who made the film. Shot with a non-Union cast and crew, the film was not restricted to specific working hours or a minimum pay scale. Most everyone involved were happy to be making a movie and the principals were satisfied to take a small percentage of the profits.

The work was grueling, with shooting continuing non-stop as long as equipment was available. The climactic scene around the dinner table was shot in one 36-hour stretch with breaks taken for only long enough to allow the cast and crew to eat. Descriptions of the experience by members of the cast make the actual shooting of the scene sound more hellish and sickening than the scene as it appears in the film (and it is certainly one of *Chainsaw*'s most repulsive sequences). All openings to the room were sealed off so that shooting would continue through the daylight hours. The lights, only a few feet from the actor's faces, heated the room to an almost unbearable temperature, recooking the barbeque and causing the chemicals injected in some the of fleshy props to release a noxious gas. But one is willing to sacrifice for art and for a percentage of earnings.

Unfortunately, after dealing with the distributor (Bryanston Films) and the investors' company (Vortex), those involved in the production have seen very little or nothing of the money that *Chainsaw* has continued to gross for a full three years. Lawsuits have been filed and bitterness still surfaces against producer-director Tobe Hooper. In view of the kind of contract Hooper signed with the investors, it seems likely they never expected that he or any of his fellow collaborators would make any money off the film. His detractors claim that Hooper was only looking to land a five-picture contract with a major company. Ironically, the big break Hooper earned may not have paid off. His next film, *Starlight Slaughters*, was previewed briefly in Austin, but has never gained national release.

It would be unfair, however, to deny Hooper the credit he deserves for *Chainsaw*. Having co-written the script as well as having produced and directed the film, his vision forms the core around which the movie revolves. Perhaps the ugliness of the way the film was made informs the ugliness of the film itself. Nevertheless, it seems no mean achievement that Hooper was able to create what is probably the ugliest film ever made. It is an accomplishment which guarantees *The Texas Chainsaw Massacre* a place in the pantheon of American film classics. The Museum of Modern Art made it official not too long ago when they purchased a print for their permanent collection.

LOUIS BLACK, ED LOWRY

VOL. 21, NO. 3
DECEMBER 7, 1981

Assault on Precinct 13 (1976)

WRITTEN AND DIRECTED BY JOHN CARPENTER

The impact in recent years of the psychoanalytic and Marxist approaches to film criticism has been such that the significance of the awareness of a dominant ideology (bourgeois capitalism) and its chief functionary (the patriarchal nuclear family) has, in an ironically pervasive way, effected a dominant critical methodology. The critic is susceptible to becoming an apologist for films whose integrity cannot be coherently argued from that perspective. The critical point of departure can become the subtly reactionary point of attack, the methodology a kind of critical hair shirt; difficult to keep on, difficult to take off.

John Carpenter's *Assault on Precinct 13* generates a unique tension between extremes of generic references, from explicit homages to directors and films to the deliberate subversion of generic expectations. The film's narrative structure ultimately reaches a point where it transcends the ideological conflict elaborated between a derelict social norm and the nihilistic alternative it has produced. The first half of the film focuses on three temporally parallel events: the closing of Precinct 13, overseen by Lt. Bishop; the relocation of death-row prisoners Wilson and Wells; and the nihilistic youth gang's apparently arbitrary attack on Lawson and his daughter. Carpenter uses superimposed titles specifying time and location of the disparate events in order to facilitate the viewer's anticipation of their convergence and thus heighten suspense. These highly localized actions set up a transition to the second half of the film, which is just as conspicuously set outside the bounds of space and time, contributing to the viewer's suspension of disbelief. The transitory status of the precinct that both is and isn't a police station, Lieutenant Bishop's temporary assignment in his old neighborhood and Wells and Wilson as prisoners no longer confined create the necessary impetus for the possibility of transcending generic milieu in the attack on the precinct which occupies the second half of the film.

This is a society of "horrible neighborhoods," where people are strangely absent from the streets and an ice cream vendor carries a gun. Police are said to have been driven to deplorable extremes, and the voiceover radio announcements suggest a state of emergency, an atmosphere of martial law. "There are no heroes anymore," for heroism has been replaced by men who follow orders; political action has been usurped by bureaucratic extension.

Lt. Ethan Bishop is a man who still believes in heroism, "a man of faith" whose emergence from the Anderson ghetto has been dependent on an implicit belief in and assimilation into the very system whose failure has turned Anderson into a jungle. That his need/quest for heroism is met with such hostility results in a personal crisis, a call for some modification of this insular faith, this cultivated naiveté; heroism by this society's dominant standards is simply no longer possible. Napoleon Wilson, meanwhile, is a romantic hero whose own *personal* moral code has made his integration into society an impossibility. A synthesis of the Western hero and the hardboiled detective (and Darwin Joston looks and acts eerily like a cross between Gary Cooper and Alan Ladd), Wilson's heroism is dependent on his isolation from a society that is corrupt. He states that he believes in only one man, himself, but also that a man must never run away from two things, "even if they cost him his life": "one is a man who's helpless and can't run with him" and the other is a woman he loves. This disclosure, plus Wilson's self-awareness that he was "born out of time" and his equation of woman with the elusive essence of life itself, make him the quintessential romantic hero whose absolutism assures both his demise and his spiritual transcendence.

The second half of the film abandons the highly localized events of the first half for timeless points of reference more closely allied to the classic Western than to the streets of a Los Angeles ghetto. The precinct becomes a frontier fort that is under siege. This attack on the precinct has been prompted by a desire for vengeance, specifically on Lawson, who has killed the white war lord, a blood brother, and generally in retaliation for the murders of the gang members by police at the beginning of the film. The murder of Lawson's daughter is symbolic though frighteningly arbitrary and the actions of the gang cannot be regarded as totally nihilistic but as rebellious, retaliatory, and ritualistic. It is the apparent randomness of the violence that is so disturbing, but insofar as it is manifest in mainstream society as well as in the gang's actions the line between absolute evil and absolute good is obliterated. It is the precinct, uniquely placed outside the law and society it supposedly represents, which affords the possibility of transcendence, of making sense of one's existence.

Leigh, Wilson and Bishop exist apart from a society which is shown to be inefficient and impotent. The film's ideological crisis—the breakdown of technocratic society and the imposed isolation of one of its unwanted appendages—is symbolized by the broken phone (communication) lines and the absence of electricity. Political and therefore moral problems have become administrative, technical problems; Julie is convinced that the phone company will sense their situation and somehow correct it. It is this isolation which interjects the idea of moral accountability and the possibility of moral triumph. For Julie, socially moral obligations exist only insofar as they are functional, and problems that cannot be seen do not exist. She recoils from this moral/ethical responsibility, from the "civilized look" whose scrutiny she feels threatens her chances of survival, and is ready to sacrifice Lawson in exchange for a return to the pre-crisis social norm.

Assault on Precinct 13, like Hawks's *Rio Bravo*, depicts its heroes as united in a common defense and by a common ethos but isolated from mainstream society. Survival depends not only on trust, on the absence of sides, but on how good one is; the personal code must not only be articulated and meticulously followed, it must work. Though the film is modeled after *Rio Bravo* and has many references to it (e.g., the editor credit on *Assault* is listed under the name of John T. Chance, the John Wayne character in *Rio Bravo*), *Assault* is concerned with the personal code of individualism celebrated in other Westerns, as well as in other male-oriented action genres. Part of Carpenter's talent, and an integral function of his style, is his remarkable ability to assimilate into his films visual and narrative homages, dialogue, thematic concerns, plot structures, images and whole scenes from other films. The cigarette scene between Leigh and Wilson could have been in *To Have and*

Have Not; the shot of Wilson catching the rifle thrown to him by Bishop, turning and firing is reminiscent of John Wayne and Dean Martin in *Rio Bravo* (or John Wayne in almost any film); Wilson as romantic Westerner evokes John Wayne in *Stagecoach* and Alan Ladd in *Shane*. The "potatoes" scene in which Wells and Wilson make a life or death decision by playing a child's game of chance is very like the bizarre dancing/guitar playing display of machismo by Sterling Hayden in *Johnny Guitar*, completely subverting the audience's expectations of what these characters, in their generic context, should be doing. Perhaps the most gratuitous homage in the film is to Alfred Hitchcock; when Bishop relates his story of being sent to the police station with a note from his father saying that bad boys should be put in jail, he is restating a story Hitchcock told repeatedly as a true incident from his own childhood.

But *Assault on Precinct 13* does not function only as a moviegoer's movie; it is the consummate exploitation film, a catalogue of generic hyperbole. It explicitly and with as much sensational detail as possible addresses the complex social problems raised by the dominant presence of a decadent, degenerate unworkable system of societal norms. Through his use of generic conventions and their selective and careful subversion or romanticizing, Carpenter demonstrates how closely the ironic approaches the mythic in its effect.

> My whole philosophy of movies is that movies are not intellectual, they are not ideas ... movies are *emotional*, an audience should cry or laugh or get scared. I think the audience should project into the film, into a character, into a situation, and react. | JOHN CARPENTER

A young girl, wearing pinafore, braids and ribbons stands before an ice cream truck and asks for a vanilla twist. A man, dressed in black and seen in profile, turns silently, with almost balletic grace and without hesitation, points a huge automatic revolver with silencer at the little girl and shoots; the little girl, still holding a now blood-splattered ice cream cone, falls to the ground dead. And whether to laugh, cry, get scared, get angry or all of these remains the critical bugaboo, a most fascinating dilemma.

———

ANN LAEMMLE

Original Scanned CinemaTexas Note

NIGHT OF THE LIVING DEAD (DIR. GEORGE ROMERO, 1968)
BY KELLY GREENE

PROGRAM NOTES

Vol. 21, No. 2
November 12, 1981

The Night of the Living Dead (1968)

Interviewer: George Romero has called his original story for the film an
               "allegory." . . . Do you agree with him: Is NIGHT OF THE
               LIVING DEAD an allegory?
John Russo: I don't agree with him.
Karl Hardman: I don't either.
Russell Streiner: No, I don't.
John Russo: I think the film is an attempt to make money.

> --from an interview with NIGHT OF THE
> LIVING DEAD's producers (Karl Hardman
> and Russell Streiner) and screenwriter
> (John Russo).

In 1975, three of the principals involved in the making of NIGHT OF
THE LIVING DEAD suggested that the project they worked on was anything
but the auteurist vision of George Romero. From script to screen, an
active group of six to ten people purportedly made a series of choices
and revisions in order to make a film that turned a profit. The choice
of a black man as the lead performer apparently came by way of default
and not by liberal design. The job of director was passed around and
finally accepted by Romero with the relish of the Ancient Mariner receiving his albatross.

We can speculate about the accuracy of the comments of these men,
but even with the tinge of sour grapes taken into account, one feels
that *their* bodies and souls no doubt lent a great deal to the creation
of NIGHT OF THE LIVING DEAD. The interview itself stands as an effective reminder of the limitations of an auteur theory imposed upon a
collective form of expression.

No brutalizing stone is left unturned: crowbars gash holes in the heads
of the "living dead," people are shot in the head or through the body
(blood gushing from their backs), bodies are burned, monsters are shown
eating entrails, and--in a climax of unrestrained nausea. . . .

> --*Variety*,
> October 16, 1968.

SERVICE OF THE DEPARTMENT OF RADIO/TELEVISION/FILM · UNIVERSITY OF TEXAS AT AUSTIN

I can't help thinking that when you drop your kids off in front of the show and the marquee says NIGHT OF THE LIVING DEAD, you should know it isn't going to be a Disney film or HANS BRINKER AND THE SILVER SKATES.

--Russell Streiner

In 1968, THE NIGHT OF THE LIVING DEAD was something of a stylistic anomaly, sporting a look that included 1) a propensity for hand-held camera work; 2) the use of amateur or unknown actors; 3) grainy black-and-white film; and 4) a story line that many viewers, such as the *Variety* reporter, assorted parents' clubs, and a young film critic named Roger Ebert, felt was strung together solely as an excuse to show graphic scenes of violence. In short, many felt that NIGHT OF THE LIVING DEAD was a porno film that had merely substituted violence for sex.

Of course, from the retrospective viewpoint of 1981, we might feel that viewers and critics overreacted to the "pornography of violence" angle of NIGHT OF THE LIVING DEAD. Films such as FRIDAY THE 13TH, HAPPY BIRTHDAY TO ME, SCANNERS, and I SPIT ON YOUR GRAVE transform LIVING DEAD into an anemic bystander by comparison. But even before NIGHT OF THE LIVING DEAD, individual scenes and even complete films had displayed similar outrageous acts of violence. Under the sanctified umbrella of Art, for example, UN CHIEN ANDALOU (1929) had slit an eyeball in extreme close-up (though God knows Bunuel and Dali's film continues to outrage and shock plenty of viewers), and VIVA LA MUERTE (1966) repelled audiences with dismemberments, punctured eyes, rains of defecation and vomit, and a finale in which a cow is slaughtered and the main actress sewed inside its belly.

The most startling filmic predecessors to NIGHT OF THE LIVING DEAD (and which spilled far more blood) were the exploitation movies directed by Herschell Gordon Lewis in the mid-1960s (BLOOD FEAST, TWO THOUSAND MANIACS). John McCarty, in his chronicle of film gore entitled *Splatter Movies*, feels that Lewis' films, when stripped of their dubious humor, resemble "Nazi death camp films restaged as entertainment."

How, then, did NIGHT OF THE LIVING DEAD receive so much publicity as state-of-the-art gore? Three vital factors influenced this phenomenon: 1) A sort of social boiling point with regard to violence had been reached by the fall of 1968 (the Viet Nam conflict on the evening news; the assassinations of King and Kennedy; the riots in slums and campuses, etc.); 2) NIGHT OF THE LIVING DEAD introduced to audiences the proper

etiquette for eating raw animal entrails (members of the crew dubbed
this scene "the last supper," and it involved hand-held camerawork,
minimal match-action cutting, and possibly some discomfort and even
degradation on the part of the actors); 3) The use of Russell Streiner's
daughter, Kyra Schon, in similar scenes of graphic violence, raised the
metaphorical ante from the notion of pornography of violence to *child*
pornography of violence, a filmic taboo rivaled only by the "snuff film."

Today, NIGHT OF THE LIVING DEAD receives an "R" rating at theatrical
screenings. This would seem to be testimony either of a more flexible,
tolerant society or of one that is rapidly decaying.

NIGHT OF THE LIVING DEAD is one of those films combining the science-
fiction theme of loss of identity with the horror fear of death . . .
a horror film without hope, a film about facing death that gives us no
reassurance.

> --Stuart Kaminsky

There is one hypothesis that seems to me consistent with all the foregoing:
The evolution of the limbic system involved a radically new way of viewing
the world.

> --Carl Sagan,
> *The Dragons of Eden.*

What do Carl Sagan and NIGHT OF THE LIVING DEAD have in common? Both, it seems, have a great interest in the neurophysiology of the human brain. To qualify this statement, let's first look at the latest breakdown in the workings of the brain, known as the triune brain model.

The Reptillian Complex (irrelevant to our discussion) operates like a permanent motor governor to control aemotional ritualizing, territoriality, and social hierarchies. The neocortex, among other things, controls our linguistic skills, mathematic computations, abstracting abilities, and our attempts at rationalization and analysis.

The limbic system, however, determines our emotional states. Its functions range from happiness, sadness, fear, rage, and sex drives to the control of the endocrine systems and the pituitary gland. When we dream, or when we trip on LSD, mushrooms, peyote, etc., the neocortex becomes largely dormant as the limbic system in our brain lights up in a storm of electrical activity.

Carl Sagan theorizes on a world view dominated by the limbic system as one in which:

> . . . we encounter vivid sensory and emotional images and active intuitive understanding, but little rational analysis; where we are unable to perform tasks requiring extensive concentration; where we experience short attention spans and frequent distractions and most of all, a feeble sense of individuality or self, which gives way to a pervading fatalism, a sense of unpredictable buffeting by uncontrollable events.

In this statement, Sagan has described what sounds like a thematic credo of horror movies in general, and of NIGHT OF THE LIVING DEAD in particular. This implies to me a strong correlation between an active limbic system and an appreciation of the Romero film.

For instance, a rational or intellectual reading of LIVING DEAD hardly leaves the viewer shaking in his or her boots. The viewer would tend to

question the validity and/or likelihood of a world ruled by ghouls
that eat their victims, who then become ghouls. Arithmetically, it
makes no sense, unless the devoured bodies are recycled. Furthermore,
the capacity of these slow, somnambulant creatures to somehow catch
their nimbler human prey reveals a distinct disdain for certain tenets
of natural selection.

This sort of rationalization, stimulated by an active neo-cortex,
should be suspended if one wishes to enjoy NIGHT OF THE LIVING DEAD
as a horror film, and not as bizarre slapstick (although it is certainly
that as well). Some of us can do it willfully (Coleridge called it the
"suspension of disbelief"). Others must be lulled into the world of
the limbic system by LIVING DEAD's dream-like imagery. By this I mean
the characters' loss of control (a trademark of most dreams), their
acceptance of their situation on an emotional level despite its irrational-
ities (how many dreams make sense when we retell them?), and even the
film's black-and-white nighttime photography (one body of dream research
holds that dreams take place in a dark, colorless world, although there
is as yet plenty of controversy on this point).

When the limbic system takes over in the viewing process of NIGHT
OF THE LIVING DEAD, snorts of scepticism become gasps of fear. The
analogy of a horror film to a nightmare or a bad drug trip becomes a
physiological reality. We squirm and sweat, turn from the screen, test
the reality of the floor, talk nervously to the person next to us, only
to be drawn back to the film more intensely than ever. It's only a
movie, of course, but when we go home to our empty apartment, we check
the closets. . . .

A conclusion to these musings would suggest that the horror film
genre demands this overpowering engagement of the limbic system (more
than any other genre), due to its dreamlike nature. One suspects, however,
that the scientific testing of this hypothesis may be infinitely delayed
in its realization.

--Kelly Greene

Suggestions for further reading:

"Anatomy of a Horror Film," *Cinefantastique*, IV, No. 1, (1975).
McCarty, John. *Splatter Movies*. Albany NY: Fantaco Enterprises, 1981.
Sagan, Carl. *The Dragons of Eden*. New York: Random House, 1977.

Bibliography

Agee, James. *Agee On Film: Volume I*. New York: Grosset and Dunlap, 1958.

Althusser, Louis. *For Marx*. New York: Vintage Books, 1970.

Anger, Kenneth. *Hollywood Babylon*. San Francisco: Straight Arrow Books, 1975.

Anobile, Richard J. *John Ford's Stagecoach*. New York: Avon Books, 1975.

Atkins, Thomas R. *Graphic Violence on the Screen*. New York: Monarch, 1976.

Barthes, Roland. *S/Z*. New York: Hill and Wang, 1974.

Baxter, John. *The Hollywood Exiles*. New York: Taplinger, 1976.

———. *The Cinema of John Ford*. New York: A. S. Barnes, 1971.

Bazin, André. *What Is Cinema? Vol. II*. Edited and Translated by Hugh Gray. Berkeley: University of California Press, 1971.

———. *Orson Welles*. Paris: Éditions du Cerf, 1972.

Bessy, Maurice. *Orson Welles*. New York: Crown, 1971.

Biskind, Peter. *Easy Riders, Raging Bulls: How the Sex-Drugs-and-Rock 'N' Roll Generation Saved Hollywood*. Simon and Schuster, 1999.

Bliss, Michael, and Christina Banks. *What Goes Around Comes Around: The Films of Jonathan Demme*. Southern Illinois University Press, 2014.

Bogdanovich, Peter. *John Ford*. Berkeley: University of California Press, 1968.

———. *Who the Devil Made It?: Conversations with Legendary Film Directors*. Ballantine Books, 2012.

Bordwell, David. *Narration in the Fiction Film*. Madison: University of Wisconsin Press, 1985.

———. *Making Meaning: Inference and Rhetoric in the Interpretation of Cinema*. Cambridge, MA: Harvard University Press, 1991.

Bordwell, David, and Kristin Thompson. *Film Art: An Introduction*. Boston: McGraw-Hill, 1979.

Brakhage, Stan. *Film at Wit's End: Eight Avant-garde Filmmakers*. Edinburgh, UK: Polygon, 1989.

Britton, Andrew. *American Nightmare: Essays on the Horror Film*. Toronto: Festival of Festivals, 1979.

Brown, Karl. *Adventures with D. W. Griffith*. New York: Farrar, Straus, and Giroux, 1973.

Byron, Stuart. *Movie Comedy*. New York: Penguin Books, 1977.

Cameron, Ian. *Movie Reader*. New York: Praeger, 1972.

Capra, Frank. *The Name above the Title*. New York: Macmillan, 1971.

Cawelti, John G. *The Six-Gun Mystique*. Bowling Green, OH: Bowling Green University Press, 1971.

———. *Adventure, Mystery, and Romance*. University of Chicago Press, 1976.

Chion, Michel. *Film: A Sound Art*. New York: Columbia University Press, 2003

Clover, Carol J. *Men, Women, and Chainsaws: Gender in the Modern Horror Film*. Princeton University Press, 2015.

Combs, Richard. *Robert Aldrich*. London: British Film Institute, 1978.

Cook, Pam. *The Cinema Book*. London: British Film Institute, 1985.

Corliss, Richard. *Talking Pictures: Screenwriters in American Cinema*. New York: Overlook Books, 1974.

Cowie, Peter. *The Cinema of Orson Welles*. New York: A. S. Barnes, 1965.

Crowley, Aleister. *Magick in Theory and Practice*. New York: Gordon Press, 1974.

Curtis, David. *Experimental Cinema*. New York: Universe Books, 1971.

Dejeune, C. A. *Cinema*. London: Alexander Maclehose, 1931.

Deleuze, Gilles. *Cinema 1: The Movement Image*. Paris: Éditions de Minuit, 1983.

———. *Cinema 2: The Time Image*. Paris: Éditions de Minuit, 1985.

Denby, David. *Awake in the Dark*. New York: Vintage Books, 1977.

Deren, Maya. *An Anagram of Ideas on Art, Form and Film*. Yonkers, NY: Alicat Book Shop Press, 1946.

Durgnat, Raymond. *The Strange Case of Alfred Hitchcock*. Cambridge, MA: MIT Press, 1974.

Eisenschitz, Bernard. *Nicholas Ray: An American Journey*. Farber and Farber, 1996.

Everson, William K. *American Silent Film*. New York: Oxford University Press, 1978.

Farber, Manny. *Negative Space*. New York: Praeger, 1971.

———. *Farber on Film: The Complete Film Writings of Manny Farber*. Library of America, 2009.

Ferguson, Otis. *Film Criticism of Otis Ferguson*. Philadelphia: Temple University Press, 1971.

Fitzgerald, Frances. *Fire in The Lake*. New York: Vintage Books, 1972.

Flynn, Charles, and Todd McCarthy. *Kings of the Bs*. New York: E. P. Dutton, 1975.

Ford, John, and Dudley Nichols. *Stagecoach*. New York: Simon and Schuster, 1971.

Fordin, Hugh. *MGM's Greatest Musicals: The Arthur Freed Unit*. Boston: Da Capo, 1996.

Friedrich, Otto. *City of Nets: A Portrait of Hollywood in the 1940's*. Berkeley: University of California Press, 1997.

Gallagher, Tag. *John Ford: The Man and His Films*. Berkeley: University of California Press, 1988.

Gardiner, Dorothy, and Katherine Sorley Walker. *Raymond Chandler Speaking*. Boston: Houghton Mifflin, 1962.

Garnham, Nicholas. *Samuel Fuller*. New York: Viking, 1971.

Geduld, Harry M. *Focus on D. W. Griffith*. Englewood Cliffs, NJ: Prentice-Hall, 1971.

Gilbey, Ryan. *It Don't Worry Me: The Revolutionary American Films of the Seventies*. London: Farber and Farber, 2003.

Gish, Lillian, with Ann Pinchot. *The Movies, Mr. Griffith, and Me*. Englewood Cliffs, NJ: Prentice-Hall, 1969.

Gottesman, Ronald. *Focus on Citizen Kane*. Englewood Cliffs, NJ: Prentice-Hall, 1971.

Grant, Barry Keith. *Film Genre: From Iconography to Ideology*. New York: Wallflower, 2007.

———. *Auteurs and Authorship: A Film Reader*. Malden: Wiley-Blackwell, 2008.

Halliday, Jon, ed. *Sirk on Sirk*. New York: Viking, 1972.

Halliday, Jon, and Laura Mulvey. *Douglas Sirk*. Edinburgh Film Festival, 1972.

Hardy, Phil. *Samuel Fuller*. New York: Praeger, 1970.

Harris, Mark. *Pictures at a Revolution: Five Movies and the Birth of New Hollywood*. New York: Penguin Books, 2009.

Hart, James. *The Man Who Invented Hollywood: The Autobiography of D. W. Griffith*. Louisville, KY: Touchstone, 1972.

Harvey, James. *Romantic Comedy in Hollywood: From Lubitsch to Sturges*. Boston: Da Capo Press, 1998.

Haskell, Molly. *From Reverence to Rape*. New York: Penguin Books, 1973.

Henderson, Robert M. *D. W. Griffith: His Life and Work*. New York: Oxford University Press, 1972.

Higham, Charles, and Joel Greenburg. *Hollywood in the Forties*. New York: A. S. Barnes, 1968.

Higham, Charles. *The Films of Orson Welles*. Berkeley: University of California Press, 1970.

Hodgson, Godfrey. *America in Our Time*. New York: Vintage Books, 1978.

Hughes, Robert. *Film: Book 2; Films of Peace and War*. New York: Grove, 1962.

Huss, Roy and Norman Silverstein. *The Film Experience*. New York: Harper and Row, 1968.

Isenberg, Noah. *Edgar G. Ulmer: A Filmmaker at the Margins*. Berkeley: University of California Press, 2014.

Jensen, Paul. "Dudley Nichols," in *The Hollywood Screenwriter*. Edited by Richard Corliss. New York: Avon Books, 1972.

Johnston, Claire. *Notes on Women's Cinema*. London: Society for Education in Film and Television, 1973.

Kael, Pauline. *The Citizen Kane Book*. Boston: Little, Brown, 1971.

———. *Kiss Kiss Bang Bang*. London: Marion Boyars, 1973.

———. *5001 Nights at the Movies*. New York: Holt, 1991.

———. *For Keeps: 30 Years at the Movies*. New York: Plume, 1996.

Kaminsky, Stuart M. *American Film Genres*. Dayton, Ohio: Pflaum, 1974.

Kitses, Jim. *Horizons West*. Bloomington: Indiana University Press, 1970.

Kolker Robert. *A Cinema of Loneliness*. New York: Oxford University Press, 2011.

LaValley, Albert J. *Focus on Hitchcock*. Englewood Cliffs, NJ: Prentice-Hall, 1972.

Lewis, Jon. *American Film: A History*. New York: W. W. Norton, 2007.

Levy, Emanuel. *Vincente Minnelli: Hollywood's Dark Dreamer*. New York: St. Martin's Press, 2009.

Mackendrick, Alexander. *On Film-Making*. London: Farber and Farber, 2004.

Maland, Charles J. *Frank Capra*. Boston: Twayne, 1980.

Maltin, Leonard. *The Great Movie Shorts*. New York: Bonanza Books, 1972.

Manvell, Roger, ed. *Experiment in Film*. New York: Arno, 1970.

Mast, Gerald. *The Comic Mind*. Indianapolis: Bobbs-Merrill, 1973.

McArthur, Colin. *Underworld U.S.A.* New York: Viking, 1972.

McBride, Joseph. *Orson Welles*. New York: Viking, 1972.

———. *Focus on Howard Hawks*. Englewood Cliffs, NJ: Prentice-Hall, 1972.

McBride, Joseph, and Michael Wilmington. *John Ford*. New York: Da Capo Press, 1975.

McCarthy, Todd. *Howard Hawks: The Grey Fox of Hollywood*. New York: Grove, 1997.

McPherson, Bruce. *Essential Deren: Collected Writings on Film*. Documentext, 2005.

Metz, Christian. *The Imaginary Signifier: Psychoanalysis and the Cinema*. Bloomington: Indiana University Press, 1982.

Miller, Henry. *Tropic of Capricorn*. New York: Grove, 1961.

Mitry, Jean. *The Aesthetics and Psychology of the Cinema*. Bloomington: Indiana University Press, 1997.

Mulvey, Laura. *Visual and Other Pleasures*. London: Palgrave Macmillan, 2009.

Murray, Gabrielle. *This Wounded Cinema, This Wounded Life: Violence and Utopia in the Films of Sam Peckinpah*. Santa Barbara: Praeger, 2004.

Naremore, James. *More Than Night: Film Noir in its Contexts*. Berkeley: University of California Press, 2008.

———. *The Films of Vincente Minnelli*. Boston: Cambridge Film Classics, 1993.

O'Brien, Geoffrey. *The Phantom Empire: Movies in the Mind of the 20th Century*. New York: W. W. Norton, 1993.

O'Dell, Paul. *Griffith and the Rise of Hollywood*. New York: A. S. Barnes, 1970.

Place, J. A. *The Western Films of John Ford*. Secaucus, NJ: Citadel, 1973.

Potamkin, Harry Alan. *The Eyes of the Movie*. New York: International Pamphlets, 1934.

Powell, Michael. *A Life in Movies: An Autobiography*. New York: Farber and Farber, 2000.

Prince, Stephen. *Savage Cinema: Sam Peckinpah and the Rise of Ultraviolent Movies*. Austin: University of Texas Press, 1998.

Rabinovitz, Lauren. *For the Love of Pleasure: Women, Movies, and Culture in Turn-of-the-Century Chicago*. New Brunswick, NJ: Rutgers University Press, 1998.

———. *Points of Resistance: Women, Power, and Politics in the New York Avant-Garde Cinema, 1943–1971*. Champaign: University of Illinois Press, 2003.

Reich, Wilhelm. *The Mass Psychology of Fascism*. Translated by Vincent R. Carfagno. New York: Farrar, Straus and Giroux, 1970.

Renan, Sheldon. *An Introduction to the American Underground Film*. New York: E. P. Dutton, 1967.

Rich, B. Ruby. *Chick Flicks: Theories and Memories of the Feminist Film Movement*. Durham, NC: Duke University Press, 1998.

Robinson, David. *Buster Keaton*. Bloomington: Indiana University Press, 1969.

Rodowick, D. N. *Gilles Deleuze's Time Machine*. Durham, NC: Duke University Press, 1997.

———. *The Difficulty of Difference: Psychoanalysis, Sexual Difference, and Film Theory*. Abingdon, UK: Routledge, 1991.

———. *The Crisis of Political Modernism: Criticism and Ideology in Contemporary Film Theory*. Champaign: University of Illinois Press, 1989.

Rosenbaum, Jonathan. *Placing Movies: The Practice of Film Criticism*. Berkeley: University of California Press, 1995.

———. *Discovering Orson Welles*. Berkeley: University of California Press, 2007.

Rosenberg, Bernard, and David Manning White. *Mass Culture*. New York: Free Press, 1957.

Round, Richard. *Cinema: A Critical Dictionary*. London: Secker and Warburg, 1980.

Rybin, Stephen, and Will Scheibel. *Lonely Places, Dangerous Ground: Nicholas Ray in American Cinema*. New York: SUNY Press, 2014.

Sarris, Andrew. *Interviews with Film Directors*. New York: Avon, 1967.

———. *The American Cinema: Directors and Directions 1929–1968*. New York: E. P. Dutton and Co., 1968.

Schatz, Thomas. *Hollywood Genres*. New York: Random House, 1981.

———. *The Genius of the System*. Minneapolis: University of Minnesota Press, 2010.

Schickel, Richard. *The Men Who Made the Movies*. New York, 1975.

Scorsese, Martin. *A Personal Journey with Martin Scorsese Through American Movies*. New York: Farber and Farber, 1997.

Sennett, Mac, and Cameron Shipp. *King of Comedy*. Garden City: Doubleday, 1954.

Seydor, Paul. *Peckinpah: The Western Films*. Urbana: University of Illinois Press, 1980.

Shadoian, Jack. *Dreams and Dead Ends*. Cambridge, MA: MIT Press, 1979.

Sherman, Eric, and Martin Rubin. *The Director's Event*. New York: Signet, 1972.

Silver, Alain, and Elizabeth Ward. *Robert Aldrich: A Guide to References and Sources*. Boston: G. K. Hall, 1979.

Sitney, P. Adams. *Visionary Film: The American Avant-Garde*. New York: Holt, Rinehart, and Winston, 1974.

Smith, James L. *Melodrama*. London: Methuen, 1973.

Smith, Julian. *Looking Away: Hollywood and Vietnam*. Scribner, 1975.

Spillane, Mickey. *Kiss Me Deadly*. New York: New American Library, 1952.

Stuhlmann, Gunther, ed. *The Diary of Anaïs Nin, Vol. 4*. New York: Harcourt Brace Jovanovich, 1971.

Sturges, Preston. *Prestion Sturges: His Life in His Words*. New York: Simon and Schuster, 1990.

Thomson, David. *A Biographical Dictionary of Film*. New York: William Morrow, 1976.

———. *Suspects*. New York: Knopf, 1985.

———. *Rosebud: The Story of Orson Welles*. New York: Knopf, 1996.

Thompson, Kristin, and David Bordwell. *Film History: An Introduction*. McGraw-Hill College, 1994.

Thrower, Stephen. *Nightmare USA: The Untold Story of the Exploitation Independents*. FAB Press, 2007.

Truffaut, Francois. *Hitchcock*. New York: Simon and Schuster, 1967.

Turan, Kenneth, and Stephen F. Zito. *Sinema*. New York: Praeger, 1974.

Ursini, James. *Preston Sturges: An American Dreamer*. New York: Curtis Books, 1973.

Vogel, Amos. *Film as a Subversive Art*. New York: Random House, 1973.

Walsh, Martin. *The Brechtian Aspect of Radical Cinema*. London: British Film Institute, 1981.

Wead, George, and George Lellis. *Film: Form and Function*. Boston: G. K. Hall, 1977.

———. *The Film Career of Buster Keaton*. Boston: G. K. Hall, 1977.

Wellman, Paul I. *The Indian Wars of the West*. New York: Curtis Books, 1963.

Whyte, William H. *The Organization Man*. New York: Simon and Schuster, 1956.

Willis, Donald C. *The Films of Frank Capra*. Metuchen, NJ: Scarecrow, 1974.

———. *The Films of Howard Hawks*. Metuchen, NJ: Scarecrow, 1975.

Wittemore, Don, and Philip Alan Cecchettini. *Passport to Hollywood*. New York: McGraw-Hill Book Company, 1976.

Wood, Robin. *Howard Hawks*. New York: Doubleday, 1968.

——. *Hitchcock's Films*. Cranbury, NJ: A. S. Barnes, 1969.

Wollen, Peter. *Signs and Meaning in the Cinema*. London: Thames and Hudson, BFI, 1970.

Wright, Will. *Six Guns and Society: A Structural Study of the Western*. Berkeley: University of California Press, 1975.

Youngblood, Gene. *Expanded Cinema*. New York: E. P. Dutton, 1970.

Zinoma, Jason. *Shock Value: How a Few Eccentric Outsiders Gave Us Nightmares, Conquered Hollywood, and Invented Modern Horror*. New York: Penguin Books, 2012.

Contributors

VALENTIN ALMENDAREZ

Val Almendarez is the collection archivist at the Margaret Herrick Library of the Academy of Motion Picture Arts and Sciences. He received degrees in English and film studies from the University of Texas at Austin.

NICK BARBARO

Nick Barbaro received his degree from the Department of Radio-TV-Film at the University of Texas at Austin, having survived his undergraduate work in English at UCLA. He is a cofounder of the *Austin Chronicle* and SXSW. His taste in film runs toward such existential comedies as *Love and Death*, *Godzilla's Revenge*, and *In Cold Blood*. The one rule which governs his critical approach is "There are no bad films, only bad film critics—and occasionally bad popcorn."

MARJORIE BAUMGARTEN

Marjorie Baumgarten is a film critic and senior editor at the *Austin Chronicle*, where she has worked in many capacities since the paper's founding in 1981. She has been the *Chronicle*'s Film Reviews editor for the last twenty-five years, and her work has also appeared in *Variety*, *The Hollywood Reporter*, and *Film Comment*.

CHARLES RAMÍREZ BERG

Charles Ramírez Berg is University Distinguished Teaching Professor in the Department of Radio-TV-Film at the University of Texas at Austin. He has authored several books, most recently *The Classical Mexican Cinema: The Poetics of the Exceptional Golden Age Films* (2015), as well as *Latino Images in Film* (2002); *Cinema of Solitude: A Critical Study of Mexican Film, 1967–1983* (1992); and *Posters from the Golden Age of Mexican Cinema* (1997). In addition, he has written numerous articles on Latinos in US film, Mexican cinema, film history, and narratology.

LOUIS BLACK

Louis Black cofounded the *Austin Chronicle*, where he is editor, and SXSW, where he is a director, and was a founding board member of the Austin Film Society. He has written extensively on film, music, and politics. Executive producer of *Be Here to Love Me: A Film about Townes Van Zandt*, he was also a producer on the Peabody Award–winning *The Order of Myths*. In recent years, he has produced restorations and reissues of classic Texas films, including Eagle Pennell's *The Whole Shootin' Match* (1978) and *Last Night at The Alamo* (1984) and Tobe Hooper's *Eggshells* (1968). In 2016, Louis and Karen Bernstein directed the documentary *Richard Linklater: Dream is Destiny.*

ELLEN DRAPER

Ellen Draper (BA Wellesley; MA English, MA Radio-TV-Film, PhD English UT Austin) has taught film and English at Emerson, Clark, Boston College, and Simmons. Her essays have been published in *Inventing Vietnam, Jean-Luc Godard's Hail Mary, Controlling Hollywood, Wide Angle*, and *Film Quarterly*.

STEVE FORE

Steve Fore retired in 2017 from the City University of Hong Kong's School of Creative Media, where he was one of five founding faculty members in 1998. In SCM, Steve taught classes in animation studies, surveillance studies, new media theory, technology and culture, science fiction film, and documentary media. Back in the day, he wrote twenty-three CinemaTexas Program Notes and served as CinemaTexas coeditor with Louis Black.

DON HARTACK

While waiting for his film career to take off (it didn't), Don Hartack began working part-time in the late 1980s for a sports statistics startup. Jump-cut ahead almost thirty years, and he is still with *Stats*, providing research notes and support for televised games in all the major sports. He has won two Emmy Awards for his contributions to major-league baseball broadcasts, including the World Series. Don and his wife oversee their colony of dogs, turtles, and quail in a fashionably shabby section of Los Angeles.

BRIAN HANSEN

Brian Hansen was a film scholar, a musician, an artist, and a filmmaker. *Speed of Light*, a film he made with Paul Cullum, earned a legendary cult reputation. Bernardo Bertolucci said, "It is a cinema symphony in red." Hansen was in *True Stories*, worked on music videos for The Clash and Talking Heads, and worked with Jonathan Demme in the early conceptualization of *Stop Making Sense*. Unfortunately, Brian died in 1986. Demme's *Married to the Mob* is dedicated to him.

JOHN HENLEY

John Henley graduated with honors from the University of Texas at Austin School of Journalism in 1977. After a period of graduate study in the Radio-TV-Film Department, he worked for local businesses until 1988, when he returned to UT and became procurement officer of the University of Texas Libraries. John retired after twenty-eight years in that position on Halloween 2016. A native Texan, he lives in South Austin with his wife, cat, guitar, piano, and William Beaudine film collection.

ANN LAEMMLE

After studying film and receiving her bachelor of science in Radio-TV-Film from the University of Texas, Ann Laemmle graduated from the University of Texas School of Law and practiced law in the New York, London, and

Hong Kong offices of Cleary, Gottlieb, Steen, and Hamilton LLP and in the New York and Zurich offices of Credit Suisse. She lives in the Adirondacks in upstate New York with her husband, Paul Willcott, and tries not to let the practice of law interfere with watching movies.

GEORGE LELLIS

George Lellis is professor emeritus at Coker College, where he taught in the communication program for thirty-five years. He received his PhD from the Department of Radio-TV-Film at the University of Texas at Austin. He is author of *Bertolt Brecht, Cahiers du Cinéma and Contemporary Film Theory*, and coauthor, with George Wead, of *The Film Career of Buster Keaton* and *Film: Form and Function*. He is coauthor with Hans-Bernhard Moeller of *Volker Schlöndorff's Cinema: Politics, Adaptation, and the "Movie-Appropriate."*

ED LOWRY

Ed Lowry as editor and programmer at the University of Texas RTF Department's CinemaTexas influenced and guided a couple of generations of film students. A cofounder, he was the first editor of the *Austin Chronicle*, finishing his dissertation the same year. He taught at Southern Illinois University and was at Southern Methodist University in Dallas, Texas, when he died in 1985. Friend, editor, teacher, leader, and programmer, many of us have missed him almost every day since his death.

MARIE MAHONEY

After receiving her master's degree in Radio-TV-Film from the University of Texas, Marie Mahoney moved to the Chicago area in 1991. She has been working at Rush University Medical Center in Chicago for most of the intervening years. She is currently a senior director in the medical center's Department of Strategic Planning, Marketing and Communications, where she manages a team responsible for content strategy, web operations, and social media.

LAUREN RABINOVITZ

Lauren Rabinovitz's current research and teaching interests include early cinema and culture, feminist film history and theory, and theories and history of visual spectacles. Her books include *For the Love of Pleasure: Women, Movies, and Culture in Turn-of-the-Century Chicago*; *Points of Resistance: Women, Power, and Politics in the New York Avant-Garde Cinema, 1943–1971*; and *Electric Dreamland: Amusement Parks, Movies, and American Modernity*. A pioneer in recognizing the scholarly and pedagogical possibilities of digital technology, her interactive projects are "Yesteryear's Wonderlands," on early twentieth-century amusement parks, funded by a National Endowment for the Humanities Educational Development Grant, and *The Rebecca Project*, which she coauthored, one of the first CDs to use new media as a tool of film analysis for Alfred Hitchcock's 1941 movie *Rebecca*. She is also the director of the University of Iowa's Center for Ethnic Studies and the Arts.

D. N. RODOWICK

D. N. Rodowick is Glen A. Lloyd Distinguished Service Professor at the University of Chicago where he teaches in Cinema and Media Studies and the Visual Arts Departments. He is the author of numerous essays as well as eight books, including most recently, *What Philosophy Wants from Images* (2017). After studying cinema and comparative literature at the University of Texas at Austin and Université de Paris III, he obtained a PhD at the University of Iowa in 1983. Rodowick subsequently taught at Yale University, the University of Rochester, and at King's College, University of London. Before coming to the University of Chicago, he was William R. Kenan Jr. Professor of Visual and Environmental Studies and director of the Carpenter Center for Visual Arts at Harvard University. Rodowick is also a curator and an award-winning experimental filmmaker and video artist.

MICHAEL SELIG

Michael Selig is an associate professor of media studies at Emerson College, where he has also served as director of the film program and chair of the Department of Visual and Media Arts. He is a former editor of *The Journal of Film and Video*. He has published on a wide range of film topics in a variety of journals, including *Wide Angle, Screen, The Velvet Light Trap*, and *Gender*.

WARREN SPECTOR

Warren Spector earned his bachelor's degree in speech from Northwestern University in 1977. In 1980, he completed his master's degree in Radio-TV-Film at the University of Texas at Austin. In 1983, he dropped out of UT's PhD program to begin a career in game development. (His mother cried for ten years . . .) Best known for his work on the *Deus Ex* and *Disney Epic Mickey* games, early in his career, he also worked on several entries in the *Ultima* series. In addition to his game work, he is a published novelist (*The Hollow Earth Affair*, 1988) and comic book author (*DuckTales: Rightful Owners*, 2012). From 2013 until 2016, he was the director of the Denius-Sams Gaming Academy in the Moody College of Communication at the University of Texas at Austin.

Index

Page numbers followed by f indicate figures.